UNFREE MASTERS

REFIGURING AMERICAN MUSIC

A series edited by Ronald Radano and Josh Kun

Charles McGovern, contributing editor

MATT STAHL

UNFREE

MASTERS

Recording Artists and the Politics of Work

Duke University Press *Durham and London* 2013

© 2013 Duke University Press
All rights reserved
Printed in the United States of
America on acid-free paper ∞
Designed by Amy Ruth Buchanan
Typeset in Minion by Tseng
Information Systems, Inc.
Library of Congress Cataloging-
in-Publication Data appear on
the last printed page of this book.

To Adam McCauley and Nat Parsons

CONTENTS

ACKNOWLEDGMENTS

Thanks to Adrian Arrancibia, Tildy Bayar, Rick Biernacki, Geof Bowker, Jericho Burg, Jonathan Burston, Pauline Chin, Melanie DeGiovanni, Jewlia Eisenberg, Gil Eyal, Catherine Geanuracos, Dorothy Geller, Jim Haaland, Susie Haaland, Val Hartouni, Alison Hearn, Dave Hesmondhalgh, Ken Holt, Robert Horwitz, Alison Huber, Steve Jackson, Christina Jimenez, Keir Keightley, Kris Langan, Steven Lee, Regina Marchi, Chandra Mukerji, Yuri Ono, Jeff Pooley, Jean Retzinger, Tony Rojas, Michael Schudson, Graham Smith, Sophia Snow, Heide Solbrig, Geoff Soule, Geoff Stahl, Tad Stahl, Will Straw, Amber Vanderwarker, Katie Vann, Dawn Vitale, Lexa Walsh, Greg Wilson, Jay Yarnall, and Ferruh Yilmaz for insight, support, and critique.

Thanks to Catherine Fisk, Mary Francis, Josh Kun, George Lipsitz, Michael Mascuch, Rick Matthews, Katherine Meizel, Carole Pateman, Ron Radano, Paul St. Amour, Jason Toynbee, Steve Waksman, a roomful of graduate students at the University of California (UC), Santa Barbara, and two anonymous reviewers for their attention to and comments on the manuscript; any remaining errors and omissions are my own.

Thanks to Jane Stahl for translations from the French.

Thanks to the Robert and Colleen Haas Scholars Program at UC Berkeley, the UC San Diego Humanities Fellowship, the Law and Humanities Junior Scholar Workshop, the Faculty of Information and Media Studies at the University of Western Ontario, and the California State Archive.

Lyrics to "Wild Wild Workweek" are by Joe Sloan, ©1990 Spot 1019, used with permission.

Portions of chapters 1 and 2 originally appeared in *Bad Music: The Music We Love to Hate*, edited by Chris Washburne and Maiken Derno (New York: Routledge, 2004), 212–32; and in *The Media and Social Theory*, edited by David Hesmondhalgh and Jason Toynbee (New York: Routledge, 2008), 231–47, respectively.

People in music enjoy a
freedom completely unknown
to the organization man.

—**Robert Curtis**,
Your Future in Music

INTRODUCTION

Popular Music and (Creative) Labor

The stars of popular music often appear to be so free and to be doing such enjoyable, expressive, and fulfilling work that it almost seems strange to think of them as working people. In contrast to the apparent freedom of Lady Gaga, Jay-Z, or Bob Dylan to decide how and where and when to record or perform, work for most people, most of the time, is not particularly free, enjoyable, or fulfilling. For most people, work generally requires doing what you're told or suffering the consequences, which can include discipline, harassment, or termination. Most people have no right and little ability to take a meaningful part in making decisions regarding the policies or organization of their place of work. For most people, most of the time, in other words, work is characterized by "democratic deficits" that "exist (to different extents) in any employment relationship."[1]

Unlike most working people, successful recording artists enjoy exceptional autonomy in their work, as well as a strong property interest in the songs they record. Typically they receive their pay in lump sums (advances) before they begin the work of recording, and although they might be required to work with a particular producer and keep to a schedule for the delivery of their finished product, they nevertheless determine to a great extent what they do and where, when, and how they do it. As an artist becomes financially successful, she may be in a position to renegotiate her contract to gain more freedom, money, or both. Once her sales or other income have produced enough money to recoup, or pay back, the record company's advance, she may begin collecting royalties, putting her in a position similar to that of a landlord collecting rent on a desirable property. Successful artists often appear to us as paragons of autonomous self-actualization. If, as John Stuart Mill believed, "the end [the goal or object] of man is the highest and most harmonious development of his powers to a complete and consistent whole," then recording artists today seem to enjoy the fulfillment of some of democracy's loftiest promises.[2]

But recording artists also typically work under unequal contracts and must hand over long-term control of the songs and albums they produce to their record companies. Typically, these contracts are exclusive, meaning that without getting special permission to do otherwise the recording artist is allowed to record only for the company with whom he has a contract. The contracts are also typically assignable, meaning that they (and hence, in a certain sense, the artists) can be bought and sold, most often along with the companies who hold them.[3] When a company is sold, the recording artists under contract to it can find themselves obligated to a new company or executives they don't like or respect. And the new company may not honor the promises made or implied by the old company. Moreover, recording contracts are typically written in terms of successive album options rather than fixed periods of time. Option contracts can keep recording artists under obligation to one company for career-length periods of ten, fifteen, twenty, or more years, closing off their access to a competitive market for their skills. The realities of contracts appear to contradict or undercut the autonomy usually attributed to successful recording artists, and in fact artists and the companies they work for frequently wrangle over their contractual relationships, often in courts, but also before legislators at the state and federal levels.

The recording artist—the successful recording artist, in particular—is a double figure. On the one hand, she is a symbolic figure offered for our consumption, contemplation, and identification; she enacts forms of expression, autonomy, and desirability, seeming to encapsulate some of our society's most cherished virtues and values. On the other hand, she is a political and economic actor, a working person whose contractually governed relationship to her company is sometimes one of real subordination. In this doubleness, the recording artist embodies a paradox: as an agent of self-expression under contract to a major entertainment conglomerate or a subsidiary company, the recording artist is both autonomous and the target of control. He must be free to generate new material and unfree when it comes to the labor and intellectual property covered by the contract. Promotional narratives in the media highlight the individuality and originality of aspiring and established stars, celebrating performers' commitments to authentic self-expression and personal and artistic autonomy. Yet the legal arrangements undergirding stardom and its cultivation constitute stable structures of authority and subordination, of property creation and appropriation. Like the steel I-beams that stabilize masonry buildings in earthquake-prone areas, these arrangements join and reinforce constellations of artists, companies, markets, legal structures, and consumers. The purpose of this book is to explore the symbolic and social figure of the recording artist through the juxtaposition of cultural and political-economic analyses; to draw out the special significance of the recording artist both as object of fantasy, identification, and commerce and as skilled working subject integrated into legal and economic structures; and to foreground popular music as a social and symbolic field of unique conceptual value in the early twenty-first century.

This book's title, *Unfree Masters*, comes from the political theorist Carole Pateman's influential 1988 book *The Sexual Contract*. She coins the term in her discussion of husbands in market society. In the nineteenth and twentieth centuries the husband was "that curiosity, an *unfree master*," because although his legal role in the household was that of an autocrat (wives and children had very few rights), in the workplace, where he earned the wages necessary to support the family economically, his own rights were severely constrained.[4] In the public realm, the husband could participate in governance through voting and other political activities. However, in the private realm of the economy and the household, the husband was situated in a hierarchy of authority: he ruled the wife and children, but the employer ruled him. I adapt this term from Pateman to accentuate the paradoxical position of the professional recording artist. Like the husband in past centuries, today's professional recording artist under contract to a record company (or, increasingly, to a concert promoter or management company) is a master in some areas and a servant in others. A primary area of mastery is the artist's control over his or her labor process. However, as will become clear later in the book, many recording artists are also employers, masters of others in small domains of production, who nevertheless remain subject to the contractual commands of their record companies. The autonomy and authenticity—or, in related terms, the power and value—of some popular music performers rest on the discursive and legal abasement of others, much as the husband's power in the nineteenth and twentieth centuries depended on the subordination of the wife, as Pateman argues.

Unfree Masters explores the relationship between recording artists' autonomy and their contractual bondage against the backdrop of a critical perspective on the institutions of employment and intellectual property. It traces this set of relations from the center stage of highly publicized, mass-mediated representations of music making in a major television talent show and "rockumentary" film to the backstage of legislative battles over the ground rules that set the legal parameters of the artists' relationships with their record company paymasters (relationships that are public in a different sense). Conceiving of recording artists as workers, and considering them in relation to working people in other sectors, this volume offers new insights into the social relations of the music industry. The contradictions and paradoxes discovered therein are not unique to the music or entertainment industry: they illuminate much broader problems in American society that derive from core propositions of liberalism, such as the paramount value of the freedom of contract. When held up together for critical scrutiny, the complementary mystifications of the artist's autonomy and freedom of contract each reveal aspects of the other. Moreover, the presumed autonomy of the creative cultural-industry worker, exemplified in the figure of the rock star, is a function of mystification by the culture itself. Rather than developing as the result of a capitalist conspiracy, it is a legacy of the proliferation in and appropriation of Romantic myths of the artist as rebel and outsider by our culture. In situating this figure in economic and legal contexts, this book also seeks to demystify this presumption.

The contradictory relationship between recording artists' autonomy and their subordination brings to the surface tensions between employment and democracy in liberal society. They highlight mounting problems associated with work and social mobility in an economy and society increasingly organized around neoliberal principles. "Neoliberalism" names the hegemonic political philosophy of the turn of the twenty-first century which advocates and justifies (among other things) the expansion of employers' power to dominate their employees, and I take it up at greater length in chapter 1. The ongoing (and increasingly contested) neoliberalist transformation of contemporary society and culture poses a primary context for the analysis offered in this book. Accounts of neoliberalism differ in their analyses and emphases, but the impacts on and implications for working people of these transformations is central to many of them. An overarching theme is the accelerating erosion of working people's socioeconomic security and political and bargaining power in the name of individual freedom, sometimes referred to as individualization or de-institutionalization. To capture an organizing theme in one of his examinations of neoliberalism, David Harvey cites poignantly a lyric from Kris Kristofferson's countercultural anthem "Me And Bobby McGee": "Freedom's just another word for nothing left to lose."[5] In this world of thought and policy, the emphasis is on freedom *from* interference from the state (in the form of labor protections, for example), rather than freedom *to* enjoy an independent individual existence.

There are both push and pull aspects to the proliferation of neoliberal logic into the social world. The push is largely political, evident in attacks on workers' rights and state-provided social entitlements and benefits by neoliberal politicians, think tanks, and industry associations, in the retreat of employers from pension and other obligations, and in the individualization, pathologization, and effective criminalization of vulnerable social groups. These and related trends push greater numbers of people into states of increased vulnerability and a decreased capacity to say no, for example, to work offered on unfavorable terms. The pull is more cultural, evident in implicit and explicit propositions that processes of individualization and de-institutionalization are enhancements of individual autonomy. As scholars of reality television make clear, the mass media are preeminent sites for the dissemination of new discourses of self-governance and self-responsibility, new modes of thinking and comportment through which people are invited and exhorted to adjust to or remake themselves in accordance with the neoliberal image of the working person:[6] one who expects only law and order from the state and only a wage from employers, who is ready to change jobs willy-nilly at the convenience of employers.[7]

Understood as workers, recording artists point simultaneously to the future of work as well as to employment's traumatic emergence in the early modern era. They exemplify the individual autonomy promised (in different registers) by democratic and neoliberal ideology and institutions as well as the routine subordination of individuals demanded in and by liberal market society. Recording artists appear as examples of the "creative worker," a term often used to suggest a dominant (yet still largely aspirational) labor paradigm of the postindustrial economy. Observers use this term, often in the context of policy polemics, to characterize positions ranging from software developers to fashion designers, event planners, and consultants of all stripes: varieties of position and activity policymakers hope will offset postindustrial social and economic decline. In light of this proliferating discourse, *Unfree Masters* offers a critical study of the contemporary culture and politics of labor focused on the figure of the recording artist. Neoliberalism has taken root in America at least in part because rhetorically it identifies itself as the enhancement of individual freedom, even while it diminishes individual freedom by eroding the political-economic bases for working people's choices, such as access to employment insurance and low-cost education. In abstract terms, then, neoliberalism does not contradict this core American value even as it destroys its practical foundation for most people. Recording artists' paradoxical autonomy and subordination—as well as their paradoxical proprietorship and dispossession—reveal hard truths about the definitions, promises, and limits of freedom for working people in American society. None of these hard truths can finally be dissolved by "creativity," no matter how it is defined.

The exigencies of paid work create obstacles to most people's "highest and most harmonious development of [their] powers to a complete and consistent whole." Lacking income-producing wealth, most people have to sell their capacity to labor to others, often consigning control over large portions of their powers, as well as the valuable results of the exercise of those powers, to others on a routine basis. This situation is often referred to as "alienation." Robert Blauner writes that in work, in general, "alienation exists when workers are unable to control their immediate work processes, to develop a sense of purpose and function which connects their jobs to the overall organization of production, to belong to integrated industrial communities, and when they fail to become involved in the activity of work as a mode of personal self-expression."[8] By this definition, successful recording artists would seem to escape alienation almost entirely as they engage in creative work that "permits autonomy, responsibility, social connection, and self-actualization," in Blauner's words[9]—the "harmonious development" of their powers, to use Mill's language. Unlike many if not most working people, recording artists are not routinely "controlled and manipulated by other persons or by an impersonal system"; rather, they are able to control their own work to exceptional degrees. Recording artists "work on unique and individuated product[s]" that are saturated with meaning. Especially in the case of members of bands, they appear integrated into professional social worlds in music. Most of all, their work appears self-expressive and self-actualizing in that it "permits the expression of present capacities and the development of innate potentialities," two principles of democratic theory emphasized by Mill.[10] Moreover, copyright law appears to vest authorship of their recorded output with recording artists, constructing them as proprietors who license their recordings to record companies (see chapter 5).

Successful recording artists are indeed unalienated in many ways. Yet the ways in which they are alienated are of such far-reaching significance that they merit the sustained focus and multidisciplinary approach offered here. To clarify this argument, I want first to explore the ways in which the work lives of creative workers (of which recording artists are an example) have been understood by contemporary scholars in communication, media studies, and related fields to be largely unalienated. In the following sections, I examine and highlight important themes of this scholarship, on which I build throughout this volume.

Popular Musicians' Autonomy

Numerous scholars of the cultural industries have explained the unusually autonomous and proprietary nature of the work of creative cultural-industry workers. For David Hesmondhalgh, "creative autonomy" is essential to work in the cultural industries because "autonomy itself is bound up with the interests of cultural-industry businesses"; without freedom from constant monitoring and control, creative workers would not (the industry fears) be able to come up with potentially valuable new cultural properties.[11] But autonomy is not distributed equally among creative workers. According to Bernard Miege, "the very conditions of creation . . . vary from sector to sector: artists' autonomy, the collective or non-collective nature of the work, division or non-division of labor, insecurity, and also social prestige" can manifest themselves very differently in different "sectors" of the cultural industries.[12] "For the majority of artists," in Miege's view, "autonomy is a pure façade: it allows them to be paid at a rate markedly lower than the value of their labor power" because the pleasures associated with autonomous creative work induce people to discount their labor in order to gain cultural-industry employment.[13] The appeal of creativity and autonomy is especially effective in persuading young people to accept low wages and uncertain working conditions.[14] Nevertheless, because cultural industries require novelty, they cannot control creative workers the way employers in other sectors can: "Owners and executives make concessions to symbol creators by granting them far more *autonomy* (self-determination) than they would to workers of equivalent status in other industries and to most workers historically."[15] A quid pro quo is implied here: we give you (relative) freedom; you give us creativity.

Music making stands apart in this regard; it constitutes a limit case of cultural work—an extreme case whose features are so pronounced that they illuminate characteristics of more run-of-the-mill cases. The autonomy of successful popular music performers is exceptional among those creative workers who work under employment contracts.[16] Jason Toynbee is one of the few scholars to analyze the question of popular music performers' autonomy as unique, without a precise equivalent in other areas of cultural production.[17] Music making, in his analysis, "has always been a relatively autonomous activity taking place beyond the supervision of the firm for the most part."[18] Toynbee finds two main explanations for what he calls the "institutional autonomy" of popular music makers in the commercial record industry. On the one hand, "fans claim a direct link to musicians, and subcultures, from jitterbug to speed garage, wrap 'their' creators in an embrace which, initially and relatively but always significantly, protects these musics from corporate control."[19] Fans' collective capacity to buy or not buy recordings, concert tickets, and so on mitigates artists' alienation: the artists who enjoy such fan support are more able to keep doing what they like, so long as their products are selling. However, other industry-specific factors also work to hold the line for recording artists, as Toynbee shows in his discussion of the performing and recording purveyors of swing (a highly danceable, "whitened" variant of jazz that became popular in the middle 1930s) and their legacy. Swing bands, like the rock 'n' roll and rock groups that succeeded them, "were able to sell their services directly to several buyers and so avoid dependence on any single one."[20] (I analyze the importance for independence of the ratio of sellers to buyers of musical services in chapter 3.) Toynbee notes that the economic "mobility and autonomy of the bands was mirrored in the way they made music." To satisfy themselves, their audiences, and the institutional buyers of their services, "they needed to be self-sufficient innovators, capable of generating new performances on the move."[21] This self-sufficiency has shaped the norms and terms of record deals and has become institutionalized in the form of popular music makers' characteristically robust autonomy.

Of course, record companies typically resist that autonomy, applying pressure to maximize their own profitability and stability in a risky industry. Musicians' collective self-sufficiency continues to shape the way they interact with the recording industry as only one of many possible buyers of their services.[22] The two parties' contractual relationships reflected the record companies' dependence on the musicians' independence: musicians' ability to generate income from numerous sources subsidized record companies' investments in them, but it also limited the companies' capacity to control the musicians' labor and products.[23] The autonomous and entrepreneurial modes that have come to define popular musicians' patterns of working come into conflict with the business imperatives of the recording industry. The industry's function is to collect profit: "If it licenses a certain amount of institutional autonomy, accommodation between [musicians'] social authorship and capital is surely a contradiction in terms."[24] This tension has been central to the popular music industry for at least the last several decades. Indeed, the rock band's apparent self-sufficiency and comradeship, Keir Keightley points out, enable its members to seem "to escape that alienation of musical labour and expression which an involvement in the cultural industries would otherwise imply."[25] In this view, the autonomy—or, to use a differently inflected term, the de- or nonalienation—of many popular music performers is an institutionalized contradiction in terms.

However, while a recording artist's balance of autonomy and alienation is variable in its historical particulars, the core themes and problems of autonomy and alienation are quite persistent. Recording artists' peculiar positions with respect to the firms for whom they work put them into real, existing patterns of relationship that have grown out of historical interactions between musicians, companies, audiences, the law, changing technologies, and so on. In order to keep their jobs, contracted artists must produce new music that is commercially acceptable to the companies, on a schedule; this music must generate sufficient revenue; and the companies must have clear control over the labor and output of the artists. In other words, recording artists must (to meaningful degrees) obey their company's executives and turn over their recordings to the company.

These characteristic patterns of interaction between artists and companies are themselves conditioned by and reflect more deeply seated liberal institutions: employment and intellectual property. Employment may be understood as the exchange of obedience for a wage (see chapter 4) and intellectual property as a way of constructing cultural expressions that are subject to state-enforced monopoly control by the license holder. Employment and intellectual property intersect in copyright's doctrine of "work for hire," whereby intellectual property produced in the workplace is typically the property of the employer (see chapter 5). To remarkable degrees, the historical interactions of musicians and their employers demonstrate the stretching (but not breaking) of these alienating institutions, with the result that recording artists do not in any obvious way seem like employees. Relative to most other working people, in short, professional recording artists enjoy real privileges.

Prefiguration and Atavism in Cultural Work

The patron saint of musicians is Saint Cecilia, who, it is said, sang to the Christian deity as she was dying. In today's context, a more appropriate figure may be Janus, the Roman god of doorways and gates, of beginnings and endings. Ancient artifacts represent Janus as a head with two faces, simultaneously looking inside and outside, ahead to the future and back to the past. This ancient deity serves as a useful tool for considering the symbolic meaning and social position of the creative cultural-industry worker, given that contemporary analyses of creative work's characteristic combinations of autonomy and vulnerability suggest an essential doubleness. On the one hand, scholars position the creative worker as forward-looking, the herald of a likely future for many (if not most) other sorts of workers — perhaps analogous to the proverbial canary in the coal mine. On the other hand, they see this figure as backward-looking, recalling or reenacting otherwise outmoded forms of work from the distant past.

The present study combines these perceptions of prefiguration and atavism and uses them to explore how creative cultural work and workers can appear so Janus-like, and how recording artists present a limit case of this phenomenon. This book suggests that creative cultural work can have such a dual appearance because these forms of work and their characteristic tensions make visible the political skeleton of labor in capitalism. The traumatic and violent early modern formation of the institution of employment makes its hegemonic political content clear. Indeed, the violence of some of the earliest English labor laws — the 1349 Ordinance of Labourers and the 1351 Statute of Labourers — and the doctrines of master and servant that they codified laid the foundations for the development of the institution of employment.[26] (It is, I believe, this ancient yet still functional political content that is becoming increasingly perceptible at the outer margins of labor under neoliberalism, as well as in right-wing attacks on labor law, collective bargaining, and working people in general.) Creative cultural work juxtaposes social forms that appear to be only distantly related, at most, and it is the specific character of their marginality that renders recording artists such remarkable figures in this respect.

Avatars of the Future

In a career guide aimed at high-school students in the early 1960s, Robert Curtis highlighted the marginal and precarious nature of the musician's work. Curtis cautioned that the unusual freedom enjoyed by people in music "may also include . . . inopportunely . . . the freedom not to work."[27] In other words, professionals in what Curtis celebrated as "the fascinating world of music" typically live in a state of what has been called "bird-freedom." They are at liberty to flit from place to place, from employer to employer, but they are simultaneously free (bereft, that is) of any substantive claims on the means of making a living, in the meaning of this phrase widely attributed to Marxist thought. Creative workers' many privileges still come at the cost of the heightened insecurity and individual risk about which Curtis warned teenaged American baby boomers: many may be called, but few are chosen; fewer still will become settled in stable careers or organizations.[28] In the recording industry, as most observers note, fewer than 20 percent of artists earn enough profits and royalties to repay their record companies' financial investments in them (known as "advances" and often treated as loans); only around 5 percent of artists actually exceed repayment and achieve profitability. Success is elusive. The recording industry is kept afloat by the small number of performers who reach star status. Failure, as Mike Jones notes, is the record industry's principal product.[29]

Television talent shows and rockumentaries are stories in the mass media about success and failure that reveal much about the logics—the systems and principles—in operation at different levels of the music industry. But as the statements of an *American Idol* judge about how average people can succeed and stay on top and a rockumentary filmmaker about how they can "follow their lives right"[30] suggest (see chapters 1 and 2), the shows and films are much more than that. Makers of popular music are creative workers who are more or less integrated into systems of production and profit. These systems are increasingly understood to model—to put into preliminary shape—forms of work organization that are increasingly perceived by academics, public intellectuals, and policymakers to be proliferating outward from the cultural industries into much more conventional worlds of work. In other words, in the view of many scholars and researchers, as well as in those of music industry insiders and independent filmmakers, creative workers in the cultural industries have much to teach us about how to succeed in the neoliberalizing economy and society.

This prefigurative view of creative cultural labor sees in it the impending future of work organization, a blurring of the boundaries between the worlds of art and work. Jacques Attali presents music itself as a social form that "implies and heralds a general mutation of the social codes"; music making appears to offer a model for the "reappropriation by all creators of their valorized labor."[31] Attali's view, which appeared in French in 1977, and English in 1985, is hopeful, in contrast to those characteristic of later contributions. In Scott Lash and John Urry's 1994 formulation, "ordinary manufacturing industry is becoming more and more like the production of culture. It is not that commodity manufacture provides the template, and culture follows, but that the culture industries themselves have provided the template."[32]

More recent scholarship has developed this insight considerably. To Richard Sennett, neoliberal transformations in the world of work are exemplified by the information and culture industries, which "exert a profound moral and normative force as a cutting-edge standard for how the larger economy should evolve."[33] The "small slice of the economy" represented by these industries, he writes, "has a cultural influence far beyond its numbers"[34] because "the avatars of a particular kind of capitalism have persuaded so many people that their way is the way of the future."[35] What he calls the "new capitalism" is an economy in the process of reconfiguration around the model provided by these industries, invoking and eliciting a normative new self "oriented to the short term, focused on potential ability, willing to abandon past experience."[36]

Pierre-Michel Menger focuses even more explicitly on artistic and creative work. Rather than appearing in their old guise as "the reverse of work," he writes, artistic and creative activities "are, on the contrary, increasingly claimed to be the most advanced expression of new forms of production and of new work relationships resulting from recent changes in capitalism." This has implications for the social meaning of the artist in popular culture and managerial discourse, as well as in the survey and demographic data Menger analyzes. The creative worker becomes, in Menger's words, "a model figure of the new worker." Through this figure we may see "transformations as decisive as the breakup of the salaried world, the growth of autonomous professionals, the magnitude and undercurrents of contemporary disparities, the measure and the evaluation of competence [and] the individualization of work re-lationships": a range of developments, some of them distinctly antisocial.[37]

In general, scholars in the humanities and social sciences understand the development of this new model for the worker as bad news for most working people. The "magnitude and undercurrents of contemporary disparities" appear great and growing, and the degree to which the artistic worker becomes a model for new forms of work organization corresponds, in this view, to the degree to which working people may lose the ability to find or demand transparency in their treatment, or to make claims on employers and the state—and the degree to which, consequently, they become more vulnerable to new forms of social insecurity.[38]

Nonetheless, this new model has its boosters, for whom insecurity and vulnerability are coded as flexibility and mobility—in a word, as liberty. Working people from all walks of life, according to this perspective, should learn to become more like creative workers in order to adapt successfully to the neo-liberalizing society and economy. Mark Deuze, invoking a handy neologism (and oddly overlooking the high rate of union membership in the entertainment and media sectors) asserts that, like the artist, the worker of today must prefer "individual independence and autonomy over the relative stability of a lifelong workstyle based on the collective bargaining power of a specific group, sector, or union of workers."[39] "Flexibilization" along these lines, according to Deuze, has many upsides. In the context of the destabilization of institutions and social bonds, "it is perhaps the perfect paradox in contempo-rary . . . life" that "those workers caught in the epicenter of this bewildering shift also express a sense of mastery over their lives, interpreting their pro-fessional identity in this context in terms of individual-level control and em-powering agency."[40] Citing Ulrich Beck, Deuze indicates that "mastery" and "empowerment" in this context appear as "biographical solutions of systemic contradictions," the results of individuals' struggles to accommodate forces far beyond individual control.[41] Nevertheless, in Deuze's formulation this im-portant sociological critique is merely descriptive.[42]

The forms of work organization that the more critical prefigurative ap-proach sees as operative in cultural work, and as on the horizon in other sectors, can be understood to incorporate new modes of labor control. Em-ployers leaning toward neoliberal social forms see models of flexible work and of workers in cultural industries, and those employers appear increas-ingly to believe that following those models would excuse them from a range of conventional employer obligations. Like artists, critics of this shift point out, workers are increasingly pressured to take responsibility for their own training, successes, and failures and to accustom themselves to short-term, uncertain, "project-based" employment. The minimization of employer obligations through the recasting of routine work on the model of artistic work decreases economic and other forms of friction as firms seek to adapt to and exploit marginal shifts in markets. In Goetz Briefs's view, "from the standpoint of efficient management, the ideal production material is described as follows: It is obtained at the lowest possible cost but is nevertheless 100 percent effective; it is highly adaptable, is economical to use, and is readily movable from place to place; it is a calculable quantity, can be used without unwelcome side effects, and can be replaced at a moment's notice." He concludes that "from the point of view of one who manages a plant or a great industrial enterprise, that 'material' which is labor comes up to the ideal when it shows these same characteristics."[43] That "'material' which is labor" shows these same characteristics when workers have lowered expectations and make minimal demands regarding their rights, the security of their places in the economy, their ability to depend on social provisions such as health care and unemployment insurance, and so on. Restraining the kinds of demands that workers can make or can imagine making on their employers liberates employers; the model of artistic or creative work helps to exemplify, legitimize, and generate discourse about this kind of shift. The ideally flexible worker expects and requires relatively little of her employer or the state and can therefore be used with fewer "unwelcome side effects" than a worker accustomed to greater public and private entitlements.

There is yet a third variant of the prefigurative approach that largely brackets questions of the "new model worker." Mark Banks proposes a "liberal-democratic" view that recognizes the rationalizing and disciplining of creative work, and the ways creative workers often perform discounted creative labor with little or no job security.[44] But the "individualizing" tendencies of modern economic life also bear promise in this view. New media and new media channels support the proliferation of "critical world-views." The "necessity of choice" native to creative cultural work, Banks contends, has liberating effects on those who create for a living. In the cultural workplace, choice and reflexivity "open up opportunities to break away from social prescriptions that would seek to contain individuals in traditional roles largely determined by, and beneficial to, capitalist institutions." In his view, "encouraging people to 'be independent' and 'think for themselves' runs the risk that one day they may actually do it," portending challenges to overarching political and economic structures.[45]

The individualization characteristic of creative cultural work, decried by critics like Menger (because it represents the narrowing of access to welfare-state institutions) and praised by boosters like Deuze (because it underwrites radical new degrees of freedom and mobility), is cautiously embraced by Banks. He sees both tendencies and holds out hope that new visions for social reform can be nurtured and take on preliminary, prefigurative form among increasingly socially insecure—but necessarily relatively autonomous—cultural-industry workers.[46] However, Banks never really defines or explains what he means by "liberal-democratic": the concept remains something of a black box in his analysis. The coupling of liberalism and democracy is not, as he seems to think, self-evident. As the discussions in chapters 3 and 4 indicate, liberalism and democracy can be shown to exist in sometimes extraordinary tension, even under conventional definitions.

Critics of the prefigurative character of creative cultural work suggest that norms of cultural work should remain marginal, and that workers in other sectors should not be asked to give up security in exchange for freedoms of unproven value. Celebrators of that character argue the opposite, and the cautiously optimistic in between look for unseen benefits. However, underlying these views, as well as the atavistic perspective outlined below, is the assumption that creative cultural work is essentially different from other forms of work because it involves the production of individual, novel symbolic goods whose chief distinction is their capacity to be meaningful.[47] The perspective developed in this volume, however, suggests that downplaying that distinction can give us theoretical and critical leverage in our examination of cultural labor as a component in the social division of labor.

Emissaries from the Past

Scholarly analysis of creative cultural labor also looks backward to older forms of work and organization for help in explaining the peculiar forms that creative cultural work takes. In different branches of cultural production, in Miege's view, "capital is put to work in very different ways, which in part relate back to the historical conditions which determined capital's original penetration of these different branches."[48] To many scholars, creative cultural labor appears anachronistically to preserve or retain artisanal or craft forms of work and work organization in the context of contemporary global capitalist industry.[49] For example, in his 1970 study, Robert Faulkner observed in passing that the "performers who work in the Los Angeles recording studios are anachronistic in our age of large-scale industrial organizations."[50] These anachronistic relations appear as the obverse of the cultural capitalists' requirement for continual innovation in cultural products; the one requires and supports the other.

Bill Ryan explores what he calls "the contradictions of the art-capital relation," arguing that the culture and organization of the cultural industries are characterized by legacies carried into the present by the durable conventions and discourses of art. Generations of cultural capitalists have modified these legacies: they have "reconstructed the original artistic division of labour around new technological forms and reconstituted the artist as an enormous variety of specialised occupations." Yet each of the artistic occupations, as it underwent capitalist reconstruction, "retained residues of its origins."[51] This view explains the unusual autonomy of artistic or creative workers as, in significant measure, a relic of decentralized craft control. Cultural industries' characteristic autonomy "has been carried over from preceding eras," agrees Hesmondhalgh.[52] Creative workers appear in this view to retain or preserve less-alienated forms of work and work organization. This translates into their integration into firms in global cultural industries in a generally loose manner, although numerous heterogeneous forces work to tighten this integration. In cultural industries "workshops," Banks finds "the endurance (and indeed necessity) of creatively led, craft systems of production even in advanced industrialized contexts."[53] Keith Negus offers a contrasting elaboration of this anachronistic principle along complementary lines in his discussion of the "rock aristocracy," musicians "who have used their economic wealth to invest in land, property and businesses." Negus sees successful artists establishing themselves effectively as country squires through the acquisition of estates and works of art, expressing, in Pierre Bourdieu's words, "the art of living of the aristocrat . . . indifferent to the passage of time and rooted in things which last."[54]

In general, these conceptions of the anachronism of creative cultural labor are ambivalent and do not benefit from references, for example, to art history, labor history, or economic history sources. Miege's ambivalence is exemplary; he argues that "the 'handicraft' structures of artistic creation continued to function despite the development of industry."[55] He also notes that "even with the cultural industries, creation still proceeds largely by handicraft methods." The reason for this is "the fact that most of the creative people are outside the scope of the wage structure, and that the division of labor is less developed than in other branches of industry."[56] Yet Miege claims elsewhere that this view is ideological: "For a long time it was believed that in the production of art—including reproducible works—craft or pre-industrial methods were still the rule, and that disruption by industry was limited to the stages of reproduction and distribution." However, he continues, "this point of view, already highly debatable for certain commodities such as books, films, or records—but a highly convenient argument to convince artists to accept low prices—is a serious obstacle in understanding contemporary cultural phenomena."[57] I argue that both prefigurative and atavistic positions are useful and that they are particularly illuminating when taken together.

Nonsynchronicity

The significance of the pronounced forward- and backward-looking characteristics of creative cultural labor has not yet, in itself, been much developed for the insights it can provide, even by scholars who perceive both divergent dimensions, explicitly or implicitly. The usefulness of an adequate historicization and theorization of creative cultural labor for understanding the highly naturalized and largely submerged politics of work and employment is made clearer by foregrounding its Janus-faced nature.

Standing apart from the range of perspectives that sense (while leaving largely underexplored) the significance of creative cultural labor's Janus-like appearance are the views of Fredric Jameson. He suggests that we see historical modes of production as multimodal and "differential" in that "each 'more advanced' mode of production includes the earlier ones, which it has had to suppress in its own emergence." He adds: "These are therefore sedimented within a mode of production like capitalism, in which the earlier forms, along with their own specific forms of alienation and productivity, persist in a layered, 'canceled' fashion." Drawing on the work of Ernst Bloch, Jameson observes that "vanquished modes of production from the past . . . survive in the 'nonsynchronicity' of the present mode."[58] This concept of "nonsynchronicity" is not unidirectional; Jameson also endorses a prefigurative approach: "It is also clear that future modes of production are also at work in the present and can be detected most visibly in the various local forms of class struggle."[59] From this perspective, it becomes clear that "no mode of production exists in any pure state." Jameson's view highlights the "contradictory overlay and structural coexistence of several modes of production in tension with one another."[60]

Although Jameson does not see this "overlay" as occurring only or mainly in cultural production, he does note that it is heightened in creative cultural work. "Modern art," he writes, "drew its power and possibilities from being a backwater and an archaic holdover within a modernizing economy. . . . Aesthetic production . . . offered the Utopian vision of a more human production generally." Noting the symbolic resonance of creative cultural work, Jameson adds: "In the world of the monopoly stage of capitalism it [modern art] exercised a fascination by way of the image it offered of a Utopian transformation of human life." Debates about postmodernism aside, popular music (as Simon Frith, Keir Keightley, Warren Zanes, and others have argued) appears in this light as a durable bastion of modern utopian practices and values, having absorbed through multiple channels a range of discourses of aesthetic and personal autonomy that are now often bundled together under the heading of authenticity. The modern perspective on "aesthetic production," Jameson suggests, foregrounds autonomy. That perspective holds that, in contrast to the "human beings in the streets outside," the artist's "feeling of freedom and autonomy . . . comes when, like [James] Joyce, you can make or at least share in making your own decisions." "As a form of production," Jameson writes, "modernism gives off a message that has little to do with the content of individual works: it is the aesthetic as sheer autonomy, as the satisfactions of handicraft transfigured."[61] Jameson suggests that the autonomy of the artist has a significance of its own, that the artist occupies a status that has meaning beyond the content of the work. I find this to be a very provocative insight. In fact, much of the argument of this book reflects an attempt to clarify the social significance of the artist or creative cultural-industry worker along these lines, through an extended examination of the symbolic, political, and economic aspects of the popular music recording artist.

Unfree Masters takes the idea of "nonsynchronicity"—"the coexistence of realities from radically different moments of history—handicrafts alongside the great cartels, peasant fields with the Krupp factories or the Ford plant in the distance"—as a point of departure.[62] I contend that it is not a perspectival contradiction to see creative work and workers as embodying and representing both the past and the future of work. It is, rather, to recognize something specific about the nature of creative cultural-industry labor as an example of labor in capitalism. Framing this study around this ambiguous overlay and coexistence of different modes of production, as well as their associated "specific forms of alienation and productivity" in cultural labor, brings to the surface provocative linkages between cultural labor and other forms and moments of work that existing scholarly literature has largely bypassed. Specifically, *Unfree Masters* focuses squarely on the Janus-faced appearance of music makers in the commercial music industry. It perceives them as confronting apparently long-settled principles of domination and appropriation in employment and rendering them controversial, while at the same time prefiguratively instantiating processes of individualization, appropriation, and domination now ratcheting up at the margins. The confrontations of artists and their employers or investors on the issue of control of creative labor and property atavistically hearken back to and enact formative moments and basic principles of capitalist development, while at the same time making visible the laws and logics that govern contemporary forms of employment and contracting. Televisual and cinematic narratives of entry into the recording industry instruct workers of all kinds in modes of comportment and new sets of values appropriate to the coming regime, while at the same time telling stories about somewhat de-alienated forms of artisanal or craft labor that appear to "persist," despite widespread transformations of the labor process in modern society.

Creative Workers

Unfree Masters focuses on the representation and regulation of relations of power and property that characterize the relationships of recording artists to each other and to their present and prospective employers in the recording industry. Throughout the book, I keep constantly in mind the fact that although the artists and their employers engage each other through otherwise outmoded or vanquished organizational forms, they do *not* operate outside the broader political, economic, societal, and legal structures that form the scaffolding for most contractual relations of labor and property.

The book starts from the novel assumption that, as creative agents, US recording artists (and many other workers in creative cultural industries) also hold jobs in a capitalist system and therefore have much in common with all other employees. Creative cultural workers, like other employees, are subject to control by their employers and to the appropriation of the products of their labor. This is an inescapable fact of employment that so far has escaped the interest of scholars of cultural industries, possibly because it seems so normal and institutionalized that it is not worthy of discussion, and possibly because, despite their legal status, many creative cultural-industry employees do not appear to be employees.[63] Taking the employment form as an objectively existing factor of creative cultural work (that is, a factor that exists independent of its perception by participants or scholars), I argue, opens up the significance of the unusual autonomy and proprietorship of recording artists and other authorial cultural-industry workers in political terms as a marginal—but not anomalous—social form. The actual forms taken by control and appropriation differ in different sectors of work, but the principles remain constant: they are intrinsic to the employment relation and to accumulation in liberal society. Without the legal capacity to control labor and appropriate its products, the cultural industries as we know them could not exist. The same is true for capitalist enterprise in general. I argue that awareness and consideration of this similarity, however obvious and therefore unremarkable it may seem, advances the development of political and theoretical conceptions of work in the cultural industries.

If creative cultural-industry labor heralds new ideological and organizational shifts in noncultural sectors, this can be the case only because shared elements of sociopolitical status renders workers across the board vulnerable to similar kinds of treatment. What is shifting in the broader economic field and the field of social power is where lines are drawn to demarcate zones of greater and lesser vulnerability (and therefore to differentiate between more and less vulnerable workers), the ways in which vulnerabilities and protections are being reallocated, and the range of choices available to different kinds and groups of actors in particular historical contests. If, at the same time, creative labor embodies anachronistic social forms, this is only because it shares essential features with earlier forms of work—not just in terms of their appearance, as the scholars of cultural industries seem to suggest, but also in terms of their political-economic structures and relations.

This "nonsynchronicity" between dominant and marginal or residual modes of production accounts in some degree for the puzzles that confront legislators when they intervene in contests over creative labor and property in the cultural industries. Taken together, these ideas reflect an impetus to push the analysis of creative cultural work in new directions, to examine its social form and its politics against a broader political and historical background than has so far been the norm in research on cultural industries, and to imagine the roles such an analysis might play in generating and supporting solidarity across established ideological, sectorial, and class divides. Creative cultural work can be understood as both prefigurative and atavistic because the "specific forms of alienation and productivity" that comprise it reflect its position at the margins of (but not outside) employment, where control of labor and appropriation of property are not settled but remain matters of contest.

Representation and Regulation

Unfree Masters examines social relations of and stories told about commercial music making in late-twentieth-century US society. Drawing not only on the communication, media studies, sociological, and social-theoretical sources familiar to scholars of popular culture and popular music, but also on less familiar legal and political-theoretical scholarship, the book presents detailed accounts of revealing encounters — on television, in film, and before the law — between players in a high-stakes, highly hierarchical cultural industry. It treats professional (and professionalizing) music makers as workers with exceptionally autonomous relationships to their labor processes, the products of their labor, the executives and managers who oversee the fulfillment of their contractual obligations, and the companies they work for.

Unfree Masters analyzes not only relationships and stories about them, however. It also analyzes the laws that govern these relationships, the linkages between those laws and the struggles over them to dynamics that have historically been specific to the music industry, and the roles and perspectives of the lawmakers in whose democratically delegated power it is to alter or preserve those laws. Political economy, in Isaac Rubin's view, "deals with human working activity, not from the standpoint of its technical methods and instruments of labor, but from the standpoint of its social form. It deals with *production relations* which are established among people in the process of production."[64] Using this definition, this book is a political-economic analysis of the social forms of creative labor in the music industry. It explores the ways in which individuals and groups are configured as "recording artists" as they are integrated into the industry and set to work largely on its terms, and it examines the political and legal relations of labor and property that characterize the institutions in which they struggle for and sometimes achieve profitability.

At the same time, *Unfree Masters* explores and theorizes the relationship of creative work in the music industry to the broader world and history of work, suggesting a new conception of creative cultural work. The struggles of aspiring recording artists for success in *American Idol* and as treated in rockumentary films, and those of established artists over the regulations that govern ownership of musical property and control of musical labor, I argue, are intimately related not only to each other but to emerging as well as longstanding problems in work more broadly conceived. Stories about creative work in the music industry and the politics of cultural work around which those stories are constructed articulate pivotal issues in the politics of employment, a foundational (yet mutable) institution of liberal market society, sometimes with startling clarity, sometimes "through a glass darkly." This perspective represents not so much a synthesis of ideas about the anachronisms in creative cultural-industry work as an exploration of what makes it possible for cultural work to represent so much to so many.

Axes of Alienation

The framework developed here translates the conventional dualistic perspective on cultural work that highlights cultural capitalists' need for both novelty and stability into the observation that different social and historical forms of work can be understood to take place at different points on what might be called axes of alienation. In other words, labor that produces things or services of value is subject to forms of alienation of different kinds, of which two stand out as basic: first, social-psychological; and second, political-legal. The social-psychological axis, introduced above, focuses on alienation as something experienced in largely subjective terms. Working from categories initially described by Marx, Blauner identifies aspects of workers' experience of work as locatable on continua that he names "powerlessness," "meaninglessness," "social isolation," and "self-estrangement."[65] Recording artists and other creative cultural-industry workers represent a happy model to the boosters in the prefigurative camp because they seem to be so free of these forms of alienation. They represent a dismal model to those followers of Michel Foucault whom Banks calls "governmentalists." To these scholars, overcoming alienation in some or most of these terms is an essential part of creative workers' actual subjugation, integrating microrelations of freedom and autonomy ever more completely into ultimately disciplinary regimes in which individuals with lowered social expectations are called on to regulate themselves.[66] Banks, in contrast, finds these gains real and meaningful, though under constant threat, and they form the basis for his cautious optimism.[67]

I agree that the forms of de-alienation enjoyed by creative cultural-industry workers along these lines are real and substantial. But drawing on critical scholarship in political economy and political theory (as well as law), I propose and develop a second, complementary political-legal axis, which highlights categories of alienating work relations registered in terms that are more objective than subjective because they exist independently of individuals' experience of them. Here I refer to the relations of command and appropriation that are codified in the contracts governing the power and property relations of employers and employees, and the laws that determine the contents and enforceability of those contracts. Along this axis, then, are two continua: self-government (less in a governmentalist than in a more classically democratic-theoretic sense) and property appropriation. The former measures not workers' experience of powerlessness, but rather the capacity of employers to control their employees' labor: the legal, practical, and contractual lineaments of what Pateman calls "civil mastery" and "civil subordination."[68] The latter measures the degrees to which creative workers enjoy property rights (or quasi-proprietary rights) over the works they produce under contract. Just as all employees can be said to experience their work as more or less alienating along the subjective lines Blauner suggests, so they can be said to have more or fewer legal and contractual rights to control their labor and its associated or resulting products (in this case intellectual property), independent of how they might feel about the presence or absence of these rights. These axes allow revealing comparisons between creative cultural-industry workers and those in more mundane worlds of work.

For most employees, being insufficiently powerful to bargain for control and ownership is so normal that ownership and control do not present themselves as possibilities. In contrast, the creative cultural-industries worker often sees a threat to or lack of bargaining power as an indignity, if not an outrage. Recording artists (for reasons that emerge over the course of this book) are paradigmatic in this regard. *Unfree Masters* presents creative workers in the cultural industries as a limit case of employment, as employees at the far end of the liberal employment relation. And it presents recording artists as a limit case of a limit case, workers whose sensitivity to the problems of domination and appropriation inherent in and essential to the liberal employment relation bring to light politics that are constantly at work in employment but that are obscured under mountains of accumulated liberal common sense.

Creative cultural-industry workers are a limit case because in general they are positioned closer to the less- or unalienated poles of these axes than most other working people are. If they are not close enough to enjoy all the benefits of de-alienation all the time, creative workers are nevertheless close enough to perceive that there is an unalienated pole that can function as an ideological North Star for them, even if only in ideal terms.[69] They are positioned close enough to know, for example, that the placement of the line between those who can be considered authors (and who on that basis may be eligible for ownership of the intellectual property they produce while at work) and those who can't is essentially political and subject to struggle and negotiation (see chapter 5). In a colloquial if not a legal sense, creative workers sometimes understand themselves as authors; this is why the bald appropriation of their work, although legal, can strike them as outrageous. In other words, where the worker understands herself to have made conceptual or authorial contributions in the course of working on a cultural product, an employer can find it difficult to obscure the fact that he is appropriating that property and the income associated with it, especially if that product goes on to have a long and successful life in critical or commercial terms.[70]

As recording artists gain in fame, sales, and licensing ventures—as they and their products increase in value—the terms of their original contracts (signed when they were unknowns) often seem increasingly exploitative. Moreover, in a context where a creative worker has the subjective experience of de-alienation (through the experience of his work as meaningful and self-expressive), employers' political and legal alienation (that is, their appropriation) of her property and income can engender her resentment and resistance, which can disrupt or threaten the employer's power to appropriate. Creative workers, however, do their jobs in volatile, highly risky cultural-industry enterprises, where they often enjoy significant degrees of autonomy and even proprietary or quasi-proprietary rights over the unique designs, narratives, songs, characters, images, and other cultural goods that they produce.[71] For such a worker, every new contract is an opportunity to negotiate for (in fact, more likely an opportunity to lose) control and ownership. The relative market strength of the parties to any given contract at any given time will determine who gets to control how much of the production process and who gets to own how much of the final product.

Creative cultural-industry workers are positioned more or less precisely at the "point of alienation,"[72] where law, liberal philosophy, and social convention enable employers to separate employees from the valuable goods (material, intellectual, and emotional) they produce in the course of their work, as well as from control over their own labor. Along with more or less universal suffrage and public education, employment is one of the defining institutions of modern society; along with other institutions, employment undergoes major historical changes while nevertheless retaining core features. These features include its widespread integration of individuals without means of their own into profit-seeking corporate enterprises, which are governed by their owners or their owners' designated agents. Enterprises are empowered to alienate—to separate, in legal and political terms—employees from claims on or rights to self-government and the property and value produced in the course of work. Stan Weir puts it starkly: "The moment that any of us goes on employer time, whether or not we are physically present on company property, supervisors do not have to deal with us on the basis of the rights concepts contained within the Constitution. We become an extension of the employers' private property, and so in large part, have left the jurisdiction of the regular law. From this view, it can be seen that every place of employment is a separate domain that has its own private government." He continues: "The seriousness of this situation comes into clear relief when we bring to mind a fact so obvious that it is mainly ignored: most of the waking hours of the work force are spent on the job."[73] What is a problem to Weir (and to other thinkers discussed in the second part of this book) appears to most people, most of the time, as the routine, unremarkable, voluntary exchange of properties: one person's work in exchange for a wage or salary from another. I sacrifice my autonomy for eight hours a day of doing what you tell me to do; you pay me a wage; and any profit you accrue is yours alone to keep. The exchange of obedience to the boss and surrendering all claims on the products of labor for a wage is "accepted as part of the furniture of the social world."[74]

Charles Taylor proposes that in contemporary society, the artist "becomes in some way the paradigm of the human being, as agent of original self-definition."[75] Popular music makers, in particular, in Toynbee's words, appear to be "exemplary agents" enjoying apparently unalienated conditions of work and extensive powers of original self-definition.[76] They generally don't even appear to be employees; common sense often casts recording artists as independent contractors, entrepreneurs, or petty capitalists in their own right, autonomously producing unique and expressive intellectual properties that they license to record companies and from which (should they succeed financially) they derive royalties. Royalties, in fact, are a kind of rent; their receipt makes successful artists appear even more like capitalists in the form of *rentiers*—those who make money from property and investment. Contemporary talent shows, rockumentary films, and other televisual and cinematic stories of music makers and music making present musical work as compelling, individual, expressive, self-actualizing, fun, rewarding, enriching, autonomous, proprietary—a model of de-alienating work and success to be emulated far and wide. But this utopian capitalist model of work is saturated with politics: participants at all levels are slotted into hierarchical systems of property allocation and power relations. As long as records are selling, income and advances keep debt under control, regulations appear suited to norms of business practice, and things are going smoothly, most of these power relations remain in the background. However, in moments of transition or crisis, the rules of the system, both ancient and futuristic, come into dramatic focus.

The Chapters

Chapter 1 analyzes *American Idol*'s narratives of success and authentication and of failure and humiliation in the context of an examination of its formidable ratings success. It considers the ways *Idol*'s narratives propose strategies for individuals' simultaneous negotiation of contemporary economic conditions and construction and maintenance of authentic selves. Just as dramatic stories of succeeding and failing bids for social mobility in a high-stakes occupational ecology amplify the appeal of *American Idol*, the musical performances around which the show is built provide the magnetic pole that aligns the attention of an unusually wide audience to these stories. The fragmentation of work and the end of the lifelong career put American workers increasingly in the position of having to audition continuously to get and keep their jobs. Chapter 1 suggests that popular music, work, and narrative are linked through the metaphor of the audition, and *American Idol* is all about auditions, successful and unsuccessful.

Chapter 2 examines the 2004 rockumentary film *Dig!* as it follows the diverging career trajectories of two West Coast "indie rock" bands. The Dandy Warhols and the Brian Jonestown Massacre (BJM) start out the film as peers: the former group has just signed a record deal with a major label, and the latter seems on the cusp of a similar deal. Their shared path splits as the Dandys work their way up to bigger international audiences, and as the BJM appears dragged down and sabotaged by its leader's entropic mental state. This chapter's analysis of the film and aspects of its context—including the professional trajectory of the filmmaker—shows that in the course of indie professionalization, authenticity is something to be managed in relation to another element in the constellation of values at the center of this book: autonomy. The story of the Dandys' careful management and attenuation of their claims of authenticity, however useful it might be as a model for individuals seeking to live their lives right, is overshadowed by the arguably less helpful story of the BJM leader's disintegration. This is what I call the bait and switch in *Dig!*: first the bait, consisting in the lure of real autonomy; then the switch, the substitution of a less-secure form of autonomy that is the obverse of what the contemporary rockumentary's typical career narrative represents.

Chapter 3 recounts an episode in the history of the American recording industry that has been little discussed outside of legal scholarship. In 1987, in response to heavy lobbying by the Recording Industry Association of America (RIAA), the California legislature enacted a law that effectively excluded recording artists from the protection of the state's century-old "seven year rule," a law that prohibits the enforcement of employment contracts beyond the period of time indicated by its name. This chapter examines the conditions that drove the RIAA to seek the change and analyzes the arguments offered for and against it at the time, making use of political-economic theories deriving from works of economic history and economic sociology. In the context of intensifying rounds of industry consolidation and companies' increased dependence on blockbusters, the "Olivia Newton-John problem" brought to light certain limits on record companies' power to capture recording artists' labor. I argue that the RIAA's member companies sought to enhance their power by making recording artists—whose contracts had been limited to seven years, just like those of all other California employees—vulnerable to contracts of effectively unlimited duration. The chapter recounts the process by which the final form of the law was enacted, showing the perseverance of ancient logics of labor control in a cutting-edge, global enterprise and offering new evidence and arguments about the ways in which cultural-industry corporations and trade associations manipulate the law to gain favorable business terms. (The labor laws of California discussed in this chapter and the next are important for the nation's music industry. This is partly because of the large amount of contracting that takes place in the state, as well as the large number of recording artists and companies based there. But it is also partly because in states where no equivalent laws exist, California laws offer a standard that local courts sometimes consider when asked to adjudicate contractual matters.)

Chapter 4 tells the story of the 2001–2 attempt by recording artists, their allies, and sympathetic legislators to overturn the 1987 exception examined in chapter 3. In this case, however, the focus is not so much on recording industry history as it is on the rhetorical strategies engaged in by the artists and their employers in the struggle over this controversial amendment. The empirical center of gravity is the testimony offered at 2001 and 2002 legislative hearings over contract practices in the record industry and proposed repeal legislation. I argue that, in their attack on this law, the recording artists' colorful invocation of slavery and indentured servitude actually raised critical questions about the nature of employment and contract in a liberal democracy. These questions, I argue, demand a critical consideration of the tensions between liberalism and democracy that are evident in the employment relation. However, as I show, when faced with the mesmerizing starkness of contractarian arguments that they signed their contracts voluntarily and therefore had nothing to complain about, the artists were unable to marshal compelling arguments to support their demand for the right to terminate their employment. In this rhetorical failure, I argue, they missed an opportunity to foster and draw on real solidarity beyond the offices of their own unions and lawyers, and the public missed an opportunity to examine the politics of employment critically through the lens of the recording artists' dramatic struggle.

Finally, chapter 5 examines another encounter between recording artists and their employers, this time in front of a committee of the US Congress. In late 1999, the RIAA engineered a change to copyright law that turned "sound recordings" (songs and albums) into "works made for hire." Work for hire is controlled by the part of copyright law that allocates to the employer the authorship and ownership of intellectual property produced in the context of an employment relation. Thus, under this new definition, the legal author and owner of the sound recording is the company that employs the artist. The law's passage outraged and drew protests from recording artists and their allies. The artists were able finally to compel repeal of the 1999 change by invoking their status as independently contracting employers. What decided the matter was not the question of who actually authored the songs or albums, but who was an employee and who was an employer within a given division of authorship and in legal terms. In contradiction of their arguments before the California legislature, the recording artists' position was that they were, first, the employers of numerous other creative and technical workers. They argued that their status as employers gave them the power of appropriation under work for hire.

Unfree Masters demonstrates that the assertions by a range of analysts that creative workers can and should be understood as avatars of the coming neoliberal regime of work are intriguing and well supported, and that anxieties over what that fact portends for most working people are warranted. But it goes further, showing how nonfictional representations of the professionalization of music makers (as just one example of creative workers) help to sell the rest of us on these new work arrangements. It shows how varieties of domination and appropriation—which are close to the surface in creative work but largely obscured in other forms of work—are re-naturalized through these processes and their representation. Moreover, the book foregrounds the shared aspects of creative and other forms of work as it follows the politics of music making behind the screens of representation and into the realm of legislation. This is the arena in which music industry players argue over and sometimes change the contents of contract and copyright law, the main forms of legislation that structure the playing field of professional and commercial cultural production. These struggles force music makers to declare themselves in political terms, in order to be recognizable to the law and to further their legislative projects and goals. As either employees or employers (they appear as both in the second part of this book), they are irremediably political and economic subjects operating in the same legal world as all the rest of us, engaging with and struggling over laws that affect all workers in a given jurisdiction (in these cases, either the United States as a whole or California).

Stories about contemporary media making help us see the shape of things to come in the neoliberalizing world of work; contract and copyright law bear the traces, and codify the results, of struggles between workers and employers over issues of autonomy and property going back centuries. Holding up for scrutiny both the stories that the media tell us about creative work and the legal struggles over the basic terms of creative work enables the central features of each to deepen our understanding of the other. It brings into focus the significance and the stakes of creative work in the context of a political economy undergoing tectonic shifts.

Let me echo Robert Curtis's exhortation: "Yes, come and join me in the wonderful world of music."[77]

Discourses of creativity . . . play
an important economic function.
—**David Hesmondhalgh,**
The Cultural Industries, 2nd ed.

PART I
REPRESENTATION

P art I of *Unfree Masters* brings into relief some of the ways popular music making becomes narrativized in contemporary America and how narratives of music making align with and become part of American socioeconomic discourse. The representation of popular music making in the mass media has a long history and a strikingly consistent set of story lines, whether presented as fictional or nonfictional. Warner Bros.' pioneering 1927 sound film *The Jazz Singer*, for example, tells the story of a young Jewish man for whom popular music is a mode of activity through which he can navigate between the traditional roles and social identities of the Old World culture of his immigrant parents and ethnic community and the exciting, alluring American scene in which he finds himself. For *The Jazz Singer*'s Jakie Rabinowitz, popular music is a form of expression that enables him to define himself as an authentic, self-actualizing young American, in a richly rewarding, highly autonomous profession, embedded in a booming entertainment industry composed of similarly fascinating, individuated, ambitious people. Numerous films, radio programs, and television shows have presented the professionalization of music makers and aspiring stars along these narrative lines, many of them focusing quite intensively on the challenges to musicians' conception of themselves as authentic, individuated self-actualizers by the commercial imperatives of the American music industry.

Such narratives often seem to offer substantial insights to people of all kinds regarding their socioeconomic mobility and the harmonious development of their powers. In this part of *Unfree Masters*, my aim is to explore and analyze the narratives of work, failure, and success offered in two very different representations of musical activity. The television talent show *American Idol* and the 2004 rockumentary *Dig!* trace the struggles of aspiring young musicians toward professionalization in the pop and indie rock fields, respectively. Each of these productions focuses on the problems and complications that confront people who, following in the footsteps of Jakie Rabinowitz, seek authentic, self-actualizing individuation as they pursue a career in professional music making. Part I analyzes the stories that *American Idol* and *Dig!* tell about the work of music making and the challenges of professionalization in the highly competitive recording industry. But as authoritative voices in and around *American Idol* and *Dig!* make clear, these stories are also about comportment and advancement in worlds of work outside of the cultural industries. Along with some of the scholars discussed in the introduction, these voices argue that the strategies of musical professionalization of aspiring pop singers and indie rockers are instructive for working people of all kinds faced with an occupational and career terrain undergoing neoliberal transformation.

As Katherine Meizel shows, *American Idol* tells stories about its contestants' professional and personal lives; these stories typically focus on themes of religious, regional, political, ethnic, racial, and gender identity.[1] In addition to these dimensions, however, the contestants' success and failure to navigate the various obstacles and tests on the way to their desired professional position is another salient dimension of the program. Chapter 1 focuses on these narratives of success and failure in terms of the program's humiliating or authenticating treatment of the aspiring singing stars. *American Idol* presents itself both implicitly and explicitly as offering useful lessons about how to prepare oneself for a career in the music industry and how to navigate the path from the privacy of the family home or dorm room to the public stage and on to the brass ring of the record contract. At the same time, the program and its participants frequently relate the dynamics of success and failure in professional music making to those of what Richard Sennett calls the "new capitalism."[2] Chapter 1 explores these interrelated narratives and social structures.

Dig! offers a complementary form of instructive narrative. However, where *American Idol* seeks and enjoys mass audiences, *Dig!* is aimed at a smaller, more rarefied crowd. The art-house audiences of this documentary, which won a prize at the 2004 Sundance Film Festival, possess different kinds of cultural capital than many *American Idol* fans, yet the film's narratives of success and failure are also framed in terms of their much broader usefulness. My analysis suggests, however, that the two bands featured in the film are not the only characters to whom we should pay attention. The contemporary conventions of the documentary put the filmmaker (and even, to some degree, her collaborators) into the frame and narrative of the film. She too is a cultural producer on the path to professionalization, and this complicates the picture. The steps encompassed in a season of *American Idol*—from a convention center audition to Hollywood and then, for a lucky but certain few, to a record contract—are huge. In *Dig!* professionalization is incremental. The filmmaker and one of the bands experience career advancement; the other band disintegrates; but nobody in *Dig!* experiences a scalar or temporal transformation equivalent to *American Idol*'s construction of a fast lane from rags to riches.

Both of these productions show actual and aspiring music makers negotiating the limits of freedom and autonomy in creative cultural-industry work. *American Idol*'s hopeful singers, attracted to pop stardom at least in large part for its freedom and autonomy, must be careful not to overstep their limits as they try to create space for themselves in a highly competitive and hierarchical industry. The appropriate attitude and approach toward their goal involves (among other things) a tricky balance of self-assertion, expression, supplication, and obedience. Similarly, among the main distinctions between the succeeding Dandy Warhols and the discombobulating Brian Jonestown Massacre are their very different attitudes toward the power structures of the record industries. Evident in the bands' trajectories are their more and less successful strategies for pleasing those in positions of power and for framing those strategies in ways that enable them to say that they are making it on their own terms.

In his *Discourse on the Origin of Inequality*, Rousseau speculates that inequality emerged at a point when individuals become capable of accumulating an embryonic form of wealth or capital he called "public esteem." The first cultural medium of the dawning process of social ranking is not wisdom or learning, not the manipulation of the natural environment, not storytelling or oratory, but music. For Rousseau, it appears, the linkage between music making and social hierarchization is so self-evident that at this pivotal point in the *Discourse* he imagines and proposes musical performance as both the preeminent site of distinction and the first act of social mobility. The origin of inequality, he argued, could be located in the moment when "singing and dancing, the true offspring of love and leisure, became the amusement, or rather the occupation, of men and women . . . assembled together with nothing else to do [because they had learned to satisfy their basic survival needs]. Each one began to consider the rest, and to wish to be considered in turn, and thus a value came to be attached to public esteem. Whoever sang or danced best, whoever was the handsomest, the strongest, the most dextrous, or the most eloquent, came to be of the most consideration; and this was the first step towards inequality, and at the same time towards vice. From these first distinctions arose on the one side vanity and contempt and on the other shame and envy: and the fermentation caused by these new leavens ended by producing combinations fatal to innocence and happiness."[3] Music is the matrix of inequality; being handsome, strong, dexterous and eloquent all have value in this account, but not one comes before singing.

Starting out on the same stages, at conference centers and hole-in-the-wall nightclubs, the protagonists in *American Idol* and *Dig!* experience radically different social trajectories as they lay claim to public esteem and then succeed or fail to accumulate it. Winners and losers regard each other as their paths diverge; television and cinema audiences—promised helpful clues in exchange for their attention—also look on. Vanity, contempt, shame, and envy are crucial themes in the narratives of music and social mobility I examine in these chapters.

O passion to gain distinction, of
what are you not capable?

—Jean-Jacques Rousseau,
*Discourse on the Sciences and Arts
(First Discourse) and Polemics*

CHAPTER 1

American Idol and Narratives of Meritocracy

Early in September 2002, a former waitress from Texas is crowned the first "American Idol" in the season-ending episode of the Fox network's new reality TV/talent show. In the final moments of the program, giving way to tears and apologizing midsong for her lack of self-control, the twenty-year-old Kelly Clarkson sings: "I can't believe it's happening to me . . . some people wait a lifetime for a moment like this." Clouds of confetti flutter from the rafters as the other finalists gather around her on stage, singing along in emotionally imperfect harmony, their occasional sobs audible through Clarkson's microphone. Finalists, their families, the two hosts, and others crowd together on stage, hugging and weeping in a display of moist, vaguely patriotic sentiment. Finally, Ryan Seacrest, one of the program's hosts, breaks away and intones earnestly: "Thank you all so very much for watching. Thank you for all your support. If you think you could be on this stage, keep on watching. It could be you in a matter of months. An audition will be coming to a city near you soon, so watch out, this could be you, one year from now."[1] The camera remains focused on the swaying young contestants and others gathered on the stage, still embracing or holding hands, savoring this culminating moment. Through a rigorous, months-long process of competition and winnowing, *American Idol* has revealed and refined Kelly Clarkson's capacities and introduced this everywoman into the vertiginous echelons of the pop music elect.

Producing moments like this since 2002, *American Idol* has attracted unparalleled numbers of viewers, launched pop careers, and generated enormous profits as well as international franchisees and imitators. *American Idol*'s ratings climbed steadily across each of its first six seasons, from an average of thirteen million viewers per show in the first season to around thirty million for its late 2000s seasons.[2] In 2003, one Fox executive went so far as to call the show "ratings crack."[3] Because of its rapidly escalating audiences, advertising rates on *American Idol*—in retrospect a steal at around $200,000 per thirty-second spot in 2002—typically crested around $1,000,000 toward the finales of the first few seasons. Those figures too increased: by 2006, the average spot had doubled in price, and an ad during that year's finale cost up to $2,000,000.[4] Opportunities to sell increasingly valuable advertising time also expanded. The first season totaled about twenty-two hours of programming, but the second and third each totaled almost forty. This figure remains high, as the program often airs two or three separate episodes per week. The first season produced windfalls of exposure for advertisers and millions of fans for Kelly Clarkson and several of her runners-up. Subsequent seasons have advanced this trend; winners and finalists have won numerous Grammy, American Music, and other awards; have sold dozens of millions of albums; and have helped to sustain the American recording industry through a period of turmoil and uncertainty.[5]

Combining the democratic principle of an audience vote and the narrative principle of a months-long competition, *American Idol* has been a music-marketing phenomenon of unprecedented efficacy. However, its social and cultural power do not derive just from grooming performers and selling recordings and associated commodities in staggering numbers, but also from the program's development and distribution of compelling stories about what it means to be a pop singer. *American Idol* has reframed and revalued the institution of the popular music performer's career and contributed to discourses of success and social mobility in the early twenty-first century. The program has established itself as both an actual route to professional positions in and around the US music industry and as a set of stories that implicitly and explicitly present the trials, failures, and triumphs of its aspiring young pop stars as instructive for Americans of all ages and skill sets. Kelly

Clarkson's crowning moment at the end of *American Idol*'s first season encapsulates one of the program's main narrative threads: the idea that a correct approach toward the position you desire reflects a sincere respect for the institutions and gatekeepers involved, combined with a high degree of self-confidence and gumption, an absence of guile, and the willingness and ability to take risks and direction. These orientations in turn reflect shared perceptions of what constitutes an authentic self-presentation in the context of the program, a key part of *American Idol*'s recipe for success. "Authenticity," in Richard Dyer's view, "is established or constructed in media texts by the use of markers that indicate lack of control, lack of premeditation and privacy."[6] Clarkson's tearful performance in the season finale, her impromptu, intimate welcome of runners-up onto the stage, and their shared embraces around her microphone may have prevented a more "professional" performance of "A Moment Like This" that night, but it ratified her consecration in a way that no flawless performance could have. The title of her debut album— *Thankful*—captures this attitude economically.

American Idol exemplifies ways in which the institutions, narratives, and social relations of popular music making self-consciously offer prefigurative insights into work and society. In this chapter, with a close focus on the program's first season (June 11–September 4, 2002), I explore how *American Idol* weaves its highly constructed rites of passage (and of denials of passage) into narratives of opportunity, comportment, and social mobility. I suggest that the program departs from reality TV conventions in its coupling with a global industry and in the actual transitioning of some of its winners and runners-up into professional positions. This linkage lends the program an unmistakable gravity and constitutes an especially inviting space of imagination and identification, evidenced in part by the enormous crowds who flock to the program's mass auditions. I zero in on two of the primary forms of *American Idol*'s storytelling: stories of authentication (biographical and autobiographical vignettes that construct contestants as moral beings) and of humiliation (scenes of dramatic shaming for misplaced aspirations and poor auditions).[7] The program's resonance has much to do with the ways it presents participants and their travails as revealing secrets and offering tools for success in the entertainment industry and for social mobility in the emerging neoliberal economy. Furthermore, this chapter suggests that *American Idol*'s pedagogical narratives of authentication and humiliation shore up liberal-democratic promises of voice and self-actualization in a society in which such promises are fulfilled on increasingly unequal terms. *American Idol*'s narratives of earned pop consecration and righteous humiliation dramatize and legitimize the reconfiguring of the life course into a series of high-stakes auditions. At the dawn of the twenty-first century, the linear, progressive biography from adolescent experimentation to stable adult commitment is a thing of the past; second chances appear increasingly remote; the sorting of the deserving from the undeserving is swift and consequential.

The Show

Like the liberal market society that gives it its general form, *American Idol* derives from a British institution. In 2001's *Pop Idol* had been a commercial success in the United Kingdom, and Fox imported it virtually lock, stock, and barrel for US audiences. Each season begins with mass auditions, attracting tens of thousands of hopefuls. Typically, the first round of auditions results in a pool of over 100 singers; this group is then brought to Hollywood (actually Pasadena until 2009) and winnowed to a smaller number. The remaining contestants then compete live on television, before a panel of expert judges, seeking to win the phoned-in votes of the viewing audience.

The judges come from the upper reaches of the music industry. The original lineup of three participated in the first eight seasons; as of the tenth season only one of them remains. Simon Cowell is a British record industry executive with a string of pre-*Idol* hits to his credit; he remained on the program for its first nine seasons. Paula Abdul is a singer and dancer who had a high-profile career as a choreographer and recording artist before joining the show; she lasted eight seasons. At ten seasons and counting, Randy Jackson is a successful musician, music director, and artists and repertoire (A&R) executive who has worked with such big-name acts as Journey and Mariah Carey. *American Idol* has also featured numerous guest judges drawn from pop's pantheon, as well as from other realms of popular culture.

Once the initial rounds of eliminations are complete, a routine takes shape, with the singer receiving the lowest number of audience votes each week being dropped from the contest. This piecemeal elimination process continues until the winning contestant is revealed; the initial contract signed by each of the tens of thousands of aspirants commits the winner to a full-bore recording and management deal. (After weeks of exposure, however, several other finalists will have emerged as bankable talents and will walk away from the program with music contracts or receive other opportunities in the entertainment industry.) The winners' contracts are with the show's creator and executive producer Simon Fuller, architect of the Spice Girls and the *Pop Idol* program; and Simon Cowell, record label executive and lead judge for the program's first nine seasons. Cowell and Fuller also retain contract options on each of the ten finalists.[8]

Through their votes over the course of the season the audience registers interest and even emotional investment, which provide some indication of the *American Idol* finalists' market promise. The release of the first season's first recordings fulfilled this promise beyond expectations. *American Idol*'s producers commissioned songs for the first season's finalists (to be released, of course, on the producers' own label). Kelly Clarkson's recording of the song written especially for the climactic final episode of the first season—"A Moment Like This"—entered the *Billboard* pop charts at number 52, and within a week it had soared to number 1. It was reported then that, up to that time, the closest rival for this sort of chart movement had been the Beatles' 1964 "Can't Buy Me Love," which had advanced from number 27 to number 1 in a single week.[9] That this level of audience investment could be sustained for months following the final show and the release of the CD single was demonstrated by the mid-April 2003 debut at the top of the *Billboard* pop charts of Clarkson's first album, the appropriately titled *Thankful*. Within a few years, *American Idol* became an internationally franchised institution, with dozens of versions taking place all over the world. Regional networks and local stations have also imitated its format (*Protagonistas de la Musica*, for example, followed on the American Spanish-language network Telemundo).[10] A 2003 feature film starring Clarkson and first runner-up Justin Guarini (the screenplay was by Kim Fuller, brother of *Idol*'s executive producer Simon Fuller and writer of the Spice Girls movie *Spice World*) flopped, but the film's commercial failure did nothing to slow Clarkson's meteoric rise or the *Idol* juggernaut.

American Idol *and Reality Television*

American Idol hitched its wagon to the constellation of reality TV, a major recent development in media and society. According to many scholarly accounts, reality TV is an active participant in an ongoing, epochal transformation of society. Numerous analyses suggest that the genre is playing cultural handmaiden to a systematic reconfiguration of social, economic, and political institutions under the banner of neoliberalism. Neoliberalism (also known as "advanced liberalism") is a utopian political and economic philosophy that has as its lodestone a utopian conception of a self-regulating market and as its practical goal the proliferation of free-market mechanisms into vast areas of life. The advance of neoliberalization requires the virtual elimination, for example, of governments' abilities to limit the impacts of market players and forces on citizens' access to social goods such as education, health care, pensions, and to elements of commonwealth such as clean air and water, non-toxic food, nature, and so on. One of this philosophy's most consistent themes is that individuals are entitled, essentially, to nothing that they have not inherited or purchased. In particular, they are not entitled to the rights, protections, and provisions (such as the welfare states' social entitlements established after World War II and attacked by right-wing radicals in the early twenty-first century) that relieve people from certain degrees of dependence on markets. One of the principal aims of the neoliberal project is to render people more dependent on markets and employers, thereby increasing the need for people to accept work on the terms on which it is offered: with stagnating or lowered wages, few or no benefits, and little if any dignity or security.[11] Reality TV, many analysts agree, plays a role in producing a cultural or ideological environment conducive to these transformations. Reality TV's "obsessive" focus on labor is substantiated in terms of its arguments for the importance of grooming oneself and competing for, obtaining, and keeping desirable forms of remunerative work—and moving up to still-more-desirable forms.[12]

According to Laurie Ouellette and James Hay, reality TV is a "cultural technology" that "becomes a resource for inventing, managing, caring for, and protecting ourselves as citizens," as entitlements and protections disintegrate under the neoliberal assault. The authors suggest that television functions as a sort of "integral relay,"[13] whittling away at individuals' expectations of social and economic security, and enticing and assisting them into positions of increasing vulnerability. But reality TV is more than just a midwife of the neoliberal order. It is also itself a set of workplaces and markets for low-wage, insecure labor, a site of material as well as ideological production. "In the simplest sense," in the view of Alison Hearn, "'reality television' names a set of cost-cutting measures in broadcast television production enacted by management." At its very point of origin, at the heart of its foundational logic, reality TV bears the imprimatur of neoliberal capitalism's mode of operation: it is both an example of and it is about the transformation of relations between capital and labor at the dawn of the twenty-first century. Reality TV programming "can provide insight into . . . more general claims about the changing nature of work on a global scale because reality television is, itself, a significant site of production," structured according to the dominant logic of contemporary employment: increase corporate profits and flexibility by reducing payments and obligations to labor. Reality TV can be understood, in other words, as both "a representational expression of, and ideological legitimation for television's economic rationalizations and post-Fordist capital's desire to externalize its labour costs."[14]

There is good reason to understand *American Idol* as an emanation of the reality TV logic. It is a largely unscripted contest, stretched out over an entire season, in which individual participants compete to valorize — to add value to — themselves and keep and enhance their social places, and it does make extensive use of low-cost amateur talent and vulnerable, underpaid, nonunion production labor.[15] *American Idol* similarly sells viewers on a new range of sociocultural, political, and economic norms; its authority is founded in the reality TV principle that "mediated reality is somehow 'higher' than, or more significant than, nonmediated reality."[16] Like other reality TV shows, the program itself tells us that it is practically useful to the navigation by all subjects of the neoliberalizing world. Ouellette and Hay suggest that *American Idol* be considered as "a form of makeover TV to the extent that experts, teachers, and judges seek to transform raw human potential into coveted opportunities for self-fulfillment through the realization and expression of talent."[17]

But *American Idol*'s relationship to the genre of reality TV is complicated by a number of specificities: it participates in a long-standing tradition of amateur music on television that has brought a discourse of opportunity to mass audiences since the 1940s; it invokes widely distributed cultural knowledges and skills, articulating themes central to the American character; and it is about producing professionals for and in an established entertainment industry.[18]

First, *American Idol* enacts social relations and industrial synergies that have their roots in television's very emergence as a mass medium. As Murray Forman shows, television in the late 1940s and early 1950s was a preeminent distribution point of a musically themed "rhetoric of opportunity and promise." The new medium of television appeared to performers as a "new apparatus of opportunity"; an appearance on a televised amateur talent contest or variety show was "imagined as either a goal for musicians as they advanced their careers or a portal to success on a larger scale in the entertainment industry." Basic aspects of *American Idol*'s die were cast decades ago: by 1950 it had become clear to music executives that television performances were helping to sell records and that television was an effective medium for introducing and promoting artists to the viewing public.[19] Game shows and other progenitors of reality TV such as *Candid Camera* are also important to early television. The difference here is that musical performance has been both a widely shared hobby and a highly public profession for a long time (in which most Americans who attended public school prior to the 1980s would have had some training), and the boundary between the two is quite porous.[20] Appearances of amateur and professional music makers on television take place in relation to (and can meaningfully alter) trajectories of skill and occupational development in an established field of practice.

Second, *American Idol*'s resonance points to its complex relationship to contemporary American society and culture. In her examination of the treatment by *American Idol*'s producers, audiences, and contestants of themes of gender, race, religion, geography, and democratic discourse, Katherine Meizel demonstrates that the program's inflated cultural stakes reflect competing beliefs and investments in the American dream and American character, to which the program appeals and which it enacts. Her account brings into focus the ways the program's basic dialecticism illuminates long-standing, "fundamental tension[s] . . . between multiculturalist and individualist understandings of American identity," between competing values of "individualism and community."[21] The skills and knowledges required and exhibited even by unfit *American Idol* contestants are those of popular music, a highly democratized range of cultural texts and practices with barely perceptible barriers to entry. *American Idol* makes itself legible and accessible to its audience by invoking love of, knowledge of, and expertise in popular music, as well as by drawing on existing and emerging television conventions. In comparison to the themes of other "job/talent search"[22] reality TV programs—such as cooking, fashion design, and business management—popular music seems to offer both a medium for and access to deeply seated social-psychological and philosophical material.

Finally, *American Idol* departs from the run of reality programs because its claim to reality is more substantive than most: *American Idol* delivers on some of its signal promises. If a preoccupation of reality TV is the multiplication of revenue-generating commodities, then *American Idol*'s institutional connections with the music industry place it in a privileged production position. The music industry's operating model is undergoing potentially far-reaching change; nevertheless, the business still has a century's worth of expertise and momentum in the production of massively distributed and consumed commodities.[23] As an adjunct of this industry, *American Idol* is a producer of revenue-generating commodities par excellence. Fuller, the program's creator, and Cowell, record executive and celebrated *Idol* judge, moved into television from the music industry with the express intention of using a television program to create musical hits and stars. *American Idol* is, and has been since its inauguration, institutionally joined with a world of professionals and investors for whom the market success of *Idol* contestants, *Idol* music, and related commodities bodes well. *American Idol* not only benefits and benefits from the music industry, however; the program also demonstrates to audiences and aspiring stars (which are overlapping identities, as Meizel makes clear) that its integration with the music industry has enabled virtual nobodies to become famous professional singing stars. It is the reality of this promise that defines *American Idol* as a communicative, political, and economic object without parallel that has set and kept in motion a virtuous circle of material and ideological production.

Reification and Utopia

Narrative, Fredric Jameson suggests, is the principal cultural mechanism through which people apprehend and negotiate the social world. Mass cultural texts like *American Idol* are "socially symbolic acts" and "individual utterance[s] of that vaster system . . . of class discourse" that mediates between the cultural and social worlds—the realms of meaning and of institutions (to oversimplify). It is through narrative that we activate ourselves, develop cultural and class identity and identifications, and understand and navigate around and between social positions.[24] In its capacity to deliver on (at least some of) its promises—to produce actual pop stars out of (talented, perhaps musically trained) cocktail waitresses and mass communication majors—*American Idol* adds weight to the utopian side of Fredric Jameson's conception of popular cultural narrative as simultaneously symbolically reinforcing and gesturing beyond the dominant culture.

Jameson argues that in order to capture imaginations and to elicit identification on a mass scale, narratives like *American Idol* must point beyond the state of things to an aspired-to world. *American Idol*, to be attractive simultaneously to capital and audiences, must maintain a balancing act between these poles of "reification and utopia."[25] *American Idol* narratives embody this dual character. On the one hand, they are social scripts produced by experienced marketers and intended to cultivate and manage profitable attachments between audiences and stars. In their production, they depend on and reproduce systems of stratification and exploitation of the groups of young people from which *Idol* finalists (not to mention the workers who actually produce the program) emerge. On the other hand, these narratives depend for their effectiveness in large part on suggested symbolic resolutions to widely shared social tensions. The program's effectiveness is intensified because it can and actually does serve as a route to real positions and careers as professional pop singers. The invitation to overcome one's social starting point through an arduous yet rewarding trek toward the status of idol is not entirely symbolic.

Narrative is a site where discourse takes on materiality by shaping the cultural conditions of and resources for social practice. Taken together, the authentication and humiliation narrative that I discuss below are features of what Richard Sennett calls "the culture of the new capitalism": through their construction (by example and by contrast) of an "idealized self," these forms of narrative participate in the adjustment of working people's expectations and aspirations."[26] This process incorporates the mass media of popular music and television, as well as ancillary forms such as magazines, computer games, and the Internet. *Idol* narratives work in varied and sometimes contradictory ways, nourishing the bonds between performers and audiences through reference to actual social positions of the fans- and idols-in-training, as well as to a substantively open and level utopian playing field. A further aspect of the program's utopian presentation is the way in which it frames its appeal to viewers and potential contestants in terms of a sort of democratic intimacy and camaraderie that seems quite robust in the face of its relentless and ruthless meritocratic winnowing process.

One particularly important way in which *American Idol* distinguishes itself from other reality TV programs is the way it releases contestants from direct competition with each other by putting the audience in the position of reducing their number every week. The mitigation of the *American Idol* contestants' impetus to direct competition is evident in contestants' frequent assertions of solidarity. For example, when asked by the host in the penultimate show of *Idol*'s first season what it was like for the two finalists to compete against each other, Kelly Clarkson responded, "We don't think of it like that, we're in support of one another." Justin Guarini added that, rather than compete with each other, "We go out and we compete against ourselves."[27] By foregrounding the biographies and moral trajectories of contestants as they audition again and again, and by reducing the pressure of intragroup competition, this hybridized talent/reality show behaves more like a dramatic series, the plot of which is tied institutionally as well as thematically to the music industry. The character development that is so central to *American Idol*, however, suggests a more complex and compelling set of narratives than had generally been the norm in talent and reality genres. Again, the program's capacity to generate such rich narratives and sustain such audience investments is enhanced by its participation in the world of popular music and by its ability to invoke widely shared cognitive resources regarding musical practice and professions.

Authenticity and Exposing the Apparatus

Although the later programs of *American Idol*'s first season projected fraternity and sorority, the critical response to the program was not so warm and fuzzy. Beyond poking fun at the first weeks' off-key performances, music and media critics stridently derided *American Idol*'s music along two primary lines. First, they argued that the music featured on the show was bland and derivative: "The music and arrangements are trite, full of wannabe Whitney Houston and Stevie Wonder wails. Originality is a losing strategy," opined Caryn James of the *New York Times*.[28] Second, more odious to many critics than the music's blandness was the fact that the show makes visible a whole process of production that would otherwise be obscured: a highly rationalized process of selection, construction, and marketing.

As Motti Regev has shown, drawing on the work of Pierre Bourdieu, popular music's artistic value derives in part from extra-textual discourses of production norms and practices that conform to ascendant Romantic models.[29] Most of the first season's mainstream critics employed criteria of value steeped in the "ideology of autonomous art."[30] In these critics' opinions, the conditions of production and distribution play a role in determining music's cultural value; the preeminence of commercial motives in *American Idol* devalues the program's music. "'*Idol*' . . . is a slick new step in music marketing," grumbled the *Boston Globe*'s Matthew Gilbert. "It's not some kind of altruistic attempt to give a young performer a chance at the big time; it's the first leg in a marketing campaign that will culminate in CD sales. We aren't the TV audience—we're the focus group."[31] The first season's prerecorded karaoke-style accompaniment often seemed downplayed, as if too much attention to it would distract from what was really at stake: the contestants' presentation of themselves as worthy, creditable, authentic individuals. (This situation has changed somewhat as live musicians have been incorporated into the program, with the bandleader even becoming a minor character.) According to this logic, no such obviously "inauthentic" musical product, conceived, manufactured, and marketed in an openly rational and instrumental way, could carry anything other than commodity value. Although middle-brow critics—sometimes promoters of a "cultural dupes" thesis—dismissed the music of *American Idol* for its apparent inauthenticity, it is exactly authenticity that was and remains a primary theme in *Idol* narratives, and a concern for finalists and fans.[32]

However, cutting against the principle that exposure of the construction process threatens artistic legitimacy, it is exactly such processes of exposure that authenticate people in front of the cameras in more personal terms.[33] Mark Andrejevic shows that many people and institutions have come to see surveillance and exposure as processes of validation and means to personal growth and self-knowledge in reality TV. Being "real" in front of the cameras "is a proof of honesty, and the persistent gaze of the camera provides one way of guaranteeing that 'realness.'"[34] The identification process so important to the success of the venture is all the more powerful because it is reciprocal, linking performer and viewer in a circuit of legitimacy and value. This process authenticates both viewer and performer through the production of a highly visible (if highly edited) backstage, purporting to open to public view certain previously hidden elements of the selection and professionalization processes.[35] The program validates the viewers' investment in the performer through its assertions that the performer is worthy of investment, legitimating the viewers as the performer's worthiness is reflected back on them.

The possibilities of authentic, unitary subjecthood and of meaningful participation in a democratic society are characteristic of the kind of utopian fantasy and identification that popular music supports.[36] Therefore, the authenticity of the musical idol is paramount in this view. Popular music's democratic promise—linked notions and discourses of equal opportunity, social mobility, and self-development—is what makes discourses of authenticity around popular music so powerfully relevant in a postmodern, and even in a postrock, scene. The star has a legitimate right to be seen and heard because her authenticity underwrites her public position. But authenticity is a resource that is in principle available to all: fans and other dwellers in more mundane realms of life draw degrees of social power from their ability to perceive and argue for value and authenticity in their chosen performers. In the words of Regina Bendix, "declaring something authentic legitimate[s] the subject that [is] declared authentic and the declaration in turn can legitimate the authenticator." If this principle sounds circular, that is because it is circular: "The search for authenticity is fundamentally an emotional and moral quest"—that is, it cannot but result in emotional and moral arguments. Unsurprisingly, "this experiential dimension does not provide lasting satisfaction, and authenticity needs to be augmented with pragmatic and evaluative dimensions."[37] Where do these dimensions arise? They arise in the polemics that characterize arguments for the authenticity of some musical act or another.

By most scholarly measures, popular music carries a heavy social, psychological, and symbolic load in this era of widespread social disembeddedness. However, popular music's ability to carry this load is under constant threat: can any of its individual practitioners ever, finally, be established as reliable, authentic porters? As targets of such projection, can any of them ever achieve unassailable legitimacy? Joshua Gamson's history of celebrity in American culture indicates that legitimate, "deserved and earned" celebrity requires the development of a paradoxical relationship. To be legitimate, aspiring idols must demonstrate both ordinariness and specialness with respect to cultural norms.[38] They must demonstrate both distance and closeness, both difference and similarity, with the target audience. *American Idol*'s narratives of authentication and humiliation balance these contrasting themes in the program's efforts to cultivate and manage the relationship between idol and fans. Stories told in the pretaped narrative segments edited into the program (most fulsomely in the first season) describe the careers of contestants as they leave their prosaic pasts behind and confront music business gatekeepers, each other as competitors, and the judgments of voting audiences. Such stories are not new with *American Idol*, as Forman's research shows; the reiteration by contestants in early televised amateur talent contests of "an ideal image of success in show business is clearly measured against the descriptions of their actual [day jobs] . . . described in terms of boredom and monotony."[39]

Leading characters in the humiliation sequences usually make it only as far as the initial confrontation before they are exiled. However, there are exceptions. Most notable among them is William Hung, an Asian American contestant whose awkward and earnest performance of Ricky Martin's "She Bangs"—and its ridicule by Simon Cowell—launched his unusual but not unprecedented career as a "spectacular failure."[40] Other exceptions include the subsequent recruitment of several of the more dramatic subjects of this kind of humiliation for a cleverly edited montage of off-key performances of "Sing,

Sing a Song," specifically prepared for and presented during the finale of the 2003 season;[41] the reprising during season finales of notable bad auditions from early in the season; and the inclusion of numerous disastrous auditions in the *American Idol: The Best and Worst of American Idol, Seasons 1–4* DVD. These stories braid together aspirants' moral and professional trajectories as they struggle to demonstrate their qualifications to the on-camera judges and the voting audience at home. At their most literal, they constitute both a set of claims about the morality, authenticity, and legitimacy of the aspiring idols and a set of stories about entering the entertainment business. At their most allegorical, they are a set of guidelines concerning the appropriate entry into and performance within the perilous, but still officially meritocratic, neo-liberalizing economy and appropriate attitudes toward that economy's re-wards and punishments, along with utopian glimpses of a classless opportu-nity structure.

Narratives of both types feature the contestants in situations that view-ers can readily understand and, because of their familiarity, readily analyze and evaluate. The program frequently shows contestants at home; at work or play with friends and family or with other contestants; and in the audition or professionalization process. Most audience members, it is probably safe to say, have never auditioned or professionalized themselves in precisely this way. Nevertheless, the situation of being judged by a teacher or employer, for example, while struggling to master new sets of rules and behaviors in school or at work, is more common and provides a basis for legibility, iden-tification, and engagement. Heather Hendershot observes that the reality TV judge "functions like a boss doing an 'annual review,' assessing an employee's strengths and weaknesses and deciding whether to grant a worker a promo-tion or to show him or her the door."[42] *American Idol*'s regime of evaluation, promotion, and rejection illustrates the growing importance of this kind of increasingly perilous encounter in the experience of work in the early twenty-first century.

Authentication

Authenticating biographical vignettes concern individual aspirants and often follow patterns of surveillance, interviews, and direct address found in con-temporary reality programming. Especially during the first few seasons, *American Idol* places contestants in highly scripted contexts in which they may perform (as) themselves—visiting their hometowns, parents and sib-lings, their old schools, and places of work.[43] Such documentary productions typically focus on contestants as moral individuals, emphasizing their "family values"; church and volunteer activities; and devotion to their friends, school, and community. Clips featuring such performances of self were a regular feature of the first season (the primary focus of the present study) and appear in several contexts. In most programs, for example, a video clip about each contestant, accompanied by her or his voice-over narration, preceded each contestant's performance.

One such sequence takes place during an outing in which the finalists are taken to work with the nongovernmental organization Habitat for Humanity on a home under construction in an impoverished Los Angeles neighborhood, thus identifying the contestants, in this case, with new home construction and social service, perhaps gesturing toward a barely remembered Great Society.[44] The contestants wield hammers and carry boards. One after another, they are singled out to say a few words; behind each foregrounded contestant several of the others are visibly at work. In one such vignette, the first season's winner-to-be, Kelly Clarkson, nails a piece of siding to the house. In a voice-over, she tells us that her father is a contractor and that working on this house is the most at home she has felt since coming to Los Angeles. Vignettes like these enable and require contestants to produce and display personal characteristics, individualizing and authenticating themselves, appearing as regular persons despite their growing celebrity.[45]

The mother of Justin Guarini, the first season's first runner-up, appeared in a "Coca-Cola Moment" (a series of heavily sponsored sentimental segments) in which the mothers of the three remaining finalists say a few words about their increasingly famous offspring. As if to stave off an excess of ordinariness threatened by the display of his baby pictures, she declares from her sumptuous living room sofa that "there's just an aura around Justin. When you meet him, you see it. From the time he was very small, when he was five and a half, it was just evident that he was special."[46] The difference between pictures of Justin as a five-year-old and his present appearance might prompt one to wonder: was his specialness more evident after his nose job? Authentication narratives underwrite the paradoxical relation of difference and similarity between fan and idol. Whether articulated by contestants or family, friends or fans, the narratives contribute to the ever-expanding back story on which all of the contestants' musical and nonmusical performances build, as well as to the narrative self with which their onstage utterances may be judged as consistent or contradictory.

Humiliation

Narratives of this type are drawn from the preliminary auditions that take place in cities around the United States and are featured most prominently at the beginning of the series, when the show delivers a general picture of the rough ground from which the diamond will emerge, and during its final weeks, when the finalists' legitimacy is being fortified. In subsequent seasons, in response to audience demand—registered largely via web-based fan chat rooms—the percentage of each show taken up by these narratives has increased; it now stretches over many weeks. Among the many ancillary media products is a "worst of" DVD culled from seasons 1–4, which features dozens of edited bad auditions as well as several unedited sequences that show entire interactions of contestants and judges (and occasionally security guards). In a typical humiliation scene, a singer enters the performance area and greets the three judges (occasionally, the panel includes a fourth guest judge, a celebrity drawn from the charts of the present or the past—or, as in the case of Clive Davis, the executive suites), who are all seated at a long table. The doomed auditioner, placed before a corporate trade show–style backdrop, often dances inexpertly, sings a few bars a cappella, and is typically stopped midsong by the judges (sometimes with a tinge of sympathy, but more often with an exclamation of impatience, scorn, or even outrage). The judges criticize the auditioner's gestures, clothing, facial expression, and manner along with his voice, sometimes with deadpan sarcasm (the specialty of the panel's most aggressive judge, Simon Cowell). The critique is followed by reaction shots in which the auditioner typically breaks down in tears, stares in disbelief, and sometimes argues with or verbally attacks the judges. Later seasons have further capitalized on the intensity of the brief encounter between contestants and judges by, for example, providing a little booth in which contestants may videorecord themselves conveying postaudition messages to the judges (and, of course, to the producers, editors, and viewing audience), and by having mobile cameras at the ready to track angry, heartbroken, or otherwise telegenic rejects as they make their way out of the audition room and sometimes the building.

Consider the following representative snippet from a segment in the first season titled "Top Five Worst Auditions." The narrator barks: "And the absolute worst, dead last out of ten thousand hopefuls, Jennifer's rendition of 'Genie in a Bottle' left us hoping that someone would put a cork in it!" Jennifer sings a verse and chorus for the three judges. Cowell, dubbed "Mr. Nasty" by the British press during his tenure as judge on the first version of the show, says to Jennifer, "That was extraordinary." Jennifer lights up, eager to hear more. Cowell continues, "Unfortunately, extraordinarily bad." The camera zooms in on Jennifer's face, as her look of joy turns to one of shock.[47]

Idol Narrative

What kind of cultural work do these narratives perform? The stories appear intended for a diverse, youthful, media-consuming audience. They aim to convince audiences of the value of the aspiring idols and the legitimacy of the process by which the idol is chosen. Like the "program-length commercials" aimed at children of the 1980s, they are narratives constructed to promote a planned set of commodities.[48] Yet by their nature as popular culture products, they contain multiple and contradictory voices and depend for their popularity on being able to reach audiences at many levels, from many angles.[49] These narratives combine stories of humiliation, authenticity, discipline, and growing up with concepts of labor, failure, and success. They incorporate both harsh lessons about adjustment and adaptation to the "new ruthless economy"[50] and ideologically saturated stories about a utopian level playing field—the transparent, equal-opportunity meritocracy that is the ideological foundation of the American dream.

Keeping It Real

Idols have to be special, but they have to be ordinary too; thus, the program balances images of the star as star with narratives of the star's ordinariness. *American Idol* constructs ordinariness: like other reality TV programs, through its surveillance and serial logic, it allows and compels contestants' characters to develop over the course of a television season. Since the contestants are not professionals, not fully socialized into the entertainment industry, they are not as socially different from their audience as established pop music stars are. Richard Dyer points to the importance of authenticity in the construction of film stars, but most discussions of authenticity in popular music, following the critical lines indicated above, have denied the possibility of authenticity in commercial pop.[51] Where academics have identified such discourses, the locus of authenticity claims is largely extramusical. For example, the quintessentially commercial Spice Girls enacted a form of authenticity distinct from the critically privileged rock authenticity, legitimizing themselves by weaving stories of their extramusical ordinariness into their music videos and feature film. Their authenticity derived from their ability to imply that idol and fan had the same identity.[52] An analysis of Jennifer Lopez's and Britney Spears's discourses and self-presentations has resulted in similar findings.[53]

But whereas Simon Fuller (creator and executive producer of the Spice Girls as well as of *American Idol*) kept the process of turning young women into Spice Girls hidden, presenting the Spice Girls as fully formed, *American Idol* invites audiences into an intimate relationship with idol hopefuls by making visible a (highly edited) selection and training process. The Spice Girls spoke not for but as their audience. Fuller has advanced that principle a step further: he draws the aspiring idols from the audience in a dramatically visible way. The democratic promise of equal opportunity to become an idol is held out to every singing person between the ages of fifteen and twenty-eight who is able to get to an audition site, exemplifying and vouchsafing the promise of equality of opportunity in a liberal democracy. During the premier episode of the series in 2002, standing on the stage of the empty Kodak Theater in Hollywood, the two hosts of the first season delivered the following lines:

> *Brian Dunkleman*: Three months from now, live on this very stage, an as-yet-unknown talent will be launched into superstardom.
> *Ryan Seacrest*: We don't know who that is yet. Right now they could be parking cars or even waiting on tables. Who knows?
> *Dunkleman*: What we *do* know is that by the end of the summer, that person's life will change forever.
> *Seacrest*: Because you at home decide who will become the next American Idol.[54]

A valet parking attendant or a waiter, the hosts suggest, could become the next American Idol through the conferral of recognition and privilege by a popular entertainment electorate. In fact, Kelly Clarkson, the first season's winner, worked as a cocktail waitress in Texas before her rise to fame.

Moreover, although successful authenticity claims alone are not enough to carry a contestant through to idolhood, without them a contestant stands little chance. In the utopian meritocracy presented by *American Idol*, social class, race, and gender often appear trumped by character.[55] Character is developed and demonstrated through the frequent biographical and documentary vignettes offered by the show (discussed above) and also through the stances taken by contestants in the face of the nearly constant criticism directed at them from the judges. In an interview featured in *American Idol*:

The Best and Worst of American Idol, Seasons 1–4, Paula Abdul remarks that contestants have "got to take the good with the bad, [they]'ve got to recognize the talent that [they] do have and be open to constructive criticism." Some contestants let criticism get the best of them, and "weird things happen when [they] lose composure as an artist and [they] start fighting back with Simon or whatever, the audience will go either way, they'll say 'I don't like the way they reacted, you know, Simon's [just being] Simon, everybody knows Simon is Simon. They just took it wrong.' And then the votes'll go down." In fact, in an informal poll I conducted, young fans told me that the first thing they judge in a contestant is the graciousness with which he responds to criticism. Fans and idols are entwined by the telling of a story of success based on character and merit, of the hard work of honest folk being rewarded, and of the hard knocks delivered by a tough but fair system. However, widespread belief in the inherent star quality of the contestant—like belief in the natural, if unevenly distributed, inherent talents of those rewarded in a meritocracy—is also important to the legitimation of individual success and failure, the rhetorical victory of equality of opportunity over other possible regimes.[56] The fan-idol relationship is thus made all the deeper through the representation of an initial social identity between performers and audience; contestants and viewers, assured at least of the possibility of possessing star quality or inherent talents, undertake this journey of social mobility together.

Back to Square One

Narratives of the humiliation and attempted humiliation of poorly prepared losers are thus not outtakes or bloopers included for mere comic relief or pathos. These narratives are instructive tableaux of punishment and vengeance that serve simultaneously as further legitimation or authentication of those in whom the desired talents inhere and as graphic warnings to all those considering an attempt to enter a field for which their talents are not appropriate. William Ian Miller suggests that a principal form of humiliation is enacted around what he calls "structural pretension, . . . an inherent consequence of ranked social difference." The person engaging in this form of pretense is asserting a higher social status than they have any "moral or social right" to claim.[57] In this context, "humiliation is the emotional experience of being caught inappropriately crossing group boundaries into territory one has no business being in."[58] Unprepared, unworthy aspirants' pretenses are exposed by the rationalistic reciprocity of Simon Cowell, the lead judge. With his businesslike lack of patience, reinforced by his industry track record, he treats their auditions as insulting pretensions. In a promotional spot that aired before the series began and was included in the "best of" DVD, Cowell said: "I'm here to do a job, and I'm going to do something which I think is going to be a shock to the American public. We are going to tell people who cannot sing and who've no talent that they have no talent. And that never makes you popular. We are going to show the audition process as it really is because shows in the past have not shown the brutality of auditions. Auditions are horrible places to go. And I'm warning you now you're about to enter the audition from hell."[59] Miller writes that although the violence of the humiliator "will shock and appall us when we feel the perpetrator is predatory . . . [it] will provide catharsis and pleasure, both aesthetic and erotic, when we feel the violator is justified, as when he acts with righteous indignation and vengefulness."[60] Vengeance can make for pleasurable narrative when audiences and humiliators share an understanding of the rules and conventions that govern the correct crossing of the social boundaries highlighted by *American Idol*.[61] Cowell's withering excoriations have been very popular and he has become a celebrity in the United States, appearing on magazine covers and in a range of other media. *Idol*'s strategy of featuring the more aggressive dressing-downs is well suited to the needs of the producers: it fills airtime with the entertaining foibles of unpaid offenders or victims who have been alienated, through the show's draconian contract, of rights over their images and voices of the right to refuse to allow their auditions, tears, and/or outbursts to be made public. Miller observes the background assumptions underlying this form of humiliation: "[i]t is for the community to determine the social position to which you justifiably belong. Your job is to know where they are likely to put you, based on both your knowledge of the relevant standards of judgment and how you stack up in relation to them. And you will be punished if you are unable to do so. It is the temerity, stupidity, or whatever not to know where you stand and then to claim a higher place for yourself than you deserve which makes others see you as humiliating yourself. You make yourself the justifiable object of their ridicule and scorn."[62]

Miller's argument points to the audience's familiarity with the rules and boundaries governing social and economic mobility outside as well as inside the entertainment industry. He highlights audiences' capacities to draw pleasure from the application of shared cultural conceptions to TV personalities whose positions at the gates of the music business parallel those of employable people of all ages pursuing opportunities and advancement. The show is about and aimed at young people who are in or close to their first jobs—on the borderline between subordination and emancipation; between the private world of adult-controlled home and school, with its mostly low-status, low-stakes work and high-stakes leisure, and the public world of adult freedom, discipline, responsibility, and commitment. To cross from childhood to (young) adulthood is to become responsible for one's own failures and successes. The humiliation of the pretentious dramatizes the harsh punishments awaiting those who fail to prepare and evaluate themselves correctly and who subsequently overstep their bounds.

I have argued elsewhere that the balance of play and professionalism attributed to pop musicians changed considerably in the translation of serially televised boy bands from the 1960s to the beginning of the twenty-first century.[63] This change reflects, I argued, the relationship between a quarter-century of economic decline and popular conceptions of how young pop performers ought to conduct themselves in their approach to their musical career paths. In a fashion very similar to *Making the Band*'s (ABC 2000–2002) serious departure from *The Monkees*' (NBC 1966–68) spontaneity and playfulness, *American Idol* tells us that music industry professionalization will not generally bear experimentation or play, nor does the industry provide resources to assist (except by example) the unprepared auditioners into their desired positions. In the "special features" section of the *American Idol* first season DVD, several finalists are asked to offer advice to those hoping to audition for the second season. Nikki McKibbin advises hopefuls to "take criticism well, 'cause it happens, unfortunately, and it happens a lot." E. J. Day reiterates that aspirants should "just be ready for criticism and just be open, because you may think you're the bomb in this small little town and then you go to this audition and they will put you in your place so fast that you will not even be ready for it."[64]

The show's appeal across age groups, however, indicates that the nature of the paths and obstacles between who and where the aspirants are (in terms of the social structure) and who and where they want to be remains compelling to a very wide demographic and suggests some further interrogation. Youthful contestants, by trying out the role of pop star—along with youthful as well as older audiences, by doing so vicariously—are not just making adolescent-style bids for freedom and identity: they are playing with a particular kind of adult role that seems to offer a high degree of autonomy. Why is it that the music industry is one "to which numerous young people aspire and for which many train"?[65] One explanation is that facing a future in "McJobs," positions "earmarked for youth or for other transient workers" in the low-wage, no-benefit retail and service sectors, along with increasingly bleak prospects for economic security and social mobility, people find an alternate, if riskier, tactic increasingly attractive.[66] To cross into adulthood as a hot property such as a pop idol is a way to literally incorporate within oneself valuable property- and ownership-producing elements of the means of production. The employment relation in the United States puts people in "the legal role of a non-adult, indeed a non-person or thing."[67] In contrast, the recording artist's contradictory status—as "employee" under state employment law and "independent contractor" under federal copyright law—makes artists quasi-proprietary partners with the record company when it comes to the intellectual property of sound recordings they make under contract, which even the most vulnerable artists typically license rather than simply hand over to record companies (see chapter 5). This special situation preserves a degree of autonomy not found in the standard employment relationship. The blurring of the lines between employee and independent contractor is related to attempts by downsized or vulnerable professionals to refashion themselves as consultants in the face of uncertain employment (but see chapters 3 and 4 for complicating factors).[68] The attempt to step out as an entrepreneur is a high-stakes bet for most people, especially for older adults; but along with increased uncertainty, it holds out a promise of increased freedom and mobility as well as increased responsibility for and control over one's own conditions of labor. The prospect of making this move under the tutelage of a major music industry institution such as a record or music company promises measures of de-alienation that are in some measure protected by the investments and logics of the institution.

Bidding to be excused from increasingly insecure conventional structures of employment and welcomed into a realm of increased autonomy and proprietorship, auditioners open themselves to scrutiny from evaluators and observers that threatens, even promises, to expose hubris and pretense. Unpreparedness, in the *Idol* perspective, is a lifestyle choice, not a structural problem; neither *American Idol* nor the shrinking welfare state is there to assist the unprepared. In contrast, when the "good guys" of the show—the thirty finalists who make it to Hollywood for the live televised competition—are subject to criticism, they have another opportunity to demonstrate their worthiness by taking that criticism graciously, and, if they disagree with it, to also do that graciously.

Success and Failure

The contemporary expansion of the communications media recalls the late 1940s television landscape described by Forman, in which an increased appetite for content drives the adaptation of existing cultural forms (such as popular music performance and the radio talent show) to the new medium.[69] Meanwhile, music performance and contest genres again provide valuable resources for the production of what David Lusted calls "light entertainment." Audience pleasure in such televisual material derives from performers' and audiences' shared sense of "the *risks* at stake" in the improvisatory and contingent nature of the light entertainment form: "Part of the pleasure of game shows, quizzes and 'talent' contests is precisely that they foreground the risk of failure."[70] A shared sense of risk is indeed a powerful contact point between fan and idol, one that enables identification through social homology. As the notion of the "secure individual"[71] who navigates a stable structure of opportunity and advancement becomes a thing of the past, more and more workers learn the currency of the old Hollywood adage: "You're only as good as your last picture."

In his discussion of the mid-twentieth-century Hollywood musical, Dyer suggests that entertainment is not merely the production of false consciousness and satisfaction of false needs; rather, entertainment "works" because "it responds to real needs *created by society*."[72] He locates the specificity of entertainment's utopia, for example, in the Hollywood musical's "nonrepresentational" communication of "what utopia feels like rather than how it would be organized."[73] *American Idol*, responding to the real needs of early-twenty-first-century Americans, and looking backstage to social structures more effectively hidden in the mid-twentieth century, shows how its utopia would be organized. The show's appeal derives at least in part from its willingness to address the core tensions of this historical moment, and to suggest what would at least initially be a leveled, classless society: anyone willing to stand in line for days is guaranteed the opportunity to audition. From the start, however, *Idol*'s narratives of individualism and meritocracy contain this utopian promise and reduce its potential, even while enacting a critique of the American occupational and social structure and highlighting the unfairnesses and risks of the new economy.

The presence of working and middle-class women and people of color in the diverse group of finalists appears to signify the inherent fairness of the meritocratic system. However, the increasing polarization and middle-class instability associated with neoliberal corporate and state restructuring, regressive taxation, and anti-affirmative-action legislation strain the legitimacy of meritocracy and set up particular tensions to be dealt with in early-twenty-first-century popular culture. *American Idol* holds out a promise of individual recognition, but its focus on biography and relationship, along with the social and material support of family and community, points to the real necessity of social ties and support for success in the arid neoliberal regime. The show deals with this tension by offering the representation of an ideal meritocracy. In this utopian society, all participants—representing all social groups in a pop culture galactic federation—represent themselves as equally unknown individuals before impartial advisors and a popular electorate, a liberal regime in which all participants have equal access to the essential resource: the rhetoric of coherent, authentic, individual selfhood.

Televised sports offer a related example; they are a "social theater" in which the fairness of the American meritocracy and the achievability of the American dream are played out before American youth.[74] All contestants, Donald Sabo and Sue Curry Jansen write, appear to "begin the game at the same starting point, but the most talented finish first."[75] They argue that this notion, like the more general notion that social and economic mobility in the United States is determined through a system of meritocratic reward, obscures the very real biases of gender and race that form the rules behind the rules of professional sports. In the mid-1990s, following the publication of Richard Herrnstein and Charles Murray's *The Bell Curve*, the legitimacy of the "starting points" and "scoring systems" that concern Sabo and Jensen became the focus of intense debate.[76] Herrnstein and Murray's assertions that the American meritocracy neutrally rewarded people with higher IQs and that IQ was unequally distributed among "races," as well as the ensuing flood of scholarly and popular refutations, made the reward structure of the American meritocracy a target of scrutiny in popular as well as academic discourse. *American Idol* draws on the same set of narratives of success and achievement as do the sports narratives analyzed by Sabo and Jensen, but the program presents an updated model of a more transparent, and therefore more legitimate, post–*Bell Curve* meritocracy.

Alternating narratives or scripts of authentically inherent talent and authentic lack of pretense incorporate two contrasting qualities whose performance is essential for success in a democratic market society: "possessive" individualism and respect for hierarchical social structure.[77] Michael Mascuch points out that the modern "individualist self" is a persisting product of early modern narrative conventions, a narrative construction: "Without acting first and foremost as an author, the individualist self would have no script of life to follow as a character. . . . This authoritative stance best epitomizes the generic self-identity of the person under individualism. In its position as the subject of its own life story, the individualist self is the creator/medium/product unified as a single, autonomous totality: the trope of the author as the hero and originator of his heroism."[78] The construction of a historically suited self-narrative is a necessary part of the navigation and creation of coherent identity in modern society.

Richard Sennett affirms the idea that coherent selfhood in industrial society is enabled by a narrative framework, contending that the development of a viable self depends on the stable economic and social structures in which individual narratives may sprout and grow. In its requirement that individuals be prepared to change tracks and start over at any time, postindustrial society produces a net loss in the sense of coherent selfhood. Increasingly fugitive, evanescent, flexible postindustrial institutions, in Sennett's view, disable the production of linear life narrative: "There is no narrative which can overcome regression to the mean; [in the new economy] you are 'always starting over.'"[79] Like the 1990s workers in Sennett's study, *American Idol* contestants need to audition repeatedly just to stay in the running; they have no apparent security. Yet *American Idol* does appear to suggest one solution: certain kinds of cultural work offer more reliable forms of security and mobility. As will become even clearer in chapters 3 and 4, forms of cultural work that depend on unique faces, voices, skill sets, and expressive styles underwrite strong claims for a worker's irreplaceability and increased control over her working conditions. This may be one reason why morality and character are so decisive in an audience-selected idol: in an era in which organized labor is considered suspect — even corrupting — by the press as well as the public and private sectors, we must be careful who we allow to have such a voice.

American Idol *and the Adolescent Moratorium*

American Idol contestants are late adolescents and young adults. James Côté and Anton Allahar combine the view of this period in the lives of Western youth as a "moratorium" — a period of social, political, and economic sequestration, during which a range of identities may be explored — with a synthesis of economic and sociological data concerning the changing situation of youth in the North American welfare state. They argue that, without proper resources, adolescents cannot make meaningful use of this moratorium and are likely to experience traumatic identity crises that will affect their life chances. The current hollowing out of the welfare state, bifurcation of the occupational structure, and acceleration of credential inflation have advanced the "deterioration in quality of life and opportunities [for young people], particularly since the 1950s, when the current occupational structure began to take shape."[80] They write:

> The paramount problem the young person faces today in many advanced industrial societies is how to formulate a viable and stable identity under uncertain and even hostile circumstances. . . . [Y]oung people, especially teenagers, have limited legal rights and economic resources; they are not considered to be fully responsible and are generally treated as incomplete human beings. But . . . the ego normally grows and remains strong by *acting* in the social world in a meaningful and socially accepted manner. Many young people, however, are denied this. Thus, they often face the dilemma of having to develop a sense of identity—a sense of temporal and spatial continuity—without the proper resources.[81]

The formation of a viable and stable identity is linked to, among other things, meaningful rather than marginal participation in the workforce, the sequestration of youth, the depression of youths' wages, and the shift from a manufacturing to a service economy—all of which bode ill for young people not blessed with deep familial pockets. The adolescent moratorium is a period of projection of the self into possible future positions that makes use of available symbolic and material resources, and new economic barriers to those resources foreclose opportunities for the exploration of possible selves.[82] In fact, a study of adolescent and teen use of media confirms this understanding of the relationship between those situated in this moratorium and the kinds of representations of young adults on television. The study suggests that "children and teens tend to be 'aspirational viewers'—that is, they are particularly attracted to shows featuring . . . older characters [who] hold the keys to their future, guide their expectations of things to come, and provide templates for their behavior."[83] These characters, according to the study, "inhabit the stage of life which young viewers are about to enter."[84] Interviews conducted by these researchers additionally suggest that "young people compare their own lives and situations to life on screen in order to assess whether they were 'getting it right.'"[85] But cannot adults also be "aspirational viewers"? If childhood and adolescence are historical constructions,[86] cannot adulthood be understood in a similar light?

I'd like to suggest that the notion of the adolescent moratorium could be expanded as a means of understanding not just the political, economic, and sociocultural sequestration of youth in Western society, but also the situations of members of other age groups who experience deprivations of social power similar to those long associated with childhood and youth. These deprivations are characteristic of the employment relation in general, and they have historically been mitigated through welfare capitalism, progressive taxation and social programs, and organized labor.[87] Anya Kamenetz's book *Generation Debt* supports this idea with respect to the economic realm. In her analysis, the emergence of what some commentators have called the "adultolescent" is due not to the personal failings or laziness of those born after 1970, but to a transformed American society in which the attainment of legal adulthood can no longer be understood to be necessarily associated with social or economic independence.[88] Kamenetz argues that baby-boomer parents of twenty- and thirty-somethings "unduly personalize the public conversation about emerging adulthood"[89] when they ignore structural social change and write and read such bestsellers as *When Our Grown Kids Disappoint Us: Letting Go of Their Problems, Loving Them Anyway, and Getting On with Our Lives* and *Mom, Can I Move Back In with You?* The increasingly common nonlinear transition to adulthood and self-sufficiency, Kamenetz argues, is more properly seen as a product of political and economic change, and not reflective of the character of American young people. "The common thread joining all members of this [young adult] generation," Kamenetz writes, "is a sense of permanent impermanence. It's hard to commit to a family, a community, a job, or a life path when you don't know if you'll be able to make a living, make a marriage last, or live free of debt."[90] American youth today encounter drastically reduced opportunities for advancement and unprecedented levels of vulnerability as college tuitions have risen faster than inflation; the Social Security system, aside from political parties' polemics, faces a reckoning, if not a crisis; and job growth—where it exists at all—is in sectors characterized by low wages, no or poor benefits, and temporary positions.[91] This puts youth in much the same situation as workers who have been downsized or are trying to change jobs. More and more workers are threatened with an increasingly negative version of this adolescent moratorium unrelated to their age: the need to construct an identity adapted to the neoliberalizing economy under conditions of reduced resources and social power, perhaps while in the low-wage ghetto of temporary and service work previously reserved for youth and other marginal populations.

Conclusion

The foregrounding of *American Idol* contestants' moral and professional trajectories highlights the homology between struggling to be a star, struggling to grow up (whether in terms of age or in terms of the social achievements that this process is often understood to signify), and struggling to succeed as a self-governing economic actor. Representations of singers in this context are representations of individuals undertaking a form of work that appears more responsible, less alienated, and less infantilized, and that combines the harmonious development of one's powers with the possibility of economic and social advancement and an unusual degree of proprietary autonomy, compared to the trend in most sectors.

American Idol's biographical and bad-audition narratives, collectively, tell useful stories of work and life in the neoliberal economy; these stories are the kind of resources required for the staking out of an identity in the manner suggested by Côté and Allahar. *American Idol* dramatizes the struggle of individuals in the society that Côté and Allahar describe: a society in which there is very little institutionalized social support; little freedom for youth to play, take chances, or fail; and a decreasing likelihood of long-term and secure, let alone meaningful, employment. This society is defined by the overriding necessity to struggle and compete on an individual basis, maybe with help from family and friends, but ultimately as an individual up against the impersonal machineries of the meritocracy and the market.

Pop music, work, and narrative are linked through the metaphor of the audition; *American Idol* is all about auditions, successful and unsuccessful. On the last night of the show's second season, moments before the 2003 idol was announced, Paula Abdul offered some final words of advice: "You know, life is like an audition; you're going to have to keep competing to stay on top."[92]

Whoever does not adapt his manner
of life to the conditions of capitalistic
success must go under, or at least
cannot rise.

—Max Weber, *The Protestant Ethic
and the Spirit of Capitalism*

CHAPTER 2

Rockumentary and the New Model Worker

The documentary genre has been enjoying such a considerable renaissance in recent years that a *New Statesman* review of Interloper Films' *Dig!* (2004) opened with the quip "another week, another documentary."[1] But *Dig!* is a rockumentary—a documentary film that centers on rock music as a social form—one of a growing accumulation of nonfiction portrayals of rock musicians at work. The film follows two West Coast bands over the course of seven years of gigging, touring, recording, negotiating with label personnel and managers, hanging out, using drugs, fighting, and stalking. Starting out as mutual admirers and "buddy bands" in the mid-1990s, the Brian Jonestown Massacre and the Dandy Warhols trace different trajectories as one group spirals into dissolution and the other achieves international fame and moderate fortune. Following a musician or group of musicians across a period of time is a familiar rockumentary approach. *Dig!* follows this convention with a twist: it narrates the divergent progressions of two bands.

This chapter examines *Dig!* as a representative instance of an ongoing boom in rockumentary production, which includes films on the Ramones,

Wilco, Radiohead, the New York City underground rock scene, Metallica, the Minutemen, the Clash, the Sex Pistols, and numerous other rock bands. Like the television program *American Idol*, *Dig!* engages and produces narratives that interweave discourses of popular music and political and economic autonomy with themes of musical professionalization, self-actualization, and the achievement of social mobility. *Dig!* is a logical choice for analysis in this context in part because, like *American Idol*, it frames, tracks, and narrates both success and failure; the film also complements *American Idol* in its cultural work, addressing audiences for whom the television talent show might be too mainstream or pop oriented to compel interest or identification.[2] What distinguishes *Dig!*, however, is its narrative bait and switch. In a real way, *American Idol* is what it says it is: through it, a cocktail waitress can become a pop star. In contrast, *Dig!* is not what it says it is. *Dig!* also offers a detailed narrative of musically driven social mobility, one that promises to show audiences how to manage the conflicting demands of autonomous self-actualization and fruitful market participation. However, it obscures the essential, mundane routines necessary to the commercialization of indie cultural production behind the screen of a more sensational story of a bandleader's supposed mental illness. Accounts of these routines could actually be of use to individuals interested in replicating some of the successes evident in and around the film. *Dig!*'s superficial advocacy of harmonious self-actualization and its substantial narrative of an unstable bandleader, hoisted by his own petard of authenticity, obscure an arguably more practically useful but perhaps (in the context of rock discourse) slightly odious tale of instrumentality and opportunism. Hidden behind the divergence of two colorful indie bands is the chronicle of the mundane dealings through which the filmmaker and the more well-adjusted of the two featured bandleaders bargain their way into positions of social and cultural power.

The new crop of rockumentaries differs from those milestones of the late 1960s and early 1970s—among which *Gimme Shelter* and *Monterey Pop* are the best known—that established the rockumentary genre. Whereas films of that era tended to focus on the spectacular dimensions of a dominant form of popular music in young white America, contemporary rockumentary takes for its focus the quotidian aspects of the rock group's working life. As one musician once told me about indie rock band life, ironically reversing the US Navy's recruiting slogan of the late twentieth century, "it's not just an adventure, it's a job."[3] For all their participation in rockumentary-style myth making, musicians' daily slog is grindingly evident in *Dig!* and other films in its category.

The new rockumentary focuses on the frequently unspectacular (and often grim) social relations and relatively routine (though no less potentially ruinous) crises of rock music making in the early twenty-first century. If the rockumentary has moved from the macro level of celebration, spectacle, and mystification to the micro level of examining the mundane—from rock as "adventure" to rock as "job"—what kinds of changing sociocultural or structural factors might be reflected, affected, or effected by this shift? Chapter 1 proposed that media narratives about performers' attempts to enter and succeed in the music industry offer uniquely instructive stories of work and social mobility in the neoliberalizing world. This chapter explores the notion that the growing production and popularity of intensive, longitudinal cinematic studies of rock musicians' careers are particularly well suited to the production of value-laden knowledge pertinent to the navigation of the class system in the United States. *Dig!* exemplifies the contemporary rockumentary's focus on strategies for achieving social mobility by aspiring autonomous professionals in an emerging and unstable stratum of creative workers.

American Idol has engendered a massive popular audience and an institutionalized entertainment industry treadmill (with tens of thousands of aspirants showing up and often camping out to audition for each season). In contrast, contemporary rockumentary presents a less spectacular career path to a smaller audience. It invokes a savvier subject, endowed with appropriate social and cultural resources, whose encounters with the music industry— particularly once he has gained good notices or "buzz"—are less fleeting, condensed, or individually decisive than those of *American Idol*'s transposed cocktail waitresses and mass communication majors with that program's judges. To these indie music makers, the record industry is less the seamless, towering monolith outlined in *American Idol* than a more horizontal system of social and professional networks with more porous boundaries and numerous personalized points of contact and access. Entry into this system is to be negotiated incrementally, not with a jump from dealing with production assistants to consorting with heavyweights like Simon Cowell, but through cultivation of contacts with relative corporate underlings positioned in or alongside music scenes. *American Idol* cultivates a reserve army of institutionally oriented proletarian peddlers of entertainment labor power by holding out the absurdly remote promise of stratospheric stardom. As aspiring *Idol* contestants approach and win or achieve runner-up status in the final contests of the season, their infamously restrictive contracts prevent them from translating their growing success into Lady Gaga or Jay-Z–style autonomy. In contrast, media devoted to the workaday world of semi-professional cultural producers engaged in extra- or quasi-institutional cultural production can be seen as appealing more rationally to the interests of those who themselves are aiming, perhaps more realistically, a bit lower: for indie rather than mainstream success, for less institutionalized, more autonomous, and only moderately elite status.[4] From indie band rockumentary-subject perspective, the industry is individuals (rather than voting audiences and celebrity executives) such as the A&R scout who may be the same age as and essentially the peer of the musician. These individuals are attached to institutions that include other people with decision-making or signing power—such as the scout's boss, an executive who might be persuaded to pay attention to this band or that one on the scout's recommendation.

Richard Sennett distinguishes between the positions and outlooks of elite and mass workers in the "new capitalism" along these very lines. "The new elite," he writes, "has less need of the ethic of delayed gratification, as thick networks provide contacts and a sense of belonging, no matter what firm or organization one works for. The mass, however, has a thinner network of informal contact and support, and so remains more institution-dependent."[5] This "new elite"—among which indie-level music industry players can be counted—can also be included in the population that the labor analyst Robert Reich once labeled "symbolic analysts" but whom he now prefers to call "creative workers," a group that, in his view, comprise "the highest paid 25 percent" of American workers.[6] Rock music makers are "creative workers" par excellence, even if they don't all fall in that income quartile; it is on the basis of what they share and don't share with growing numbers of professionals that the social dimensions of the rockumentary's contemporary proliferation (as, among other things, a form of economic education) can best be understood. Before discussing *Dig!* and its filmmaker in detail, I will outline aspects of the social and historical context in which the rockumentary emerged and which influenced its general contours.

Rockumentary

Many of the crop of rockumentaries from which I have selected *Dig!* depend on the extensive use of filmmaking techniques first pioneered under the banner of "direct cinema." Direct cinema was the name chosen by its founders for a documentary movement that began to capture public attention in the early 1960s, often colloquially referred to as "American cinéma vérité." Direct cinema is, in fact, the social and creative milieu and genre in which the rockumentary first came into its own in the 1960s. Three of the first rockumentary filmmakers, Albert and David Maysles (*What's Happening! The Beatles in the U.S.A.* [1964] and *Gimme Shelter*, featuring the Rolling Stones [1970]) and D. A. Pennebaker (*Dont* [sic] *Look Back*, featuring Bob Dylan [1967] and *Monterey Pop* [1968]) had worked together in the late 1950s through 1962. Along with the cinematographer Richard Leacock, this team pioneered the technology and philosophy that would bring a new form of documentary into mainstream television and thus into the American public sphere. The conditions in which this cinematic form was developed, as well as the philosophy behind its development, help to illuminate the form's affordances as a defining component of the new rockumentary.

For most of the first half of the twentieth century, documentary was largely didactic and propagandistic—mostly associated with state and corporate projects and having to do with issues such as public health, government projects, industry, and consumption. The technological constraints of sound-film production reinforced the stylistic conventions of documentary. The size, weight, and crew needs of synchronized-sound filmmaking equipment required that subjects had to orient themselves to the camera; filming was most successful on sets, where conditions could be controlled. Mobile cameras could not easily capture audio. The result was that conventional documentaries tended either to be stiff and stilted or overlaid with "voice of God" narration and music.

Direct cinema emerged around 1960 as an alternative to this established form of nonfiction film. Photojournalist-turned-filmmaker Robert Drew and the handful of filmmakers he assembled under the aegis of Drew Associates in the late 1950s are widely understood to have pioneered this new documentary form. Funded by *Life* magazine and its parent company, Time, Incorporated, Drew, the two Maysleses, Leacock, and Pennebaker developed compact, portable synch-sound rigs that required only two people to operate, and a new approach to the use of camera in recording social life. Minimally encumbered, guided by an observational attitude of relaxed alertness and sensitivity, these two-person crews could enter intimate settings and follow people and events in order to convey to the viewer what Leacock called "the feeling of being there."[7] These filmmakers sought to position the viewer in such a way that he or she could observe what Albert Maysles suggests "would have happened had we not been there" in surroundings where old-style synch-sound cinematography could not have operated: in a car, a small office, a hotel or dressing room or onstage at a rock performance.[8] When this group of film-makers emerged into the media mainstream in the early 1960s with a series of films produced for ABC, they captured the public's attention and garnered wide praise for their new style.

Robert C. Allen and Douglas Gomery argue that the portable synch-sound technologies developed by these filmmakers (now virtually omnipresent in the form of handy- and digi-cams) were the technological components or expressions of a filmmaking philosophy rooted in what they call "American liberalism." American liberalism is a postwar political mood and orientation rooted in the idea that the improvement of society will come through ratio-nal action and gradual, piecemeal change guided by expert (social) scientific knowledge, "rather than in a total and drastic [that is, revolutionary] reso-lution of all its problems."[9] The "implicit philosophy" of direct cinema—the notion that the truth of a given situation can be discovered and recorded by an unbiased observer wielding a camera—constitutes the basic assumption behind its reformism: presented with facts, viewers could and would make rational judgments and participate in the public sphere and democratic po-litical processes on that basis.[10] In Leacock's words, the films of Drew Asso-ciates "presented you with data to try to figure out what the hell was really going on," letting the individual, rational member of the audience evaluate cinematically recorded facts that were speaking for themselves."[11]

The New Individualism and the "Mass Society Critique"

Direct cinema emerged in the context of, exemplified, and advanced the post-war formation of what Axel Honneth calls "a new, late-modern stage of con-scious individualism."[12] The cultural obverse of this new individualist ethos was what Thomas Frank has characterized as the popularization of the "mass society critique" (exemplified in David Riesman's influential book *The Lonely Crowd*, first published in 1950) and the ensuing intertwined countercultural and business revolutions of the 1960s.[13] According to Frank, the twin devel-opment of business and countercultural revolutions—in which sensation-seeking middle-class youth and intrepid ad agency creatives rejected con-formity and endorsed individuation and self-actualization more or less simultaneously and on a large scale—resulted in the institutionalization of "a hip consumerism driven by disgust with mass society itself."[14] This mid-twentieth-century cultural logic has persisted into the present with grave con-sequences, in Honneth's view, and appears as an animating force in the new rockumentary, most especially in *Dig!*

Honneth observes that the early twenty-first century is saturated with "ideologies of deinstitutionalization," increasingly pervasive individualist attitudes that enable and accept the ongoing neoliberal evisceration of the welfare state and imposition of insecurity on working people. The enabling ideologies that have greased neoliberalism's gears appear as the perverse consequences of a so-called democratization in the 1950s and 1960s of values of self-actualization that were previously the province of an economic and cultural elite. In conjunction with a widespread relaxation of traditional behavioral norms and the continuing growth of experience-oriented consumption, Honneth argues, postwar expansions in income, occupational choice, social mobility, and education supported the development of working people's demands for more opportunities to realize and express themselves in the workplace. Intersecting structural and cultural factors fomented in the expanding middle class a "tendency to think of the various possibilities for personal identity as being the stuff of experimental self-discovery," leading to "the appearance on a large-scale of individualization of a 'qualitative' kind: individuals were trying out various ways of life in order to be able, in light of these experiences, to actualize the core of their own personalities, which is what most clearly distinguished them from everyone else."[15] During this era of postwar economic, social, and cultural expansion, the conception of the individual life as what Anthony Giddens calls a "reflexive project of the self" began to spread beyond the overlapping realms of the elites and marginal bohemians and to take root in vast groups of the population whose members had previously been less troubled by, for example, the radical separation of work and personal life.[16] The perverse consequences of this shift, according to Honneth, are evident in the transformation of self-actualization from an option into an obligation.

Honneth's observations about the emergence of the new individualism focus on what could be called a push: *by* working people *on* institutions, for greater opportunities to actualize and differentiate themselves. In contrast, Frank's study of the Creative Revolution in American advertising in the mid-twentieth century is a detailed account of the development of a complementary pull: *by* institutions *on* working people, to encourage individuals to imagine themselves as self-actualizing, individuating nonconformists. Frank's account shows how elite concerns regarding the social and cultural perils of a society increasingly dominated by a vast system of interlocking state, corporate, and union bureaucracies struck responsive chords in the mass media, leading to the widespread popularization of a "mass society critique." Mid-century intellectuals' analyses of the "lonely crowd" and the "organization man" primed the discursive pump and, "by the middle of the 1950s, talk of conformity, and of the banality of mass-produced culture were routine elements of middle-class American life."[17] The mass endorsement of the mass society critique is a stunning contrast to present-day conceptions of that period as one of staid state and corporate monoliths populated by vast armies of drones in gray flannel suits, opposed only by ragtag bands of youthful bohemian visionaries, outcasts, and radicals. Frank's account limns "the democratization of the modernist impulse, the extension of high-brow disaffection with over-civilization . . . and [the spread of] elite concerns with individual fulfillment to the widest possible audience." Values of individual self-actualization and a hostility toward hierarchy and conformity, Frank shows, were widespread throughout society, from the most "far out" reaches of the counterculture to corporate America's bean-counting company men. Just a few years later, in the 1960s, "bohemia itself would be democratized, the mass society critique adopted by millions of Organization Men, and the eternal conflict of artist and bourgeoisie expanded into a cultural civil war."[18]

In this atmosphere, the rejection by this group of filmmakers of documentary conventions that seemed to construct audiences as populations to indoctrinate and manage makes a great deal of sense. The object of these filmmakers, rushing out to examine the experiences and lives of individuals who were often at crossroads or in crises, was to create person-sized "spaces" in otherwise inaccessible social situations into which audiences could imaginatively insert themselves, and from which they could observe and form their own opinions of "what the hell was really going on." Their desire to produce for audiences "the feeling of being there" drove them to reject ever more firmly conventions such as narration, interviews, extradiegetic music and to understand themselves to be observers only—led by the actions of their subjects, totally subservient to the situation in which they found themselves. Leacock wrote that early in their collaboration, the members of Drew Associates had begun to subject themselves "to a rather rigid set of rules. If we missed something, never ask anyone to repeat it. Never ask any questions. Never interview." He said that "we rarely broke [these rules] and when we did we regretted it."[19] Other comments made by these filmmakers seem to suggest that they understood themselves to be participating in a moment of invigorating change. Albert Maysles later recalled that during the filming of *Primary*, "we were on fire with enthusiasm, and we knew exactly that we were creating a revolution."[20] "For Ricky [Leacock], . . . Maysles and myself,"

Pennebaker informed an interviewer, "it was something of a religious experience."[21] Maysles's and Pennebaker's language presents their practice almost as cinema's equivalent of rock music, multiplying the salience of the term "rockumentary." The simultaneous engineering of their own release from the didactic, stilted, institutional modes of the documentary and of their ability to address distinct, self-directed individuals at the crest of a wave of new individualism and mass society critique, through the development of a technological and philosophical representational apparatus of their own design must indeed have been exhilarating.

As both Honneth and Frank are at pains to make clear, however, the movement toward mass individualization and self-actualization carried in itself the seeds of its own destruction. At this time, working people were pushing for opportunities for self-actualization and, to some degree, de-alienation in work; business revolutionaries, academics, and artists were railing against "organization men"; and direct cinema was constructing television audiences as critical, capable, choosing individuals. But American business was simultaneously advancing individualization and self-actualization for its own ends, to what would become the detriment of organized labor and working people in general. Indeed, before, during, and after their social activist, reformist, public sphere–oriented collaborative filmmaking, some of these same filmmakers produced non-theatrical films that addressed citizens and employees as self-actualizing individuals for the purpose of aligning them with administrative and pro-business initiatives.[22] The Maysles' 1965 AT&T film *Employee Barriers To Good Service*, for example, exhorted workers through discourses of self-improvement to internalize managerial imperatives.[23]

Direct Cinema Modes in Rockumentary

Almost the entire corpus of films from which I have chosen *Dig!* makes use of techniques officially shunned by the originators of American cinéma vérité or direct cinema (such as interviews and extradiegetic sound), and *Dig!* in particular makes very interesting use of voice-over narration. But these films' rhetorics of authenticity and truth—the cinematic strategies on which they ultimately depend for their status as representations of reality—are based solidly on their extensive use of direct cinema's techniques and approaches. Indeed, the films are largely composed of direct cinema–style hand-held location shots that are distinctive for their intimacy, and are inflected with a sense of radical transparency. Many reviews of *Dig!* locate the film squarely in the direct cinema tradition, and Ondi Timoner, the filmmaker, has frequently expressed her understanding of herself as a "vérité" filmmaker and has often explicitly acknowledged the influence of the early work of Maysles and Pennebaker on her production.[24]

Cinema vérité is a form of nonfiction filmmaking, practiced primarily in France in the 1950s, which involved a provocation on the part of the filmmaker, who would then film his or her subjects' responses to this provocation. As I've noted, American vérité—or direct cinema, as it came to be called by its practitioners and film studies scholars—is characterized by its avoidance of such provocations and its commitment to finding a person or people in an existing situation and allowing the unfolding flow of events to direct the filmmaking.[25] Almost directly quoting some of the pioneers of this cinema form, Timoner handily sums up the direct cinema philosophy in which she sees herself participating: "form should follow content" and, with this approach, "your subject matter can dictate how it should be shot, how it should look, how it should feel, what the story is."[26]

The origins of the direct cinema filmmaking style suggest directions for the analysis of the contemporary rockumentaries that depend on this style. Whether as a set of rules for the production of complete films or as one of a number of methods (or of filmmaker identities or subject positions) to be combined within a given documentary, we can understand direct cinema as an example of a "text genre," whose selection "places a variety of constraints on what can be said and how it can be expressed."[27] But the selection of a "text genre"—in the case of documentary production, one of a number of possible "mode[s] of documentary representation"—not only constrains but enables: direct cinema's "American liberal" philosophy, politics, and origins shape what can be said and how, on the occasions when its methods or ideologies are engaged.[28]

Most of the new rockumentaries are not unalloyed works of direct cinema, but neither were many of the works produced by the pioneers of direct cinema themselves.[29] *Dig!*—like *Metallica: Some Kind of Monster* (2004); *End of the Century* (2003), about the Ramones; *I Am Trying to Break Your Heart* (2002), about Wilco; *Meeting People Is Easy* (1999), about Radiohead; and a host of others—is an amalgam of documentary styles that have accumulated during the last several decades. "Older approaches" to the documentary, writes Bill Nichols, "do not go away; they remain part of a continuing exploration of form in relation to social purpose. What works at a given moment and what counts as a realistic representation of the historical world is not a simple matter of progress toward a final form of truth but of struggles for power and authority within the historical arena itself."[30] The power of a documentary to convince is a function of the relation of its form to its time and place. Nevertheless, despite their adaptations of or departures from direct cinema's rules, the new rockumentary depends a great deal on direct cinema's rhetoric of truth and its legitimation over the last half-century. Direct cinema is both a text genre that can be drawn on to construct stories or arguments about the social world and a tradition, made up of a group of filmmakers and a body of canonical works, that continues to influence and to be engaged by contemporary filmmakers.

The intimate connections of direct cinema with key social institutions in the 1950s and 1960s, the collaboration of direct cinema with these institutions toward the production of new individualist citizens/workers/consumers, and the changing relations between those institutions and individuals point toward a hypothesis concerning the political baggage and perspectives contributed by the direct cinema text genre to rockumentary. If the representations of work in direct cinema (and in those non-theatrical films produced by Maysles, Pennebaker, and other Drew Associates alumni) also model and prescribe preferred orientations to work, how might the selection of this text genre by rockumentarists shape what can be said in or by their films? How might rockumentary's ambivalence—simultaneously advancing the new competitive individualism and American liberalism's prosocial agenda—participate in the production and proliferation of new and future working subjects that articulate this odd tangle of self-actualization, discipline, responsibility for oneself, freedom, and authenticity? An analysis of *Dig!* will help frame these questions more concretely and advance an understanding of the political, economic, and cultural role of rockumentary today.

Ondi Timoner and Dig!

After graduating from Yale University, Ondi Timoner moved to Los Angeles to get into the film industry, bringing with her a student documentary she had made that told the story of a woman prisoner in a Connecticut prison. Her hope had been to get her film produced as a full-length feature, but what she encountered was a succession of industry sharks looking to reshape her property to suit their commercial purposes. Smarting from this awakening, and reflecting on it through her own experience as an amateur musician, Timoner developed a project that would focus on "what happens when art and industry meet." Titling this project *The Cut*, Timoner sought out and began filming ten Los Angeles bands with the intention of tracking their progress through their anticipated impending interactions with industry.[31]

Dig! begins in 1995 with the meeting of the filmmaker and Anton Newcombe, the leader of the Brian Jonestown Massacre (BJM), in San Francisco. In Los Angeles, working on *The Cut*, Timoner had heard the group's music and had "thought they were from the 1960s, and then somebody told me 'no, they're alive and well in SF and everybody wants to sign them.' So I went up there to meet them and I was blown away by the characters and . . . I also liked the music."[32] In comparison to the BJM and the Dandy Warhols (with whom, according to Newcombe, the BJM would "kick off a full musical revolution"[33]), the bands Timoner had been filming in Los Angeles suddenly seemed less compelling. "Instantly from meeting the Brian Jonestown Massacre," she told an audience at the London Film Festival, "I encountered people who were willing to play the game on their own terms only . . . and I just saw a gutsiness that I didn't experience with the bands in L.A. so much; and I think that [the L.A. bands] were sort of cowering in the shadows of the industry trying to be what the business wanted them to be . . . whereas these guys were just living for the moment, and that's what attracted me to making a film about them."[34] Newcombe told her to "forget about the other bands, 'cause this is a whole 'nother level of American underground that I'm going to help expose."[35] According to Timoner, Newcombe "said he was going to take over my documentary and I thought 'ha ha' and then he did."[36] Newcombe's presence ended up dominating the film.

Timoner abandoned *The Cut* and joined San Francisco's BJM and Portland's Dandy Warhols shortly after the bands' first meeting in the mid-1990s. *Dig!* follows the groups from then until 2003, by which time the former group had dissolved in the face of Newcombe's own downward spiral and the latter group had established itself as a successful, savvy recording and touring unit. With seven years' worth of documentation, including some 1,500–2,000 hours of film and video footage (accounts differ), Timoner compressed a complex story into a hundred-minute documentary. While contrasting the two bands' personalities and trajectories, the film nevertheless focuses primarily on the more dramatic, crisis-ridden coming apart of Newcombe and his dysfunctional band.

In the first moments of the film, we learn that the two bands impress each other musically—each has its own brand of sixties-revivalist psychedelic rock music—and also bond with each other over a shared devotion to drugs, parties, outrageous vintage fashion (including musical instruments), and a cocksure, "stick it to the man" attitude (although the Dandys have just signed with a major label). In their first years of association, the bands play gig after gig together in venues up and down the West Coast. The film offers evidence of this togetherness in the form of clips from these gigs that show band members sharing stages with each other (playing gigs together usually means sharing a bill in succession, not sharing a stage simultaneously, but footage of stage-sharing conveys this collegiality very economically). "It was *rock*," intones Courtney Taylor, the leader of the Dandy Warhols and the film's narrator. The mutually reinforcing cultural value of the bands' and the film-maker's projects is established early on through the intercutting—amid the direct cinema-style sequences of parties and gigs—of clips of music industry authorities pronouncing alternately on the genius of the two bands and on Newcombe's reputation as a visionary and his view of success and integrity as "mutually exclusive," as the culture critic Carlo McCormick puts it in *Dig!*

A Synopsis of *Dig!*

Newcombe and Taylor, as leaders and frontmen of the two bands, are the film's main characters; other band members have supporting roles (which are not always supportive). After their first couple of years of "rocking" in this reciprocally admiring fashion, Newcombe moves his band to Portland to advance the cause with the Dandys. The Dandys, however, are busy "being productive," according to the keyboardist Zia McCabe,[37] and they rebuff the members of the BJM, who appear to have planned to actually move in with the Dandys to jointly further the revolution. Before too long, however, Bomp! Records, an indie label with a good reputation, invites the BJM to Los Angeles, where they settle into a small house (which Bomp! has rented for them) that will remain mostly free of furnishings (other than musical instruments and equipment) for the duration of their stay.

In Los Angeles to meet with Capitol Records, Taylor plays for Newcombe "Not If You Were The Last Junkie On Earth," an upcoming single that will also appear on the Dandys' album then in progress. Newcombe appears to think the song is about him, and the rivalry that occupies much of the film's dramatic core appears to be initiated at this moment. Relations between the bands are further strained when the Dandys, in Los Angeles again for a big-budget video shoot, arrive unannounced at the BJM's still barren but some-how messy house to be photographed for a spread in the music journal *Alternative Press*. The members of the BJM sense that the slumming Dandys are exploiting them (I discuss this exchange further below). Meanwhile, Newcombe appears to be accelerating his use of heroin, and his violent temper manifests itself in increasing frequency and scale.

After recording an entire album in five days (a feat which included a riposte to Taylor, "Not If You Were The Last Dandy On Earth"), the BJM embark on a national tour. *Dig!*'s tour montage follows the band from one dingy club and tiny audience to the next. Their experience is contrasted with that of the Dandy Warhols, whose coinciding tour places the Dandys before bigger audiences and entails more glossy, well-adjusted fun, compared to the BJM members' constant fights and breakdowns. Taylor, however, returns from the Dandys' tour to a record company unimpressed by the group's too-slowly-growing commercial success. Dispirited, Taylor joins the BJM's tour in Detroit, hoping for some inspiration—the film frequently suggests that Taylor uses Newcombe as a source of inspiration and a barometer of integrity, coveting Newcombe's genius. Taylor travels with the BJM to New York, playing music and taking drugs with them yet remaining detached, having no stake in the conduct or outcome of the tour. At this point, the film undertakes an extended meditation on the music industry through the lens of the BJM's courtship by a "baby" A&R scout and the group's eventual signing by a "major indie" label, TVT Records.[38]

In New York, at the storied nightclub CBGB, another outburst of Newcombe's temper results in the severing of the BJM's relationship with its long-time manager. Newcombe hires the booking agent who had arranged the tour as the group's new manager. Fearing that Newcombe's drug use and temper will derail the developing deal with TVT, the new manager tells the label that Newcombe is sick and sends the group's tambourine player to New York to sign the contract instead. Back on the West Coast, Newcombe begins stalking the Dandys in earnest; it remains unclear to what degree he is expressing jealous anger over their success and to what degree he is playing up a rivalry in the tradition of the Beatles and the Rolling Stones, or the British pop bands Blur and Oasis, with the possible aim of generating media attention. The BJM-TVT deal, however, results in worldwide exposure for the band and cuts short Newcombe's stalking with a trip to Tokyo, where huge, enthusiastic crowds get the band's hopes up.

Before going to Tokyo, Newcombe had used the TVT recording budget to purchase recording equipment and instruments and rent a house in Los Angeles for the production of the group's first TVT record. When they return from Japan, however, the band members' hopes fade as Newcombe begins to use heroin at a perilous rate. The group's new manager hires an engineer to facilitate the recording process, but Newcombe fires him in a drug-fueled fit of pique. An onstage argument at a Los Angeles gig results in the departure of one of Newcombe's long-time collaborators (between 1990 and 2004, the band had burned through dozens of members). In the meantime, the Dandy Warhols are back on tour in Europe. Their song "Bohemian Like You" had been used in an advertisement by Vodafone, the European cellphone company, and raised interest in the group from Stockholm to Madrid. The film presents a succession of glamorous press interviews and performances before tens of thousands of people, parties, with a shot of Taylor leaping around a hotel room in his underwear shouting "Hello! We love it!" about the band's escalating fortune. Back in Los Angeles, the BJM crumbles as drug use and fighting continue apace.

After their triumphant return from Europe, the Dandys take their "promo budget" (the amount advanced by a label to be spent on making a video) and, following in the footsteps of the Who (and other "rock aristocrats"), invest in real estate: they construct a practice space/recording studio/theater/ nightclub of their own design.[39] In the black with their record company,[40] the Dandys have become proprietors and are "grown up" and "taking [their] jobs seriously."[41] Winding down at this point, the film closes around a shocking incident involving Newcombe at the Knitting Factory in Hollywood. During a lull in the performance, an audience member makes an audibly critical comment, and when Newcombe belligerently invites him to come closer to the stage, the attendee does so, only to be met with a brutal kick in the head from Newcombe's booted foot. Newcombe is handcuffed, arrested, and shown weeping to the filmmaker in the backseat of the police car. The film ends with the (probably former) TVT A&R person observing that people who have worked with Newcombe have gone on to significant success, while he's managed to stay "exactly where he was before."[42]

What Happens "When Art and Industry Meet"?

In a discussion of some of the very interesting technical aspects of the film, Timoner gives a little more detail about her motivation for making the film. "I had made a documentary, *Nature of the Beast*, about a Connecticut woman who is serving a life term in prison for murder," she tells *American Cinematographer*. "I went to L.A. to try to turn it into a film or TV movie to help bring her story to more people. As all of these players became involved in the process, I started to realize how the purity of art is thrown [off balance] when it becomes a commodity. That's why I started filming bands on the verge of getting signed."[43] She approached her topic with a stake in the problem (one is tempted to say an ax to grind): a perception of the similarities in her situation as a young filmmaker coming to Hollywood and that of an independent band approaching and negotiating the boundaries of the music industry. And not just any band either: the L.A. bands she had been filming paled in comparison with the "gutsier" groups to the north, who apparently conformed more to her sense of what the meeting of art and industry should look like. She was immediately captivated by the BJM's Anton Newcombe, becoming a willing "conscript"—"Leni Riefenstahl to Anton's revolution."[44] She emerged nearly eight years later with a major Sundance prize and distribution deal; offers of new, fully funded, high-profile projects;[45] and a film with a distinctly social purpose—which was, as she told *The Age*, to "inspire other people to explore their own creativity and their hearts, to see if they are following their lives right."[46] *Dig!* offers a prescription, through its invocation of sixties-style counterculture and social relations, for following one's life right in today's political economy.

Just as the BJM and the Dandys shared interests in and commitments to a set of cultural signifiers and practices, so did Timoner—first with the BJM and then with the Dandys, to whom she was introduced by Newcombe. Some details can be added to this homology between indie bands and filmmaker. Timoner tells an interviewer at the 2004 L.A. Film Festival that she and the bands "grew up together": "You can see it in the film, in the filmmaking, in the style, how it became sort of, more steady, less enthusiastic, less zooming at the end."[47] This is particularly striking with respect to her filming of the Dandys, with whom her relationship, for reasons I suggest below, appears far more comfortable than her relationship with the BJM. She and the Dandys grew together in "steady" self-confidence as well as in material wealth and professional status. Her growing up along with the Dandys is reflected in the changing technologies that become available to and affordable by Timoner and her partners as their own business, Interloper Films (which they tended between *Dig!* shoots), flourished. In an interview included in the special features of the *Dig!* DVD, Timoner explains that "the medium goes from 8 millimeter, hi-8 millimeter (hi-8 video), to 35 millimeter film."[48] It happens, she reports, that the BJM "really feel like a Super 8 band; their sound is so nostalgic and 'imperfectly perfect,' much like Super 8." She notes that "later on, we decided to start shooting 16mm of the Dandy Warhols to reflect their success," and the fact that that tool and its expensive stock and processing were within Interloper's reach at that point testifies to the changing fortunes of Timoner and her partners themselves.[49] But their social homology and "growing up together" have more dimensions than just the intertwined professional success of both the Dandys and Timoner. The commonalities of both bands and filmmaker are rooted in deeper sociological soil: their sharing of critical elements of habitus—that is, class-based, sociocultural predispositions.[50]

Timoner allows that her "greatest feeling of the film was that, I think that a lot of us grew up, or at least I did, with the feeling of 'I want that, I want that feeling of the 1960s, I want that feeling of a revolution.'"[51] When she encountered these bands, she recalls,

> I felt, just like the names Brian Jonestown Massacre and the Dandy Warhols, there's an obvious reference to the '60s, and I think that I was also drawn to the subject matter because these bands were in the mid-90s trying to find something to fight against and hearkening for a time when there was a true counterculture, and when music—you know, the music industry was really fresh. And so I think there's certainly the personal and the political and all that is mixed together, but I think certainly they're coming from that perspective. [Newcombe] kept using the word "revolution," but I was like, I wasn't sure, I just knew he was going to do it.[52]

Newcombe, according to Timoner, "was longing for that Sixties camaraderie he'd read about in books about The Beatles and the Stones" and appeared to have found it with Courtney Taylor and the Dandy Warhols.[53] Based on Timoner's construction of her film, as well as her statements about it, it seems that she was inclined to work with the direct cinema form at least in part because of that form's association with the new individualism and the mass society critique, as well as the seductive character of the collaborative relationship of direct cinema filmmakers to their rock star subjects. The Brian Jonestown Massacre, the Dandy Warhols, and Ondi Timoner shared enough of an orientation to the cultural artifacts, collective memory, and what they perceived as the social relations of cultural production of the 1960s to come together for this long-term, intimate collaboration. But the shape that their three-way relationship takes as the project progresses suggests the presence and determining power of distinctly contemporary forms of classed sociality.

Three Agents, Two Divergent Paths

The film is thus not simply about the diverging trajectories of the two bands, as the reviews and interviews suggest, but about their trajectories and that of Timoner, and what the comportment and trajectories of all three have to tell us about lives and careers in the contemporary economy. The bands and filmmaker come together in the mid-1990s under the banner of a few features of shared habitus: 1960s music and fashion, youthful urban partying, and indie cultural production. The divergence that takes place is not, as is suggested by many reviewers, between two bands holding contrasting attitudes toward the music business. Rather, the divergence traced by *Dig!* is that of groups of cultural producers drawn to particular, shared, or homologous forms of indie cultural production from different social positions. They share an interest in a narrow band of cultural tropes, practices, and artifacts, but the bands and filmmaker approach them with different orientations and expectations, bringing with them different amounts and kinds of resources. Seemingly minor differences of habitus and social origin become major as their relationships develop. What Timoner and the Dandys have in common that is not shared by the BJM ultimately seems to eclipse what all three shared initially. Common intentions and conceptions—a shared value of "hold[ing] onto their integrity in the face of commodifying their art"[54] and the binary conception of social relations that such a position entails—intersected in their initial moments of courtship and cultural camaraderie. As they pursued their goals, however, these two groups—Newcombe and his bandmates on the one side, and the Dandys and Timoner on the other—ultimately put these cultural signifiers and practices to work in different ways, to different purposes, and with different results.[55]

In many places in the film and its special features, Taylor and Timoner argue that Taylor and the Dandys provide Newcombe with a "foil" of commercial success against which he could understand himself as musically and ethically pure. I think more can be learned from this film by reversing that framework. Without, I hope, reducing the tangle of issues here either to purely psychological or sociological arguments, I want to offer an alternate reading of the film: Newcombe's apparent madness provides the Dandys with an irrational Other whose flagrant self-sacrifice on the altar of authenticity reciprocally makes plain the soundness and reasonableness of the Dandys' approach and allows Timoner to avoid dealing with the probably thorny problem of trying to reconcile her overdetermined initial critique with a less dramatically exciting but perhaps more challenging—not to mention practically instructive—story of successful rather than failed, frustrated, ill-starred, or self-sabotaged collaboration with capital.

What this, in turn, makes possible is the pedagogical presentation of a model orientation toward work and the economy that reinforces the ties between 1960s-esque, authenticity-driven cultural production and evolving entrepreneurial subject positions. Individualization continues unabated, emerging in new, more extreme forms in a new, more extreme era. Contemporary changes in social relations take place, as they did in the 1950s and 1960s, amid a variety of pedagogical media. In the present case, however, the media we are concerned with is not the savvy, sophisticated, Creative Revolution–driven forms of advertising produced by giant corporations of the mid-twentieth century that wanted to impose business-friendly models of nonconformist consumer subjectivity on members of Riesman's lonely crowd. This is media produced by people who are struggling to harmonize the self-directed development of their powers with the needs of capital for other people who are increasingly compelled to do the same. With contemporary rockumentary, as exemplified by *Dig!*, the filmmakers and their musician subjects are the offspring—arguably, the fulfillment—of Frank's popularized mass society critique and Honneth's new individualism of the 1950s and 1960s: sensation-seeking, risk-taking creative workers whose very visible and audible work models intense self-actualization, offered as an example for people to make sure they're "following their lives right."

Bearing with them familiar critiques of the bureaucratic, risk-averse corporations that dominate their respective fields, both Timoner and the Dandys set out to make it on their own terms. This valuation of authenticity and relative autonomy is not built on a rejection of exploitation, but rather on an acceptance and even enjoyment of forms of exploitation that do not appear to compel them to be (or to pretend to be) other than who they believe themselves to be—that do not appear, in social-psychological terms, to alienate. Employees in the intensifying neoliberal elaboration of new individualist regime must, as Honneth puts it, "be ready and willing to present every change of position at work as flowing from their own choice."[56] Thus the deeper story of *Dig!* is one of collaboration and alignment with capital that highlights and renders even more attractive—through its selective association with 1960s counterculture—the new "freedoms" associated with what Honneth calls "de-institutionalization." Analyzing this more subtle of *Dig!*'s themes illuminates the film's participation in the proliferation of neoliberal subjectivity.

Timoner meets Newcombe and—galvanized by his music, charisma, and charm—abandons *The Cut*. He introduces her to his "gutsier" San Francisco scene and to the Dandy Warhols. Wielding her camera onstage during performances, sharing drugs afterward, she films both bands playing gigs, partying, and driving around in tour vans. Newcombe's volatile, occasionally violent, character becomes more and more of a problem for the BJM and for Timoner (she reports having been ordered out of his presence more than once) as the Dandys' oft-repeated, self-proclaimed status as "the most well-adjusted band in America" adds to the rapidly deepening contrast between the two bands. The topic of the film begins to shift markedly from "what happens when art and industry meet" to what happens when a guy with a personality disorder fixates on a particularly rigid construction of authenticity and then alienates his friends and collaborators and destroys his business relationships. Newcombe's personality is increasingly the focus of amateur psychological detective work, diagnosis, and pseudoclinical portraiture, while Taylor and the Dandys, in comparison, are normalized and flattened with respect to their origins, personal lives, and career and social trajectories.[57] The Dandys' role soon devolves into a cinematic fulfillment of the band members' perception of themselves as a well-adjusted foil to Newcombe's rigid personality; their portraits in *Dig!* remain superficial in comparison to that of Newcombe.

A selection from the *Dig!* DVD's special features, titled "The Reckoning," shows Timoner near despair at a moment about a year into the project. Newcombe is giving her a hard time regarding permission to use the BJM's music in the film, probably having trouble distinguishing her documentary (or cultural capitalist) interest in his music from the economic (or plain old capitalist) interest of others. Timoner says: "I've poured so much—we've poured so much into this band, so much into this project. Our release form is good [valid], it is! And if we [can't] have any Brian Jonestown Massacre music, we [won't] have any Brian Jonestown Massacre music. We can literally create a short film of a person experiencing multiple personalities, going from angelic to fascist—um, scared, vulnerable. We can do a portrait of a madman, that'll be—probably win Sundance."[58] It cannot have been an easy decision to include this moment in the special features of the DVD. It is revealing: even though her release form *was* good and there is a great deal of BJM music in the film, the portrait of a madman/Sundance strategy appears to have carried the day and the film. Including the amount of time spent by the Dandys talking about Newcombe's personality problems and the BJM's troubled career, approximately 75 percent of the film is about Newcombe and his band's dramatic dissolution and failure (of course, the Dandys' discussions of Newcombe and the BJM tell us a lot about the Dandys as well). Indeed, almost every interview of people not in one of the bands (including other musicians, record label employees, and critics) concerns Newcombe and his personality.

The effect of this shift is to forestall what I believe are more provocative questions about "what happens when art and industry meet" *and get along really well*. What happens when rebellion, resistance, authenticity, and bohemianism—including, among other elements, indie cultural production and massive, frequent, illegal drug use—slot happily into institutions like Capitol Records, Vodafone, the Sundance grand jury prize, and distribution by Palm Pictures? The question of art and industry meeting is only partially addressed: the unspectacular yet probably very useful story of mutual alignment and adjustment in the course of the successful integration of art and industry is obscured in favor of a dramatically tragic story of psychosis and dissolution. It is my sense that this shift happens for two reasons. First, Newcombe's behavior and pronouncements make for compelling viewing, and his dissolution gives appealing shape to the narrative. The second reason, which I explore here, is that framing strong resistance to capital—the desire for radical autonomy—as crazy (an easy task, given Newcombe's personality) allows a lot of room to legitimize collaboration with capital under the banners of well-adjusted sanity and relative autonomy.

Timoner and the Dandy Warhols appear quickly to recognize (or at least intuit) that the more pertinent homology at work is that between their own intertwined and complementary trajectories and fortunes in their respective industries, rather than simply the three producers' starting positions at the margins of the cultural industries and shared interest in 1960s-style culture and social relations.[59] These trajectories in turn are related to their class positions and their possession of various forms of capital. As the differences between the positions, trajectories, and capitals of Timoner and the Dandys and those of the members of the Brian Jonestown Massacre become more apparent, a shift of attention toward the "madman" and how he wrecks every relationship and opportunity that comes his way deflects attention away from the relatively smooth integration of art and industry going on in the professional lives of Timoner and the Dandys. It is an explicit argument about how not to be, and an implicit argument about how to be, if you want success in the cultural industries on your own terms. The secret: it's far easier to make it on your own terms if your terms are already closely aligned with the cultural movements of capital.

Pathologizing Newcombe

In her review of *Dig!* in the *Village Voice*, Laura Sinagra recalls that "in 1994, Minneapolis's *City Pages* ran a cover story about the 'privileged poor'— bohemian kids moving in from the burbs to haunt midsize-city coffeehouses." She continues: "The '90s economy hadn't yet bubbled, and a Slacker aesthetic encouraged an off-the-grid communalism of band houses and barter networks. But you always knew who could buzz home for extra cash and who was really flying solo. [*Dig!*] captures the essence of that split."[60] The film makes plain that Newcombe was indeed "flying solo," to his very great disadvantage. Newcombe's familial origins appear to have been quite ignoble. His mother brags to the filmmakers that she called the police on her son several times for growing pot and refused to take him home after he was arrested for violating a curfew. His father—an alcoholic who had been diagnosed with schizophrenia—admits to having left the family while Newcombe was still a toddler. A particularly chilling moment in the film occurs when the father's image is frozen on the screen and drained of color following his brief monologue, and a superimposed caption informs viewers that he took his own life on Newcombe's next birthday.

In concert with the direct cinema footage of Newcombe's violent blow-ups (the longest non-narrated shot is of his violent attack on bandmates at a record label–sponsored party at the Viper Room in Los Angeles), the film makes clear through interviews with his parents that Newcombe's repeated failures and self-sabotages are to be linked to his alleged mental illness, aggravated by a horrible childhood and frequent drug use as an adult. Much of the movie focuses on Newcombe's violent temper and irrational outbreaks, presenting moments of apparent paranoia ("really incredible" paranoia, according to Timoner in her commentary on the DVD)—such as when he talks about being stolen from in ways that he does not define, and when he beat band members inside and outside of venues, has highly charged arguments with audiences and collaborators, and behaves erratically in other contexts. But also brought into relief are elements of what would appear to be a savior complex, his pronouncements that he is "love" and that he is the "son of God," pronouncements that seem all the more bizarre when presented adjacent to sequences of abuse and invective. Much of this material, particularly with respect to his temper, is presented in the context of statements, discussions, or filmic evidence of his drug use. According to one record company employee, who appears in the film as an authority on music and the music industry, Newcombe's TVT-financed home studio "was just a smack house; it was reeking of death. I thought [my visit] was actually the last time I would see him."[61]

His drug use, which does seem to affect his ability to maintain both working and intimate relationships, is characterized by Timoner as "self-medication." According to her, "Anton cultivates a certain edge: he denies a home, he denies self-comforts, he self-medicates, he denies himself psychotropic drugs which may help him stabilize because he cultivates and maintains that edge."[62] The Dandys' drug use, on the other hand, is never a matter of concern; if anything, it is a subject of the filmmaker's wonder and admiration. Early in the film we are introduced to Zia McCabe, the Dandys' keyboardist, as she is driving the filmmakers around during an interview. Voice-over commentary of Ondi Timoner and her brother David, provided in the *Dig!* DVD's special features, accompanies this moment:

> *Ondi Timoner*: We were crashing with Zia—
> *David Timoner*: Yeah.
> *Ondi*: —who was cutting up various drugs for us in the evening.
> *David [chuckles]*: But they were the most functional people who also cut up drugs, it was really together.
> *Ondi*: It was incredible, yeah—like warm breakfast in the morning but ecstasy at night, you know?[63]

This admiration betrays a shared productivist orientation between Timoner and the Dandys that functions not simply as a moderator of excess but as a component or goal of excess. Honneth proposes that under the aegis of the new individualism, "mounting claims to self-realization are transformed into a productive force in the capitalist economy"; *Dig!* limns the outer (illegal) limits of a corresponding form of what Honneth calls "experiential consumption."[64] An undercurrent throughout the film suggests that there is excess and there is excess: the wanton excess of Newcombe and his fellow band members is contrasted to the productive excess of the Dandys and their new filmmaking friends. In the contemporary economy, wanton excess disturbs and derails, but productive excess aligns, smoothing the way.[65] Productive excess, *Dig!* suggests, plays a role in forming the kinds of professional networks that are crucial for the success and upward mobility of promising young cultural producers and, increasingly, aspirants in a range of fields.[66] The Brian Jonestown Massacre is portrayed as a grim, doomed, "heroin" band, wantonly destroying support systems and resources in orgiastic potlatches of social capital. The Dandy Warhols, described by one critic as having a "generation Y industriousness,"[67] are portrayed as a shiny, turbo-charged, "ecstasy" band, productively cementing friendships and expanding networks, in part through intense partying.[68]

We are told very little about the Dandys' backgrounds, though it's surely easy for anyone versed in American culture to sense their economic and cultural privilege. One moment, however, is telling. In one of the special features on the *Dig!* DVD, Timoner films two of the Dandys in their separate hotel beds. McCabe, the keyboardist, recounts how earlier that day someone asked her to sign his guitar. She jokes that "he's just cashing in, he's one of those smart investors like Pete's dad. Knows a gold mine when he sees one." A filmmaker concerned with financing herself, Timoner's ears understandably prick up: "Is Pete's dad an investor?" McCabe answers, "Nah, he just lucked out." Timoner turns the camera on Pete in the adjacent bed as, somehow both sheepishly and proudly, he says that his dad "was the thirty-fifth member of Intel [Corporation]." He waits a beat and adds, deadpan, sounding almost rehearsed, "he took the stock option."[69] The only reference to the Dandys' backgrounds in the film itself is offered directly after the harrowing interviews with Newcombe's parents. Over shots of the band frolicking sweetly together—in a field, on a sidewalk—Courtney Taylor remarks that "when we all got together we realized all our parents were still married, and we're like, 'we're the most well-adjusted band in America.'" He repeats himself: "We're the most well adjusted band in America."[70] (The "adjustment," class positions, and professional trajectories of the Dandys are further substantiated in the film's closing scenes, as well as in the "Where Are They Now" special feature on the DVD.)

We learn almost nothing about Timoner in the film proper, and next to nothing about her as a person in the DVD's special features. But an article in the *Miami Herald* notes that her father, Eli, was an airline magnate—the founder of Air Florida—and that, in the words of David Timoner (Ondi's brother and *Dig!*'s coproducer), the Timoner children were "pretty privileged." Eli Timoner, according to the *Herald*, "was a widely regarded businessman and philanthropist, a 'pillar of the community' type." However, at the age of fifty-two, when Ondi and her siblings were approaching adolescence, the senior Timoner suffered a stroke that left him incapable of remaining in his professional position. At that moment, reports David, "everything unfolded. We fell back to earth." "Falling back to earth" in economic terms, however difficult it may have been, did not, of course, result in a loss of cultural capital. All three siblings attended Yale; the elder sister became a rabbi in the Bay Area; and Ondi and David started Interloper Films in Los Angeles.[71] It is not a stretch to suggest that, on account of her background and life experiences as the daughter of a successful capitalist, an overachieving teenager in reduced circumstances, an Ivy League student, and a struggling filmmaker, Timoner had much in common with both of her sets of subjects. Indeed, as she notes jubilantly in her online "production diary" about her experience in Paris with the Dandy Warhols, "my subjects love me!"[72]

Her other subjects may not have loved her quite so much during one particularly revealing episode in the film, mentioned briefly above. While in Los Angeles filming a video, the Dandy Warhols are booked by *Alternative Press* for a photo shoot. Courtney Taylor fixes on the BJM's unkempt, unfurnished Bomp! Records–financed L.A. house as an ideal location. "What I want to do," he tells the *Alternative Press* crew, "is go out to this really fucked household" and arrive without warning, to use it as a backdrop. The BJM had had a very successful party the night before, attracting even marginal movie star and recording artist Harry Dean Stanton, for drug- and booze-soaked jams into the wee hours. Taylor, who was not at the party, nonetheless knows that the house (and the BJM band members) will have been demolished. He, the Dandys, the filmmakers, and the photo crew show up there before any of the residents has woken up, let alone shaken off hangovers or cleaned house. McCabe remarks retrospectively, voicing over shots of the Dandys poking around in the wreckage of the party, "I just couldn't believe it. They had no furniture, hardly, everything was on the floor. It was like a squat, a hovel. [I thought:] 'How do you guys live like this?'"[73] As Taylor scampers impishly around the house scouting locations, Timoner follows the barely recovered Matt Hollywood, a long-time BJM member, with her camera, almost taunting him: "Matt Hollywood, there's a lot of people walking into your house right now, there's a whole photo shoot about to happen, and your house is *trashed*. You guys partied last night!" The magazine's photographer shoots the Dandys in the bathroom, around the kitchen table, on the floor in front of the television. Some of the BJM's members discuss the politics of the situation with Taylor; they maintain a joking tone, but the power dynamics here indicate the gulf between the BJM on the one side, and Timoner and the Dandys on the other. The BJM's tambourine player (and "speed addict"[74]), Joel Gion, observes to Taylor, "You're pumping our whole gig; [you're visiting, but] we have to live that, baby." Jeff Davies, a guitar player for the BJM ("fresh out of rehab"[75]), asks "How much do we get paaaiiid [for letting you use our house]?" To which Gion adds, "We're talking about dough, baby, where's the dough? Where's the dough? Where's the dough?" Hollywood, however, puzzles the problem out from a slightly different angle: "Now, if we take pictures in our own house, people are going to accuse us of ripping you guys off, in our own house." This sequence of events testifies to the BJM's usefulness to the Dandys, as well as to the BJM's role in the relationship between the Dandys and Timoner (for whom both bands are useful).

Self-Actualization, Deinstitutionalization, Work, and Rock

I want to return briefly to some key concepts from the earlier discussion of American liberalism, the production of subjects in direct cinema, and ideologies of self-actualization and deinstitutionalization in the arena of work in order to develop a clearer sense of the relevance of *Dig!* and documentary in general for the production of entrepreneurial, neoliberal economic subjects.

Direct cinema is a reformist medium—it suggests that the overarching system is essentially sound, and that corrections can be made to improve its exploitive or unfair elements without necessitating radical change. Direct cinema fits into this scheme in part because of its invocation of an individual, rational subject, understood to be capable of occupying the place of the observer and making up his or her mind as to "what the hell was really going on." *Dig!*'s formal participation in direct cinema is fractional: the film continually relies on the direct cinema text genre in short stretches as a means of presenting evidence. For example, in scenes where what's happening appears obvious, the absence of narration or captions or extradiegetic sound adds to the truth of the depiction. But through her constant references to "vérité" and favorite films produced by Albert and David Maysles and D. A. Pennebaker, Timoner aligns herself explicitly with the direct cinema tradition. Her initial approach to the film—"what happens when art and industry meet"—is classic subject material for direct cinema: musicians' professional careers as upward or downward trajectories and their interactional styles, struggles with market forces, and modes of dealing with crisis recall many of the early direct cinema films.[76] Moreover, the film posits the cultural industries as essentially just and fair—they don't stand in the way of the Dandy Warhols' apparently meritocratic success, and they can't be held responsible for the Brian Jonestown Massacre's failures. The music industry is populated by reasonable people (and perhaps a few scoundrels), and real talent is recognized (even if it can't always be disciplined). You and I are presumed to be rational viewers capable of inserting ourselves into the person-sized space opened by the agile, mobile camera and judging for ourselves, based on this accumulation of evidence. The individuals under scrutiny are presented in a way that allows us to feel that we comprehend their situations and can evaluate their choices.

But is it really so simple? The shift in perspective I've pointed out has significance here. From very early in the film, as Newcombe is increasingly pathologized and his band's progress disrupted by his drug use and temper (which also tend to obscure any other problems that may exist between the band's members), the position occupied by Courtney Taylor and the Dandys and the position of the filmmaker very quickly become virtually indistinguishable. This eclipsing or overlapping manifests itself in concrete terms in the selection of Taylor as narrator of the film. Timoner is vague about why exactly Taylor ended up narrating. The narration, she told the L.A. Film Festival interviewer, "was something where I had written it but I didn't know who was going to say it. It was gonna be me for a while; people were trying to convince me, friends were trying to convince me that it was my story. But you know, every film is made by a filmmaker. It's not really my story and, of course, my life is totally woven in that tale. But it's really a story strong enough to stand on its own, which is why I continued with it for seven years."[77] It would appear, if it were anybody's story at all, to be that of Anton Newcombe—who, incidentally, was angry about his portrayal in the film, feeling "strongly that the Jerry Springer-esque vilification of his nature is an inappropriate, mis contextualized [sic], and exploitative use of the footage."[78] Responding to the film on his website, Newcombe stated that "Several years of our hard work was [sic] reduced at best to a series of punch-ups and mishaps taken out of context, and at worst bold-faced lies and misrepresentation of fact." "A perfect example," Newcombe writes, "is footage shown of me getting arrested in Georgia. The narration and editing suggest that I am being arrested for drug possession. It was actually Ondi who was arrested for possession, and rightly so, as the drugs were hers. I happened to have an expired license." Newcombe also asserts that whereas Timoner's filming of the Dandys continued through 2003, she ceased filming the BJM in 1997, leading "the viewer to believe that I fell off the earth in a drugged-out downward spiral of insanity. Nothing could be farther from the truth. I quit heroin over 5 years ago, thank God, and have been more productive than ever making albums and touring all over the world."[79] Consistent with contemporary "interactive" and "reflexive" documentary practices,[80] Timoner does not try to excise herself and the filmmaking process completely from the story, but her use of Taylor as the reader of her narration (written so that he can use the first person, no less) obscures the degree to which she is a character in this story.

I'd like to suggest that the story is in fact hers and the Dandys' and that the flattening in the film of the Dandys' story relative to that of Newcombe and the BJM reflects the Dandys' and the filmmaker's growing sympathies. Months and years go by, and their professional careers progress as together they simultaneously draw away from and focus critical attention on the train wreck that is the BJM, constituting Newcombe and his band as the center of personal and narrative gravity, deflecting critical questions about what happens when the art of the Dandys and Interloper Films meets industry. The film is about Newcombe and the BJM's path of self-destruction. But it does not suggest that we follow our lives right through inviting us to insert ourselves into the position of the supposedly neutral direct cinema documentarist, where we may choose a model against which to evaluate our lives—in fulfillment of direct cinema's avowed approach. Rather than invite us to occupy the position of an uninterested observer (or even credibly aspiring to this direct cinema conviction), *Dig!* stealthily invites us into the position of up-and-coming cultural producers embodied by the Dandys on the one hand, and by the mostly absent presence of Timoner and her partners on the other. Through the film's early shift of focus from the imminent, jointly led musical revolution to the swallowing up and spitting out of one band by a tornado of drug use, alleged mental illness and even scapegoating, we are invited to join the functioning band and the recorders of the saga in the safe but obscure territory of white, middle-class well-adjustedness. The Dandy Warhols are shown enjoying reasonable, productive drug and alcohol use; responsibility; marriage; home ownership; and family—an apparently economically secure lifestyle secured through their sufficiently successful music making. Yet we are invited to identify with the success they suggest that they have achieved through moderately autonomous cultural production undertaken "on their own terms" in the absence of any explanation of how that success has been achieved, how they managed the meeting of their art with industry in so successful a manner. *Dig!*, in other words, invites us into a political and economic subject position oriented to the convergence and melding of individualistic self-actualization with savvy, well-adjusted, relatively autonomous entrepreneurialism while keeping the mechanisms of this achievement secret. What is made clear, however, is that while a moderate commitment to authenticity—to "one's own terms"—appears both necessary and productive, a zealous, absolute commitment is pathological, something from which to distance oneself. The progressive alignment of the filmmaker with the more successful band obstructs a more balanced narrative that would be more in the aspirational tradition of American direct cinema.

From yet another angle, *Dig!* invites us to consider more normal and thus more desirable an approach to work that conceives of work as a, if not the, dominant mode of orienting toward one's self and the world. Viewed from the perspective of the Dandy Warhols and their filmmaker colleague, all dimensions of life—including rock, drug use, fashion, hanging out, parties—are part of the self-actualizing mode of value production in the new individualism Honneth describes. The Dandys' path to minor rock stardom and, more graphically and explicitly, the BJM's destruction on the rocks of stardom (and, less explicitly, Timoner's path to the status of Hollywood phenomenon) offer instruction in how to construct what appears to be a life in which work is the authentic expression of a self autonomously aligned with global entertainment capital.

Homologies of Arts and Employment

Both Frank and Honneth argue that the historical phenomena they describe are at the root of many contemporary problems in Western society. Frank's critique addresses the relentless penetration of all realms of life by capitalist frameworks and the legitimation of those frameworks through countercultural rhetorics of revolution and resistance. The counterculture's rejection of mass conformity all too easily becomes the rebel consumer's rejection of unhip brands; the "craving" of countercultural youths "for deeper satisfaction" and their "accelerated lifestyle experimentation" all too easily harnessed to capitalists' drive toward "accelerated obsolescence."[81] Honneth's critique points to the ironic and perverse foundation of a new iron cage on rhetorics of freedom and self-actualization. He writes that the desire of individuals for further integration of self-development and work "brought about changes in the functioning of institutions and organizations and were added to the list of the latter's expectations, over the following decades, so that individuals were confronted with them as though they were demands issuing from without."[82] Accelerated lifestyle experimentation, expressive consumption, and self-actualization become institutionalized demands on individuals.

The research of Pierre-Michel Menger directly concerns the role of discourses of art and cultural production in the accumulating demands on individuals at the turn of the twenty-first century. He suggests that these new demands are mediated in contemporary society through the figure of the artist, noting that ongoing changes in the shape of Western employment and social relations are prefigured in the normal relations of twentieth-century artistic labor. For most of the last century, artists—broadly defined—have been accustomed, for example, to long periods of unemployment, the need to provide their own benefits, a general lack of socioeconomic security, and uncertain, project-based employment. Ominously, artists have long been subject to systems of evaluation and reward not conditioned by any ethic of fairness or seniority, with advancement and employment based on subjective judgments of quality. Such determining judgments do not rely just on aesthetic quality. They also depend on the way artists present themselves, their cultural and social capital, as suggested by the diverging fates of the participants in *Dig!* Moreover, such determining judgments also depend on the promises that the cultural capitalists who invest in artists believe (and in some cases contractually require) those artists to have made: promises to meet deadlines and budgets, promises not to tear themselves apart, promises to continue to comport themselves in suitably eccentric ways in suitably fashionable circles, and so on.

Deinstitutionalizing capital seeks working subjects who have low expectations of employer loyalty and state services. Through trends in management training and the pronouncements of business gurus, capital does what it can to amplify the promise and attractiveness of a narrow conception of one form of freedom—the freedom to pursue certain forms of self-actualization and autonomy in work—and minimize the apparent threat of another form of freedom—the freedom from means of subsistence, social collectivities, and institutional supports. I believe that the representations of discourses and practices of rock music making in documentary film are rhetorically powerful in considerations of freedom, self-actualization, work, and economic peril because of their very ambivalence. If we are to understand that the artist is the harbinger of the worker of the future, then who better to promote the limited positive side of the transformation than a person who embodies and becomes wealthy and powerful through, as Keightley notes, the paradoxically popular and commercially successful mass society critique?[83] The critique of mass society and conformity (which still operates as an organizing feature of popular and business culture[84]) in part drove the production of self-responsible, self-motivating, mobile individuals primed to accept and even trumpet the deinstitutionalization of Western society, a transformation which neverthe-less promises heightened peril for the vast majority. The trick is that the thrust of the mass society critique is now attached to a new critique of resistance and collectivism in the name of self-actualizing and enjoyable entrepreneurialism. In Menger's artful prose, we see in "the machinery of measuring talent and its price-setting supplies, under the painless and exciting guise of a pathway to the stars, the most astounding defense of competition among individuals."[85] Substantial creative or artistic challenges to this dominant culture, *Dig!*'s por-trait of Anton Newcombe suggests, are pathological.

Segmentation and "Matching Up"

The sociopolitical heart of creative work, and the coming reality for workers in noncultural sectors, can be seen to operate in some empirical details in and around *Dig!* One way to understand the manner in which workers are in-creasingly summoned by employers hoping to enjoy the benefits of creative workers' innovation and self-responsibility in the context of cultural-industry style flexibility is to conceive of a dual process of segmentation on perpen-dicular axes. On one axis, segmentation occurs horizontally: each person is separated from his or her neighbors as, for example, a bearer of a unique set of competencies. On the other axis, the segmentation is vertical: each person is subject to incremental rankings of quality and value.[86]

Both segmentation processes have long been exemplified in the relations of creative production; when applied as a model to work in general, how-ever, they produce a devastating combination. The first—horizontal—is com-monly understood among analysts of the cultural industries as having to do with "product differentiation."[87] In the broader work world, it can be under-stood as the individualization of work, skill sets, and career trajectories in a way that, for example, normalizes competition and makes solidarity (which could perhaps have transformed the relationship between the Brian Jones-town Massacre, the Dandy Warhols, and Ondi Timoner and her partners) seem counterproductive. But it is in combination with vertical segmentation that horizontal segmentation reveals the potentially perilous depths of its promise. "On the ocean of this infinite differentiation of work and talent," writes Menger, "comparisons operate indefinitely to evaluate, rank, sort, ori-ent preferences."[88] It is on this vertical axis, where minute distinctions in quality become magnified to form increasingly unbridgeable gaps, that *Dig!* indicates some of the processes at work.

Dig! obliquely communicates many of the problematic dynamics that accompany the exportation to the general world of work of forms of ranking characteristic of the world of artistic production. One of the exported mechanisms through which disparities are magnified is what Menger calls the "matching" of talents at similar levels: "The talented are matched among themselves within projects or within organizations that expect to draw advantages from the grouping of those who within each one's specialty belong to groups of equivalent reputation, in order to increase the productivity of the competencies of each member of the team and to increase the chances of success and profit."[89] What we don't see taking place between scenes shot over the course of seven years is the process of professionalization that Timoner and her partners are undergoing as they develop their business. As I noted above, *Dig!* did not just come out of nowhere to win a prize at Sundance; for years, Interloper Films had been producing commercials, music videos, and other work for a range of clients. Timoner has explained that *Dig!*'s transition through different formats as filming progressed reflected the increasing success of the Dandy Warhols. This it no doubt did, but at the same time, it also reflects the changing fortunes of this young filmmaker and her crew.

Perhaps more tellingly, this matching appears to have evolved organically and naturally, as the filmmakers and the Dandys increasingly accepted each other as professional equals on related—indeed, linked—trajectories. It is, in part, the mechanics and synergistic benefits of this matching that are obscured as the narrative centers more and more on the BJM's dissolution and shies away from a more reflective consideration—one that would have been more consonant with contemporary trends in documentary—of the Dandys' and Timoner's professional trajectories. Despite this skewed focus, however, Timoner understands herself to have produced a film that will help people follow their lives right. Surely she's not suggesting that a drug- and alcohol-fueled descent into mental illness and isolation is the answer, but this is the focus of three-quarters of the film. If you want actually to learn something about how following your creativity and your heart can bring material success, according to *Dig!*'s underlying doctrine, you should learn to think like the well-adjusted, productivity-maximizing cultural entrepreneurs obscured behind Newcombe's spectacular fall.[90]

European and North American social theorists are developing accounts of changes in work and in the political economy (in the classical sense, as the social division or distribution of labor) that suggest we are in for a bleak future. What some have called "the end of work"—productivity rates so high that entire populations will become supernumeraries—promises archipelagos of elite urban economies surrounded by oceans of the un- and underemployed.[91] There is also the obvious problem that in societies in which entitlement to various benefits depends on waged work, many people's citizenship will cease to have significance along a number of axes, such as providing the basis for access to health care or pensions.[92] Pressure to find a waged place in the productive core is increasing, and as Menger and others suggest, almost no place in that core will be secure. How can one plan? What models do we have to deal with this ongoing bifurcation of society? The closing moments of *Dig!* (not to mention press coverage of the film, its subjects, and the filmmaker since its release) offer lessons on the relative wisdom of two types of approach to the individualistic entrepreneurialism that promises to eclipse other forms of work organization in the coming years: Anton Newcombe, abandoned by his band, is hauled away in a police car, only (perhaps out of pity on the part of the filmmaker) to return (from an earlier moment in the film) among the credits looking disheveled, playing his guitar and singing about his own survival in an empty parking lot. Members of the Dandy Warhols, on the other hand, are shown getting married, driving around in a big 1970s American convertible full of bridesmaids, talking about the joys of home ownership and of taking their jobs (recalling the indie rock musician I quoted earlier) seriously.

The chickens of the postwar era's new individualism and mass society critique have come home to roost and, in conjunction with the changing organization of capital leading up to the beginning of the twenty-first century, promise a potentially devastating pecking order for vast numbers of working people in the developed countries—not to mention the intensifying immiseration of entire populations in less developed countries. The rock star (or indie rock semi-star) is a figure on whom we pin many hopes—for the possibilities of unalienated existence in the liberal market society; of a secure selfhood in which work, self-actualization, and social mobility are joined; of staying relevant and afloat; and of retaining some sense of agency as social changes beyond our control and perhaps even our comprehension alter the conditions of our existence. Contemporary rockumentary's rhetoric of direct cinema truth, in its de-scription and pre-scription of orientations to work and social mobility appropriate to turn-of-the-twenty-first century society, offers training in disciplined, rightly directed self-actualization to accommodate the very deinstitutionalizing structures made possible by sociocultural revolutions of the 1960s.

Conclusion

Contemporary rockumentary, understood as a body of microscopic examinations of work, social relations, and selfhood in contemporary society, can be usefully viewed within a broader conception of the documentary as a medium organized around sometimes explicit goals of subject production. Documentary constitutes arguments about the world that call on us to respond. Nichols explains:

> The voice of the documentary is a proposition about how the world is—what exists within it, what our relations to these things are, what alternatives there might be—that invites consent. "This is so, isn't it?" The work of rhetoric is to move us to answer, "Yes, it's so," tacitly—whereby a set of assumptions and an image of the world implant themselves, available for use as orientations and guide in the future—or overtly—whereby our own conscious beliefs and purposes align themselves with those proposed for us. We become better qualified through the knowledge provided by us by the text's argument and through the subjectivity conveyed by its rhetoric to take a specific position within the arena of ideology.[93]

Direct cinema as a particular form and text genre in documentary filmmaking can be seen to operate in a more specific manner. Allen and Gomery, though they don't use constructivist language, suggest that direct cinema participates in the construction of the liberal, public-sphere, prosocial dimension of the new individualist subject of the 1950s and 1960s, who is wary of mass society, and who values self-actualization. With the advent of flexible accumulation and deinstitutionalization, many theorists argue, the boundaries between what is and what is not work become increasingly permeable; Giddens's "reflexive project of the self" becomes not just a symbolic project but a political and economic one.[94] What for Honneth's 1960s self-actualizers was an opportunity is increasingly, today, a requirement, a new iron cage of responsibility for oneself and individualized entrepreneurship. It is an advancement of the second half of Marx's dual conception of the freedom of the worker in capitalism: free *to* flit from position to position, but also free *from* substantial claims on the means of life. Rockumentary combines the liberal and disciplinary modes of direct cinema, producing and inviting audiences into individualistic subject positions that are on the one hand rational, choosing, and reformist, and on the other hand disciplined into self-responsibility, productivity, and entrepreneurialism.

In the worlds of art and cultural production, autonomy and risk have long been two sides of the same coin, acceptable to creative workers as a dual reality because of the kinds of monetary and nonmonetary rewards they can achieve. Contemporary rockumentary narrates the trajectories of entrants in the fields of popular music, promulgating cultural concepts of work and the working subject as essentially autonomous. *Dig!*, *Metallica*, and other films offer social scripts for the adaptation of "manner[s] of life," to use Weber's phrase,[95] in accordance with the proliferation of autonomy as a desideratum in the organization of work and as the ascendant aspect of the working subject. The films frame the risk embraced by rockers as chosen voluntarily: it is part of the package of possible outcomes, some of which — stardom, for example — appear very desirable.

The combination of autonomy and risk embraced by artistic workers, however, is quite different from that increasingly imposed on workers in other sectors. The combination of autonomy and risk embraced by artistic workers, however, is quite different from that increasingly imposed on workers in other sectors. Autonomy was once associated with the choice of whether or not to enter into employment; a choice made possible for many people, prior to the emergence of fully-fledged capitalism and the consumer society, through their access to alternative means of self-provisioning (i.e., productive property, from gardens and access to common lands, to rent- and profit-producing capital enterprises).[96] Most people in the developed world do not have access to the sort of productive property on which such autonomy could be based. However, a new kind of autonomy for workers is of increasing value to capital,[97] useful in eliciting consent and legitimating the redistribution of corporate risk, while the corporation itself retains possession of the material means of making a living. In this context, the increasing autonomy of work at the cutting edge is coupled with increasing risk of vulnerability to exploitation and social exclusion.[98] To use Marx's terminology, most working people — no matter how innovative, no matter how autonomous — still have nothing to sell but their skins.

The same is not true for those popular music makers who can claim the mantle of authorship: they are the recognizable owners of potentially productive property, in the form of their songs and performances. Their autonomous work in the context of risk characteristic of art worlds is thus not analogous to that of the preferred new worker. The autonomous work of rock 'n' roll authors may not produce immediate income, but it does produce unique intellectual properties. These properties constitute a potential basis for entry into the class of *rentiers*, those who make money from property and investment.[99]

Thus *Dig!*'s bait and switch: first the bait, the lure of real autonomy, the making of rock music presented as an ideal form of work; then the switch, the substitution of a form of autonomy that is the obverse of that represented in the contemporary rockumentary's typical career narrative. What for musicians and cultural producers is the challenging and fulfilling experience of autonomous creativity turns out for other workers to be exhausting demonstrations of innovation and value-adding in contexts of heightened insecurity: the freedom *from* institutional supports and stable entitlements as the undesirable, obscured obverse of the freedom *to* work in exciting, self-actualizing ways. In *Dig!*, in creative cultural-industry work more broadly, and in the present and near future of many working people, the flip side of original, unique self-expression is individualization, horizontal segmentation, and vertical ranking—flexibility leading to radical insecurity.

The enterprise, like the state, is
a political system where power is
exercised over the governed.

—**Carole Pateman,** "Self-Ownership
and Property in the Person"

PART II
REGULATION

Nonfiction reality television and rockumentary tell different kinds of stories of the professionalization of music makers. Television viewers encounter *American Idol* contestants at the periphery of the music industry, in hotel conference rooms, convention centers, and sports arenas. A tiny fraction of these aspirants will converge in Southern California; of these, a handful will emerge with recording contracts. This journey can be broken down into one giant leap followed by a long series of small steps on the way to a position in the entertainment firmament. Independent film buffs encounter the Brian Jonestown Massacre and the Dandy Warhols in motion, also toward Southern California, from their homes in San Francisco and Oregon. The movements of these groups are less vertiginous and more peripatetic and incremental than those of *American Idol*'s winners and finalists. By the time we meet the bands, they have each already cultivated audiences without the benefit of major investments of entertainment industry capital. Although the stories of performers in the two productions have many parallels, they also have illuminating differences. These stories' ways of conceiving of work and working differ strikingly in their presentations of class mobility: where *American Idol* is pitched, almost lottery-style, to a mass audience, *Dig!*'s insiders' gloss targets more elite viewers bearing more rarified forms of social and cultural capital.

Part II of this book follows the work of popular music making into corporate and legislative arenas. Here we encounter recording artists who, having achieved professional and star status by proving their profitability, undertake different forms of struggle. Established recording artists must deal with certain institutional and structural conditions that set limits and exert pressures on their experiences of work as autonomous or heteronomous (controlled by outside forces), and their relationship to the products of their recording work (sound recordings). Contestants on *American Idol* and the rock bands in *Dig!* find themselves performing mass-mediated negotiations that are often articulated in terms of criteria distinguishing authentic talent from hubris, distinguishing making it on one's own terms from selling out. Established artists—having already made the deals, recorded the albums, and done the tours—find themselves fighting, sometimes quite publicly, over different but related dinstinctions: those between mastery and servitude, proprietorship and dispossession.

Part II analyzes struggles between recording artists and record companies over laws that govern their working and contractual relationships. These episodes offer unique insights into the political and legal dimensions of cultural-industry labor and property. They provide new evidence about and analyses of the ways in which the record industry operates in the context of copyright and labor law, which it tries to change to its benefit. Chapter 3 tells the story of a successful 1987 effort by the Recording Industry Association of America (RIAA) to make recording artists more vulnerable to record companies by excluding them from a century-old California labor-protective statute. It argues that the RIAA's action exemplifies durable principles of employer response to labor shortage that were put into operation in the context of cutting-edge global cultural-industry operations. Chapter 4 recounts the failed 2001-2 effort of recording artists and sympathetic legislators to repeal the RIAA's 1987 "carve out" amendment. Recording artists argued provocatively that the 1987 law made them "slaves," "indentured" to record companies, and their claims turn out not to be as absurd as they sound.[1] Through an analysis of legislative documents and reports in trade journals, and against the backdrop of political-theoretical critiques of employment and contract theory, it becomes evident that the recording artists' arguments simultaneously raised and suppressed real tensions between principles of democracy and employment.

I should note here that the purpose of this particular analytical frame-work, although suggested by the language of the recording artists themselves, is not to build a case against the unfair treatment of recording artists. Many of them do desperately need advocates to help them secure health and pension benefits and unpaid royalties, and organizations like the Blues Foundation—through its Handy Artists Relief Trust—have begun to do just that for less-well-off, elderly artists, most of whom are nonwhite.[2] But performers such as Courtney Love and Don Henley—arguing over conditions related to their extraordinary commercial success—do not need my help. Rather, in keeping with the general theoretical thrust of this book, the argument is that certain characteristics of recording artists' labor—its unusual autonomy, in this case—render visible a range of employment-determined tensions and contradictions that are harder to see, although perhaps even more salient, in more routine forms of work. As I argued in the introduction, recording artists' employment is a limit case of employment, at the margin of but not outside the institution of liberal employment. Examining highly dramatic struggles over employers' power to command and dispossess creative workers helps to make employers' control and appropriation rights in general more visible, and, I hope, more controversial.

Chapter 5 concerns another RIAA-driven change to law, this time to copyright law. In 1999, the RIAA managed to change copyright law in such a way that recording artists would no longer be considered the authors of their sound recordings and thus could no longer have any proprietary claim over them. In the following year, recording artists and their congressional supporters were able to get the law overturned. In 1987 and 2001–2, recording artists and their allies argued before the California legislature that recording artists are employees. But in 2000, before Congress, they argued just the opposite: they claimed that their status as employers—of their backup musicians, engineers, and so on—established their authorship and ownership. This case demonstrates not only that copyright's line between authors and nonauthors is politically determined, but also that claims of authenticity ultimately fall short when it comes to finding authority and allocating property rights. These chapters show how crises and struggles between artists and executives in the music industry (and the lawyers for each side) expose foundational principles in the heart of the liberal employment relation. These struggles and crises bring into high relief the otherwise obscure but mundane facts of employers' legal power to control labor and appropriate its products.

Contract always generates political right
in the form of relations of domination and
subordination.

—**Carole Pateman,** *The Sexual Contract*

CHAPTER 3

Carving Out Recording Artists

from California's Seven-Year Rule

From renting apartments to buying groceries, people engage in contracting behavior every day, but few contracts have as privileged a place in popular discourse and culture as the recording contract. To many popular music performers, the major label recording contract is a symbol and instrument of a very rare kind of achievement: the assumption of a public, professional position in the music industry, with fame, wealth, and freedom as the principal rewards. In the ten years since *American Idol*'s 2002 debut, tens of thousands of young people have lined up to audition for a chance to compete for that golden ticket. Winners and runners-up have emerged from the program having signed deals with US record companies and won potentially bright professional futures. The Dandy Warhols and the Brian Jonestown Massacre—the indie bands featured in the 2004 rockumentary *Dig!*—developed their acts and careers in the penumbra of the recording contract's symbolic significance and institutional reality. Each band's approach to the industry had the recording contract as its North Star.[1] For indie bands and *American Idol* contestants alike, signing with a record company enacts, confirms, and signifies their value and legitimacy. To other music makers, other companies, and audiences (as well as the performers themselves) the contract conveys the "identifiable cultural message"[2] of having "made it," of having entered the music industry's "holy of holies."[3]

Signed and established recording artists in the mass media often represent an apex of individual self-determination, artistic expression, and self-realization, a point at which boundaries between work and life are erased in a positive, liberating way. In Jonathan Burston's view, the public performer's "nearly insatiable desire for attention" has embedded within it "a distinctly non-neurotic desire . . . for unalienated labour; for work in which each of us may fully apprehend the linked dimensions of our individuality and our sociality."[4] In striving toward "unalienated labour," performers seek to overcome the isolation, powerlessness, self-estrangement, and meaninglessness of routine employment (the so-called day job) to achieve the autonomy and self-actualization that modern society appears to promise. Insofar as it seems to support and reward performers' continued, professionalized self-expression and to enable them to keep doing what they love, for more money and before larger audiences, the recording contract symbolizes the achievement of this kind of working situation.

The recording contract is not only a symbol of success, it is also a "technical artifact" that establishes "intricate frameworks of procedures, commitments, rights, and incentives—all in order to accomplish practical objectives in the governance of human transactions."[5] Yet these practical objectives do not always unfold in such an apparently neutral fashion. On closer inspection, the "governance of human transactions" is a freighted concept. In the famous words of Jeremy Bentham, "human beings are the most powerful instruments of production, and therefore everyone becomes anxious to employ the services of his fellows in multiplying his own comforts. Hence the intense and universal thirst for power, the equally prevalent hatred of subjection. Each man therefore meets with an obstinate resistance to his own will, and this naturally engenders antipathy toward beings who thus baffle and contravene his wishes."[6] Bentham's words capture the kinds of orientations, motivations, and tensions that emerge in the study of recording contracts, which govern the human transactions through which companies employ the services of performers.

A new artist signing a first contract with a major label may imagine that she is entering a partnership with an institution brimming with resources and experts on duty to help her achieve her professional goals. As she becomes successful, these resources and experts may play a significant role in supporting her work. However, as success mounts, what may have seemed like an equitable deal can appear to entail an unacceptable degree of subjection, as happened in the case of the 1980s R&B singing star Teena Marie, who signed with Motown in 1976, as a teenager without representation. Before signing the contract, she asked to take it home for further scrutiny, whereupon a Motown executive scolded her: "Don't you trust us?"[7] Two of Teena Marie's albums made Motown some $2 million in profits, and the company paid her approximately $100 per week for nearly seven years.[8] By 1982, the disparity between the label's profits and her rewards became unsupportable. At that time, when Teena Marie sought to be released from her contract, Motown responded to her contravention of their wishes by attempting to enjoin (obtain a judge's order to prevent) her from recording for anyone else. Ultimately, the court found in her favor,[9] and she went on to further (and better rewarded) success with a different company.

One of the striking features of star recording artists like Teena Marie is their unusual irreplaceability, or, more precisely, the difficulties encountered by a record company seeking to replace a successful artist who has chosen a new employer. Motown had invested in Teena Marie and was deriving a great deal of income from her recordings. No other singer could simply step into her place and sustain that particular flow of profits should she leave the label. This form of specialness is basic to the relationship between record companies and recording artists. It is cultivated, in large part, through the marketing of stars to the public and is intensified by television and film narratives of the kind discussed in chapters 1 and 2. Despite the fact that there are thousands of aspirants for every pop star position, only a very small number of artists will occupy those positions and be marketed into specialness and irreplaceability, thereby becoming stars. Companies depend on stars like Teena Marie for the bulk of their profits as well as "the capital for expansion and re-investment in new acts,"[10] and often find themselves "competing with each other for sure-fire sellers."[11] Contracts are the principal means by which companies secure control of the labor and recorded output of their stars and potential stars, preventing artists from taking advantage of attractive offers from competitors and preventing other enterprises from unauthorized access to their artists.

Like any contract, the recording contract operates within cultural, economic, and legal frameworks. The existence and success of a contract depend in part on its parties' sharing values and norms regarding good faith and commitment.[12] But the shape a contract takes also depends on the market for indications of value and bargaining power, and on laws and government for the demarcation of the boundaries of the contract—what can and cannot be bargained for—and for the contract's enforcement. In market terms, conditions of specialness and irreplaceability can be quite favorable to the recording artist (or any kind of worker with rare or valuable skills or endowments) because they increase that person's bargaining leverage with respect to his or her employers. When a musical act is in demand, "it can use the competition for its services to improve both its financial returns and its musical control."[13]

However, an act can take advantage of a competitive market for its services only when and where it is legally free to do so, and record companies work hard to constrain successful artists' ability to change employers. This dynamic has a long history and is strikingly evident in the forms of labor legislation that proliferated in England and elsewhere in Europe in the wake of the Black Death. Just after the plague's peak, laborers and artisans were able to take advantage of "the competing needs of employers, and the clash of interests they provoked," frequently changing employers and localities in order to obtain higher wages and better conditions.[14] In response, "in the whole of 'civilized' Europe at this period . . . an astonishingly similar set of royal or municipal ordinances appeared, which . . . aimed to prevent mobility in work" as well as to foreclose other means by which those who had no property could survive outside the authority of the local landholder.[15] Manifest in England's Statute of Labourers (1351), for example, are several principles that continue to haunt the contracts of valuable recording artists, including penalties for failure to work and for the luring away of an employee by a competing employer. The aim of European landholders, monarchs, and parliaments was to use such legislation "to control servants and laborers."[16] Recording contracts enshrine these principles of control. Under contract to Motown, Teena Marie was not free to find another employer with whom she could realize an income proportionate (by industry standards) to the revenues her work earned. Once a court declared that Motown could no longer enforce the contract, Teena Marie had access to an open market for her talents and persona.[17]

Contracts between companies and recording artists are governed by the numerous laws that limit what such a contract can include or require and that specify the rights of the parties and the range of conditions under which the government will enforce the contract. Teena Marie was able to show that

Motown had not complied with a labor law that would have allowed the label to enforce the contract through injunction.[18] This chapter focuses on another of the labor laws that affect contracts in the music industry: California's so-called seven-year rule, a law that since 1872 has limited the length of time during which contracts of employment (such as a recording contract) may be enforced. The importance of this law to the recording industry became clear in 1979, when Grammy award-winner and film star Olivia Newton-John stopped recording and delivering records to MCA Records, in breach (violation) of their contract. The record company's ensuing lawsuit and its resolution took place just as the industry was undergoing an alarming slump. Among the industry's responses to the drop in profits was the further development of a nascent blockbuster business model that would intensify companies' dependence on stars like Newton-John. This increased dependence, in turn, increased the bargaining power of those artists to the point where it appeared to pose a threat to the industry, an unintended consequence.

Newton-John's conflict with MCA sent shock waves through the industry. In the context of a profit crisis, the capacity of superstar artists to quit at the seventh anniversary of the signing of their contracts directly threatened both crucial streams of income and the capacity of companies to act and react in a changing market with a minimum of friction. Record companies responded to a drop in profits in much the same way that medieval European landholders did to a post-plague decline in their incomes. One of the companies' principal efforts was to turn to lawmakers for help in increasing their control over workers. Through the RIAA, they pressured the California legislature to exclude recording artists from the century-old seven-year rule, making the artists vulnerable to long-term domination and exploitation by the companies. In 1987, the RIAA member companies' goal was achieved when the legislature "carved out" recording artists from the seven-year rule's coverage. This chapter examines the combined efforts of record companies (and sympathetic California legislators) to alter the regulatory framework of recording contracts, and the arguments that recording artists and their allies leveled against these actors. This effort to pry recording artists out from under the protection of this law—in other words, to render a formerly inalienable employee right alienable for this one occupational group—is linked to the record industry's perceived need to change its business model in the face of the early 1980s profit slump and its burgeoning global reorganization. Ending a decade of steady growth and increased external investment, the 1979–80 slump devastated the industry. Yet the later 1980s and 1990s show not just recovery but an escalation of profits. The RIAA's focus on enhancing member companies' power to lock stars in for potentially interminable periods played an important role in stabilizing the industry and creating a basis for its reinvigoration. The chapter analyzes the legislative contest between record companies and recording artists as a contest between capital and labor, over the terms on which they could bargain, in the context of an alarming financial crisis.

Alienation

"Alienation" has had many definitions since Marx explored the concept in his *Economic and Philosophical Manuscripts of 1844*. In the introduction, I outlined contrasting concepts of alienation in social-psychological and political-legal terms. The former is highlighted in classic social-scientific studies such as Robert Blauner's *Alienation and Freedom*; the latter is discussed in the political-theoretical analyses that I engage in this part of this volume. These two axes are closely related: if employment means the legal conversion of a person into an instrument through the hiring relationship,[19] then how could anyone be surprised when employment is also sometimes experienced as alienating? However, to be legally alienated from the power to control your labor or to claim property rights in the things or value that you produce does not necessarily mean that you will have an experience of alienation. Much management literature is devoted to banishing workers' subjective experience of alienation in environments of political-legal alienation. The stories I tell in this chapter and in the two that follow are examples of how these two dimensions of alienation can sometimes be tied very tightly to one another.

As introduced in the 1950s by Melvin Seeman and refined by Blauner a few years later, the social-psychological conception of alienation pertains to people's experience of work. As I mentioned in the introduction, Blauner distinguishes powerlessness, meaninglessness, social alienation, and self-estrangement, and explores evidence of these forms of alienation that he finds in workers' descriptions of their experiences and perceptions of work, gathered through interviews and surveys. Both Seeman and Blauner perceive alienation as a constellation of subjective experiences tied to broader social and technological changes, a phenomenon that social science research could measure and compare. Blauner finds that different forms of work are alienating to different degrees and in different ways, but each form of alienation "makes it more possible to use people as means rather than [treat them] as ends."[20] These categories appear implicitly and explicitly in the words of scholars of and participants in the contemporary music industry. Mike Jones offers a perspective on the politics of the "music industry as a workplace," and on recording artists as workers, that brings problems associated with alienation into the foreground.[21] Jones, a former professional pop musician, analyzes aspects of "artist development," an organizational approach of the recording industry that, since the late 1960s, has played a role in the cultivation of potentially bankable stars. To Jones, "artist development" is a "feel good" phrase that "masks . . . a process that is likely to be experienced by the pop act in anything but a pleasant way." "Artist development" is an institutional terrain on which artists, managers, and record companies engage in the process of transmuting the sound, image, and narrative of an act into an attractive commodity. In this organizational setting and process, the musical act is "structurally disempowered."[22] In this process of disempowerment, "the act cedes not only a vital degree of control to someone who is or becomes inculcated in the methods of the industry, but they also ensure their own separation from, and ignorance of, the very methods by which commodification takes place."[23] In Jones's analysis, artist development exemplifies social-psychological powerlessness, described by Blauner as a worker's "loss of freedom, initiative, and responsibility."[24]

Working people's experiences of alienation offer evidence of institutional mechanisms of alienation, even while they may also involve under- or overestimation of the alienating powers of the governing institutions. The relationship between the recording artist and the record company is codified in and governed by the recording contract, which exists independently of individuals' experiences or perceptions of that relationship. The recording contract conveys to the company rights over the labor and the recorded output of the artist (and, increasingly, over a range of other activities by the artist). The contract, in other words, plays a role in commodifying and alienating the artist's labor, her recorded output, and the rights to them. The struggles analyzed here bring to light a problem provocatively framed by the economic historian Karl Polanyi. Labor, Polanyi argued, is a "fictitious commodity": "the alleged commodity 'labor power' cannot be shoved about, used indiscriminately, or even left unused, without affecting also the human individual who happens to be the bearer of this peculiar commodity."[25] As numerous scholars have shown, the "sale" of labor is more properly understood as the rental of one person by another, with all of that word's instrumentalizing and objectifying connotations. This jarring conception is clearer in the British usage of the word "hire" to mean both rental and employment.[26] Whether or not working people experience this relationship as disempowering, socially isolating, or self-estranging, or their work as meaningless, the fact of their being hired necessarily installs them in a system of structurally alienating legal definitions, obligations, and constraints.

In order for the cultural industries to accumulate profit with any kind of predictability, investors and employers must be guaranteed some degree of control over the labor of their workers and over the cultural products produced under contract. That is, there must be clear and stable structures that ensure that employees can legally and contractually be alienated from control over their labor and the songs and records they produce. In some cases, viewed from some angles, the relationship between capital and creative labor appears to take the form of a "delicate balance" between "art" and "commerce."[27] This chapter offers evidence and analysis that support a view of employment as a site of domination, where the degree and type of domination is influenced in part by employers' perceived market challenges. It suggests that the "balance" between art and commerce may not always be so "delicate" and that, in fact, the "blood and dirt" with which Marx argued "capital comes dripping from head to toe, from every pore," may never be completely washed off.[28] In 1944, Judge Charles Burnell of the Los Angeles Superior Court found California's seven-year rule to be a bar against the enforcement of "peonage," "serfdom," and "life bondage" of workers by their employers.[29] From his perspective, the efforts of the RIAA and its member companies to exclude recording artists from that law's protection would appear quite striking.

Key Contractual Terms

Are major-label recording artists actually employees? They appear to be more like entrepreneurs—delivering finished recordings that they conceive and make on their own schedule in their own way, paid in lump sums and then royalties (if they're lucky) rather than wages or a salary, and so on. That is, they appear rather to be independent contractors. To accept this appearance as reality, however, would be misleading.[30] Some recording artists do achieve the heights of independence necessary to support that status. Nevertheless, Sidney Shemel and M. William Krasilovsky, authors of a respected reference work on the music industry (now in its tenth edition, with Krasilovsky as the lead author), state unequivocally that "a recording agreement is an employment contract."[31] It may be that the wealth and autonomy of many successful recording artists obscures the legal definition of major-label recording artists' work, but all that wealth and autonomy does not counteract the power of the companies for whom they work to use the employment contract to set the terms on which they work.

In the context of the worldwide casualization of labor, record companies' preference for the employment form of the use of labor (rather than the independent contracting form) is an exception that proves the rule: employers prefer the form of labor that gives them the most freedom in the market. Tracing the trajectory of labor law from England in the mid-fourteenth century to the United States in the early twenty-first century, it appears that the subordinate political status of employees enabled the long-term capture and control of labor by employers. Through the late nineteenth century this status was evident in many workers' vulnerability to criminal prosecution for refusing or failing to work. Karen Orren points out that working people's historical political debility, articulated in the law of "master and servant," "supported and stabilized changes in technology, industrial organization, and population." Employment, as a subordinate legal status, "provided a basis of stability for both politics and industry" up through the first third of the twentieth century. Seen from another angle, the legal "foundations, molds, fixed boundaries, [and] barriers" imposed by employment on employees were essential to the management of markets for labor according to the requirements of entrepreneurs in a developing market society.[32] Record companies tend to prefer employment over the independent contractor relation because the employment contract overrides the wealth and autonomy of even the most successful recording artists.[33]

The intensification of record companies' power over the labor of their star recording artists played an important role in the industry's strategies of recovery from its late 1970s downturn. Pivotal to this intensification were particular contractual terms: "exclusivity," "assignment," and "duration." The last of these three occupies center stage in the legislative encounters examined in this chapter and the next one. Each of these terms operates as a formal instrument of legal—and, according to the commonsense view, consensual—alienation. Through "exclusivity," the artist alienates his right to offer his recording services to anyone else for the duration of the contract. "Assignment" is less self-explanatory, and its political content is somewhat subtle. It refers to the transferability of the contract, what Krasilovsky and Shemel call the "unfettered freedom" of a company to sell the contract to another company. This ability "can be injurious to an artist, particularly when the new owner lacks the same interest in the artist as the original record company."[34] Assignability is a standard feature of the recording contract that very few artists have the power to contest; it is another means by which a recording artist alienates the right to choose for whom or what company he records.[35] On rare occasions, very powerful artists may be able to mitigate assignability through what are known as "key man" clauses. Such clauses link the artist's obligation to the continuing presence in the company of a "key man," typically an executive with whom the artist has a close or trusting relationship. Should that person be fired or move to a different company, the artist with a "key man" clause has the option to terminate the contract.[36]

"Duration" determines the length of time for which the contract may alienate these aspects of control of one's labor. Without the ability to govern the length of time during which a recording artist can be locked into an exclusive contract (which might be bought and sold without her approval), few recording contracts would have the power and value they do. Keith Negus highlights the decisive nature of a contract's sunset: "The company's control is limited by the fact that at some future point the artist may be contractually free and have the choice to stay or go elsewhere and earn a vast amount of money for a competitor."[37] Duration is the motivating issue in many contract disputes; it was the impetus of the 1980s and early 2000s encounters between artists and companies in the California state legislature that I examine in this and the following chapter. Duration in recording contracts is determined through the structure of "options" and "option periods." The standard recording contract consists of an "initial period" followed, typically, by four to six "option periods." The initial period covers the production and marketing of the first album. Should the first album's market performance suggest a profitable future for the artist, the subsequent option periods enable the record company to require the artist to record further albums for the company. Typically, each period is nine to eighteen months long, but it can be much longer, particularly if extensive touring is undertaken subsequent to a release. In today's contracts, as Krasilovsky and Shemel note, a period does not end until the label has accepted delivery of a "technically and commercially satisfactory" recording, an album typically understood to be "not less than 10 individual selections totaling not less than 50 to 55 minutes duration." Under the standard agreement, "no record company will accept a unilateral right of termination by the artist . . . the artist does not have the right to terminate the contract no matter what the circumstances."[38] Only the record company can exercise an option; this feature of the contract facilitates the company's spreading of risk among multiple artists. The option contract offers "a get-out clause for the party with the superior bargaining power: Sometimes the party with greater power wants a relationship based on trust and cooperation but also wants to reserve the power to hold the other to the letter of a written document which is to its advantage." Option contracts "possess an inbuilt mechanism that makes the contract potentially more restrictive (in terms of length if not reward), the more successful the artist becomes."[39] The entertainment attorney Donald Passman warns artists: "DON'T BE FOOLED! OPTIONS ARE NEVER GOOD FOR YOU!! They only mean you'll get dropped if you're not worth the price, or you'll get too little if you're a smash. So repeat after me: 'OPTIONS ARE NEVER GOOD FOR ME!!!'"[40]

In many ways, duration undergirds the other rights and duties allocated in a recording contract. California is the only US state that limits the duration of employment contracts (although courts in other states sometimes consider California law when adjudicating recording contract conflicts).[41] Through the seven-year rule, the state, as a matter of public policy, will not enforce an employment contract beyond seven years from the commencement of the service under it. The 1937 version of the law, which stood for fifty years, states that "a contract to render personal service . . . may not be enforced against the employee beyond seven years from the commencement of service under it."[42] This law is of enormous significance for the entertainment industries' use of option contracts. Its public policy rationale was most clearly set forth in a 1944 case: workers in the state have the right to change employers at least once every seven years, no matter how many options their contracts may contain.[43] "As one grows more experienced and skillful," the presiding judge in the case wrote, "there should be a reasonable opportunity to move upward and to employ [one's] abilities to the best advantage and for the highest obtainable compensation." The judge also commented on the importance of the inalienability of the right to change employers every seven years:

> If the power [of the employee] to waive [the seven-year rule] exists at all, the statute accomplishes nothing. An agreement to work for more than seven years would be an effective waiver of the right to quit at the end of seven. The right given by the statute can run in favor of those only who have contracted to work for more than seven years and as these would have waived the right by contracting it away, the statute could not operate at all. It could scarcely have been the intention of the Legislature to protect

employees from the consequences of their improvident contracts and still leave them free to throw away the benefits conferred upon them.[44]

This labor-protective statute (and its rigorous interpretation by the court) regulates the terms of the employment contract. No matter what the contract says, no one may be held to an agreement to work for a single employer for more than seven years. The employee has the inalienable right to say no to continued service under the contract, no matter how dependent on one's work is the continued success of the enterprise, once the seven-year anniversary has passed. The seven-year rule stakes out an inalienable resource of employee bargaining power that limits the power of employers over employees. Moreover, the court asserted that seven years meant precisely that. The court found that Warner Bros. Pictures' extension of the contract beyond seven years, to account for time during the seven years when Olivia de Havilland's contract was under suspension, was contrary to this public policy, and that "we cannot believe that the phrase 'for a term not beyond a period of seven years' carries a hidden meaning. It cannot be questioned that the limitation of time to which section 1980 [the first appearance of the seven-year rule] related from 1872 to 1931 was one to be measured in calendar years."[45]

In the text of the law, "personal service" refers to "service" (labor) that cannot be carried out by anybody but the contracted party. Most considerations of "personal service" suggest that the term relates only to the work of "stars," who cannot be replaced on account of their "specialness." "Duties are nondelegable if pertaining to a contract based on artistic skill or unique abilities"—in other words, Madonna cannot delegate her work to someone who is not Madonna.[46] However, this is not the interpretation of the court in the de Havilland case, which conceptualized creative workers as not essentially different from their brothers and sisters in other economic sectors. Judge Clement L. Shinn wrote for the court: "It is safe to say that the great majority of men and women who work are engaged in rendering personal services under employment contracts. Without their labors the activities of the entire country would stagnate. Their welfare is the direct concern of every community."[47] It was evidently the opinion of the court that "personal service" refers not simply to creative, "special" workers but to all California workers.

As the decision notes, the state's limitation on the duration of personal service contracts had been in existence since 1872. At that time, the limit was two years. The state legislature extended the limit to five years in 1919, and then to seven in 1931.[48] In the mid-1980s, however, the RIAA succeeded in pressuring the California legislature to exclude recording artists from the protection of the seven-year rule. Effectively, since 1987, the state has given up its power to protect recording artists—alone among all California employees, contrary to the stated public policy in the de Havilland case—from contracts lasting longer than seven years. The remainder of this chapter tells the story of how this happened and suggests why it did and what this change to the law represents.

The US Recording Industry: Late 1970s to Early 1980s

In the context of waves of mergers and acquisitions and a disastrous fall in profits in 1979, the outcome of MCA's suit against Olivia Newton-John revealed weaknesses in the record companies' ability to maximize returns on their investments in star performers. In this section, I focus on several interrelated phenomena that clarify the stakes perceived by the RIAA and its member companies in contracting practices and the laws that governed them.

For most of the twentieth century, "the recording industry [was] in a state of tight oligopoly."[49] As a number of observers have pointed out, waves of expansion, diversification, and consolidation have punctuated the basic oligopolistic condition of the recording industry.[50] Steve Chapple and Reebee Garofalo, for example, recount the merger mania of the 1960s and 1970s, noting that "companies in the music industry were especially attractive to merger-hungry conglomerates. Earnings at music companies were high, 10 to 15 percent after taxes . . . , and the companies were part of the entertainment field which was growing in the affluent sixties."[51] They quote the felicitously named record company president Arthur Mogull, who observed in 1969 that "brokers realize that the return on capital [in the music industry] is much more rapid than in, let us say, the motion picture business." This perspective was supported by a spokesman for the Commonwealth United Corporation, who stated around that time that "frankly, we've made marketing studies of the music industry and we see definite signs of an unlimited growth potential in the field."[52]

The activities that transformed Warner/Reprise into Warner Communications Inc. present an illuminating case study. In 1966, Seven Arts, a motion picture company, purchased Warner Bros., which included the record company Warner/Reprise. The new company, Warner/Seven Arts, immediately acquired Atlantic Records. As longtime Warner executive Stan Cornyn recalls, "the quickest way to build [corporate value] was to buy undervalued companies, add them to what you have, and make the two worth three. It was called 'conglomeration,' and it was all the business rage."[53] In 1968, this new conglomerate was itself taken over by Kinney National Services, a company that until then had largely been concerned with funerals, car rentals, and parking lots. The Warner companies' rise to market dominance in the early 1970s is widely attributed to their capitalization by Kinney's owner, Steve Ross, and his "hands-off" attitude toward the recording operation. With Kinney's capital, "Warner Brothers [could] become a proper rock label," paying massive advances to up-and-coming rock stars, and reaping enormous profits through investments in long careers.[54] According to Cornyn, Ross understood the value of the record executives' autonomy "and assured his chiefs of it, with only one proviso: You bring home good profits. Do that, and the world is yours."[55] The company's next target was Elektra Records, acquired in 1970. Among its assets was a highly profitable budget-line label, Nonesuch. This imprint licensed European recordings of works in the public domain at minimal costs for release and distribution in the United States. In 1971, Kinney spun off its entertainment assets into Warner Communications Inc. (WCI), which then absorbed Asylum Records. Shortly thereafter, the labels under WCI's umbrella joined the ranks of the major labels by forming WEA (Warner/Elektra/Atlantic), its own distribution system.

The buying and selling of record companies by bigger companies continued throughout the 1970s. Some of the deals involved major US holding companies like Transamerica and Gulf+Western; some involved European record companies like EMI and PolyGram; but most of them took the form of a major (a company with its own distribution system) buying up independents (companies depending on others for distribution). In many cases—through the assignability of contracts—the majors got as part of their purchases the expertise of the indies' executives, whose knowledge of developing musical trends was quite valuable, as well as the indies' contracts with star or potential star artists. When Led Zeppelin, an Atlantic Records group, "hit," for example, "they all but paid for the label's acquisition" by Warner/Reprise.[56] When WCI bought David Geffen's Asylum Records, the smaller company had Jackson Browne, Linda Ronstadt, Joni Mitchell, and the Eagles under contract. The Eagles were to become one of the best-selling groups of all time.

The most important development of the late 1970s was the rise of disco music and of profits associated with this new musical trend. As the popularity of disco music grew in the mid-1970s—and with it the profitability of independent disco record labels like RSO and Casablanca—the major record companies began to recruit disco producers and performers and buy interests in disco record companies. During this time, industry profits escalated by 28 percent from 1976 to 1977, and by 18 percent from 1977 to 1978, cresting at an all-time high for US companies of $4.1 billion in 1978.[57] The cross-media success of the disco-themed film *Saturday Night Fever* (1977) and the retro musical *Grease* (1978) was accompanied by a "wave of euphoria" as their soundtracks sold in unprecedented numbers in 1978.[58] Yet by the spring of 1979, it became clear that an industry downturn was under way, and by the end of that year, sales had dropped almost 11 percent. In the ensuing years, sales would rise incrementally, but not until 1984 would wholesale revenues exceed those of 1978.[59] Observers attributed the slump to a range of causes: the economic recession of the time, home taping and the recession-driven business innovation of retail record rental, expanding costs associated with the recording and promotion of records, demographic changes and baby boomers' aging out from record-buying categories, and the inability of record companies to institutionalize disco along the lines it had established in the marketing of rock-related musical forms in the early 1970s. In their scholarly analyses of the industry, however, both Serge Denisoff and Will Straw perceive that the anomalous success of disco obscured deeper problems; in Denisoff's words, "*Saturday Night Fever* had postponed the inevitable."[60]

The "inevitable," in Straw's analysis, was the stagnating effect of the record industry's operational strategy of artist development (the target of Jones's critique, discussed above), a "temporal logic" that had come to dominate the marketing of rock-related music in the 1970s. Seeking to produce long-term stability in popular music markets, record companies directed resources toward the cultivation of artists and their audiences over the course of several single and album releases, live appearance tours, and other promotional activities. According to Straw, "the principles of 'artist development' were rooted in the assumption that the success of a current recording would affect the sales of previous and subsequent recordings by the same performer. This success would contribute to the development of an audience for future releases, and stimulate the sales of earlier, 'catalogue' products." The failure of disco—and the failure of the industry to bounce back after disco's demise—revealed problems with the artist development model and the industry's focus on cultivating fans even as they aged out of the main music-buying demographic. By the late 1970s, this misallocation of resources toward "the promotion of bestselling albums" had, Straw concludes, "resulted in an under-capitalization of two practices necessary to long-term stability within the recording industry: the maintenance of catalogues of older materials, and the long-term development of new artists to replace those who were currently popular." Behind the veil of disco's success, the artist development model had overpowered and largely halted other key activities in the marketing of popular music.[61]

The tactics and means of industrial recovery were numerous, and although mass layoffs and reductions in both new artist signings and option renewals for "marginal" performers had immediate effects,[62] most of them took several years to bear fruit. (Straw's analysis focuses particularly on the fortuitous developments associated with New Wave.) One strategy, however, was an intensified reliance on stars and an orientation toward the production of blockbuster or "megaplatinum" albums like the soundtracks of *Saturday Night Fever* and *Grease* that would sell across traditional age- and race-based market segments.[63] As a result of the slump, the artist development model was dealt a major blow: "The record industry's increased reliance on blockbuster successes . . . led it to incorporate comprehensive strategies of audience-building within the promotional itinerary specific to any individual album," rather than along career-spanning trajectories.[64]

Many observers argue that it was primarily the strength of two 1983 albums, Michael Jackson's *Thriller* and Bruce Springsteen's *Born in the USA* (which sold a combined forty-five million copies), that levered the industry up and over 1978's previous high-water mark.[65] The biggest-selling albums, according to a WEA distribution executive, were "hitting numbers we thought might no longer be attainable."[66] This sentiment was echoed in many corporate offices. For example, an official with MCA concurred: "We are getting more sales volume than a year ago, but it's all predicated on product at the top."[67] The difference between the revenues associated with "normal" artists and superstar artists capable of producing blockbusters is evident in a comparison of the fortunes of the Hooters, which had signed with Columbia Records in 1984, and those of Michael Jackson, signed to Epic Records (a subsidiary of Columbia). The Hooters themselves broke even, while the company grossed $3 million on sales of 450,000 albums. Michael Jackson's artist royalties alone totaled over $50 million on sales of twenty-five million copies of *Thriller,* and the record company took in half a billion dollars in profits from sales of the album and its seven hit singles.[68] Garofalo puts a fine point on the logic of the situation: "If a single artist can move 40 million units, [companies] reasoned, why shoulder the extra administrative, production, and

marketing costs of 80 artists moving half a million units each?"[69] The critic
Robert Christgau wrote in early 1984 that "the dollar volume of only four
albums — *Thriller*, *Flashdance*, Def Leppard's *Pyromania*, and the Police's *Synchronicity* . . . —probably made up most of the industry's total 1983 gain."[70]
In the years following the *Thriller*-led resurgence, smaller numbers of artists
would generate an increasing proportion of revenues. As Al Teller — an executive with CBS, the parent company of Columbia and Epic — put it in 1986,
"the superstar is the giant bonanza. The big hit is to develop superstar careers.
That is the biggest win you can have."[71]

The shift toward the blockbuster out of the wreckage of disco and the (at
least partial) failure of the artist development model created a new strategy
for dealing with the risk inherent in the record industry. It was complemented
in short order by the emergence and rise to power of MTV (which, through
the new requirements of video-heavy promotional strategies, further raised
costs and increased companies' reliance on massive sales) and the CD boom
(and that format's inflated retail pricing); both of those phenomena drove
revenues up across the board. In the mid-1980s, a new wave of mergers and
acquisitions began to pick up steam as the "exorbitantly high rates of growth"
associated with the blockbuster syndrome and CD sales "attracted investors
from outside the industry." Most notable among these were the German publisher Bertelsmann, which purchased RCA in 1986; Sony, which purchased
CBS in 1987; and Matsushita, which purchased MCA in 1990.[72] This wave of
acquisitions differed from that of the late 1960s and early 1970s, however.
In large part because of the force and logic of the blockbuster strategy and
record companies' intensified, high-stakes dependence on superstars, this
latter series of corporate takeovers was also accompanied by a substantial
and potentially threatening increase in the bargaining power of the blockbuster recording artists.

As recovering record labels fought to attract the most promising new
(potential blockbuster) talents and retain established stars, artists' attorneys
fought for maximum album advances and royalty rates, further escalating
costs and stakes. In 1981, the artists' attorney Jay Cooper wrote: "For many
years it was considered standard in the industry to give a new artist . . . a
royalty of 5% of the suggested retail list price of records sold."[73] In 1974,
that was the standard rate at Columbia Records, and even Bob Dylan was
able to achieve only a 10 percent rate on his return to that label from Geffen Records.[74] "Recently," Cooper continued, "new artists begin with between
6% and 9% of retail, and in some cases, even more."[75] By 1983, according

to one industry observer, it was possible for a new artist "to negotiate for a royalty of eleven percent or twelve percent of the retail price of each album sold; an established recording artist may have the bargaining power to get up to eighteen percent."[76] This new average was two or three times the average of less than a decade before. Michael Jackson, the star at the center of the blockbuster model, enjoyed at this time "the highest royalty rate in the record business—approximately 42% of the wholesale price of each record sold," which was over 20 percent of the retail price.[77] In the context of the new blockbuster-driven balance of power, record companies' stability and profitability depended on their ability to control the labor of the successful recording artists in a way that had not been possible or necessary since the advent of the rock era. The companies' need for this power was made painfully obvious in 1979, when the dispute between Newton-John and MCA rocked the industry to its core.

Olivia Newton-John and the Imperative of Control

Few of the professional reference works treat the topic of the sale and purchase of music industry companies; Krasilovsky and Shemel is a rare exception. They quote an unnamed industry veteran who compares the purchase of two different kinds of companies. This veteran advises: "When buying a music-publishing firm, treat it like the purchase of an insurance company annuity with some side benefits available. . . . When buying a record company, treat it like the purchase of an expensive jet liner already flying high in the air and make sure that you have a qualified pilot and enough gas."[78] Krasilovsky and Shemel elaborate on the valuation of record companies: "Ongoing exclusive artist recording contracts, as well as . . . [other] value-added factors can result in a negotiated price as high as 20 times current net earnings."[79] The metaphors of the jet liner, pilot, and gas suggest the dizzying stakes involved in such deals. The jet, obviously, represents the company; the pilot, the executives with "signing powers"; and the gas, the recording artists and their creative output—the economic fuel of the record company. Naturally, the buyer of a "jet liner already flying high in the air" is going to want to be as sure as possible that the tank has "enough gas" and moreover, that there is no possible way for that gas to leak out or otherwise vanish from the tank.

In order, in other words, to make the sale and purchase of record companies in a period of consolidation as smooth and transparent as possible and to facilitate increased growth and the maximal reward of executives, entrepreneurs, and investors, the stability of artists' long-term contracts must be as certain and calculable as possible. The facts and the generally accepted interpretation of the 1979 lawsuit between Newton-John and MCA made the importance of this principle plain. As I noted above, this suit was decided just at the point where the record industry "went into the toilet," in the words of A&M Records president Gil Friesen.[80]

In April 1975, Newton-John, then a rising star, and MCA entered into a five-year, ten-album deal. They agreed that Newton-John would record and deliver two albums per year for an initial period of two years.[81] Following that initial period, MCA could require six more recordings, two per year for three additional one-year periods. If Newton-John should fail to deliver according to schedule, MCA could suspend the contract until delivery and extend its term to account for the lateness. Newton-John delivered the first, second, and third albums on the biannual schedule; the fourth album (probably in the works at the same time the star was involved in *Grease*) was delivered late. By this time MCA had paid out approximately $2.5 million in advances and royalties and was anxious to keep the star producing under contract. Therefore, it exercised its option to renew and extend the agreement. Newton-John did not deliver the next optioned album. On May 31, 1978, MCA and Newton-John filed breach-of-contract actions against one another. The Los Angeles Superior Court ruled in favor of MCA, granting it a preliminary injunction—an action whose major purpose "is to preserve the [contractual] status quo pending a final judgment," usually in cases where the "employer would be more likely than not to win the trial on the merits."[82] This injunction, the court said, could extend past the five-year terminus of the original contract and through to April 1982, the end of the seven-year statutory period. Newton-John appealed. Although her request to void the injunction was denied, the appellate court ruled that the period of injunction could not be extended past the 1980 end date of the original contract. "If defendant had performed under the contract," the court reasoned, "plaintiff would not be entitled to prevent her from recording for competitors at the end of the five-year term of the agreement. We have grave doubts that defendant's failure to perform her obligations under the contract can extend the term of the contract beyond its specified five-year maximum."[83] The injunction survived the appeal, and Newton-John was enjoined from offering her recording services to any other company until the end of her original five-year commitment. The question is: who actually won in this case?

Despite the appellate court's endorsement of MCA's injunction, the generally accepted interpretation is that the recording artist rather than the record company was the clear victor. The precedent was now set: to get out of an unwanted contract, an artist had only to be prepared to accept a degree of recording idleness for a period equal to the difference between her time under contract so far and the seven years allowed by law (unless the contract, like Newton-John's, specified a shorter period). Moreover, the decision seemed to promise an immediate way out for artists whose contracts had already exceeded seven years.[84] A recording artist's certainty regarding a fixed exit point from an employment agreement constitutes a concrete form of bargaining leverage. With this certainty, an artist has the capacity to say no to terms she finds unfavorable or executives she finds unsympathetic, secure in the knowledge that she will be free at a definite future date. In other words, the recording artist may feel alienated in a contract and not want to continue to deliver under it. At the same time, she has legally alienated the right to change the terms of or terminate the contract. The court's finding here suggests that the legal alienation has a fixed term that cannot be extended without a new contract.

The Newton-John decision not only reminded record companies that California law limited California contracts to seven years. It also gave notice that if the original contract term was shorter than that, the companies could expect enforcement only for the specified contractual term. "The effect of the Newton-John decision upon the recording industry," one industry observer noted in 1981, "has been tremendous."[85] It demonstrated to the industry the danger posed by a contract with a fixed duration and spurred executives, attorneys, and lobbyists to create a way around this newly discovered hazard.[86]

The Industry's Response to the Olivia Newton-John Problem

The industry was shaken by the Newton-John decision and responded in two ways. First, companies dealt with weaknesses in their contracts, then (through their trade association) they dealt with contract law. An early 1980s overview of changing contracting practices indicates that "as a consequence of the Newton-John case, to preserve the remedy to enjoin competing employment by a breaching artist for a full seven years from the initial contract date, several record companies have redrafted their contracts to eliminate references to a term shorter than seven years." In addition, this observer notes, contractual option periods are "now often defined by the date albums are delivered, rather than the expiration of a certain number of months." This also gives companies a much longer period during which to promote and market a popular album — a decisive gain in a blockbuster-driven, multiplatform marketing system. Finally, "to ensure that the artist is not able to deliver too quickly, thereby giving the contract a life span shorter than seven years, some contracts prohibit the artist from delivering a particular album earlier than a certain number of months after the company has requested the album."[87] This last shift in contract norms was reportedly prompted by Frank Zappa's alleged simultaneous delivery of four albums in order to complete his Warner Bros. contract early.[88] This shift is manifest in contractual language requiring the artist's satisfaction of commercial rather than merely technical evaluative criteria on delivery of an album. As virtually every legal and professional reference notes, in words to this effect, "largely as a result of [the Newton-John] lawsuit, record companies quickly changed their recording contracts to base them upon the number of *albums* to be recorded, rather than the number of *years*."[89]

The first prong of the industry's response was thus to fix the obvious "leaks" in their "gas tanks" by changing their contracting practices to ensure that every contract with a successful artist would extend to the seven-year maximum term. But it was clear from industry practice that seven years is not that long a time when it comes to long-term artistic careers. The artist development model for the construction of popular recording artists' productive trajectories as long-term careers was itself driven in part by a need for organizational stability in a frustratingly unpredictable market.[90] The "Olivia Newton-John problem"[91] only clarified a deeper problem: under the artist development regime, it could take much of the first seven years of an artist's career just to reach a break-even point. This amount of time generally did not allow record companies to accumulate the kind of profits to which they believed themselves entitled. This problem only intensified as the blockbuster syndrome became more firmly established and a new wave of merger mania gathered momentum in the second half of the 1980s.

As one legal analyst put it, "a record company's financial status depends on its long-term contracts with successful artists"; this value, in turn, hinges on the contracts' security (established through the terms of exclusivity and assignment) and duration.[92] Another contract lawsuit throws this principle into high relief. When Sony defeated George Michael's petition to be released from his contract in 1994, "stock values for many record companies increased right after the decision came down."[93] The seven-year limit on contract duration also imposed a limitation on the value of contracts, and hence of the companies holding collections of contracts. Buyers of record companies could be assured only of the limited amount of time remaining on each of the contracts held by a given company; sellers could not be sure that buyers would perceive the time-limited contract "tanks" as holding enough "gas"—that is, recording artists' future recording and promotional services. This is where the second prong of the industry's response comes in, an action that would embed the changing logic of the contract—from options of fixed duration to potential number of deliverables—in a new system of obligation.

1985–87: A Change Made to California Labor Law

According to Simon Frith and Lee Marshall, although it might seem "that what the industry does . . . is determined by what the law allows it to do," such a conclusion would be "misleading." Rather, they point out, "if individual music companies have to ensure that what they do is lawful, the music industry devotes much of its energy as an industry to seeking to change the law." This axiom, proposed in an essay on music and copyright, is more provocative than it may appear. It suggests that the music industry frequently seeks to contravene public policy, and that it therefore engages in "ceaseless lobbying" to change the law and render legal practices that were formerly illegal practices legal so it can do just that.[94] In the United States, the record industry does this through its trade association, the RIAA. In this case, the aim was to enable companies to keep recording artists under contract for more than the seven years allowable by law, contrary to century-old public policy enacted (as California courts had found) explicitly for the protection of workers. The practical problem that the industry faced was to change the California Labor Code in order to eliminate or alter the seven-year rule so that the companies could secure artists' productive compliance for longer terms.

In 1987 the RIAA obtained this desired change when the California Legislature appended subsection (b) to section 2855 of the California Labor Code, the seven-year rule. Subsection (b) adds three parts to the law. First, using the lawyerly term "notwithstanding," the original seven-year limit, contained in what is now subsection (a), now notes that a different set of rules applies to parties to contracts "to render personal service in the production of phonorecords in which sounds are first fixed."[95] Second, according to these new rules, "in the event that a party to such a contract is, or could contractually be, required to render personal service in the production of a specified quantity of the phonorecords fails to render all of the required service [according to the contract's schedule], the party damaged by the failure [the record company] shall have the right to recover damages for each phonorecord as to which that party has failed to render service."[96] Finally, the new rules specify that these damages can be recovered during or after the point beyond which the state will no longer enforce the contract—the seven-year point.[97] This legislation singles out a group of California workers for special treatment. The reference to "phonorecords" (albums) that "could contractually be" required is generally read to refer to unexercised album options, and the language of subsection (b)(2), by allowing recovery of damages beyond the seven-year limit, is generally read to erase the seven-year period. Donald Engel, an artists' attorney, testified in a 2001 hearing held by the California State Senate Select Committee on the Entertainment Industries that, citing subsection (b), the record label from which one of his acts was attempting to disaffiliate itself told him that $100 million was the "minimum damages" the act would have to pay to exit the contract, based on the number of unexercised album options remaining in the contract.[98] As Jay Cooper later argued, "the threat of a lawsuit is the same as an injunction"—the same, that is, as allowing injunctions to extend past the seven-year limit, because either an injunction or sufficiently high damages can effectively stop a career in its tracks.[99] This section of the chapter offers an account of the RIAA's successful efforts to carve out recording artists from the protection of the seven-year rule, and the failed efforts of recording artists and their allies to prevent this change.

Senate Bills 469 (1985) and 1049 (1987)

In February 1985, Senator Ralph Dills introduced Senate Bill 469, titled "An Act to Amend Section 2855 of the Labor Code, Relating to Employment," on behalf of the RIAA. Over the next eighteen months, SB 469 would be amended eight times, largely in response to arguments made by opponents of the bill. The governor ultimately vetoed it because of a technicality. In March 1987, Dills reintroduced the legislation as SB 1049. This time, the bill was amended twice and finally signed by the governor in September 1987. Through the thirty-month process of debate and amendment, the bills' core purpose remained unaffected: to change the law so as to make recording artists vulnerable to record company control well beyond the seven-year limitation enshrined in California law. This chapter's analysis focuses principally on SB 469 because it was around this bill that the most contention took place; the final form of SB 1049 is virtually unchanged (minus the technicality) from the version of SB 469 vetoed by the governor.[100] The main contests over the legislation addressed a handful of recurring themes: the length of time to which the state should limit the enforcement of employment contracts, the singling out of recording artists from other workers, the meaning of midcontract renegotiation, and the institution of damages as a means of achieving the desired goal of the record companies.

The first, February 20, 1985 version of SB 469 would have covered all employees in the state. It said that if the service expected by the employer (for example, the production of a certain number of albums) could have been performed in seven years but wasn't, then enforcement could take place for up to ten years after the commencement of service under the contract. It also asserted that a renegotiation before the end of the contract constituted a new contract and thus a restart of the seven- or ten-year clock. Chester Migden, executive director of the Association of Talent Agents, expressed immediate opposition. He argued that since a "ten-year period frequently encompasses an entire professional career," the new law would underwrite contracts that would amount "to an indenture rather than a personal service contract." The new legal weight of a renegotiation to constitute a new contract for the purpose of the statute would, he argued, "destroy common law principles tested for hundreds of years"; moreover, the law's "total impact runs counter to public policy."[101]

If Dills replied, there is no record of it. But the core terms became clearer in the April 8, 1985 version of the bill. Occasioning the most substantial arguments, this version limited the law's application to the employment of recording artists. It noted that contracts call for specific numbers of records, and that if the failure of the employee to complete the terms of the contract were the fault of the record company, then the seven-year limit would be honored and not extended to the ten-year limit still in the bill. An analysis of the April 8 bill by the committee's legislative consultant notes that the RIAA—the bill's sponsor—is its lone supporter and that its opponents include the California Federation of Labor, a member of the AFL-CIO; American Federation of Musicians Local 6; San Francisco and Los Angeles locals of the American Federation of Television and Radio Artists; Association of Talent Agents; Directors Guild of America; Eye of Newt Productions; Screen Actors Guild; and "individual attorneys who represent recording artist[s]." This document succinctly records the policy positions of the two sides. On the one hand, "proponents argue that the bill is necessary to ensure that recording artists comply with personal service contracts to complete a specified number of recordings within the terms of a contract." On the other hand, "opponents argue that the bill would result in the long-termed exploitation of recording artists, especially in cases where an artist becomes a star in a relatively short period of time. In these cases the recording artist would not have adequate bargaining power to receive just compensation for a period of seven years with the possibility of an extension to ten years in cases that he or she refuses to complete all of the recordings as specified in the contract."[102]

Main Arguments

Industry arguments for the bill were presented in detail in a position paper prepared around this time by Gang, Tyre, and Brown, a Beverly Hills law firm, and JLA Advocates, a Sacramento lobbying firm, both engaged by the RIAA.[103] This document avers that the capacity to keep recording artists under contract for more than seven years is critical to the survival of the industry. The authors argue that "current law in California has been used as a weapon by prominent, highly successful recording artists." Because of their ability to invoke the seven-year rule, recording artists, the position paper claims, can "force their record company employer/financiers into renegotiating contracts under circumstances in which the record company is not even sure it will get the benefit of the new bargain." If the record companies don't submit, "the alternative to renegotiation is that the artist will sit out the balance of his contract term with impunity." The artist's bargaining power — implicitly conceived as his right to say no to unfavorable terms — is enhanced "because he can and does earn substantial sums from 'live' entertainment tours and personal concert appearances" that reduce his dependence on the recording agreement for income. Dills's bill, the position paper argues, corrects these "inequities."[104]

Gang, Tyre, and Brown and JLA Advocates employ a range of rhetorical strategies to support their position, including ten "case studies" of "inequities" visited on labels by recording artists emboldened by the seven-year rule; a detailed legislative history; interpretations of the few cases in which the seven-year rule figured prominently; and a consideration of the distinction between employee and independent contractor based on a test emerging from a mid-1960s case involving the rule. From the perspective under development here, an explanation of why the RIAA sought the change at that particular moment is illuminating. According to the position paper, "over the past ten years competition for the services of leading recording artists has become increasingly intense. Advances payable to artists and royalty rates earned by them have escalated markedly. Consequently, the problems created by the ambiguities and uncertainties in the seven-year rule have become magnified and threatened the entire functioning of the business. Accordingly, the California-based record companies have determined that they can no longer wait for the law to develop in the usual course of judicial decision making."[105] The structural changes in the recording industry I discussed above are here presented as facts of nature. It is as if, between 1975 and 1985, the pool of capable, charismatic, potentially popular, or otherwise qualified recording artists has somehow mysteriously dried up; it is as if advances and royalty rates have escalated on their own accord, and not (at least in part) as a result of the transformation of a range of business strategies. To be sure, as individual superstar recording contracts become evermore important to a company, any limitation on their fungibility will "become magnified," and in the aggregate this limitation might indeed "threaten the entire functioning of the business," especially if one assumes widespread artist hostility, venality, or recalcitrance. In the context of escalating blockbuster profits and the CD boom, as multinational electronics firms increasingly purchased entertainment businesses with creative-labor contracts, seeking sources of valuable properties, and as major record labels preened themselves before those salivating multinational corporations, the "usual course of judicial decision making" must have seemed positively glacial. The "gas" became more valuable and volatile the higher and farther the "jet liners" aimed to fly.

On May 15, 1985, shortly after the RIAA's position paper was distributed to state lawmakers, Cooper issued a "Background Paper in Opposition to Senate Bill 469." In addition to being an artists' attorney, Cooper was special counsel for the American Federation of Television and Radio Artists and the Screen Actors Guild. His paper argues that the proposed change to the law was not necessary to the continued functioning of the record industry, and that the record companies' bargaining power remained overwhelming despite the new blockbuster model. Cooper even suggests alternative changes to the law that would increase artists' bargaining power. In its arguments about the problems posed by the existing law to the state of the industry, the RIAA's position paper argues in general terms about the law's supposed impediment to organizational efficiency and the ambiguities resulting from the scanty litigation in previous decades about details of the relationship between record companies and recording artists (most disputes had been settled out of court). In contrast, Cooper's analysis focuses on the political specifics of the standard recording agreement's boilerplate terms and the class power of record companies. It therefore serves as a useful exposition of the politics of the recording contract from the standpoint of labor.

Cooper argues that the problems highlighted by the RIAA are exceptional, not routine, and that the proposed law will heighten the excessive bargaining power of the record companies because the existing contract is already weighted heavily in favor of the companies, even with respect to the most successful performers. No one disputes the fact, he notes, that approximately nine out of ten recording artists' contracts fail to lead to profitable relationships. On that basis, several points must be recognized: most artists are not wealthy and therefore do not have robust alternative income streams to relieve the pressure on them to record for their record companies; most artists—even those whose records do make a profit—have careers lasting fewer than four years; most artists are not heavily promoted by their labels, which focus the bulk of their promotional dollars on their most sure-fire hits; and, for these reasons, "the vast majority of artists faithfully honor their commitments and are fearful of angering their labels, knowing full well that the company can substantially injure or effectively put an end to a recording career."[106] (One way a company can threaten recalcitrant or refractory artists is through suspension. The contest between Sammy Hagar and Capitol Records in 1980 and that between Kathy Dalton and Discreet Records in 1974 are examples of suits over the labels' suspensions of the singers' recording agreements. Although the details are rarely reported in the legal literature, suspensions of this kind often appear intended to compel the artist to obey the label. With exclusivity in place, suspensions effectively put artists in professional limbo.[107])

In the context of this political economy, Cooper points out, the routine structure of recording contracts is notoriously one-sided. Contracts for options exercisable at the sole discretion of the employer serve to displace risk from the employer to the employee and increase employees' dependence and vulnerability. Contract boilerplate plainly releases the company from any obligation to produce, manufacture, distribute, or promote records, whereas the option system enables a company to "tie up an artist by requesting album after album even though they have no commitment to the artist's career."[108] Through what are known as "pay or play" contract clauses, the recording agreement typically stipulates that, merely by paying the recording artist union-scale wages for the amount of hours it could have taken to record an album, the record company can release itself from advancing the full cost of production for an album ($200,000 or more, at the time), should executives change their mind even after exercising an option. In that case, "the artist is thereby left in a situation where he will receive no benefit in terms of compensation or career unless the record company chooses to proceed." Contractual features like these minimize the risks posed to buyers of record companies. But problems associated with assignment also take place when executives move between companies. Highlighting the alienating aspects of ongoing industry restructuring, Cooper notes that "almost all of the record companies over the past several years have changed their leadership at least once, if not more. When this happens, artists may find themselves bound for a long term to a company run by executives whose views are diametrically opposed to their own careers and talents. Compounding the problem is the fact that incoming record executives tend to put an emphasis on their own new 'signings' with a correlative de-emphasis on the artists signed by previous executives for fear of proving that the former executives were right in their choice."[109] Carly Simon's situation illuminates some of these issues: "I was signed in Elektra by Jac Holzman in 1970 and made my first record in 1971. . . . Jac left the company in 1972 or 1973, and then I was with David Geffen, who brought in Asylum Records. All of a sudden I didn't get the same attention I did with Holzman. Then Geffen left, and Joe Smith came along. You begin to feel like a stepchild, once removed, and then twice removed. What is a company . . . but the people involved, and you sign with a company because of the people. And if the people leave, it's like being orphaned."[110] According to Cooper, the practice of "key man" clauses—tying the artist's obligations to a company to the presence of a particular executive in that company—"has virtually ceased." Cooper notes ironically the contrast of executive versus artist mobility: "Many artists of unique style have found themselves the victim of such label jumping by company executives with results that have been totally frustrating to the artist."[111]

Moreover, Cooper points out, contract law and the standard recording contract already offer very substantial remedies to record companies whose artists breach their contracts by "sitting on their hands," refusing to deliver optioned records. When a recording artist fails to meet a delivery deadline, the company may sue for breach of contract. If the suit is not resolved by the seventh anniversary of the contract, even under the old seven-year rule, the action for damages may continue beyond the existing statutory time limit. "The right of a record company to sue immediately for non-delivery or late delivery is not unique to California," notes Cooper. "The principle is well-settled at common law."[112] Furthermore, as cases brought by Olivia Newton-John, Redd Foxx, and Teena Marie demonstrated, California's "minimum compensation" law makes it very inexpensive to keep the remedy of injunction available. In the 1980s, under this 1919 law, an employer needed only to guarantee an employee $6,000 per year in order to be able to enjoin that person from working for anyone else for the duration of his or her contract.[113]

Tacking

By defining a midcontract renegotiation as the beginning of a new contract and a resetting of the seven- or ten-year clock, the proposed law appears directly to contravene the public policy articulated in the de Havilland case. In industry jargon, this practice is known as "tacking," with a new contract being "tacked" onto an existing one. The RIAA maintained that this kind of renegotiation satisfied the standard of the de Havilland case, that a worker should be free every so often to obtain the highest possible compensation. Cooper argues that "tacking" does not allow access to a competitive market: "An artist with, for example, three years remaining under this recording contract with his record company will not be compensated at his true fair market value if he is forced to renegotiate with that company only; the company, after all, essentially presents the artist with a new offer which is merely their idea of what the artist is worth." Cooper notes the politics implied here: the artist is under pressure to respond positively to this offer to start a new seven-year contract, and "if he does not, the record company always has the implied ability to stop supporting the artist's career in retribution."[114]

Slightly more than a week after Cooper's paper was circulated among lawmakers, the Senate Committee on Industrial Relations, generally considered somewhat sympathetic to labor, rejected the bill. Industry observers "credited [Cooper's paper] with a major role in bringing about the defeat suffered by the bill" and noted in articles in trade journals that vigorous opposition to the "tacking" provision of the proposed bill, as well as the stark legislative analysis by the committee's consultant (cited above), contributed to the bill's failure in committee. According to Mark Alan Farber of the American Federation of Television and Radio Artists, tacking "just continues slavery."[115] The legislative analysis supports this kind of interpretation: "Under current law, no matter how many contracts are signed, only seven years can be enforced."[116] This is clear in the de Havilland case (and would be further clarified with respect to all workers not engaged in the production of "phonorecords" in the 2001 lawsuit by boxer Oscar De La Hoya to be released from his promoter's contract[117]). "With this bill," however, according to the legislative analysis, "you can make each contract enforceable for up to seven years, and it could be 21 years for three successive contracts."[118] The bill's coauthor, David Roberti, a powerful state senator, appears to have strong-armed committee members to overcome a Senate rule and reconsider the bill. Shortly thereafter, with the reduction of the proposed ten-year limit back to seven years, but still retaining the tacking provision, the committee approved the bill.

Damages

In the course of numerous amendments, a governor's veto, and the introduction of a new bill (SB 1049), tacking gradually gives way to damages as the industry's preferred way to ratchet up control of recording artists' labor. In the June 1985 amendment, tacking is restricted only to contracts with recording artists (rather than applying to all California employees); the January 1986 version allows tacking only where the renegotiation of a contract results in a "material improvement of benefits" for the artist. Finally, in Dills's new bill of March 1987, tacking has disappeared and the damages provision carries the entire weight of employer power.

Damages had always been available to employers within the seven-year rule's ambit. Indeed, the very first (February 1985) version of the bill stipulates that "nothing in this [new] section shall affect the right of any party to a contract to obtain damages for a breach of the contract occurring during its term." The new, more robust provision for damages first appears in August 1986. It is at this time that the option structure of the contract comes into the law as a component not just of the customary but of the legal regulation of recording artists' labor. The law now moves beyond its previous limitation to two dimensions—dealing only with the length of contracts and the specification that contracts with recording artists may be treated differently than other contracts. It now adds a third, distinctly different dimension by engaging directly with the one-way, option-based constituents of control and autonomy specific (but not unique) to the recording contract. It is at this point that the language cited above regarding parties who "could contractually be required to render personal service in the production of a specified quantity of the phonorecords" enters the bill. This new approach is qualitatively different because of its specification of a unique form of vulnerability to which recording artists alone will now be subject. Renegotiation and "material improvement" of contract terms are no longer requirements that record companies must satisfy in order to extend a contract's term beyond the seven-year limit, and the contract term is no longer effectively limited to seven- or even ten-year increments. The shift from an emphasis on contract duration and tacking to product commitment shifts the balance of power. Artists' liability for damages renders them vulnerable to economic coercion as long as the record company deems their obligations unfulfilled (through, for example, the companies' boilerplate right to reject delivery of finished recordings), even after the end of the seven-year term.

I have briefly mentioned some of the political-economic and political-theoretical issues associated with this legislation and the arguments for and against it, and I have implied several more. The next section of the chapter takes these perspectives on explicitly, moving rapidly from a general analysis of the record industry to a broader exploration of the industry's changing historical, political, and economic contexts.

The Carve Out, Flexibility, and Rigidity

The record industry, like the music and entertainment industries more generally, is riskier than other retail commodity industries. In Paul Hirsch's famous formulation, "fads and fashions" are notoriously hard to predict or construct, and the entertainment industries' constitutive dilemma is how to reconcile the impetus toward calculability with the necessity for constant innovation by often individualistic, contrary, and willful creative workers.[119] It is the record industry's tendency to pursue measures intended to stabilize elements of the record business in times of accelerated growth as well as of heightened uncertainty. In the 1950s and 1960s, for example, the industry began to explore "'long play' institutions," including "the extended performer career as the ultimate goal of both artist and label," a strategy that was to reach its apex in the artist development model.[120] Company executives explicitly conceived of marketing plans as market stabilization measures. One Capitol Records executive argued in 1952 that the "most important function" of a "well-balanced and administered album program" is that, by "featuring a wide variety of products and continuing appeal to a broad market, it furnishes both the diversification so highly regarded by investors and a more stable base of operation for the company."[121]

In recent decades, global corporations' desideratum of flexibility has increasingly overshadowed commitments to "long play" strategies for the stabilizing of the record industry's modes of production and accumulation. In the mid-1980s round of "merger mania," previous modes of stabilization gave way to new ones. As sales flagged and the reconfiguration of income flows around the new blockbuster model grew increasingly attractive to new investors, the industry's stabilization strategy enlarged its focus to include the further locking down of musical labor. In particular, as this chapter has shown, corporate labor strategy included the elimination of a century-old form of labor protection that inserted newly unacceptable degrees of friction and unpredictability into the management of artists' contracts, as fungible assets of companies that were themselves commodified in global reorganizations. The next section explores the historical context of the seven-year rule's origin as a way to bring to light the broader forces at work in the 1985–87 contest over the carve out.

Labor Mobility

The interlocking themes of labor mobility and labor regulation that I mentioned in connection with medieval Europe are points of departure for a more broadly political conception of this 1980s encounter. Maurice Dobb has articulated the relation between the two in a provocative way:

> There seems to be at least *prima facie* evidence for connecting periods when the policy of the State in a class society moves in the direction of economic regulation with periods of actual or apprehended labour-scarcity, and periods when State policy is inspired by a spirit of economic liberalism with an opposite situation. . . . The hypothesis [thus entailed] has, at least, a good deal to recommend it, that freedom flourishes most under Capitalism, when, by reason of a superabundant proletariat, the mode of production is secure, whereas legal compulsion stands at a premium as soon as jobs compete for men and the mode of production becomes less profitable as a source of income on capital and less stable.[122]

Put more simply, Dobb's cautiously phrased but trenchant axiom holds that when compelled to compete for valuable workers, employers call on the state to assist them in limiting the mobility of that labor, to make it more difficult for the bearers of those valuable skills to avoid working on the employers' preferred terms. In the context of the 1980s recording industry, "compulsion" took the form of rendering alienable (at least for recording artists) the formerly inalienable right to change employers every seven years. The inalienability of the right had been explicitly argued by the court in the de Havilland case to be necessary to its effectiveness. The effect of the 1987 change was to turn that inalienable right into an alienable bit of property that could be bargained away in the negotiation of a record deal. In order for an artist to preserve the pre-1987 status quo in a contract, she would have to get the company to agree to waive the damages provisions so that the seven-year terminus could not be obviated by a demand for lost profits on unoptioned records. Of course, as is clarified in the following chapter, the language of "compulsion" is controversial: record company executives like Jeff Ayeroff (who plays a significant role in the contest discussed in chapter 4) argue that they "don't drag people into [their] buildings off the street and force them to record," but Cooper characterizes the rendering alienable of the formerly inalienable seven-year rule as providing the record companies with "an additional weapon . . . that no other employer in the state of California has."[123]

It may seem counterintuitive to analyze the policies of the record industry through the lenses of labor mobility and shortage. As numerous observers have pointed out—and as the tens of thousands of *American Idol* wannabes, who travel great distances to line up for days to audition for the talent contest, have graphically demonstrated—there is no shortage of highly mobile aspiring performers ready to sign anything.[124] But star and superstar labor—more reliably linked to the relatively calculable production of hits—is nevertheless so expensive to develop and so valuable that its mobility poses a severe threat to the companies that depend on it. As the blockbuster complex developed and record companies became increasingly dependent on relatively small numbers of superstars as their primary sources of profit, the moods and desires of bearers of this valuable "signature" labor became increasingly important.[125] Because one company might seek to lure stars and superstars away from a competitor, rights to the creative labor of these artists threatened to become increasingly evanescent as they became more valuable. In this context, the decision in the Newton-John case is an exacerbating factor because it makes clear the fact that recording artists have the inalienable right to unimpeded mobility every seven years; every so often they enjoy the right to choose a new employer or no employer at all. The attempt to make this class of labor more vulnerable to record company fiat took place in the sphere of regulation: policymakers intervened to change the balance of power between artists and record companies by altering long-established legislation designed to protect labor. What I call cultural labor's atavism is evident in a glance back to medieval Europe. "A pattern of declining seigneurial incomes prevailed during [Europe's] post-plague years and stimulated a reaction that was to become increasingly routine," writes Elaine Clark. This reaction was the demand by users of labor for the central government "to dictate the conditions of . . . employment, and simultaneously to oversee compliance" with these conditions.[126] One response of the recording industry to the 1979 decline in its profits was a similar effort.

Liquidity

A less politically polemical formulation of Dobb's axiom (and of my invocation of atavism) is offered by Bruce Carruthers and Arthur Stinchcombe regarding what they call the "social structure of liquidity." "Liquidity" describes the ease or difficulty with which a thing (such as a record company or recording contract) can be sold. Carruthers and Stinchcombe argue that liquidity is not an inherent characteristic of a given commodity or class of commodities; rather, it must be socially constructed. They develop this argument through the examination of two processes by which formerly "illiquid" assets—the British national debt in the early eighteenth century and the US home mortgage in the 1930s—were reconfigured into more liquid, fungible assets by public and private actors. The core problem of liquidity, they argue, is a problem of knowledge: the key factor in rendering something more liquid, or more easily sold, is the degree to which buyers and sellers can be certain of the thing's value, its membership in a class of things known to be valuable, and the security with which the knowledge of that thing's value (not necessarily its actual or eventual value) is assured.[127]

In the consolidating recording industry of the 1970s and 1980s (as well as in the development of a business model in which bigger companies routinely buy up smaller ones to gain access to their catalogs and stables of developing and promising artists[128]), the knowability of the value of a record company is part of the company's vendibility. "Liquidity," Carruthers and Stinchcombe write, "presumes assets that are knowable by a large group of potential buyers and sellers"; "organizational flexibility," in this context, "depends on believable commitments."[129] As investors come to view record companies as (in large part) constellations of returns-producing assets, the perceptible stability of a company's ongoing recording commitments—as major elements of that company's value—itself becomes a factor in the valuation of the company. A company's collection of recording contracts, from this angle, is very similar to the forms of debt that Carruthers and Stinchcombe analyze. The British national debt and US home mortgages are sets of obligations whose owners may assign them to third parties. These obligations entitle the new assignee— the purchaser of the obligation—to the income that derives from it. However, the value of these obligations and the willingness of potential investors to buy them depend on the investors' certainty about their knowledge of the qualities and parameters of the assets.

According to Adolph Berle and Gardiner Means, "the owner of a nonliquid property is, in a sense, married to it"—that is, the owner and the thing are not easily separated.[130] Although technically the property may be alienable, without the attribute or appearance of liquidity, it is harder to sell. As Carruthers and Stinchcombe show, to free up assets for easy sale, the "market makers" in previous centuries had to work very hard to construct markets for portions of previously illiquid national debt and bundles of mortgages. Standardization, homogenization, and new policies were all required to create the conditions of public knowledge in which these financial instruments could become liquid. The crux of their theory extends Orren's observations (cited above) about the usefulness of restrictive doctrines of "master and servant" in providing a stable basis for state and industrial experimentation. Carruthers and Stinchcombe's finding that "liquidity in one place presumes 'solidity' elsewhere"[131] captures the RIAA's efforts in the 1980s to control the mobility of successful recording artists and make the labor market more stable. In other words, when "organizational flexibility" is a desideratum—as it is in moments of market turbulence and instability—a corresponding requirement is policies that fix certain factors in place as a basis for that flexibility. A fall in profits and a nationwide recession precipitated the period of record company conglomeration and consolidation that began in the 1980s.

Conglomeration and consolidation gathered steam in the context of reorganization around the new business model of the blockbuster. These trends took off amid the subsequent massive rise in profits associated with the emergence of new musical trends and widespread consumer embrace of the CD. The increased certainty of the effective interminability of recording contracts, secured by the 1987 change to California's seven-year rule, supported a more functional market for the buying and selling of record companies throughout this period of turbulence and reorganization. In an era when major record companies sought increasingly to buy and sell independent ones, and when major multinational corporations sought increasingly to buy and sell major record companies, the change to California's labor law helped simultaneously to standardize and homogenize and to render more certain existing knowledge about long-term recording agreements. "Flexibility," write Carruthers and Stinchcombe, "has to be compounded of a set of rigidities"; "organizational flexibility"—the basis for capitalist innovation and experimentation in the record industry's reorganization along the lines of multinational corporate structures—"like market liquidity, rests upon a firm foundation."[132] In the run of routine employment, this foundation is rendered increasingly solid as hiring patterns become more fleeting and transactional. This is why employment casualization has been the ascendant labor paradigm in recent decades. For growing numbers of employers, the ability to absorb and release labor with a minimum of friction provides a firm foundation for corporate flexibility and innovation. In the recording industry, where there is a chronic shortage of successful artists and they therefore tend to enjoy greater bargaining power, long-term recording contracts, made up of a series of one-way options, contribute significantly to this foundation.

Conclusion

The ascendance of the blockbuster model and the outcome of MCA v. Newton-John threatened to shift the balance of recording industry power from companies to prominent recording artists. All of a sudden, staring down the barrel of labor law "used as a weapon,"[133] record companies experienced a galvanizing vertigo as it realized how free its best-selling artists were to change employers, not only cutting off companies' major profit streams, but bringing them to competitors. The old machinery kicks into gear: the record industry calls forth what Marx calls "the power of the state, and uses it to 'regulate' wages, i.e., to force [recording artists] into limits suitable to make a profit . . . and to keep the [recording artist] at his normal level of dependence," so that he will keep producing.[134]

The recording industry employs recording artists, and it does so through the option contract because this makes it easier for record companies to manage their relationships with their artists so as to maximize predictability and minimize obligation and risk. Employees are by definition alienated from basic rights to control their labor; in law, as will be shown more fully in the following chapters, employees are not responsible instruments, not full persons. For most working people, this situation is normal and uncontroversial. But when high-profile recording artists—especially those who stake some or most of their public personae on their autonomy or even oppositional positioning—are required to obey or face harsh consequences, the normal arrangements start looking extreme.

Like other employees, recording artists are at a systematic disadvantage through their contractual political and legal alienation; unlike most employees, successful recording artists are often able to escape the subjective ravages of social-psychological forms of alienation. The recording contract is the instrument—the "social artifact"—that both undergirds and undermines the recording artist's autonomy.[135] It signals to the world the artist's achievement of recognition and financial support. But it is also the instrument that binds the artist to the record company in ways that make her vulnerable to the latter's almost inevitably superior bargaining power. Exclusivity alienates her from her power to choose for whom she works; assignment further intensifies this form of powerlessness because her contract can be sold and bought without her consent; duration in post-1987 contracts consigns her to potentially interminable bondage. (But didn't she enter into this deal voluntarily? I take that question up in the following chapter.) In the environment of corporate consolidation and in the wake of the Newton-John case, the recording industry discovered weaknesses in its contracts and sped to repair them. But as long as the inalienable seven-year rule was in place, no change in contracts could result in the desired effect of long-term bondage. Thus in 1985, the industry initiated the change to the California Labor Code. The variety of approaches to the desired effect of increased control intersected at the point of increased control for record companies and decreased autonomy for recording artists. The evolution from tacking to damages and the integration of the specificities of the recording contract into the law itself showed how the legislature was convinced of the legitimacy—indeed, the necessity—of this increased subjection. The legislature passed the law, the governor signed it, and a small group of employees was carved out from the protection of a century-old labor statute.

The commonsense conception of employment in contemporary liberal society equates employment with freedom: today, in contrast to the norms of preliberal societies, individuals have more freedom to choose their occupations and their employers. That is, in contrast to the heavily regulated, unfree systems of employment that predominated in Europe (and to some degree the New World) before the liberal and democratic revolutions of the seventeenth and eighteenth centuries, contemporary labor markets appear free, increasingly flexible, and largely unregulated, except around issues such as safety and discrimination. Yet in spite of this common sense, regulation remains an object of interest to employers in conditions of uncertainty and changing market conditions. When changing conditions challenge employers, as happened in the record industry in the late 1970s and early 1980s, employers often seek increased freedom to try out new strategies in order to regain some stability. One strategy toward restabilization is the pursuit of increased power over employees, and this brings regulation into focus. Employers can maximize their flexibility to adapt to new conditions, and minimize the risk of doing so, by changing the regulations that govern their use of labor in such a way as to reduce their obligations to employees or to reduce the ability of employees to make disruptive claims on employers or changes to their employment contracts. Employers as a group enjoy a monopoly on the means of making a living; their superordinate position over workers enables them to set the terms on which work will take place. When employers engage the power of the state to render employees more pliable, subordinate, or dependent in times of uncertainty, such actions can reveal the unequal power relations that characterize employment and throw into question the equation of employment and freedom, especially when they affect highly visible, even highly sympathetic employees accustomed to unusual degrees of autonomy and independence.

A peculiar kind of freedom is invoked when
it can be exemplified in subjection for life.

—**Carole Pateman,** *The Sexual Contract*

CHAPTER 4

Freedom, Unfreedom, and the

Rhetoric of the Recording Contract

Recording Artists: Slaves and Indentured Servants?

In early 2001, at the urging of his Los Angeles "talent" constituency, Democratic State Senator Kevin Murray, a former executive at the William Morris
talent agency, began looking into record industry contracting practices.
Major label recording artists had begun to complain about section 2855(b) of
the California Labor Code, the amendment to the state's long-standing seven-
year rule discussed in chapter 3. The rock star Courtney Love, who at the time
was challenging her contract with her record company, had complained quite
publicly.[1] Love and others contended that the amended rule exposed them to
virtually interminable contracts. For over a century, prior to the addition of
subsection (b) in 1987, section 2855 had limited the enforceability of employment contracts to a certain number of years, increasing to seven in 1931. The
legislature's addition of subsection (b) at the behest of the RIAA, "carved out"

recording artists from protection under the seven-year rule by adding special provisions for damages to recording contracts. Since 1987, recording artists seeking to get out of their contracts at the end of seven years have remained vulnerable to assessments of financial damages on "undelivered" recordings (from which, in theory, the company could have profited) beyond the seven-year mark, effectively extending the terms of the contract and eliminating the time limit.

In September 2001 Senator Murray convened an informational hearing before the Senate Select Committee on the Entertainment Industry, of which he was the chair. The purpose of the hearing was to give recording artists and their allies the opportunity to air their grievances regarding subsection (b) and the post-1987 contracting regime. Record company executives and their lawyers and lobbyists were also invited to explain their need for this special exemption and to respond to the artists' arguments for its reconsideration or repeal.

The hearing was a sensation. It brought music industry stars, bigwigs, and their dirty laundry before the public in Sacramento. It also publicized the artists' charges against their employers, the major record companies. The jazz and R&B singer Patti Austin told the assembled lawmakers, witnesses, and members of the audience and press that "I was always taught that Lincoln freed the slaves, and I didn't realize that he excluded recording artists from that list." "The Legislature," she added, "should join the Union"—a reference to the North in the US Civil War—"in freeing the recording artist from the bondage to which this legislation relegates us."[2] Courtney Love pointed to the political and economic principles at work in the 1987 legislation in her testimony: "It seems to me that 2855(b) is so precious to this system, [because Vivendi] would have never paid $30, $40 billion dollars for Universal if we weren't indentured, we weren't part of the deal, if our slavery wasn't part of the deal." She added: "In the last 14 years, you [record company] guys have created a real economy based on 2855."[3] That is, "you guys" have been able to develop a business model based on your ability to keep us under contract as long as you like, because you've taken away our right to depart from the contract at the end of seven years. The language of "slavery" was not as far-fetched as it might initially sound. To scholars and policymakers in the centuries-old liberal tradition, "the limitation on the duration of the contract appears to be the only thing that divides a slave from a servant or wage laborer."[4] Austin's and Love's characterization of the loss of a limit on duration is well within reason, analytically speaking.

Austin and Love are not talking about being born into slavery or being captured or conquered into slavery. They are talking about what scholars call "civil slavery"—"civil" here indicates that it is voluntary and consensual. (This interpretation is underscored by the artists' equation of slavery with indentured servitude, the latter being a form of consensual labor bondage that could be enforced by criminal sanctions.) Love acknowledged the strangeness of their complaint: they were "not here to complain that we don't have swimming pools, or, to use sort of an inverted phrase from *Bonfire of the Vanities*, 'they get the cake and they give us a little bit of the crumbs.' I have a swimming pool, all right. I have nice shoes. Nobody is sitting here saying, 'I'm so poor. Please help me.'"[5] However, in theoretical terms, the artists' leap to this language of slavery and indenture was not a long one. High-profile recording artists complaining about involuntary servitude could seem like a patent absurdity, but from another perspective it is actually a cogent, if rudimentary and self-interested, political critique.

In the 2001 informational hearing at which they uttered these charges, recording artists and their allies argued that in exempting recording artists from the protection of the seven-year rule, the Legislature made the artists exceptionally, unfairly, and excessively vulnerable to their record company employers' superior power in the labor market. Austin, Love, other recording artists, artists' attorneys, union officers, and even lawmakers used this barbed language to advance two main points: that recording artists had been unfairly singled out from all California employees for special vulnerability, and that recording artists' loss of protection under the seven-year rule deprived them of a crucial dimension of the control of their own labor. Industry insiders from both sides gave extensive testimony over the course of the hours-long hearing; in the weeks leading up to the hearing, numerous other interested parties had submitted letters and position papers for consideration by the committee. This material offered the public a rare glimpse into the inner workings and politics of the relationship between record companies and recording artists.

In January 2002, Senator Murray introduced legislation to repeal the 1987 carve out and restore to recording artists the seven-year rule's guarantee of the right to change employers or leave employment entirely at the end of seven years, without penalty. The assignment of Murray's bill (SB 1246) to the Judiciary Committee for debate led to a second public discussion of recording industry politics and minutiae. The stakes were much higher at this second debate because actual legislation was now under discussion. Accordingly, the committee's chair, Martha Escutia (a Democrat from Los Angeles), instructed participants to avoid hyperbole of the kind engaged in by Austin and Love and others the year before, and to stick closer to empirical details of the business and their relationships. However, while the recording artists' side toned down their rhetoric, the companies' side cranked theirs up considerably, spurred aggressively by Ray Haynes, a conservative Republican state senator from wealthy Orange County. The artists' side shifted emphasis, from charges of slavery and indenture to more considered arguments about the perceived degradation of their bargaining power. The record companies continued their arguments about the need for incentives and efficiency but shifted from a tentative to a radical contractarian approach, in which voluntariness and consent are the only criteria necessary to legitimate a contractual relationship. In part by giving up their more radical arguments about slavery and indenture, but also because of a myopia resulting from their deep investments in the record industry's contracting system (despite their complaints about it), and the absence in existing case law of a clear and useful critique of the carve out, the recording artists and their attorneys were caught short when faced with these absolute, misleadingly sharp, and ideologically mainstream arguments.

This chapter takes the examination of this kind of contest in a different direction. The empirical substance here is the arguments made by each side in their struggle over the reconsideration and repeal of the 1987 carve out. And not all of the arguments either: many of the arguments made in 2001 and 2002 are more or less identical to those of the 1980s (discussed in the previous chapter) and so will only get passing mention (if any) here. This chapter takes its impetus from the statements of Austin and Love and their allies about civil slavery and indentured servitude, the receptivity of the lawmakers to these statements, and their discursive trajectory over six months of debate. What kind of an argument is it to say that one's work is a form of consensual slavery or servitude? What kind of an argument is it to say that you can be held to whatever you agree to? From what kinds of broader political conversations do such contentions flow? To what kind of broader political conversations do such contentions link or gesture? What can we learn about the politics of recording artists' labor—and labor more generally—by following these arguments through these public debates?

Critical scholarly analyses of the politics of employment help clarify the arguments made by both sides in this particular conflict. These analyses also invoke civil slavery and servitude, and in a complementary way: whereas the recording artists use this language to highlight their encounters with what they believe is excessive employer power, scholars use it in the analysis of routine relations to show that modern labor is not, as liberal rhetoric has it, free in any essential way. Robert Steinfeld has studied the emergence and legal history of the system of "free labor" in the Anglo-American world of the last several centuries, showing that the categories of "free" and "unfree" change alongside other changing social and cultural institutions. He points out that "the line separating free from unfree labor is not natural, but conventional"—that is, it does not derive from inherent characteristics of the work or the relationship between worker and employer but is a social construction or story, produced by people as they interact, that can serve all kinds of social purposes. This particular story, according to Steinfeld, tells us that our work arrangements are "free" in comparison to those of our forebears before the twentieth century. But because of the socially constructed nature of the definitions of "freedom" and "coercion," Steinfeld reasons, "nearly all forms of labor not performed for sheer pleasure can be characterized [by the observer] as either voluntary or coerced," depending on the observer's definitions, or the dominant definitions, of these terms.[6] After seven years, the recording artists argued, their labor was no longer voluntary but coerced by the threat of damages. For the record companies, this was an impossibility: all parties agreed to the contract, and the terms of the contract did not change in any way at the seven-year point. However, while the recording artists' definitions of "voluntary" and "coercive" differed from those of the record companies, they did not differ either clearly or completely, and even this lack of clarity was itself obscure to the artists.

This chapter analyzes testimony and argument from the 2002 California State Senate Judicial Committee hearing against the backdrop of critical scholarly analyses of the employment relationship. It focuses in later sections on very revealing gaps in the recording artists' arguments for their return to the protection of the seven-year rule. Although their rhetoric of "involuntary servitude" points to real problems at the heart of liberal society's defining relation of employment, the artists ultimately were too invested in their existing contractual relationships to enable their critique to hit its true target. The companies' most powerful contractarian arguments were that the artists had signed their troublesome contracts voluntarily and therefore had no basis for complaint. When the artists finally encountered these arguments, they were so handicapped by the gaps in their arguments that they could not effectively refute their opponents, even though their stance was perfectly aligned with powerful and long-standing political and philosophical counterarguments.

Whether or not pressures on people to work and in work are considered coercive by dominant common sense, such pressures "take similar form," according to Steinfeld: "One person is placed in a position to force another person to choose between labor and other alternatives that are more disagreeable than labor itself."[7] However imperfectly articulated they might be, the arguments of recording artists and progressive legislators that employment agreements can give rise to coercion—even when entered into voluntarily—challenge commonsense conceptions of employment in the cultural industries and in general. Is it a legitimate exercise of freedom to give up one's freedom this way? An individual may choose to enter a contract, but in so doing, as John Stuart Mill puts it, "he abdicates his liberty" and "foregoes any future use of [his liberty] beyond that single act." The individual entering into a contract "therefore defeats . . . the very purpose which is the justification of allowing him to dispose of himself." According to Mill, "the principle of freedom cannot require that [a person] should be free not to be free. It is not freedom, to be allowed to alienate [one's] freedom."[8] By making charges of "[civil] slavery" and "indentured servitude" regarding contracts they had signed voluntarily, the recording artists implicitly invoked a Millian critique of employment, arguing that any relation that subordinates one person to the will of another is undemocratic and contrary to a strong conception of liberty, even when the relation is consensual. In making these charges, the recording artists gestured toward challenging critiques of contract, employment, and alienation. In contrast to the dominant, classical liberal contractarian logic that more freedom means freedom to alienate more things (including rights), the recording artists agreed with Mill, in principle, that people should not be allowed to alienate certain freedoms, even voluntarily. But the artists were unable, finally, to argue why that should be the case.

The recording artists' rhetorical failure is not surprising; after all, the market system in which most of us make our livings is based on alienation. What is surprising is that they got as far as they did in their arguments, and that their arguments were taken as seriously as they were by legislators. Seen in this light, this episode is significant in at least two ways: first, it offers an opportunity to explore further political aspects of the relationships between creative workers and their entertainment industry employers, especially how they work out their differences in the world of public policy; and second, it is an example of a rare opportunity (ultimately, a missed opportunity) to bring a formidable critique of both contractarianism and employment *tout court* before the public from the standpoint of labor.

Hearings on the Seven-Year Rule

The ground rules of the employer-employee relationship are "nearly always subject to challenge and may become the object of political and legal struggle at any time."[9] The seven-year rule is a California-specific example of such rules. In the mid-1980s, during a period of turbulence in the industry, the RIAA successfully challenged the seven-year rule. As I argued in chapter 3, the ability of business enterprises to achieve stability in their labor relations is a central concern during times of organizational uncertainty. In conditions where highly valuable employees—such as star recording artists—may be tempted to change employers and thereby threaten sets of income streams, contracts of effectively unlimited length are very effective in enhancing at least the appearance of this stability. In 1985, the RIAA lobbied the California Legislature to change the seven-year rule's time limit to ten years; when that approach failed, they attempted to get the law changed so that a renegotiation prior to the end of the first seven-year term would trigger a new seven-year period ("tacking," in industry jargon, technically known as "novation"); this effort also failed. Finally, in 1987 a new subsection of the law was proposed, saying that artists would be liable for damages on undelivered albums enumerated in the contract (albums that may never even have been optioned or requested by the company) after the expiration of the seven-year period, thus effectively removing recording artists from the protection of the seven-year rule's protection.[10] At the same time, the major record companies began reconfiguring their recording contracts so that they would be limited only by the number of albums to be delivered, and not by the number of years of recording services that would count as completing the contract. As a result, the 1987 addition of subsection (b) to section 2855 enabled record companies—alone among all California employers—to bind their recording artist employees to contracts of effectively unlimited duration.

The 2001 Informational Hearing

In the early 2000s, owing in large part to the rise in political power of State Senator Murray, but also at least in part to growing public awareness of the dramatically lopsided politics of the recording industry (particularly in the context of the late 1990s rise in industry profits), recording artists and their allies and advocates began to pursue reform efforts and resist further probusiness legislation, and lawmakers increasingly took up their concerns. At this time, popular recording artists (as well as recording artists and musicians at many lower strata of the industry) were beginning to see themselves and their interests represented publicly, before lawmakers in new, explicitly political ways. In 1998, for example, the RIAA attempted to change pending federal bankruptcy legislation to make it harder for recording artists filing for bankruptcy to be excused from their recording contracts. According to an RIAA press release, the organization was trying to close a "loophole" that was being exploited by "increasing numbers of agents and lawyers for popular recording artists who have been misusing the bankruptcy process to get out of long-term contracts in order to sign alternative, more lucrative contracts."[11] The RIAA's 1999 attempt to amend copyright law in the record companies' favor, against the intellectual property interests of recording artists (the focus of chapter 5), was another starkly revelatory episode. That bill's passage, the outcry over it in the trade press and on musicians' websites, and its ultimate repeal the following year, galvanized artists at all levels. Out of this contest emerged a lobbying group representing successful artists (The Recording Artists' Coalition), a promusician think tank (The Future of Music Coalition), and numerous other smaller-scale and local groups.[12]

Senator Murray's first informational hearing brought top-shelf recording artists and powerful executives with decades of industry experience together in the state capitol to talk about the nuts and bolts of the record industry's contracting practices. The witness list included the recording artists Don Henley (who, along with Sheryl Crow, had played a prominent role in the copyright conflagration the year before), Courtney Love, LeAnn Rimes, and Patti Austin (other artists, including Ronnie Spector of the Ronettes, attended but did not testify; many more sent letters of support); the record company executives Jeff Harleston (MCA), Mark Goldstein (Warner Bros.), and Roy Lott (EMI); and a handful of lawyers for each side, as well as two union officers.

The hearing took place in two parts. In the first, artists, lawyers, managers, union officers, and artists' supporters in the industry offered their arguments against the 1987 carve out. In the second panel, record company executives, a lobbyist, corporate lawyers, and two law professors followed, presented their arguments for the post-1987 status quo. Throughout, lawmakers questioned representatives of each side about aspects of their arguments and asked them to comment on those of their opponents. Between this informational hearing in September 2001 and the hearing on Murray's proposed legislation in March 2002, both sides had the time and the impetus to examine their own and the other side's arguments further, and tune their approaches more finely.

Recording Artists' Contentions

The artists argued that they were subject to civil slavery and indenture (including their ostensible legal conversion into chattels through the operation of "assignment" clauses in their contracts[13]) so that their mobility—reckoned in terms of their access to an open labor market—was unfairly constrained. This was the result, they argued, of two principal institutions: the combined operation of the option contract for "deliverables" (albums) rather than for "time" (years), accompanied by the damages provisions of 1987's 2855(b) (see chapter 3); and the closely related problem of the record labels' power to impose a "standard contract" (discussed below) on new deals. The artists also argued that the post-1987 regime more tightly bound successful artists in order to cover record labels' losses because of the labels' high rates of "failure," that the RIAA's behavior in getting the 1987 law passed was disingenuous, and that by tending to push artists toward settlements and renegotiation, the post-1987 threat of effectively unlimited damages prevented the new law from being tested in court.

Supporting their more abstractly political arguments about being singled out from among all other California workers for special vulnerability and about the constitution of their employment as slavery through the loss of a limit on duration, the artists and their allies argued a number of concrete points repeatedly. These arguments represent the artists' understandings of how the 1987 law enables record companies to enforce contracts for periods of time that would have been unenforceable before 1987. The artists made nine specific points.

1. Collectively, the big record companies have concentrated (monopsonistic) control of the market for recording artists' labor. The rock star Don Henley testified: "The five major labels comprise what the Federal Trade Commission calls a cartel. If you look up cartel in the dictionary it says, see cabal. If you look up cabal, it says, conspiracy. Sue me. This cartel wields enormous power over artists through structures and practices that come from the very earliest days of the record business."[14]

2. This concentration of hiring power enables the record labels to impose a "standard contract." As Henley argued, "while the labels portray this industry as being collusion-free, a comparison of contractual terms in the standard major label contract company by company, shows a uniformity and a consistency that is undeniable."[15] Don Engel, an artists' attorney, elaborated on this theme: "If there is not a conspiracy here, there is another doctrine, called conscious parallelism, which is also illegal. You don't have a choice. The contracts . . . are foisted upon the artist."[16]

3. A lack of mutuality, exemplified in its option structure, characterizes the standard recording contract. Ann Chaitovitz of the American Federation of Television and Radio Artists testified: "The option structure of the contract means basically, that the recording artist is stuck. If his, or her, record succeeds, the record company will exercise its option for additional albums at what [has] now been shown to be less than the fair market value of the artist. If the record does not succeed, the record company will not exercise its option, [it] will drop the artist and will walk away from the contract."[17]

4. The one-way ratchet of the contract's option structure is intensified by what the Recording Artists' Coalition called the "product commitment Catch-22."[18] That is, if contracts are figured in terms of numbers of "deliverables" (albums), and the typical initial contract calls for five to seven of these to be delivered to complete the contract, then the heavy touring and promotion schedules required of artists for maximal commercial exploitation means that each album's cycle of production and promotion could take up to three years, leading to contract durations of more than a decade. As Love put the problem, "in seven years I cannot make seven albums because they will not let me. There is no way they'll let me. I sit down with them. [And they tell me] '[y]ou have a 210-day touring schedule.'"[19]

5. The option ratchet is also intensified by the 1987 law's provision for damages even on unoptioned records—those albums that, at the time the artist seeks to leave a contract, the record company has not yet requested, but that, in the statute's language, could contractually be required. It is the threat of damages at this point that constitutes the block on an artist's mobility at or after the seven-year mark. Engel noted that one of the acts he represented was subject to "the threat of $100 million . . . as the minimum damages for the number of records in the contract;

not the number of records that they wanted or would be delivered, but the number of records, $100 million. So they are saying to you, you're still subject to the seven-year rule, just give us the $100 million. It makes no sense."[20]

6. The entire contract structure has evolved and hardened around the industry's blockbuster model and corresponding 95 percent failure rate. James Barber, an artists' manager, argued that "artists like Don, like Patti, like Courtney, subsidize the inefficient and poor business practices of the recording industry. The recording industry is so incredibly profitable; people make a lot of money; the corporations who own the record companies are very happy with the return. Who suffers are the hundreds of artists who are signed, who never get a fair shot at being marketed because the record companies don't have to worry about wasting the money on recording or inefficient marketing schemes, because they're covering their losses from the profits they're making from the successful artists."[21]

7. The law affects new artists as well as established artists because it enables record companies to suppress the potential value of an initial contract. Engel asked: "Can you imagine what would happen in the motion picture industry if an actor in his first starring role is going to have to do seven more movies at $500 a week, SAG [Screen Actors Guild] minimum [wages]? That's what they're doing to these artists."[22]

8. Record companies should not get a free pass on the regulatory constraints that apply to all other enterprises. Engel told the legislators that they should say to the record companies: "Look, an artist has to be able to leave. If you can't run your business [without] indentured servitude for more than seven years, get out of the business. Make widgets or grapes. Go into the grape growing business. Seven years is enough."[23]

9. The result is that, unlike all other employees, recording artists are prevented from obtaining their fair market value after seven years of employment. Tom Lee, president of the American Federation of Musicians, touched on legislative and judicial language in his testimony: "2855 reflects the legislative determination that after seven years an employee should be able to reassess his employment situation, change employers or occupations, and be in a position to negotiate freely with the present or new employer for compensation commensurate with his fair market value, which hopefully, has increased from the time that first contract was signed until the last contract was signed."[24]

Record Companies' Contentions

Although at one point the record companies and the RIAA did provide a list of artists who had been able to produce an album per year, and thereby complete their contracts within a seven-year period, the companies mainly focused their arguments on the familiar issue of the economic incentive necessary for them to continue to do business.[25] There are many subsidiary arguments here: that the record industry, as the RIAA likes to say, is the "epitome of risk"; that in this context, the record industry needs the increased certainty of long-term relationships with profitable artists; that it takes years for a company to recoup its investments in financial advances, artist development, marketing, and so on; and that artists should not be able to walk away from their contracts just when they're achieving substantial commercial success. The companies also argued that in other states where the entertainment industry operates—New York, Tennessee, and Texas, for example—there are no limitations on contract duration, and so effectively ending California's seven-year limit levels the playing field in the industry. As businesses under scrutiny or facing regulation love to do, the companies threatened to leave the state should they be confronted with a reinstatement of artists' inalienable right to terminate contracts after seven years (these arguments are analyzed at greater length in chapter 3).

For the most part, the record company executives, lobbyists, and expert witnesses deflected the bigger political questions of domination and exploitation during the 2001 hearing. With the exception of those concerning the existence of a standard contract, they did not directly contradict any of the artists' arguments excerpted above. (Of course, most of those arguments concern aspects of the 1987 law that the RIAA explicitly sought and so were noncontroversial.) Record company executives and their allies denied the existence of a standard contract. Jeff Harleston, senior vice president of business and legal affairs for MCA Records, argued that "there is not a typical contract; there's not a standard contract."[26] Generally, however, the company side sought, as it had in the mid-1980s, to characterize successful artists as being in a position to dominate, exploit, and harm their record company employers. Cary Sherman, the RIAA's senior executive vice president and general counsel, went so far as to argue that "the record company is at the mercy of the artist in terms of whether or not they're going to comply with their contractual commitments."[27] They reiterated their mid-1980s incentive, clarification, and certainty arguments. Exemplifying this approach, Sherman testified that, back in 1987, "the Legislature thought this was something where certainty was preferable, and so they created that certainty. To put us back into a period of uncertainty would undo all of the benefits of having a legal environment in which everybody knows what their rights are. The California artists and labels would be hurt because there would be no incentive for a record company to invest in a young artist's career developing his talent, his music, his image, if when that artist makes it, he can just walk away from his commitments to his label."[28] Miles Copeland, an executive at an independent record company, used more colorful language: "If you're trying to build a record company, and you're trying to build an asset, what you really try to do is you try to find a young artist that you can sign and develop. Those are the riskiest ones. Those are the ones where you're going to get the most return. When I go to the marketplace to try to borrow additional money, or get investment in my company, they're going to look at what are the potential returns of [my] company."[29] One of the limitations on these "potential returns," as I showed in chapter 3, is a fixed duration to a recording contract. Copeland continued, "I'm still here in the hopes that I will find a young artist; they'll break[30] on the third or fourth album and I'll have three or four more albums to make my money. And that's why I invest my money. . . . I care about my artists. I want them to succeed. But you know what, I want to succeed as well. I want them to make a lot of money, but I want to make money too. And I want the incentive, and I want to have all these guys to have an incentive, to invest in new talent, because if they don't have incentive, we all know what will happen: they will not invest."[31] That incentive, he and his allies argue, is provided in Section 2855(b)'s damages provisions.[32]

The 2002 Hearing on Senate Bill 1246

Before six weeks had passed after his first informational hearing, Senator Murray and a number of allied senate coauthors began preparing legislation to repeal the 1987 carve out.[33] At the same time, recording artists and the RIAA and its member companies began to prepare for confrontation. Chuck Philips and Dan Morain of the *Los Angeles Times* describe the marshaling of forces and resources on each side of the proposed repeal: "The musicians have formed their own trade groups . . . , amassed a $300,000 war chest and are in the process of hiring a bipartisan and high-powered team of lobbyists to push their agenda in Sacramento." In 2000, the RIAA "spent $130,000 on lobbying, hardly significant by Sacramento standards." This appeared to the reporters to be changing: "After a spate of corporate mergers, record labels are tiny divisions of some of the biggest conglomerates in the world—making their potential power huge. And the industry appears to be preparing for a giant political fight." Surveying the bicameral legislature's likely response to the bill, the reporters suggest that the Senate would probably pass the bill out of "deference" to Murray's entertainment industry expertise, while the Assembly would probably be a "tougher sell" because of its greater susceptibility to industry influence.[34]

In January 2002, Senator Murray introduced SB 1246, titled "an act to amend Section 2855 of the Labor Code, relating to employment." The bill "would declare as the policy of the state that [the seven-year rule] may not be waived by the employee, and would delete the provisions relating to personal services in the production of phonorecords and the recovery of damages for certain breaches of contracts related to the production of phonorecords."[35] (It is the damages provisions that carve the recording artists out of the protection of the seven-year rule.) In addition to deleting the damages and phonorecords language, the proposed legislation quoted language from the influential 1944 California Court of Appeals decision (also discussed in chapter 3) about the right of employees to change jobs. This decision noted that "if the power to waive" the seven-year rule's statutory right of employees to change employers after seven years "exists at all, the statute accomplishes nothing."[36] Murray's bill affirmed this reasoning, stating that this "unwaivable"—that is, inalienable—protection would, should the bill become law, "be afforded to each and every resident of the State of California."[37]

The March 2002 hearing was held while the bill was under consideration by the Senate Committee on the Judiciary. In June an amended version of the bill was passed by the committee and then by the Senate; but in November, facing an uphill battle in the Assembly, Murray withdrew the bill. Chuck Philips of the *Los Angeles Times* reported that Murray withdrew the legislation because he "did not have the votes to pass the bill" in the more employer-friendly Assembly.[38] (Later that year, Murray would return to the issue in a more technical way, introducing SB 1034, a more incremental bit of reform legislation regarding the record companies' accounting rules that would pass in a watered-down version in 2004.[39] The 2004 bill's passage was accompanied by a wave of major-label *mea culpas* over highly publicized royalty accounting abuses and of announcements of voluntary royalty accounting reform and self-regulation.[40] The record industry was thus able to avoid major challenges to its exceptional employer power and to the special vulnerability of recording artists, in the end accepting the moderate reform of some of its most egregious accounting practices.)

In addition to their continuing arguments about the details of recording industry practices and contracts, witnesses and lawmakers participating in the March 2002 hearing also expatiated implicitly and explicitly on themes of coercion, freedom, voluntarism, power, regulation, choice, and individualism as they articulated contrasting views about the essence and politics of the relationship formalized in the recording contract. The witness list included several "regulars" accustomed to appearing before government officials: Jay Cooper, an artists' attorney; Don Henley, a star recording artist; and Hilary Rosen, CEO of the RIAA. Also appearing and testifying in favor of repeal were John Branca, another artists' attorney, and Simon Renshaw, an artists' manager. Testifying against repeal were Glen Barrows, president of Concord Records, a small jazz label; Jeff Ayeroff, creative director of Warner Bros. Records; Steve Berman, head of marketing at Interscope, Geffen, and A&M Records; Jeff Harleston, head of business affairs at MCA; and Steve Marenberg, a litigator from Irell and Manella, a law firm that often represents record companies in court battles. In addition to Senator Murray, Senators Dick Ackerman (a Republican from Orange County), Byron Sher (a Democrat representing San Mateo, Santa Cruz, and Santa Clara counties), Sheila Kuehl (a Democrat from Los Angeles), Steve Peace (a Democrat from San Diego), and Ray Haynes (a Republican from Riverside) participated in the hearing, and Senator Escutia chaired it.

Contrasting Conceptions of Freedom and Contract

The battle lines between the opponents of the repeal legislation and its supporters emerged almost immediately, as lawmakers representing the two sides made opening statements. These statements seem intended to set the terms of the debate, and to encode or enforce the two sides' contrasting notions about which social and legal categories are at the center of the argument, about the definitions and parameters of these categories, and about basic assumptions, values, and norms that characterize their competing definitions. The perspective of the opponents to repeal appeared in stark and decisive clarity; that of the supporters in much murkier and ambiguous terms.

A Contractarian Framework

The 2002 hearing began with Senator Haynes's assertion of a classical liberal contractarian framework for the analysis and evaluation of the arguments to come. In response to Senator Escutia's offer to let committee members make opening comments, Haynes said that he would like to comment. He spoke at some length:

> The seven year rule I know is born out of a long tradition, at least in California and in some ways in the common law; it was originally protection against indentured servitude for a time when that was a serious problem. [At] this time [it] is not as serious a problem, and the kind of servitude we're talking about is usually fairly well compensated. I've talked to some folks and said "if this is indentured servitude then send me the money," because I'll take it.
>
> People that enter into a contract usually do so voluntarily, each side thinking they're going to get a benefit out of that. When we enact a law, we [interfere with this voluntarism], we basically say we know better than you how to organize your own business affairs, because, for some reason or another, we're smarter than you. What I would like to know from my perspective is, why the Legislature ought to stick its nose into somebody else's business and interfere with that voluntary transaction. . . .
>
> Those who want to have the Legislature interfere with that voluntary relationship have a high burden [of proof] for me, but the way you overcome that burden is to explain why the seven-year rule makes sense in your business.[41]

"Contractarianism" is the term offered by Carole Pateman in her 1988 work of feminist political theory *The Sexual Contract* to designate this important strain of liberal thought that reckons from the "standpoint of contract."[42] Following his initial jab at recording artists' privilege, Haynes's invocation of voluntarism shows his rootedness in this orientation.

The standpoint of contract emerges from Enlightenment-era conceptions of a social contract as the foundation of social order in the modern, liberal age. Theories of the social contract purport to explain why free individuals submit to governance by a central authority; they appear often to justify existing political authority. In the emerging modern world—as it was imagined, for example, by early liberal thinkers like Thomas Hobbes and John Locke— "none of the old arguments for subordination," such as God's will, brute force, custom, or tradition, "could be accepted. The doctrine of individual freedom and equality entailed that there was only one justification for subordination. A naturally free and equal individual must, necessarily, *agree* to be ruled by another."[43] The social contract is seen as the original agreement, entered into on our behalf by our forebears when they left behind what contract theorists call the state of nature, where force and insecurity prevailed, and entered what we now know as civil(ized) society, where interactions are voluntary and take place between those who are equal in the eyes of the law. To contract theorists, civil society governments are public, rule in civil society takes place by consent of the governed, and coercion is reserved to the state.

The economist and philosopher David Ellerman illuminates the nature of contractarianism when he refers to it as the "alienist" tradition in liberal thought because it tends to think of rights as alienable property.[44] Considered from what Pateman calls the "standpoint of contract, social life and relationships not only originate from a social contract but, properly, are seen as an endless series of discrete contracts. . . . From the standpoint of contract, in social life there are contracts all the way down"—not only between individuals engaging in commerce but between family members, friends, neighbors, individuals and the state and other organizations, and so on.[45]

To contractarians like Haynes—or classical liberals, to use their preferred descriptor[46]—contracts can be found operating, implicitly if not explicitly, in virtually every human relationship, every human interaction can be rendered in contractual terms, and people should be free to contract for almost anything. In Haynes's contractarian view, efforts by the state to set limits on individuals' power to contract are understood as interference, as instances of "paternalism," where "the state is acting like a father and treating individuals like sons who cannot yet act for their own good."[47] To convince Haynes of the legitimacy of this sort of interference in the right of free individuals to enter into any kind of contract they like (short, of course, of contracts to commit crimes), the recording artists and their allies have a "high burden" to "overcome." Not only is it not government's role to set or limit the terms of contracts, but the contractarian view also holds that government officials are incompetent in that regard and are bound to "screw it up," as Senator Sher said later in the hearing.[48] Employment, in the contractarian view, is nonproblematic, a routine contract like any other; if any element of servitude exists, it is legitimated by the voluntary consent of both parties, and is often well compensated—especially at this socioeconomic stratum.

The philosophical issues associated with the contractarian approach to the employment relation are particularly interesting. From the standpoint of contract, "no limits can be placed on contract and contractual relations; even the ultimate form of civil subordination, the slave contract, is legitimate. A civil slave contract is not significantly different from any other contract."[49] A "civil" slave contract is one entered into voluntarily, without the coercion characteristic of the "state of nature" (in contrast to which "civil society" and "civilization" take their meaning); basic to contractarianism is the notion that voluntarism and consent legitimate virtually every conceivable relationship or interaction (except with regard to minors and the mentally ill). When the recording artists cry "[civil] slavery" and "indentured servitude," the contractarian response is, essentially, "So what? Did you not consent to the contract?" From the standpoint of contract, consent legitimizes not only contracts of unlimited duration, but even a contract for "self-sale."[50] In a way, then, the artists are pushing against an open door: contractarianism does not disagree with them that their contracts subject them to control and domination; where the contractarian disagrees with the artists is on the legitimacy of the control and domination.

Contractarianism has an appealing appearance of clarity: when you can divide the world up into mutually exclusive categories of consent (which is free and good) and coercion (which is unfree and bad), and when a paper or implied contract is the unequivocal signal of consent, it becomes very easy to draw a line between legitimate and illegitimate relations. From this point of view, no contract to do anything that is not prohibited by law can be illegitimate; moreover, in this view, there still exist numerous paternalistic laws that stand in the way of people making contracts that ought to be legitimate. Utterly in keeping with the neoliberal thinking and discourse dominant in politics and business at the turn of the twenty-first century, this frame remained in place throughout the hearing. It was this noncontroversial understanding of contract and employment with which the recording artists and their allies had to contend in order to press their case to restore their inalienable right under a renewed seven-year rule. The most intense arguments erupted around contentions regarding the degrees of choice, voluntarism, and coercion in the recording contract.

An Opposing but Ambiguous Frame

Senator Murray, lead author and proponent of SB 1246, made his opening statement right after Senator Haynes's effort to frame the proceedings. Murray attempted to orient the discussion around a different axis, shifting from a contractarian position to another set of criteria organized around subtler ideas. First, Murray attempted to change the focus from contractarian conceptions of legislative interference to a vision of the 1987 carve out as controversial and contrary to long-standing practice. "Remember," he advised his listeners, "Section 2855 has a hundred year history in various forms and has been confirmed by numerous courts as not even being something that the artist can waive. So the question is: what was the burden at the time to create an exception to Section 2855, when, in fact, not even an individual who was subject to a personal services contract could have waived that right?"[51] Murray wanted the assembled lawmakers to consider the gravity of taking an inalienable right away from a particular occupational group at a stroke.

Where Haynes saw voluntarism and consent, Murray wanted lawmakers to see a line between legitimate and illegitimate exploitation. "The artists fundamentally believe that this is about fairness," he continued, and then shifted toward a different political reading of the situation. "At the outset," he noted, the seven-year rule "was clearly a bar against indentured servitude":

> You could argue . . . if you're in house arrest, in a castle tower with servants, whether you're under any less house arrest [than someone under house arrest in less luxurious circumstances]. But the other thing is that everyone [else], including record executives, has a limitation of seven years, and the question is . . . at what bar do you make an exception for one, single group? The question is whether or not one single group—recording artists—should be exempted from a protection, that is, a labor law, which we don't even allow individuals—who contract freely—to waive, because to do so would allow exploitation of those who are subject to the contract.[52]

Detention in one's house is a form of punishment in which a person's freedom is constrained, despite the fact that the circumstances might not be uncomfortable. House arrest in a "castle tower with servants" might be very comfortable, in fact. But what Murray wants to convey is the political condition of subordination in which a person under house arrest finds herself: regardless of the material conditions that obtain, she is not free to leave.

Murray makes it clear that, with the exception of recording artists, the state of California does not allow freely contracting individuals to waive the protection offered by the seven-year rule; if it did, that would, in Murray's terms, allow their exploitation.[53] This exception, he suggests, is illegitimate not only because it contravenes liberalism's tenet of equal treatment under the law, but also because it flies in the face of California's established public policy. With this last statement, Murray is drawing on the language and scope of the 1944 decision in the de Havilland case, which is quoted in SB 1246. In this influential decision—written during World War II, when US workers were near their apex of social power and cultural esteem—the court made three arguments about the politics of work, the legitimacy of employers' control over labor, and the legitimacy of the state's restriction of freedom of contract in connection with employment. In finding that Olivia de Havilland's contract could not be extended beyond seven years (to compensate for the twenty-five weeks when both parties had agreed to suspend her work), the court argued that first, there is a public interest in the supposedly private relations of work; second, the public interest is served when employees have rights against their employers' superior market power, such as that provided by the seven-year rule; and third, unless they are inalienable, such rights are meaningless. As Senator Murray had pointed out in the personal service contracts hearing the year before, the court "stated unequivocally that it was the policy of the state to allow you not only to get out of the contract, but to test the marketplace," to be released from the exclusive control of your (former) employer and to court other bidders for your services in order to discover your fair market value.[54]

This 1944 decision is a powerful argument against contractarian thinking about the employment relation, but it is not without its weaknesses and holes. As do the decision's obvious strengths, these flaws inhabit and shape the arguments and approach of the recording artists. The decision focuses narrowly on the specific value to employees of freedom from overlong contracts. The decision states that the Legislature's power to restrict freedom of contract is part of its "power to legislate for the purpose of preserving the public comfort, health, safety, morals and welfare,"[55] and it explains why a limit on the right to contract for more than a certain amount of time is valid. However, the decision neither specifies the nature of the forces that make that limit necessary nor refers to any principle that would explain why workers should have inalienable rights of any kind. The notions that employers often wield their market power to pressure employees into harmful arrangements; that sometimes the harm is in the excessive duration of the arrangements; and that that explains why employees must have inalienable rights are nowhere explicitly stated. The lack of clear statements along these lines in the court's decision is at least a partial explanation of the failure of the recording artists to present their own arguments more successfully.

With his opening statement, then, Senator Murray restates the main political claims of the artists. On the one hand, he asserts that recording artists were unfairly singled out from among all California employees to be made particularly vulnerable to employer power (and that the legitimacy of that instance of singling out should itself be made a topic of debate), and on the other hand, he suggests that the passage of the seven-year anniversary of work under a contract, without the possibility of free access to the market in order to test one's value, turns that voluntary contract into an instrument of domination (a sort of house arrest, as he put it) making possible a degree of exploitation that would not be enforceable in any other employment arena. In obliquely citing the robust public policy rationale behind the duration limit as articulated and endorsed by the court in 1944, Murray gestured toward an idea that he and the legislation's other supporters would struggle to articulate and contain: employee freedom is inversely related to contract freedom.

Voluntarism and Entitlement

Of all the record company executives to testify at the 2002 hearing, Jeff Ayeroff of Warner Bros. Records most vehemently engaged the artist side's still-resonant 2001 claims of domination and exploitation. He and Senator Haynes—the two most vocal participants in the hearing—combined to form a contractarian tag team to oppose arguments for restoring 2855's protection to recording artists. Ayeroff made the following five basic arguments:

1. Recording artists come to us as individuals and enter contracts voluntarily, represented by the best lawyers.
2. We are not employers; we invest in artistic careers.
3. Our contracts represent the exchange of our expertise in artist development and marketing for recording artists' creativity.
4. When the artist is successful, this investment/exchange/contract produces revenue over which we have a proprietary claim.
5. We require long-term enforceable contracts in order to be profitable.

Early in his testimony, Ayeroff articulated his contractarian belief in the power of consent to justify any particular arrangement. He told the committee that, in reflecting on the "dialogue going back and forth about artist relationships to record companies" since Murray's inquiry had begun the previous fall, "the first thing that comes to mind is 'if you don't want to sign with a major, don't sign with a major.' We don't drag people into our buildings off the street and force them to record for us. They are brought to us by very high-profile lawyers." He reiterated: "They come as individuals in their relationship to us." And he repeated a few minutes later, "We don't put ourselves in a position of forcing anybody. They come to us, they compete, they're competitive, they take the contracts as they take them."[56]

Curiously, Ayeroff had some difficulty explaining exactly what kind of relationship exists between a record company and its recording artists. The role he constructs through his roundabout description is hard to define, but it is certain that he does not see his company as an employer, nor himself as an employer's representative. "I take great umbrage," Ayeroff declared, "at the fact that someone would say that the relationship that we share with an artist has anything to do with indentured servitude. If anything, we serve them." In what capacity do the record company and he serve the artists? Ayeroff told the committee: "We are people who invest, we are a combination of investors, marketers, promoters, salespeople, and we sometimes are cheerleaders, advisors, psychologists, and we end up having a very tight relationship with many of our artists that has value; obviously there are other people in the record industry who have other relationships with them, all of us together, some sort of strange cabal, pull in the same direction toward success."[57] "We have a very tight relationship . . . that has value"; other industry people also have valuable relationships with the artists, all of us together try to maximize that value. But what exactly is this relationship? It involves capitalization, valorization, exhortation, and forms of advice and even therapy, but not, apparently, the kind of control an employment contract grants an employer.

At the core of the relationship between artist and record company, in Ayeroff's view, lies not the contract for "personal services in the production of phonorecords" by the artist, as section 2855(b) puts it, but something else: the artist's career. "When I look at an artist, because I do sign artists, I look because I'm trying to figure out how I'm going to make an investment in a career," Ayeroff said. He doesn't see himself dealing in terms of numbers of records or years, but cultivating the career of the artist, as investor, cheerleader, and so forth. How does this benefit him and his company? "When making that career," he testified, "I share . . . a certain portion of their revenues. . . . I have a relationship with the records that I've bought from them, that I own, because the only way the record industry survives is by ownership of catalogue, and by owning a certain portion of the relationship to an artist's career." These relationships—with the records, to an artist's career—are entirely different kinds of relationships than those of cheerleader or advisor: they are associated with ownership and control.[58] Here some of the deeper lineaments of the contractarian view emerge. The artists, in Ayeroff's view, voluntarily enter into mutually beneficial exchanges with the record companies. The artists offer ownership of records and a certain portion of their relationship to an artist's career in exchange for the expert professional services of the record company. Even though people could conceivably build their own cars, Ayeroff suggested by way of explanation, they prefer to buy them from, say, General Motors because "it's easier—they [General Motors] have the expertise." Artists "come to us," he said, "because we offer things" like market development, advice on visual presentation, publicity, "and relationships with places like MTV." Moreover, artists "also have the desire to make money off of that relationship and that desire isn't some sort of strange, Fagin-like relationship. . . . I just think it's a misdirection to think that we are there to exploit, as opposed to have a business relationship in an artist's career."[59] Ill-defined as it is to Ayeroff, the contract represents an agreement between equals who appear to remain equals: each party offering the other services in a business relationship that both hope will generate profits.

But in reflecting on the 1987 legislation, a sense of the power dynamic embedded in the law by subsection (b) emerges. Despite Ayeroff's expressed sense of the voluntary and equal nature of the relationship, it's clear that some degree of control must rest with the employing record label: "If there's a band that we want, that Interscope wants or that DreamWorks wants, we want it really badly . . . and we will pay the money to get it, making the risk higher. The higher you pay, the higher the risk, the more delicate the work, the worse you feel when you fail. But like good baseball players, we don't hit the ball every time, you know . . . and if we succeed, we're entitled to having a long-term relationship to be able to recoup those kinds of investments." But what kind of relationship is it that allows one person to have a long-term, exclusive, enforceable claim over the disposition and productive output of another person? What kind of relationship enables one to command another under threat of injunction or damages? Not cheerleading, not therapy, not even ownership in the way Ayeroff was using the term. He may be "emotionally there, financially there, and creatively there" for his artists, "helping them create a career for themselves,"[60] but no matter how happy and comfortable his artists may be, if they're profitable, Ayeroff will also be "there" to prevent them from leaving before he and his company are finished with them. The relationship he invokes in this last passage is that between an employer and an employee, in which the former has exclusive claims over property and activity, and the latter has to relinquish any such claims or face unpleasant consequences.

The Standard Contract

The last verbal testimony excerpted in this chapter comes from an argument between Cooper and Haynes, the senator who initially imposed a hard contractarian frame on the proceedings. In this hearing, Haynes was the single most vocal legislator, again and again speaking up along the philosophical lines he articulated at the outset, shepherding the discussion ever back to contractarian parameters and criteria.

Leading up to this exchange, Cooper testified about how hungry new artists are for their first contracts, how ready they are to "sign almost anything to get into these contracts":

> Sometimes we as attorneys and managers have to put the brakes on them, because they will give away everything. I have one horrible example just two years ago, of a label that is back East, I won't [name it], financed by a television company based in California, financed by a record company based in California (but the label is back East). [They] signed the artist to—get this—the contract was . . . for something like fourteen albums, [for] television [appearances], in which they didn't pay for any services for the first year; merchandizing, publishing, everything cross-collateralized, *and* the company back East also got the management.[61]

The RIAA's CEO, Hilary Rosen, interjected, "That just doesn't happen," to which Cooper replied, "Hilary, I will show you the contract."

After a bit more discussion of the range of contract terms, Haynes turned to the artists' side and told them, essentially, that the content of the contract is irrelevant. "A contract on a take it or leave it basis still has an option," he declaimed, "and what you're trading in that option is the benefit that's being offered for the 'take it' process." The onerous contract that Cooper had just described still had an option. In the abstract terms of Haynes's preference, the "leave it" option could mean not taking work in the chosen field, or it could mean unemployment and poverty. For Haynes, even starvation is an "option."[62]

Haynes highlights the one-sided nature of the encounter between the artist and the label in his acknowledgment that the contract is a "take it or leave it" document. (This is also known as an "adhesion" contract—one has no choice but to "adhere" to the terms if one takes the deal. Such a deal takes place when one buys a candy bar from a shopkeeper: one buys it on the shopkeeper's terms, or not at all.) This kind of contract is notable because its terms are only minimally negotiated or negotiable. Haynes's remarks here are especially interesting because, as I noted with respect to the 2001 hearing, the very existence of a standard recording contract is a matter of argument. In the course of the introductory remarks that Senator Escutia, chair of the committee, made in opening the 2002 hearing, she told participants that there is "significant debate" about "whether there is such a thing as a standardized contract for new artists." She continued: "I can tell you that both sides have given me diametrically different responses. This issue is important because everything else follows from that very first contract."[63] The first contract sets the terms on which any renegotiation would build. Unfavorable initial terms may become less unfavorable through renegotiation, but, as the artists argued, those new terms may be nowhere near what the artist could achieve in an open market for his labor.

The party offering the "take it or leave it" contract is in the position of superior power: that party sets the terms of the contract to suit it. Big companies with many artists under contract, all of whom have some potential for commercial success, have relatively little at stake in the outcome of any particular negotiation. Recording artists, on the other hand, like most other working people, must place all their eggs in one negotiating basket.[64] Outlining the politics of the standard contract in the context of the British music industry, Steve Greenfield and Guy Osborn quote Lord Diplock, a judge in a case that was ultimately decided in favor of a songwriter over a publisher. (The songwriter's victory came about at least in part because British legal conventions allow greater latitude in the examination of the power relations at work in the negotiation of an initial contract.) Lord Diplock contrasted standard contracts of "ancient origin" that "have stood the test of time" and are usually considered to be "fair and reasonable" with a second type "of comparatively modern origin." This latter type "is the result of the concentration of particular kinds of business in relatively few hands . . . (t)he terms of this kind of standard form contract have not been the subject of negotiation between the parties to it, or approved by any organization representing the interests of the weaker party. They have been dictated by that party whose bargaining power, either exercised alone or in conjunction with others providing similar goods or services, enables him to say: 'If you want these goods or services at all, these are the only terms on which they are obtainable. Take it or leave it.'"[65] In England, a finding that a contract is a standard contract supports an employee's case for terminating the contract: it helps to demonstrate the one-sidedness of the initial deal. In the United States, the focus is more on the outcome of the contract than the process by which it was initially drafted.[66]

Greenfield and Osborn observe that standard contracts pose problems for the classical contract theory. "Situations where one party is effectively able to foist their own standard (preferred) terms on the other party," they write, "offer a direct challenge to the concept of free will in classical contract theory." The free will supposedly exercised in the "meeting of the minds" that is understood by classical contractarians like Haynes to be at the core of any contract is placed in doubt when there are terms that must be accepted by the weaker party in order for the deal to be made. Nevertheless, Greenfield and Osborn continue, standard contracts "are a staple feature of business contracting and prevalent in the entertainment industry."[67] The standard contract's key features "of exclusive performance over a wide geographical area . . . for a potentially long, virtually career-length period of time are seemingly cast in stone. No matter what the status of the artist, the company . . . will not concede much in these areas."[68]

In his use of the "take it or leave it" language, Haynes acknowledges that there are systematic disparities in power between the two sides and certain terms to which virtually all recording artists must agree in order to be employed in this industry. He nevertheless insists that "taking it" and "leaving it" are legitimately voluntary; the circumstances are immaterial as long as there is a choice to "leave it." Haynes pulls back to frame the issue slightly differently: "You've got capital and you've got labor," he lectured. "Capital is saying 'we want your labor, we think we can make a return off your labor,' you're saying 'I want to make a return off my labor,' and through the process of a voluntary negotiation [you arrive at a contract]." He reiterates that "take it or leave it, by the way, *is* a voluntary negotiation" because "there is still one element of voluntariness left over, and that is the take it or leave it part of it—even if you don't like all of the terms, you still want the benefit that attaches to it."[69] Haynes sees capital and labor meeting each other in a neutral, nonpolitical market space, each as an owner bearing something the other desires. Capital sees in labor the source of a marginal return, and labor sees in capital a buyer of its services. The two choose to contract—voluntarily, Haynes stresses again—and labor "takes it" because even if labor doesn't like all of the terms of the deal, it still wants the benefit of the deal, which ultimately outweighs the costs. (Note the rather serious slippage here between the language of "negotiation" and "take it or leave it.") The voluntarism that Haynes sees in this exchange excludes any consideration of power relations—indeed, of anything external to the contract itself—and legitimizes any legal outcome (and perhaps, in Haynes's utopia, some currently illegal outcomes, such as the contract for self-sale).

Arriving finally at his principal point—the point at which the artists themselves were aiming but failed to reach because of their own investments in the status quo and their intellectual blind spots—Haynes asks why the Legislature should reinstate the seven-year rule's inalienable right. You recording artists, he admonished, are now asking us "to reassign benefits, the risks and benefits in the business":

> I have no idea what those risks are, I have no idea what those benefits are, and I don't know under what terms I would enter into such a deal—but you're asking me to rewrite your contracts. From up here [in Sacramento]. Understanding, as you said earlier, that we rewrote it a few years back. In a way to give more freedom, quite frankly, more freedom in the contractual relationship, not less. . . . I mean, the more freedom of contract we get I think is a good thing, less freedom of contract is a bad thing. . . . What I'm trying to get to here, what I'm trying to figure out, is what basis is [there] for us in interfering with an artist who freely puts pencil, or pen, to the paper and signs on the contract? Why should we engage in that? Why should we get in the middle of that?[70]

Why, he wants to know, should the Legislature, servants and representatives of the people of California, act "like a father and [treat] individuals like sons who cannot yet act for their own good?" as Pateman puts it.[71] Why should ignorant legislators, who are bound "to screw it up," put limits on the kinds of deals that the people of California should be able to make?

The basis for restricting freedom of contract in California, as the Olivia de Havilland case made clear, is that it benefits the people in the state. There are some deals that people should be prevented not only from making, but from being required to fulfill even if they do make them. As the 1944 decision implied, and as Murray and the recording artists' side stated in their elliptical way, employers' power threatens working people's substantive freedom. For Haynes and the record companies, however, the only real freedom is contract freedom.

The identity of freedom with contract freedom is a deep-seated form of classical liberal common sense. Back in 1987, in Haynes's view, the Legislature increased freedom of contract by removing a limit on the kinds of deals Californians could make, albeit in only one industry. Haynes's "major concern," he says, is that by replacing that limit, the government would be "interfering with a totally voluntary relationship, by sticking an involuntary element into it. We're going to say to these guys, 'you can't sign that deal. Even if it hurts you, or even if it helps you to sign the deal' (and it would help you guys to sign, for them to sign the deal), we're saying 'you can't do that.' And I have a problem with that, I'm concerned with that." At this point, Senator Byron Sher reminds Haynes of the intent of the law, at least as read by the 1944 court, to provide an inalienable right. Sher says, "Well, that's the way the original law was set up, was it not? The original law—" but Haynes cuts Sher off with the contractarian criterion: "As I said, you move, we moved from a restrictive, a less free, less freedom of contract situation, to a more freedom of contract situation."[72]

Section 2855 of the California Labor Code does not actually tell people they cannot make employment contracts for longer than seven years; it says only that the state will not enforce such contracts beyond seven years. Similarly, subsection (b) of 2855 does not say that recording artists cannot invoke the seven-year protection; it says merely that the company is allowed to seek damages for undelivered records past the seven-year mark. (An artist and a company could conceivably draw up a contract in which, by waiving their right to seek damages, the company conceded to the artist the right to leave at seven years, just as if the 1987 amendment had never been enacted. I have seen no evidence of this taking place.)

"What we added," said Haynes later of the 1987 amendment, "was the ability of the artists and the record companies—again this is a mutual relationship—to negotiate over an additional term in the contract."[73] This added possibility is the effect of making an inalienable right into an alienable bit of property. From Haynes's "standpoint of contract" perspective, this process expands the area of freedom of contract by including an element that wasn't there before. Record labels and recording artists are now "free" to negotiate over contracts of unlimited duration because, through the damages provisions, they will be fully enforced by the state. From the standpoint of labor, however, the process removes an element of security and bargaining power, reducing a valuable form of freedom: the right to say no to harmful bargains. Under section 2855, any worker is free to continue working for her employer for more than seven years if she chooses to do so. Turning 2855's protection into an "additional term" to be negotiated in the contract makes recording artists vulnerable to interminable employment contracts, contrary to California's public policy with regard to all other workers in the state. The irony here, of course, is that few other workers in the state actually require protection from contracts of excessive duration. (I treat this irony at greater length below, as the "artist-worker" vs. "worker-worker" paradox.)

But why shouldn't all employee rights be alienable bits of property? Why should there be any inalienable rights when it comes to private contracts between free parties who are equal in the eyes of the law? You're free to ask me to give up a right in exchange for "a return," and I'm free to either "take it," accepting the deal and losing the right, or "leave it," losing the deal and keeping the right. Cooper came very close to answering this question.

The Artists' Response

Cooper responded to Haynes's characterization with a statement from the standpoint of labor that brings the politics of employment closer to the surface of the debate. To Haynes's assertion that "we moved from a restrictive, a less free, less freedom of contract situation, to a more freedom of contract situation," Cooper responded, "I respectfully disagree, Senator. I don't think we did, I think we did just the opposite, we made it more restrictive, because now you gave a certain additional weapon to the record companies . . . that they didn't [have], that nobody else, no other employer in the state of California has."[74] By characterizing the legislation as restrictive, Cooper advances the analysis of the recording artists' side toward an understanding of how freedom of contract is neither identical with, nor the extent of, substantive liberty, as framed (for example) by John Stuart Mill. By characterizing the 1987 legislation as the state's gift of a weapon to the record companies, Cooper advances the argument that consent does not necessarily represent or produce a free relation. But what Cooper fails to note here is that, from the standpoint of contract, Haynes is actually correct: the state did expand freedom of contract by adding an "additional term" to the range of negotiable contract terms. This is an analytical gap in the artists' argument, an inability or unwillingness to answer a crucial question in a grounded fashion: What's wrong with expanding freedom of contract? It is also a social gap in their argument and makes their case for rights less legible to those people and legislators who might consider themselves to have an interest in the welfare of the state's workers. In today's employment environment, it is increasingly likely that in seven years, many if not most employees will have found new employers many times, possibly against their will. The artists never clarified why any other workers in California should care about a right they will likely never need to exercise: the right to change employers after seven years.

But this moment represents the artists' most concentrated attempt to refute the radical logic of contractarianism. Cooper has represented recording artists' interests before state and federal lawmakers since the mid-1980s, accumulating extensive experience in formulating arguments on legislation and jurisprudence, yet he encounters a major obstacle here. He cannot (at least, he does not) present a foundation for the recording artists' argument that is as robust or legible as the contractarian argument against it. He does not argue that, in a class-divided society, contract freedom is inversely re-lated to substantive freedom; that contract freedom advances at the expense of workers' rights; and that this position has been supported by formidable liberal and democratic thinkers for at least a century and a half. Cooper thus argues, without elaborating a clear ethical or philosophical principle, that the 1987 legislation "was a mistake at the time, I said so at the time, because there was nothing given for that, it was just a gift, that was handed over to the record companies, and there was no reason for it and what we're here about is that shouldn't have been done, because there was no reason, I cannot find a reason, and I don't think the record companies have made the case that there was a reason for making that gift to the record companies." From Cooper's perspective, the damages provisions were a "gift" from the Legislature to the record companies; Haynes insists on seeing this not as something that was taken away from the recording artists, but as a gift to both parties. In his view, the artists are free, juridically equal to the companies; both are voluntarily contracting individuals and any restriction on their freedom to contract is a restriction on their freedom. Rather than refute Haynes's argument with criti-cal analysis, Cooper responds, finally, with "No, I apologize, I don't see it."[75]

Senator Haynes now lays his cards on the table. "If we were to take my phi-losophy to its logical conclusion," he declares, "we would eliminate 2855 com-pletely. And then allow everybody to negotiate however they wished under these kind of circumstances. I mean there would be no seven-year limitation on anything, and *that's* what I'm saying."[76] To Haynes, the recording busi-ness appears to be just the first to see the elimination of the seven-year rule, a harbinger of the expansion of freedom of contract through the elimination of workers' rights across the board.

Haynes was not the only legislator to speak from the "standpoint of con-tract," but his was the most relentlessly and uncompromisingly articulated position. The debate continued for another hour, with Senators Sher and Kuehl taking up the contractarian critique of the artists' demand to once again restrict freedom of contract, and answers from the artists' side con-tinuing to show this basic ambiguity.[77]

Paradoxes

The Legislature did not pass Kevin Murray's bill to repeal the 1987 carve out. But SB 1246's failure had more to do with the Legislature's overall probusi-ness orientation and the resonance of neoliberal arguments than the weaknesses and blind spots of the recording artists' arguments in the hearing discussed above. In fact, the bill passed out of the very Judiciary Committee that held the hearing. The artists' arguments, however imperfect, combined with the deference of the committee members to Murray's eminence and experience in the entertainment industry (and perhaps to the celebrity and cultural power of the artists), convinced a majority in the committee. Despite their negligible role in the bill's ultimate failure, however, these weaknesses and blind spots are fascinating and provocative.[78]

The recording artists' charges of civil slavery and indentured servitude actually point to the porosity of the boundary between employment and servitude, opening an opportunity to scrutinize the employment relation in critical terms. Senator Murray's invocation of "house arrest" in his opening statement was, ultimately, as close as the artists' side came to articulating the starker arguments that previously had been central to their effort. In giving up that more critical line of argument between the first and second hearings they lost a powerful analytical tool. Moreover, hobbled by their ultimate dependence on (and overall contentedness with) a system that had enabled a tiny minority of them to build successful careers, the artists were at a loss when it came to contesting the contractarianism that became the core of the record companies' arguments. The lack in existing entertainment industry lore and case law of an accessible, clear, and useful critique of employer power as a general problem exacerbated the artists' rhetorical helplessness. They could argue that they were stuck in what Carole Pateman calls relations of "civil mastery" and "civil subordination" and have that diagnosis tacitly and explicitly accepted by lawmakers.[79] However, they were at a loss when it came to arguing why they should be protected, like all other employees under 2855(a), "from the consequences of their improvident contracts," as the decision in the de Havilland case puts it.[80]

At the core of the story lie two related paradoxes, which I call the artist-workers versus worker-workers paradox and the seven years plus one day equals slavery paradox. The first concerns recording artists' only partial understanding of the relationship of their exceptional work arrangements to the more mundane arrangements of most other employees. The second concerns the artists' only partial understanding of the politics of employment and of how those politics—as much as, if not more than, any particular bit of legislation—determine their experiences under contract.

In seeking to reinstate the artists' inalienable right to change employers after seven years, the artists and their allies argued repeatedly that recording artists had been unfairly singled out and that fairness demanded that they be treated like all other employees in the state. As Simon Renshaw, an artists' manager, told the Senate Judiciary Committee in 2002, "this is about trying to level the playing field and . . . have [California recording artists] treated in the same way as any other California citizen is treated, with respect to their employment."[81] Or as Cooper argued, "if you want to repeal it, then it's repealed for all people, not just recording artists, but on the other hand, as long as it's on the books, we just feel that recording artists should be treated equally with everybody else in the state of California."[82] Jim Guirenot, another artists' manager, testified in 2001 that "this provision separates artists from every sector of labor in California: the waiter, the insurance person, store clerks; it makes musicians separate from every single worker in California and it defies fairness."[83]

However, recording artists have little in common with the majority of California workers. For example, most employees are subject to more or less constant monitoring and surveillance, in profound contrast to most recording artists' experiences of their employment. However, in addition to such obvious differences in moment-to-moment experiences of work, there is a much broader difference to bring to the foreground here. For most working people in these times of increasing instability in the labor market and high unemployment, a long-term employment contract provides a very real experience of freedom from insecurity. For most people, the statistically common occurrence of being thrown back into the labor market at the convenience of the employer can be catastrophic: losing the wages; health care; and sense of belonging, expertise, and usefulness that can come with even the most miserable job often has disastrous effects on individuals and their families.[84] For those without inherited or accumulated income-producing wealth, long-term employment provides economic stability. The transformation of employment from a heavily regulated, collective social institution to a minimally regulated, individualistic, marketized one has been accompanied by widespread political liberalization and democratization. The capacity of some private individuals to force other private individuals to work, and the existence of criminal sanctions for the failure to work, appear to be things of the past. In the last century and a half, since the demise of indentured servitude, employers' power to control others has been scaled back considerably, enabling people in greater numbers to pursue individually chosen, even fulfilling, occupations and careers. But today, working people increasingly find themselves in labor markets where the tendency is toward the oversupply of labor and competition for positions. This is in contrast to the cases of successful or rising recording artists, who can benefit from the positive effects of competition among employers for their labor. In a very real way, because of these differences, recording artists make no sense when they complain that, unlike all other California workers, they are vulnerable to overlong contracts.

However, just as they overlooked and downplayed the real differences that separate them from other workers, rendering their claims less legible to those in other worlds of work, the recording artists also overlooked and downplayed a real similarity that links them to other workers: their shared political locations. When recording artists complain about being held to contracts in excess of what appears to be the established norm of seven years, they are complaining about their encounter with a universal feature of employment: employers' rights to control employees' work. As a small group of powerful buyers they are capable of taking a unified stance toward a large number of sellers. Record companies' monopsonistic dominance of the market for the labor of recording artists enhances their power to foist a standard contract on artists, especially new artists. Basic to this contract is the employers' right to determine what kind of behavior counts as fulfilling the contract. The delivery clause is an illustrative example: an optioned record is considered to have been delivered only if the record company accepts it.

When a successful artist reaches the seventh anniversary of work under her contract without having completed all of the albums that "could contractually be required" she remains effectively unfree. Ever since the addition of the damages provisions to the seven-year rule, the record company has been in a position to say, in effect, "the four albums you've made to date don't count as fulfilling the contract; either make us X number of albums up to our commercial standards or pay us damages based on the profits we would have made from those X remaining albums." In political terms, this is hardly different from a situation in which my boss at the sign factory tells me, "Assemble this many signs in this way so that they come out like this before the end of the day, or you're fired." Because of their difficulty in perceiving and communicating these very real differences and similarities, the recording artists' universalistic arguments in favor of the seven-year rule had little purchase. Had they invoked the general necessity of inalienable rights for workers against employers they could, I believe, have gone a long way toward overcoming this problem. The second paradox develops this point more fully.

Seven Years Plus One Day Equals Slavery

In arguing for repeal of the 1987 carve out, recording artists focused excessively on the seven-year limit. Being required to serve for longer than seven years was, according to them, an unconscionable degree of exploitation. For example, according to Senator Murray's opening statement (quoted above), to allow people to contract for more than seven years at a time "would allow exploitation of those who are subject to the contract." "In my gut, and most lawmakers' guts," Murray said at the 2001 hearing, "seven years is the appropriate length of time to limit personal service contracts for everyone, including recording acts."[85] Country singer LeAnn Rimes testified in 2001 that "recording artists are being taken advantage of by being tied to a record company contract for more than seven years. . . . Recording artists should not be tied to one record company contract for more than seven years."[86] In 1995, as a teenager in Texas, Rimes had signed a deal with Curb Records that could keep her under contract for more than twenty years. Michael Greene, of the National Academy of Recording Arts and Sciences (sponsor of the Grammy Awards), testified: "Seven years is the magic number here today."[87] Engel admonished the audience: "You can't take a young artist's life for more than seven years. . . . [I]t's unfair to go beyond seven years."[88] Indeed, this conviction echoes the forceful language of the de Havilland case (quoted at length in chapter 3), that "seven years of time is fixed as the maximum time for which [employees] may contract for their services without the right to change employers or occupations. Thereafter, they may make a change if they deem it necessary or advisable."[89]

But rhetorically, the recording artists had been backed into a corner by Senator Haynes and his less rigorously contractarian colleagues: they couldn't simply cite that case and argue that it was unfair that they'd been singled out and denied the protection of a century-old labor law. They had to demonstrate why they should have this right returned to them. The artists were happy to let "the market" determine their compensation—in fact, freedom to achieve market-determined compensation was perhaps the most important prize associated with winning back the right to leave contracts after seven years. But they did not want to leave the question of duration to the market; they sought protection from the market power of their employers. On what basis could they argue that fairness dictated a fixed time limit, or any inalienable right? The question that recording artists and their supporters could not or would not address was this one: if a seven-year relationship becomes unconscionable at seven years plus one day, then what does that say about the nature of the relationship? If it can go from legitimate to unconscionable in one day, could that relationship ever really have been conscionable in the first place?

The boundary between free and unfree labor is shifting and permeable. Carole Pateman has explored the politics of employment at least since the 1970 publication of her book *Participation and Democratic Theory*. Her analyses and critiques of women's and workers' subordination in her 1988 *The Sexual Contract* are part of a broader project of "democratization," of "reducing subordination and creating a more democratic society."[90] This process is particularly urgent in what have long been considered the private or nonpolitical realms of the family and the workplace. In *The Sexual Contract*, Pateman seeks in part to strengthen feminist arguments for women's full political personhood by clarifying the relationships of those arguments to the existing discursive and political structures that shape the public and private realms. In her view, socialist feminists have made flawed arguments in comparing the situations of women and men to those of workers and bosses. In clarifying this comparison, she develops a compelling analysis of the employment relation. And she pushes this analysis further in later work, supporting a basic income as a significant step toward democratization.[91]

According to Pateman, women, employees, and slaves (civil and otherwise) endure subordinate status, though the precise forms of their subordination differ in important ways. Nevertheless, between the employee and the slave there is no hard analytical distinction: "It is virtually impossible to distinguish the piecemeal contracting out of labor power from the alienation of the whole lifetime of a man's labour."[92] Lines such as the one frequently held to divide employees from slaves (as well as the line purported to divide authors from nonauthors discussed in chapter 5) do not correspond to any actually existing or essential difference between people in the world. The closer one looks at the phenomena these lines are supposed merely to reflect, the less substantial the connection between reality and convention appears, and the more such lines appear contingent and political. One of Pateman's contributions in this vein is her explanation of the "eminently permeable" nature of the distinction between employment and civil slavery. Far from deriving from or depending on disjoined foundations, both institutions turn on the "political fiction" of "property in the person."[93] The modern employment contract expresses the idea that "every Man has a *Property* in his own *Person*," according to John Locke's seventeenth-century formulation; "this no Body has any Right to but himself."[94] This understanding is what, in contractarian eyes, evacuates the employment relation of any non-voluntary or coercive aspect. If each person is an owner of property in the person, the story goes, then what takes place in hiring is the voluntary contractual exchange of properties between civil equals: labor for a wage.[95] As Senator Haynes put it, "you've got capital and you've got labor"—each has some thing that the other wants.[96] Labor and capital encounter each other as formally equal owners of equally alienable goods. But this is the political fiction. In fact, labor is not actually a thing, and the labor contract, as Pateman points out, is not a contract for exchange, because what counts (for the worker) as fulfilling the contract requires that worker's bodily and mental presence and effort over time, under command. It is not a swap of one bit of property for another, taking place in some temporally fleeting moment or point of exchange.[97] You have to be there, doing what you're told, for a certain amount of time. Recording artists, however, are notable precisely because they don't have to be present in a workplace under continuous command; they sign their contracts, take their big advances, and go off and conceive and make a record on their own schedule in a studio of their choosing, typically, with only a deadline ahead. The contract itself almost functions as a talisman of the artist's capacities that can be used to summon the artist bodily when necessary.

Do Pateman's analysis and contentions advance the study of music makers? I believe they do, because although the approach she develops may seem remote with respect to recording artists most of the time, it appears front and center when an artist becomes successful and hence of greater value to his employer and others. At this point the recording artist may experience the contractual restriction on his freedom to test the market and change employers more personally and concretely. When push comes to shove, Pateman continues, "the employer must . . . have access to the knowledge, skills, and experience of the worker if the capacities are to be used as the employer desires."[98] Access is guaranteed through the contract, which gives the record company the power to command and takes away—civilly and consensually— the recording artist's power freely to say no without penalty. Compared to its routine, continuous, grinding operation in other workplaces, this power usually tends to operate more intermittently, with relative gentleness and at a relative distance. But when record companies finally stop cheerleading, advising, and counseling and start commanding, their actions can strike the artist as coercive.

The political fiction is that there is such a thing as property in the person that can be alienated—as property, properly so called, must be—in the hiring bargain. "When the individual is conceived as an owner of property in the person," as liberals hard and soft (as well as contractarians) do, "rights are seen in proprietary terms. The major mark of private property is that it is alienable, so it is legitimate to alienate the right of self-government, at least in the 'private' sphere of economic enterprises."[99] To make the most compelling argument for an inalienable right against the recording artists' employers, it was not enough simply to say that the weight of a century of California public policy demanded a seven-year limit on recording contracts. The artists had to go beyond the findings in the de Havilland case in order to disrupt the mesmerizing (and reactionary) axioms of contractarian voluntarism. The recording artists had to argue against the idea that there is such a thing as property in the person, which can be alienated voluntarily in the employment contract. "The question raised by contractarians," notes Pateman, anticipating Haynes, "is why alienation should not be unlimited and apply to all rights."[100] It was this target that the recording artists hit with their vocabulary of "[civil] slavery" and "indentured servitude": the alienation of our right to self-government in our employment puts us in a condition of civil subordination through the fraudulent construction of us as owners of property in the person. It was the sight of this target that the artists and their allies lost with their shift of emphasis away from more radical-sounding arguments regarding civil slavery and indenture. No amount of consent can actualize the alienation of our factually inalienable capacity to work by fraudulently (although possibly legally) placing our capacity to work in the fictional category of "property in the person."[101] "The question that is bypassed in all the argument about the duration of the employment contract," and that was notably bypassed in most of the debate over California's seven-year rule, ". . . is how this peculiar property can be separated from the worker and his labour. All the parties to the argument, in other words, tacitly accept that individuals own property in their persons."[102] The recording artists were not about to stop signing contracts to produce records for major labels, even though those contracts would remain—must remain—premised on the very fiction of property in the person that dissolves the rights they say they require to avoid servitude. For successful artists, for the most part, the "exchange" of "property in the person" for record label employment is something that works very well for them: unlike most employees, only rarely do they come up hard against the harsh realities of their employers' actual legal control over their "property in the person."

Thus the paradox: the artists' claims of civil slavery and indentured servitude, while appearing outrageous, actually point to their real problem, the same problem that all employees face: the political fiction that legitimizes their domination. However, because artists place such a high value on their contracts with record companies (which involve the political fiction), they cannot or do not pursue the strongest arguments against their civil slavery and indentured servitude. They embrace the political fiction in order to accept the contract. One of the most provocative of these themes in *The Sexual Contract* is Pateman's critique of prominent socialist and feminist strands of argument against exploitation. As she shows, these strands buy into, rather than denounce, the political fiction of property in the person, and do so in ways that propagate its individualizing and depoliticizing tendencies. These critiques take as the basis for contestation the same liberal individual established in contract theory: if only contracts could be more free and fair, they suggest, then exploitation would subside. Pateman views this as a self-defeating approach. Contracts, she argues, cannot be rendered neutral; their essential function is to create or codify a relation of domination. It is this power relation that creates the condition of possibility for exploitation. She explains: "Exploitation is possible precisely because . . . contracts about property in the person place right of command in the hands of one party to the contract. Capitalists can exploit workers and husbands can exploit wives because workers and wives are constituted as subordinates through the employment contract and the marriage contract." Contract theorists' genius "has been to present both the original [social] contract and actual contracts as exemplifying and securing individual freedom."[103] It is the acceptance of this model of individuals as individual owners of property in the person that stands in the way of a more far-reaching conception of social domination. By taking this fictional model as a baseline and arguing in favor of reduced exploitation, without questioning the validity or improvability of contract, "certain current trends in socialism and feminism join hands with the most radical contract theory."[104]

What is paradoxical is the centrality to class- and gender-based social struggles of the Lockean idea that individuals have property in their persons. This insight of Pateman's is particularly pointed in the following observation:

Marx could not have written *Capital* and formulated the concept of labour power without [the idea of property in the person]; but nor could he have called for the abolition of wage labor and capitalism, or what, in older socialist terminology, is called wage slavery, if he had not also rejected this view of individuals and the corollary that freedom is contract and ownership. That Marx, necessarily, had to use the idea of property ownership in the person in order to reject both this conception and the form of social order to which it contributed, is now in danger of being forgotten.[105]

Similarly, women's use of the idea of self-ownership as a basis for their struggles to overcome exploitation and domination is also troubled along these lines; feminist and socialist critiques should not and do not require self-ownership. Too many critics make demands for equal treatment, Pateman argues, on contractual terms, "unaware that the 'individual' as owner is the fulcrum on which modern patriarchy turns."[106]

This was the problem that the recording artists and their allies could not or did not bring up: it is the contract itself, and the idea that a contract not only preserves but expresses political equality, that stood in their way. It is the contract itself that enables the domination and exploitation of recording artists just as it does the domination and exploitation of working people in general. Of course, it would be absurd to expect recording artists and their lawyers to perceive or make such an argument. The project here is not to help them build a case for their better protection under the law, or to excoriate them for not building themselves a better one. Rather, the project is to take their blinkered graspings for arguments that would explain why they should have an inalienable right against their employers as an opportunity to explore some of the very interesting ideas about work and power raised in the struggles of creative cultural-industry workers at the margins of employment.

Conclusion

This chapter has examined a collision of two arguments over work and power. On the one hand is the recording artists' argument that they should have an inalienable right to change employers at the end of seven years, as Section 2855 of the California Labor Code had assured them prior to 1987. On the other hand is the record companies' and legislators' contractarian argument that, since the artists sought out this employment and accepted it, voluntarily, on the terms that it was offered, they should just live with their vulnerability and indenture and enjoy their substantial privileges without complaining. Implicitly or explicitly, avowedly or disavowedly, intentionally or unintentionally, these arguments point beyond their immediate targets (the problems of recording artists and their record labels) and toward broader political horizons. The recording artists' argument points to a society in which people in their capacity as employees enjoy valuable inalienable rights, similar to those of citizens under democratic governments, that counterbalance the power of employers to set the terms of employment and make demands on employees. The record companies' argument points to a society in which there is no right that is not an alienable piece of property, a chip on the bargaining table to be struggled over or conceded.

The arguments of the recording artists and record companies (as well as the allies of each of the two sides) can be read as a sort of ventriloquy for two contrasting traditions of liberal thought. Ellerman labels these the "alienist" and the "inalienist" liberal traditions (although each has its origin in preliberal times): the former sees rights as bits of alienable property, and the latter sees them as components of full legal personhood inalienable in public or private. The alienist tradition dominates the political scene today, and the democratization of relations in the private economic sphere is a low priority. (This tension is often highlighted in contests over privatization—shall a certain element of the commonwealth be reconstituted along alienist lines?) The struggles of the recording artists for increased control over their labor, and the necessity of its protection through inalienable rights, opens a window onto these traditions and gives observers an opportunity to consider contrasting ways of thinking about the hegemonic employment relation. In the following chapter, however, in a struggle before the US Congress in which it behooved recording artists to identify themselves as employers rather than employees, the artists brought a very different set of arguments to bear about who they are and what they do.

Efficiency arguments . . . and
inalienability arguments are like oil
and water; they do not mix.

—David Ellerman, *Property and*
Contract in Economics

CHAPTER 5

Recording Artists, Work for Hire,

Employment, and Appropriation

Authorship and ownership are decisive principles in the music industry's
modes of accumulation, yet they exist in a curious relation in US copyright
law. Understood in common sense as an act of original creation, authorship
appears to underwrite ownership. However, in practice it often seems that
ownership establishes authorship—as a set of rights—retroactively. Because
it is the basis for the monopoly control of copyrights and claims on profits,
the authorship-ownership complex is fundamental to the relations of production and accumulation of popular music. The holder of the rights to a profitable recording has authority over the use of, and incomes deriving from, the
recording. Because the stakes can be high, participants often struggle over
the determination of who can and cannot claim the mantle of authorship; in
turn, the results of these contests play roles in future encounters. Whether a
given act of creation actually constitutes authorship in a legal sense depends

on rules that change over time. Whereas the previous chapters concerned recording artists' relationship to their labor, this chapter concerns the relations of recording artists (referred to as "featured artists" in the debates discussed below) to the rights to musical works they produce while under contract.

Authority over musical works is determined by copyright law. There are two copyrights associated with the commercial production of music: the long-standing copyright in the composition and the newer copyright in the "sound recording"—the recording artist's recorded performance. This chapter focuses on a contest in 2000 between artists and companies over the copyright status of the sound recordings produced under contract. In this contest, recording artists were opposed not only to their record company contractors, but also to their backup musicians, producers, engineers, and other creative collaborators. In the course of this struggle at the federal level, in direct contrast to their efforts in California, recording artists sought to demonstrate that they should not be considered employees but independent contractors, themselves the employers of others.[1] This episode in 2000 illustrates paradoxes at the heart of authorship and exemplifies a second form of struggle between creative workers and their paymasters at the upper strata of the entertainment industry, over intellectual property rights rather than over labor rights.

In addition, this episode brings to light further tensions and complications inherent in the history and nature of contractual relationships between working people—"creative" or not—and those who engage them. Employment and independent contracting are the two prevalent ways in which enterprises harness individuals' productive powers. In broad terms, employees are those workers deemed essentially vulnerable by common sense and law, and in need of protection. As I argued in chapter 4, these protections often appear in the form of restrictions on the freedom to contract; the law may forbid employers, for example, to contract employees without the guarantee of compensation for workplace injury.

Independent contractors are those who seem to fit better into the category of entrepreneurs. In contrast to employees, independent contractors seem not to be in need of protection and hence the law allows them to make more or less any deal they want. For example, an independent contractor is free to work in almost any conditions; he can work for less than minimum wage. The idea is that the law recognizes the independent contractor as an equal of those with whom he contracts in terms of his ability to manage risk. One useful way of looking at it is that while employees are dependent on a single employer for their incomes, independent contractors deal with numerous users of their services, limiting their vulnerability to the power of any one of them.

For most of its history, employment has been viewed as unhappy, undignified, and subservient conditions of last resort for the most desperate members of society. In his study of the relationship between employment and independent contracting in Anglo-American law, Marc Linder argues that the legal status of the employee was so degraded in the nineteenth century that it led to the "spectacle of employees' claiming to be independent contractors in order to escape the harsh consequences" of the laws governing employment.[2] This status has largely been reversed, as legislation to protect labor (including California's seven-year rule and, more important, legislation establishing workers' compensation, minimum wage, and workplace safety) has increased employers' obligations and employees' benefits. Today, for the most part, employment has shed its appearance of desperation and debility.

But the protections and the obligations that have helped raise the security and prestige of the employed have come at a cost to employers. Under the now-dominant neoliberal common sense, employers reject the twentieth-century regime of employee protection and security. As I noted briefly in chapter 3, employers increasingly shun employment as they shift toward more independent contracting as a way of minimizing obligations and expenses and increasing flexibility. Often this means miscategorizing de facto employees as independent contractors. The trend these days is for workers to fight for recognition as employees entitled to established labor protections. However, as Linder notes, there are still some areas in which the status of independent contractor is more desirable than that of employee because although the "modern social welfare state[s] condition their entitlements on the existence of an employment relationship,"[3] employment is still a subordinate, nonresponsible relationship—and, under copyright law, a dispossessive one.

"Perhaps the most prominent current atavistic enactment that protects independent contractors to the exclusion of employees," writes Linder, "is the Copyright Act of 1976." This act lays out a "default rule" of employer authorship and employee dispossession: when employees produce new, copyright-eligible works, the employer becomes the author and owner of the work, unless there is an explicit contract to the contrary. "Although the courts of appeals are divided on the issue of the scope of protection afforded independent contractors under this provision," Linder continues, "it is indisputable that the Act protects employers and independent contractors, while disentitling employees."[4] This chapter tells the story of recording artists' struggle in 2000 to construct and defend their identity under copyright law as employers and independent contractors in order to resist their "disentitlement" through an RIAA-driven legislative project of "accumulation by [recording artist] dispossession."[5]

In November 1999, Congress passed a brief amendment to American law that would have repercussions for the relations of recording artists, studio musicians and personnel, and the recording industry. The amendment, buried in a 1,740-page spending bill, changed the wording of US copyright law to include "sound recordings" in the list of "commissioned works" eligible for "work for hire" status. The doctrine of work for hire is that element of copyright law that governs intellectual property produced in the workplace in the course of employment and, in certain circumstances, outside the workplace under special commission. Since the beginning of the twentieth century, intellectual property produced by American employees—unless otherwise specified in the employment contract—has had the employer as its legal author and owner. For much of the twentieth century, this allocation of authorship and ownership also operated with respect to works produced under commission, by freelancers or independent contractors, outside the employment relation.

Sound recordings made by recording artists have traditionally been considered to be commissioned works. Since the 1978 implementation of the 1976 Copyright Act, the law has more closely regulated the authorship and ownership of works produced under commission, with only nine categories of commissioned works eligible for legal appropriation by commissioning parties. Sound recordings did not appear on this list. Nevertheless, for decades, most recording contracts have contained language defining the works created by the artist(s) under contract as "works made for hire." Contracts typically buttress this term with backstop language stating that, in any case, the artist assigns rights to the sound recording(s) to the company in perpetuity. The addition in 1999 of "sound recording" as a tenth category of commissioned works eligible for work-for-hire status changed at a stroke the balance of power between recording artists and the record labels that commission their work, retroactively validating the work-for-hire clauses in contracts going back decades. Copyright law would no longer recognize recording artists as the legal authors and proprietors of their sound recordings, because under the boilerplate language of the conventional record contract almost every major-label artist has agreed that sound recordings are works made for hire. (The legal category "sound recording"—sometimes called "soundcarrier," "phonorecord," or "phonogram"—includes the sonic expressions "fixed" in CDs, cassettes, vinyl records, and digital audio files; the RIAA's move would have no bearing on compositions.[6])

Within a few weeks of their discovery of this change, recording artists and their advocates began mobilizing, and soon a coalition was calling on Congress to repeal the law. The Subcommittee on Courts and Intellectual Property of the House of Representatives' Committee on the Judiciary held a hearing in May 2000, at which interested parties and experts offered testimony concerning the purpose, magnitude, and results of the change. Artists and their advocates argued that the change was an act of appropriation; the industry maintained that the change merely clarified predominant practice (companies had, after all, been using work-for-hire language in their contracts for years). By year's end, Congress had repealed the law. The artists' victory, however, ultimately depended on their ability to define themselves not as creative authors (as might have been expected) but as the employers of others involved in the production of sound recordings. As employers, recording artists were legally entitled to dispossess their employee collaborators, particularly their backup musicians, through the doctrine of work for hire. This chapter examines this interaction of copyright law, authorship rhetoric, and working conditions and the division of creative labor in the music industry.

This incident made it clear to artists that, although they may share some goals with their record companies (for example, some artists believe their interests too are served by strong copyright protection),[7] at the points of production and appropriation, their interests can be sharply divergent. Furthermore, the incident spurred the development of a movement made up of professional, labor, and advocacy groups, focused on representing and defending the rights and interests of recording artists and musicians before the US Congress and the California and New York state legislatures. Copyright's "millennial flip flop"[8]—the work for hire amendment and its almost immediate repeal—highlights copyright's role in the class politics of cultural production. It shows how featured artists' resistance to dispossession depended on and intensified stratification and inequality: the strategy of resistance involves shifting burdens and debilities onto subordinate others; artists resisted what they considered illegitimate dispossession by enforcing what they considered the legitimate dispossession of another, subordinate group.

The account in this chapter focuses on the paradoxical relationships between the rhetorics employed by the two opposing sides in this struggle over authorship and property. Furthermore, it considers the concept of the (non)responsibility of the employee and the capacity of this element of the employment relation to supply the conditions of possibility for the recording artists' response to the RIAA's legislative efforts.

Sound Recordings as Works Made for Hire

On November 16, 1999, Margaret Cone, a lobbyist working for the American Federation of Television and Radio Artists received a tip that a pending bill threatened to affect the interests of her client and its members. Buried in Section 1011 ("Technical Amendments") of the "Satellite Home Viewer Act," she found what she had been warned about: "(d) Work Made for Hire.— Section 101 of title 17, United States Code, is amended in the definition relating to work for hire in paragraph (2) by inserting 'as a sound recording,' after 'audiovisual work.'" Cone later told a journalist that when she found this passage, her "knees literally gave way." Regaining herself, she went to the offices of the Subcommittee on Courts and Intellectual Property "to find out how bad it was."[9] Within a few days, Congress passed the omnibus spending bill to which the Satellite Home Viewer Act had been affixed, and President Bill Clinton signed the bill shortly thereafter. Cone had discovered the language too late to ask for changes.

As I mentioned at the beginning of the chapter, there are two copyrights associated with any recorded pop song: the composition copyright and the sound recording copyright. The first copyright protects the song in its immaterial form of words and melody.[10] Unless a composition is the product of an employee or has been specially commissioned for use in a final product (like a film) that is eligible for work-for-hire status, its copyright is that of a composer, who may assign it to a publishing company for the purpose of promotion and commercial exploitation. The second copyright is the one associated with the embodiment of a particular performance in a recording medium—the sounds themselves, as captured on a record, tape, CD, or digital file.

Congress made sound recordings eligible for copyright in 1971, when it created a new right to protect owners of sound recordings from market incursion by counterfeiters.[11] Before the passage of the Sound Recording Act of 1971 (which took effect in 1972), copyright protection extended only to the author (or owner) of the composition, and the control of recorded music was effected only through ownership and management of physical master tapes (accounting in part for the importance of "the vaults" in popular music discourse). The typical record counterfeiter of the late 1960s "purchases legitimate records or tapes commercially for a few dollars each and then reproduces or 'dubs' the sound onto new records or tapes which he sells locally, regionally or nationally."[12] Copyright's "compulsory mechanical license," institutionalized at the beginning of the twentieth century, facilitated this practice. At that time, the player piano manufacturer Aeolian had exclusive rights to the production of piano rolls of almost all popular compositions. Fearing that monopolization and restraint of trade could hamper the booming new music industry, Congress established a "compulsory mechanical license" as part of the 1909 Copyright Act. Possession of such a license would allow any producer of "mechanical" reproductions (initially piano rolls, but soon audio recordings)[13] to record and distribute new versions of any previously published song. Thereafter, the agreement by the reproducer to pay the mechanical royalties (at the rate set by statute) for every copy sold automatically foreclosed the right of the copyright holder to deny (or put conditions on) permission to record and distribute the song. This right enables you to record an album of Beatles or Michael Jackson or Disney songs and release it, without anybody's permission, so long as you made the requisite payments. Because of this compulsory license, "record pirates only had to pay the composer the two cent royalty fee to be exempt from further liability under the Copyright Act"—in order, that is, to counterfeit legally with respect to copyright.[14] The burden of regulation and enforcement of this kind of gray-market activity fell to states, but only eight of them had laws pertaining to the practice. Arguing in 1971 that "this modern form of piracy . . . now accounts for one-fourth of the total sales in the recording industry," and that its continuation would "threaten the very economic health of the whole record industry," record companies convinced Congress to create the right for the owners of sound recordings to deny permission to copy them.[15] At the moment the sound recording becomes eligible for copyright, the owners of sound recordings become their legal authors, endowed with the authority to exercise the new right. That new copyright required the federal government to prosecute activities now classified as infringements on behalf of individuals who were now authors and enjoyers of a new intellectual property right, adding to the legal and economic power of the recording industry through the reinforcement of its monopoly.

Termination of Transfers

A work made for hire is one whose authorship (and therefore the control of the work, for the life of the copyright) resides not in the actual creator but in that creator's employer or contractor. To determine whether a given intellectual property can be considered a work made for hire, the law provides a two-pronged test. First, material eligible for copyright that is produced by an employee (as defined in the 1989 case *Community for Creative Non-Violence [CCNV] v. Reid*[16]), is by definition work for hire; regardless of who actually creates it, the legal author and owner of an employee's work is the employer. (This rule can be overcome by an employment contract that explicitly grants authorship to the employee; such contracts are extremely rare.)

The second prong concerns works made under special commission, not by employees but by freelancers or independent contractors. Under the 1909 Copyright Act, the law treated commissioned works as employee works and located authorship in the commissioners of the works. The framers of the 1976 Copyright Act, however, intended to make all commissioned works ineligible for work-for-hire status and shifted the law in favor of actual creators. In 1963, early in the drafting of what would become the 1976 act, "the Copyright Office defined 'work made for hire' as 'a work prepared by an employee within the scope of the duties of his employment, but not including work made on special order or commission.'" Under this definition, and "contrary to the case law interpreting the 1909 Act, no commissioned works would have been deemed works made for hire."[17] Nevertheless, the motion picture and publishing industries, learning of Congress's intentions, lobbied intensively and successfully to obtain exemptions for forms of commissioned works pivotal to their businesses.[18] These exemptions, reflecting the desiderata in the 1960s and 1970s of savvy producers of works eligible for copyright, constitute the nine legislated categories of commissioned works that are eligible for work-for-hire status:

— a contribution to a collective work, such as an encyclopedia or dictionary
— a part of a motion picture or other audiovisual work
— a translation
— a supplementary work
— a compilation
— an instructional text
— a test

—answer material for a test

—an atlas

If a work falls into one of these categories, and there is a contract specifying that the work is a work made for hire (which is the norm), then the contracting party is the author, and the actual creator (sometimes called the "natural author" or the "direct producer" by more critical scholars) has no rights to the work. Sound recordings were not protected by copyright law when the list was established and so did not come up for discussion.

The 1976 act declares that all copyrights, with the exception of works made for hire, revert to their authors thirty-five years after "transfer"—that is, after the assignment or licensing of the copyright to a record label, book publisher, or other party. This "termination of transfer" was intended to offer what Congressman Howard Berman (D-California) later called a "second bite at the apple."[19] "From the beginning of the copyright law revision process," Geoffrey Hull observes, "Congress sought to provide authors with some means to protect themselves against 'unremunerative transfers' made prior to any determination of the true value of the work"—that is, after the work had been marketed and become more valuable.[20] A young author might create and assign a work on unfavorable terms, and the licensee might be able to market and profit from the work. Termination of transfer allows the author, now thirty-five years older, to take advantage of the work's commercial success, either by renegotiating the license, licensing the work to someone else, or taking over the marketing of the work. Termination does not happen automatically; the author must initiate a statutory process of termination no less than two and no more than ten years prior to the termination date. It is, however, an inalienable right: you don't have to exercise it (your existing contract will remain valid if you do not, and you will remain the lawful owner), but you can't sell it; "the termination right is not one that can be contractually waived."[21] If you are a legal author, you can reclaim your copyright thirty-five years after transferring it, no matter what your contract says. If your production is a work for hire, you have no statutory right to that which you have created.

While the first prong of work for hire specifies the allocation of authorship and ownership according to the nature of the relationship between the natural author and the hiring party, the second regulates labor relations through the definition of certain kinds of intellectual properties. Depending on a determination of the legal status of the intellectual property in question, the natural author may be relegated to the status of employee or may enjoy proprietorship. In the case of commissioned works, copyright law stipulates that there must be a contractual agreement to the effect that the work-for-hire-eligible product will be the property of the commissioning party. However, the publishing, motion picture, and other mass media industries have so concentrated their market power that most freelancers in these fields have little choice but to relinquish their rights in order to practice their professions.[22]

Critical observers of the "millennial flip flop" saw what they called a "pre-emptive strike"[23] by the recording industry, through the RIAA, to secure sound recordings before the artists responsible for late 1970s hits started the termination process for income-generating songs. The companies and their trade association sought to enable the maintenance of secure catalogs far beyond the thirty-five-year termination of transfers period: in fact, for ninety-five years from date of first publication, the copyright term for record company corporate authors. "Catalog," or a recording company's copyright holdings, is a body of income properties of varying—sometimes only of potential—market value. Following the enactment of the new copyright in sound recordings, record company catalogs became considerably more valuable; the new copyright enabled companies to prohibit others from reproducing their recordings without permission. Made possible through the sound recording copyright, federally enforced intellectual property monopolies have enabled post-1972 catalog material to generate rivers of secure profit, long after costs have been recouped and with less risk in marketing. The commercial success of the recent Elvis Presley and Beatles "#1 Hits" albums are high-profile indicators of the general value of a catalog; there are likely to be vast amounts of catalogs from the 1970s, 1980s, and 1990s that will be similarly exploitable.[24] (Indeed, catalog has demonstrated a steady growth trajectory that is especially appealing in the context of the industrial turmoil of the early 2000s. One of the most vigorous responses of music industry institutions to the loss of revenues supposedly related to Internet-enabled unauthorized music distribution has been the rapidly expanding investment in catalog and an associated acceleration of marketing of catalog material.[25])

Copyrights granted after the 1976 act became law in 1978 are subject to reversion in 2013; experts on both sides disagree as to whether or not the law will consider sound recordings works made for hire.[26] Several cases, while not decisive, suggest that no matter what the contract says, if "sound recording" is not on the list of the enumerated categories of works, then sound recordings are not eligible for work-for-hire status.[27] The addition in 1999 of "sound recording" to the list of categories in the 1976 Copyright Act, however, decided the matter in favor of the record companies, without any hearings or the solicitation of comments from interested parties.

Following Cone's discovery of that addition, a battle raged in the pages of *Billboard*, the premier music-industry trade publication. Bill Holland, *Billboard*'s Washington correspondent, wrote over thirty stories about the issue—many of them cover stories, and many of which included interviews with celebrated musicians, officers of the RIAA and other industry organizations, and members of the congressional subcommittee. The controversy rated little attention in the mainstream press, for whom the ongoing Napster case was much sexier, but after weeks of argument in the trade publications, the chairman of the subcommittee, Representative Howard Coble (R-North Carolina), scheduled a hearing. In the following section, I recount and analyze the arguments that participants made at the hearing.

The Hearing on Work for Hire

The May 25, 2000, hearing on the work-for-hire amendment to the Satellite Home Viewer Act lasted just under four hours. In attendance were several artists as well as supporters, including the banjo maestro Earl Scruggs, who was recognized and saluted by Coble, and girl-group vocalist Ronnie Spector, "who burst into 'Be My Baby' after being introduced, to the delight of the attendees and lawmakers"—an appropriate opening salvo in an argument over the properties some artists describe as their offspring.[28] Following the opening statements of several members of the subcommittee, Register of Copyright Marybeth Peters testified that the change under discussion "was a substantive amendment to the law, not a technical amendment as some have claimed."[29] The witnesses offering testimony and answering the questions of subcommittee members were, in order of appearance, Hilary Rosen, president and CEO of the RIAA; Paul Goldstein, a Stanford University law professor, on behalf of the RIAA; Marci Hamilton of the Cardozo School of Law, on behalf of recording artists; Sheryl Crow; and Michael Greene, president and CEO of the National Academy of Recording Arts and Sciences, also on behalf of recording artists. In addition, letters from thirty-five interested parties, including members of the Artists Coalition (later renamed the Recording

Artists' Coalition)—a group formed (reportedly by Sheryl Crow and Don Henley) to represent the interests of recording artists in Washington—were entered into the record. No artists testified in support of the RIAA's position. That evening, Bill Holland reported, Joni Mitchell interrupted her concert at the Merriweather Post Pavilion in nearby Columbia, Maryland, to announce her support of the hearing to her audience of 6,000 fans.[30]

Efficiency versus Inalienability

The RIAA first argued that the new law was necessary to permit the enforcement of "anti-cybersquatting" legislation (it wasn't)[31] and then that sound recordings were already works for hire according to certain interpretations (which put its representatives in the position of arguing that "we didn't seek this change because we thought it was necessary"[32]). Finally, the RIAA settled on its last and most aggressively argued justification: economic efficiency. Rosen and Goldstein concentrated the bulk of their testimony around the prohibitive "transaction costs" that would result if all conceivable ownership claims made possible by the inherently collaborative process of studio recording could not be precluded by concentrating ownership in a single (corporate) entity. Goldstein asserted in his written testimony that, "by allowing the parties to definitively confer for-hire status on these works," the inclusion of sound recordings among the categories of commissioned works eligible for work-for-hire status "promotes marketability by making it possible for parties to eliminate an otherwise chaotic state of copyright title, centering full ownership in a single individual or entity and thus facilitating the secure and fluent transfer of ownership interests over the life of the copyright."[33] Because most commercial sound recordings are collaborative products resulting from the cooperation of many creative contributors, Rosen and Goldstein argued, without such concentration of ownership, the termination of transfers would require record labels wishing to continue the exploitation of a terminating grant to track down and negotiate a new license with each creative contributor or their heirs.

Rosen spoke about what she called "the most important point of all": "that work for hire status benefits everyone involved in the creation and distribution of recorded music—including artists and producers, as well as record labels—because work for hire status is essential to preserve the marketability of highly collaborative works like sound recordings."[34] She painted a picture of the industry disabled by the administrative nightmare promised by termination:

If highly collaborative works were subject to the termination right, they would get tied up in endless disputes and negotiations over copyright ownership among any and all of the individuals who had any colorable claim of authorship (not to mention their various heirs, assigns and employers). And almost everybody who participates in the creation of a sound recording would have a bona fide claim of authorship under U.S. copyright law—including the producer, the engineers, the mixers, the background vocalists, the owners of samples used in the recording, and others—along with each member of the group of featured recording artists. Regardless of whether the artists' representatives testifying today believe that is a proper interpretation, the fact is that "author" is not defined in the copyright law, and we're likely to see years of litigation over which creative participants are entitled to ownership rights in the work—exactly the result the work for hire doctrine was created to avoid.[35]

It is very likely that this argument seemed disingenuous to the musicians as well as the musicians' attorneys at the hearing. First, it is well known in industry circles that most session personnel work under contracts that specify what in the industry is called "participation"—whether, what kind, and how much of a claim on rights to any future income any of them might have related to the recording. At present, the norm is that the featured artist uses the money advanced to her by the record label to hire (rent) a recording studio, and hire (employ) a coterie of legally subordinate creative collaborators. Thus, most backup musicians, engineers, and some producers are the employees of recording artists.[36] However, many producers and some celebrity engineers will often work only when guaranteed participation in the form of percentages of the artist's royalties.[37] Second, where the contracting unit is a band, there is usually a preexisting agreement between band members as to how credit and ownership are to be allotted. Such a contract between band members could possibly preclude copyright law's treatment of "joint authors." The RIAA was aware of this standard industry practice, as were the musicians and attorneys at the hearing. It is likely that many of the subcommittee's staff members were aware of it too, if not the lawmakers themselves.

Why then did the RIAA hammer away at this point with such energy and conviction? The prospective loss of rights to a number of relatively inexpensively-maintained income properties (the "time bomb" in the record company vaults)[38] was indeed a problem for the industry and the RIAA. What drives the self-described "copyright industries" is a relatively constant impetus to turn intellectual property into the virtual equivalent of real property—to be held, for all practical purposes, in perpetuity with no obligation to (natural) authors or the public. Consider the words of the film industry's legendary lobbyist, Jack Valenti, who once told Congress that "creative property owners must be accorded the same rights and protection resident in all other property owners in the nation."[39] It is plausible that the RIAA believed focusing on this "efficiency" line of argument would deflect accusations that the change in law was unvarnished appropriation, to try to forestall a threat to revenue. The RIAA needs to preserve its relations with the artists who, Rosen admitted, "are the lifeblood of the record business"; this argument allowed the association to preserve some credibility with artists while still maintaining its aggressive profile.[40] The insistence on this argument nevertheless points to the politics of work for hire, on which not only copyright industries but recording artists themselves rely. Rosen continued with her unhappy vision:

> Think about the disruption that would ensue if, 35 years after its creation, each of the multitudes of authors involved in each and every track of an album could reclaim copyright ownership of that track. Each of such claims would have to be researched, and litigated. Imagine trying to reconstruct the facts on each such claimant 35 years after the fact. Rights in the recordings of a single group would differ from album to album if there were changes in band membership. Disagreement over the rights to a single track on an album could prevent the entire album from being sold.[41]

The RIAA's Hobbesian conception of human nature and its liberal conception of the role of markets and corporations in bringing justice and order to social life bolstered its warnings of the administrative hell to come. In this view, the fact of rights was the promise that those rights would be exercised agonistically:

> In most cases, every co-author would have an undivided right to license the sound recording on a non-exclusive basis. Thus, one of the co-authors interested in a quick buck could collect a one-time fee from a record distributor, preventing the other authors from negotiating a better deal with a competitor. Or one of the co-authors could grant a cheap license to an Internet music service to distribute the recording for free in order to attract site traffic, leaving the other artists with dramatically reduced prospects for future royalties. Since the traditional way to maximize commercial revenues is by granting exclusive licenses, any one author could hold

up all the others for a greater share or higher price as a condition of agreeing to join in a single exclusive license. Moreover, the absence of a central administrator and the practical inability to get all joint authors to sign a license could prevent certain meaningful deals from being consummated.[42]

Rosen assumed that joint authors were individualistic opportunists, considering only the "quick buck" and sparing not a thought for their coauthors, the possibility of collective strength, their own reputations, or the morrow. Work-for-hire eligibility thus would protect these conniving, cynical, amoral artists from themselves and each other. Additionally, Rosen's conception of the principal purpose of copyright was deeply self-interested. Granting exclusive licenses might "maximize commercial revenues," but not one of the major copyright systems in the Western world was founded expressly on such a proposition.[43] Finally, Rosen reminded her listeners that, thanks to the new Section 1011(D), this vision of the wheels of musical commerce grinding to a halt in the midst of a rash of litigation among band members and sleuthing for claimants was, after all, just a dream: "None of these risks actually exist because sound recordings are eligible for work made for hire status. And that is why the work for hire doctrine—which guarantees the continued ability to exploit the work commercially—is so ingrained in industry practice."[44]

In reality, the concept of work for hire is ingrained because of the unequal bargaining power of performers and companies. Ever since the creation of a copyright in sound recordings, record labels have included boilerplate language in contracts specifying that recordings produced under the contract are works made for hire. Record labels also customarily register those works with the Copyright Office as works made for hire, though the fact of such registration is in no way decisive for the status of the property.

Jay Cooper, the attorney representing Sheryl Crow, testified that, in almost all cases, it is impossible to negotiate that language out of the contract. Cooper was later to represent the recording artists in negotiations with the RIAA over repeal language, and then to become an officer of the Recording Artists' Coalition. Bob Goodlatte, a Republican congressman from Florida, questioned Cooper about work-for-hire language in recording contracts.

Bob Goodlatte: Would the record company agree to the deal if it did not contain a work for hire provision? . . .

Jay Cooper: No, it would not.

Goodlatte: Have you ever been able to simply strike the work for hire provision from a contract?

Cooper: No, I have not been successful in doing that.

Goodlatte: So it is pretty clear that the work for hire provision is essential to the entity with which you are negotiating?

Cooper: Again, it contains the alternate provision, which says basically that if it is not a work for hire, then this will be deemed an assignment [transfer] of copyright.

Goodlatte: Do you tell your client that you think the provision is invalid and you expect to challenge its validity sometime in the future?

Cooper: Yes, I do. . . .

Goodlatte: Did the initial contract you worked on for Ms. Crow contain a work for hire provision?

Cooper: Yes, it did.

Goodlatte: And once Ms. Crow gained commercial success, I imagine you were able to get a better deal for her.

Cooper: We were able to get a better deal for her, but the language is still in there.

Goodlatte: Did you revise or renegotiate her contracts?

Cooper: Yes, I did.

Goodlatte: Did the renegotiated contract contain the work for hire provision?

Cooper: Yes, it did.

Goodlatte: And did you try to get it taken out?

Cooper: Yes, we did.

Goodlatte: So you know that this provision is pretty important to the companies. Is that correct?

Cooper: Well, it has been my position, as well as many other of my contemporaries, that that language is not effective. . . . We were well aware of the fact that the copyright law never provided that recordings would be a work for hire and never listed them as one of the categories [eligible for work-for-hire status].

Goodlatte: But nonetheless you could not get that contract negotiated without it?

Cooper: That is correct. . . .

Goodlatte: Obviously, it means something to them for them to state that in every single contract.

Cooper: I would assume that it is their honest attempt to try and make it a work for hire, but I do not believe it has been effective as such.[45]

Cooper's responses indicates the power of the standard contract and the power that record companies have in negotiations (especially in the wake of the 1987 carve out of artists from the seven-year rule, discussed in chapter 3), as shown in the fact that even the most powerful stars cannot get this language out of their contracts. Holland later reported that the RIAA had been pursuing the addition of sound recordings to the categories of works eligible for work-for- hire status more or less actively for over ten years. He also reported that the entertainment industry, particularly the holders of substantial catalogs such as Universal Music Group, had been very heavy political contributors, especially to the campaigns of politicians on relevant committees.[46]

Goldstein's presentation of what another witness would later call the industry association's "chaos theory"—that the need to renegotiate licenses would throw the industry into chaos—was less florid and more direct than Rosen's.[47] Yet, as I suggested above, in addition to the contradiction of the chaos theory by the fact of artists' dispossessive employment of creative collaborators, there were also contradictions within Goldstein's arguments and between his arguments and those of the RIAA in general. Goldstein framed his reading of the chaos theory in terms of "transaction costs": barriers to the smooth flows of profits and transfers of rights raised by the necessity of dealing with unruly mobs of grasping claimants. I will briefly consider some of his testimony before turning to the recording artists' responses.

Goldstein argued that sauce for the goose is sauce for the gander. Work for hire protects featured artists from recording session personnel's future ownership claims. The fact that record labels seek to assert and protect their monopolies in albums the same way that featured artists try to protect their monopolies in songs should be seen as legitimizing the claims of the former based on the established and time-honored practices of the latter. There is no ambiguity in featured artists' appropriation of the product of side musicians' creative labor via work for hire. The categories into which fall the works they pay others to produce for them are immaterial; the mere fact of the employment relation places ownership unequivocally in the employers.

Goldstein wrapped up his brief verbal testimony (witnesses were allowed five minutes each) with a closing statement that contradicted some of the logic of Rosen's argument in interesting ways. "The genius of the work for hire concept," he told the subcommittee and the audience, "is to consolidate ownership in a single entity that will in the marketplace pay for the privilege of being the owner of the work-for-hire, rewarding the creative authors accordingly, enabling consumers to receive entertainment and information goods at the lowest possible cost, and advancing the purpose of the copyright system overall."[48] There are at least three problems in this statement. First, there is no payment required for the privilege of being the owner of a work for hire, separate from whatever payments might be made according to the wages, salary, or contract. In fact, the appeal of work for hire is that through it, further obligation on the part of the employer or commissioner is eliminated.[49] Second, there is no legal mechanism to ensure the "according" reward of creative authors.[50] Where there are no residual rights guaranteed through collective bargaining in a side musician's contract, or some other sharing of rights agreed to in the contract, work for hire is a complete denial of natural authors' ownership claims. Goldstein does not show how consumers will benefit under conditions of corporate monopoly, and as Rosen's earlier testimony suggests, nonexclusive licenses under US copyright law's codification of the rights of joint authors would be much more likely to result in lower costs to consumers. Joint authorship, as she implied, is governed by something akin to a "one drop" rule: joint authors, by virtue of that legal standing, without regard to how much they contributed to a given work, have what can often amount to veto power.[51] Finally, the purpose of the US copyright system is not to distribute entertainment and information at a low cost but "to promote the Progress of Science and useful Arts, by securing for limited Times to Authors and Inventors the exclusive Right to their respective Writings and Discoveries."[52] In her testimony, Marci Hamilton argued provocatively that "the commissioned work made for hire provision is constitutionally suspect. . . . [T]he Constitution's Framers chose . . . the term 'authors.' The word is 'authors.' They could have chosen publishers. They could have chosen guilds, like the Stationer's Company in England. They could have chosen the people. They had all those choices and they chose 'authors.'"[53]

Recording Artists' Response to the RIAA's "Chaos Theory"
The appearance in Congress of what *Billboard*'s Washington correspondent christened an "artist community" (and an "artist manager community") signaled a new era of representations of the interests of rich recording artists at the federal level.[54] I don't mean to make light of these artists by referring to them as rich. Despite the success of their record companies in marketing their work, artists such as Sheryl Crow, Don Henley, and the other charter members of the Recording Artists' Coalition occupy positions structurally

homologous to those of much more vulnerable artists. Unlike most recording artists, however, Crow, Henley, and their peers had the resources and allies necessary to protect themselves from certain degrees of exploitation. Nevertheless, these powerful artists had also come face to face with the appropriative power of the record companies in their contract negotiations and in their regular audits of their labels' account books, which almost invariably turned up unpaid royalties and produced at the very least what Crow called "hard feelings."[55] In any case, they could not but be familiar with the tragic stories of fallen stars such as Mary Wells, known as the "First Lady of Motown," who turned up in a Los Angeles hospital charity ward in the early 1990s. Suffering from a cancer that could probably have been successfully treated if it had been dealt with earlier, Wells was destitute thanks to unpaid royalties, despite having earned millions of dollars for Berry Gordy and Motown Records.[56]

This hearing signaled the arrival of a self-conscious "artist community" in Washington. This was not the first time that artists had represented their interests before legislators. For example, artists had participated in the long-running arguments over the implementation of the digital performance right,[57] as well as the arguments in 1998 over the RIAA's attempt to change bankruptcy law to the disadvantage of recording artists. In neither of those cases, however, did artists take center stage. Their presentations at the work-for-hire hearing would be their debut as a distinct political interest group, and the hearing's unfolding and outcome could set the tone and scope for musicians' participation in upcoming debates over online music delivery, piracy, and other sensitive issues concerning their livelihoods.

The RIAA had fired the first shot in this particular battle. At the May 25 hearing, the testimony of the RIAA's Rosen and Goldstein, the association's expert witness, also came first. Most of the witnesses' written testimony was deposited with the subcommittee before the hearing; verbal testimony, though ad libbed, was generally based on written testimony. In the question and answer session following the opening statements and testimony, witnesses spoke off the cuff. Even though parts of the recording artists' testimony were improvised, taken as a whole, it amounted to a carefully considered rebuttal to the bill, its logic, and the process of its passage. The artists' rebuttal was presented principally by Sheryl Crow, whose homespun self-presentation, as well as her representations of her career trajectory and labor process as a recording artist, contained strong claims about authorship and ownership. Don Henley later told Bill Holland of *Billboard* that "our official position is what Sheryl Crow enunciated in her written testimony in Washington."[58] Because Crow articulated the official position of the Recording Artists Coalition in her testimony (prepared, no doubt, in consultation with Henley, Cooper, and other members of the group), I quote her testimony extensively.

Crow introduced herself and, before beginning her testimony, asked that a stack of letters of support from recording artists (including REM, Bruce Springsteen, the Dixie Chicks, and others) be entered into the record. Crow then said that the amendment

> truly undermines what the architects of the copyright law intended. I was raised to believe America was based on the importance of ideas and the freedom to see dreams through. It was founded on hard work and the encouragement and nurturing of creativity. To let the looming presence of large organized special interest groups, working on behalf of film and recording companies, control the fate of the artist community is alarming. In the most eloquent words of Timothy White, who is a writer for *Billboard* magazine and my good friend, "It is a small change in terms of the number of words in the statute, but it is a very big change by potential implications when the heirs of recording artists discover they don't have a legacy they might have enjoyed."[59]

A thread of Jeffersonian republicanism runs throughout Crow's testimony. Her role, she said, was "to talk about what it means to be the author of a sound recording."[60] Following as it did the RIAA's strident presentation, Crow's verbal testimony departed from her written testimony in ways that seem to reflect a sense of urgency in response to certain of the RIAA's points. In the first part of her testimony, Crow declared: "If anyone in this room sat in a recording studio, you would see that the artist featured on a sound recording functions as the author of the work. Without the creative vision of that featured artist, there would be no sound recording."[61]

In Crow's written testimony, it is not the featured artist's "vision" that is the basis of a sound recording, but the less grandiose "contribution." "Vision" is much more mystifying and irreducible than "contribution"; moreover, "contribution" not only places the work of the featured artist on a level more consonant with that of her employed side musicians, it also smacks of "contribution to collective work," a conception the artists wanted to avoid reinforcing at this stage. In her written testimony, Crow added that "to legislate that the record label should be recognized and credited as the 'author' of the sound recording undermines the framers' intent of the Constitution and goes against my good Midwestern common sense. I am the author and creator of my work," and therefore entitled to enjoy the ownership of it and its fruits.[62]

Crow's written testimony continued with a description of "the process by which I and other music artists author our sound recordings, for the journey begins long before the recording contract is signed."[63] The authorship process, she suggested, begins with the first childhood or adolescent glimmerings of the person's identity as a musician; later amateur and professional activities serve as a foundation, which Crow framed almost as an investment in resources:

> My mother, who still teaches piano and my father, a lawyer and trumpet player, raised me to appreciate all kinds of music and to never fear the challenge of pursuing my dreams of becoming a musician. I went on to study music at the University of Missouri, where I received my degree in piano performance and music education. While teaching music in the St. Louis school system, I began playing in local bands. I also began working in a local studio as a jingle singer for commercials. Before I obtained my recording contract, I worked as a background singer, side musician, and wrote songs that were recorded by other artists. After many years of writing my own songs and playing any place that would have me, I finally was offered a recording contract. As you can see, the creative work that goes into making a first album begins long before the record contract is ever obtained.[64]

Crow's testimony is devoted to the construction of an authentically expressive self. Developed through a narrative of aspiration and apprenticeship and combined with a concept of authorship, this construction naturalizes a proprietary relation between the featured artist and the sound recording by locating the source of property in the unique personality of the author.[65] However, the authorship of a sound recording, generally understood to be more collaborative (not to mention highly technologically mediated), is not identical (at least in discourse) with the authorship of a composition (which still invokes the idea of a garret-dwelling songwriter). Although Crow invoked her authorship of compositions, she was careful not to dwell too much on this form of authorship. To achieve her rhetorical goal, she stayed focused on the authorship of sound recordings, while distinguishing her creative work from that of her creative collaborators in such a way as to naturalize her own proprietary role and assert the others' nonproprietary essence. Too great a focus on the personality as the distinguishing feature might tend to raise the question "why should the state recognize your creativity as proprietary, but not that of others whose contributions may also be understood as saturated with their own personalities?" (This question would arise a little later with respect to the relationship between Bruce Springsteen and Clarence Clemons.)

Rather than focusing on the creative dimensions of her authorship of sound recordings in a way that would invoke composition authorship, Crow located sound recording authorship much less ambiguously in the person of the featured artist as sponsor and coordinator of the recording session in which the sound recording actually comes into existence. "Personality" and "creativity" arguments could take her and the Recording Artists' Coalition just so far; what she and they could really stand on was the recording artists' legal status as the hiring party in the recording process. As Crow moved from talking about authorship as the embodiment of creative personality in symbolic forms to talking about it with respect to the proprietary creation of sound recordings, her emphasis shifted from the conventionally solitary process of composition to the social processes of producing recordings in recording studios. Crow thus highlighted the hiring and implementation of capital, facilities, technological systems, and personnel. In this shift, the legal and historical connections between authorship and entrepreneurialism—the law's de facto ascription of creativity and responsibility to capital—come into view.

"Because I produce my own records," Crow stated, "I am basically the captain of the ship and ultimately, the decision-maker. I must also decide what musicians I want to perform on each song, given the desired sound I want to attain, what engineering staff to implement my sonic vision, what studio will be appropriate (in my situation, I own my recording equipment which is set up in my home studio), and how much money I want to spend. The cost is very important because I pay for the recording of my own albums and a portion of the marketing out of my royalties."[66] The record label gives the artist an advance in the form of a loan that is to be repaid ("recouped") out of his royalties (before he receives any royalty payment). Rather than capital hiring artists, then, Crow wanted her audience to see the artist as hiring capital—she borrows money from a corporate investor (the record company) to produce the album, in exchange for a sizable share of the profits from its circulation in various markets.[67] The less an artist spends on production, the less the artist will owe the label, or the more the artist can spend on promotion, publicity, touring, and videos. Crow went on to describe what happens once the now-capitalized artist has hired all the human and technological resources necessary to begin recording:

This part of the process is perhaps the most difficult but also the most exciting. This is where I translate my vision for my music into a quality recording. To accomplish this, I communicate with and direct the engineer and the musicians. (In the case of an artist who does not produce himself, he will have hired a producer to facilitate the process of capturing his vision, as the artists [sic], on the recording. The producer would have been chosen with the artist's vision in mind and follows the creative lead of the artists [sic].) . . . Once the songs are recorded and mixed, I choose what songs will be included on the album and what the album will be titled. I then deliver the master tapes, completed, fully edited, and ready for manufacturing.[68]

Crow was at pains to show the degree to which she was in charge of a process of production involving multiple actors: every facet of production is polished to perfection with the purpose of reflecting her individual vision. Her description of the recording process ended with a rhetorical *coup de grâce*:

It has been argued that the work for hire amendment was necessary to clarify who is the author of the sound recording. There is no confusion in the record industry as to who creates the sound recording. It is the featured artists. A sound recording is the final result of the creative vision, expression and execution of *one person—the featured artist*. And, although the artist may respect the fine folks' opinion at the record label and may even solicit advice from them, they are, by no means, involved in the process of defining the music. Furthermore, any claims to the authorship [sic] by producers, hired musicians, background singers, engineers would be false.[69]

Jason Toynbee has characterized popular music making as "social authorship," a multiplicity of processes that have as their principal common denominator their irreducibly social nature.[70] For Crow and the Recording Artists' Coalition to reverse the movement of appropriation, however, they had to deny (or at least rhetorically downplay) certain social dimensions of music composition and production.

The postulates of individual self-ownership, freedom of contract, and the privacy of markets and production that comprise theoretical foundations of liberal society and provide the template of that society's rules establish this anti-social paradigm as the norm. John Locke famously bases his justification of the natural right to unequal property and unlimited individual appropriation on what he suggests is a natural individual right, transmitted through labor: "Whatsoever that [a person] removes out of the state that nature hath provided, . . . he hath mixed his labour with, and joined to it something that is his own, and thereby makes it his property."[71] But there is only so much stuff in the world; more to the point, there is only so much land. What happens once the "original appropriators" (who were industrious enough to have gotten there "first") have claimed all the common stock that "nature hath provided"? At the exact moment when all that stuff has become property, and there's no more for anybody to appropriate in that original fashion, labor is transformed from an instrument of the personality (through which property is created) to a commodity for sale.[72] In C. B. Macpherson's reading of Locke, "the more emphatically labor is asserted to be a property, the more it is to be understood to be alienable. For property in the bourgeois sense is not only a right to enjoy or use it; it is a right to dispose of, to exchange, to alienate."[73] Not surprisingly, this works out nicely for the original appropriators, who may now buy the labor of all those other people who were late to the party and whose labor, commodified, itself property, does not produce property. In this way, an economy in which some own productive property and the rest have only their labor power to sell is promised and justified on the basis of universal self-ownership (the "property in the person" discussed in chapter 4) and freedom of contract.

Copyright developed more or less in parallel with enclosures of common land in the eighteenth and early nineteenth centuries. Copyright law provides a means by which new productive property rights can be claimed and a new class of capitalists established, by making possible the conversion of effectively unlimited quantities of intangible stuff into appropriable property. As did the value of other forms of property, the value of this new kind of property depends on the construction and state-sponsored enforcement of boundaries around it. Intellectual property depends on the construction and enforcement of individual authorship rights that deny or defy principles of social authorship. Macpherson points out that Lockean property theory assumes that "labor, and its productivity, is something for which [one] owes no debt to civil society"; strong conceptions of intellectual property assume or at least imply the same thing with respect to creative or intellectual labor.[74]

To Locke, moreover, there is no difference between one's own labor and that of draft animals or employees: "The Grass my Horse has bit; the Turfs my Servant has cut; and the Ore I have digg'd in any place where I have a right to them in common with others, become my Property, without the assignation or consent of any body. The labour that was mine, removing them out of that common state they were in, hath fixed my Property in them."[75] Work for hire is anticipated and justified in Lockean theory; its enshrinement in copyright law is the basis of appropriation and alienation in the creation of culture. Eli Zaretsky frames this relation poignantly: "The bourgeoisie made its revolution on behalf of a specific property form—private property—which it already possessed. But the only property the proletariat possesses lies within itself: our inner lives and social capabilities, our dreams, our desires, our fears, our sense of ourselves as interconnected beings."[76] Under work for hire, those dreams, desires, fears, and self-understandings become the property of employers to the degree that they are expressed by employees on the clock.

Rhetorically, authorship begins in the personality; however, socially, politically, and economically it culminates and is fully certified in the hiring, organization, and management of capital, facilities, technological resources, and, finally, labor services. Authorship is anchored in the control of the labor processes and the legal structures that condition the relations between hiring and hired parties.

Recording Artists as Employer-Authors

As I mentioned above, there are two prongs for determining work-for-hire status: the fact of the employment relation (and the absence of a contract contravening its norms), and the relationship of the work at issue to the 1976 Copyright Act's list of commissioned works (and the existence of a contract specifying work for hire). Despite recording artists' treatment as employees under state labor law (see chapters 3 and 4), record company representatives did not try to argue that, for the purposes of copyright, legislators should consider recording artists to be alienable employees.[77] The arguments of the record companies and the RIAA therefore dealt with the second prong, either with respect to the creation of a new category of commissioned works (the way they had the law changed), or the interpretation of an existing category in such a way that sound recordings appeared to fall within it. However, artists usually employ session personnel, and the work of session personnel is usually (in the "majors," or the world of the big, multinational labels and their subsidiaries) unambiguously work for hire under the first prong.

Music industry professionals allied with the artist community offered testimony along these lines. Michael Greene, president of the National Academy of Recording Arts and Sciences, directly addressed the threat of unmarketability in his brief verbal testimony: "I have headed up over 10 recording studios and

produced armies of musicians over my career and I will tell you that this so-
called chaos theory the recording companies are advancing is merely confetti
being tossed into the air to hide the reality. All non-featured performers, such
as side musicians, backup singers, and engineers are hired to work on a song
with a contractual understanding through industry standard agreements that
their contributions are made without claims of authorship. This has been the
standard practice forever, and anyone who has contracted, recorded, or produced a record certainly knows this."[78] The academy, however, was ambivalent about repealing the amendment. Greene pointed out in his written testimony that "despite our strong position on the subject, we are somewhat
conflicted about our appearance here today. Our organization is comprised
of several strata of the creative and technical community within the music
industry. The Academy's constituency is recording artists, songwriters, musicians, producers, engineers and other professionals in the industry. As a result, it would be disingenuous for us to propose that in every instance the
performer or producer can enjoy the benefit of termination rights under the
Copyright Act."[79] The academy represents constituencies that will be at odds
over the resolution of the ownership of sound recordings; nevertheless, to include sound recordings in the categories of commissioned work eligible for
work-for-hire status would preclude other claims that might be at variance
with those of the featured artists.

Jay Cooper, Crow's attorney, also argued vigorously that it is work for hire
itself that makes it possible to arrest authorship of sound recordings at the
person of the featured artist. To determine where work for hire actually comes
into the relations in production, and in whose favor it actually operates in the
production and marketing of copyright-eligible sound recordings, he argued:

> We have to go to the contract that Ms. Crow and most artists sign. And
> in that contract, it says to Ms. Crow, "You will deliver this album. We are
> going to pay you in advance. You pay for all the recording costs. If you ex-
> ceed the advance, it comes out of your pocket. You will hire the producer.
> You will hire the musicians. You will hire the studio. You will hire the engi-
> neer. You will hire the mixer. You will hire all these people." So Ms. Crow or
> other artists of that nature—that is what they do. They go ahead and retain
> all these services and they deliver then a final product to the company. It is
> not the company that is hiring all these people. It is not the company that
> goes out and contracts with the producer. . . . She goes out and engages all
> these people to work. So if there is a work for hire at all, it would be by the

artist because the artist is engaging everybody that is concerned with the recording and not the record company.[80]

A little later in the hearing, Cooper was questioned by Congressman Robert Wexler (D-Florida), who was interested in exactly how the line between proprietary and nonproprietary authorship was drawn, and whether sauce for the goose, in this case, would also be sauce for the gander. He asked about the status of Clarence Clemons, saxophonist for Bruce Springsteen:

> *Robert Wexler*: Ms. Crow indicated which extraordinary artists apparently share her frustration in this process, and one of them was Bruce Springsteen. And it just occurred to me while you were reading what you perceived to be the law—I am worried about Clarence [Clemons], the saxophone player, because I love Bruce Springsteen. When I buy Bruce Springsteen's albums, I buy them just as much for Clarence the saxophone player as I do for Bruce Springsteen. Where does he come out in this deal? If we adopted your point of view and at the end of the game—if I understand it, then, at that point, Bruce Springsteen then says, "I am the artist, I negotiate, I make my deal." Where does Clarence come out in this? Does he have to follow Bruce? Where does he come out in this?
>
> *Jay Cooper*: I was a saxophone player, so I know this from experience. Clarence is a hired hand, a hired gun. He gets paid a salary, he gets paid fees. Bruce may decide to reward him with a royalty. But he is generally employed by Bruce Springsteen. He is not employed by the record company. He doesn't sign with the record company unless Clarence Clemons goes out and makes his own deal somewhere. But he is one of Bruce's side men, just like the piano player, the bass player, the drummer, and everyone else like that.
>
> *Wexler*: He is not a work for hire in any respect?
>
> *Cooper*: He may be in the context, but he may be under work for hire for the artist.
>
> *Wexler*: Okay. That is my point. If he is in fact a work for hire for the artist, and we then change the rules as you suggest we do as between the artist and the recording company, are we then obliged to change the rule between the artist and the "Clarences" of the world?
>
> *Cooper*: Well, I didn't quite finish what I was going to say. It may be a work for hire.
>
> *Wexler*: What if it is? Let's assume he is.

Cooper: There is one other intervening factor, which is that he is a member of the Musician's Union [*sic*]. When you contract with musicians, you contract with a certain employment form. The union sanctifies this relationship and he is paid as an employee just like any other hired hand on that particular record date. So it is not clear—

Wexler: So you are not advocating that we do for Clarence necessarily what you would advocate we do for the primary artist?

Cooper: No, not whatsoever.[81]

Wexler's questions indicate that he considers creativity to count toward authorship, and that on that basis he perceives something of a contradiction in the artists' position. If authorship were decisively coupled with or dependent on creativity, then only by denying Clemons's creativity could Springsteen treat Clemons the way that the record companies want to treat artists—as producers of works for hire. To Wexler, the difficulty of reducing an obviously creative sideman to a noncreative "hired gun" is striking, so he presses Cooper to clarify why Springsteen should enjoy authorship and Clemons should not. Cooper's responses make clear that the final salient boundary around authorship is not creativity but employment. (Springsteen could broach this boundary by deigning to offer Clemons inclusion in a copyright as joint author, but that would be an act of largesse.) In the view of Cooper and the artists, the employment relation is determinant of authorship, and their arguments are not those by which some creative people might declare other creative people not creative. Nevertheless, Wexler's questions suggest that he detects a lingering whiff of hypocrisy in the artists' position.

The ways in which many backup musicians are entitled to quasi-royalty payments, despite the absolute nature of work for hire, is evidence of the tenuous logic of the featured artists' assertions and implications regarding the creative work of their collaborators. For decades, musicians who record under the collective bargaining agreements of the American Federation of Musicians have been entitled to forms of additional compensation based on the reuse of their work, typically understood as a translation between formats. Examples include the syndication of a TV show in which their musical performance is incorporated, the release of a film in a new medium such as the DVD, the renewal of a TV commercial beyond its initial thirteen-week run, and the reuse in a TV commercial of a song recorded for other purposes. Musicians and then television writers originally negotiated these payments in the early 1950s "in the belief that if a program was rerun, then there was less employment for new product."[82] However, the payments also have come to reflect and reinforce basic notions of authorship. According to a veteran officer of the American Federation of Musicians, "the creativity level with musicians is high enough that even the playing of somebody else's material, the interpretation of it, is considered an intellectual property"; side musicians and their union colloquially consider their performances works of authorship. Reuse payment agreements between the union and employers are, in the perception of this union officer, "based on the fact that nobody, really, can totally *buy* someone else's intellectual property, [that] there's always a thread leading back to that original person."[83]

Employment, Appropriation, and Independent Contracting

Although Romantic concepts of authorship might have played a role in influencing legislators' ultimate decisions to support repeal of the 1999 amendment, the recording artists' successful bid for repeal (and the chance to claim authorship definitively in coming court battles over termination) was won in large part through their compelling presentation of themselves as entrepreneurial employers rather than employees. The law should define sound recordings as their property, they argued, because of their legal power to dispossess their creatively contributing but employed side musicians, engineers, and other participants in the division of recording labor. This is obviously in contrast, if not in contradiction, to their characterization of themselves as employees before California legislators in 1985–87 and 2001–2 (see chapters 3 and 4). Although this contrast or contradiction is not exactly the legal conundrum it might seem (many workers can occupy apparently contradictory positions when viewed through different legal lenses, without their positions or the perceptions of them rending the social fabric), from critical and scholarly perspectives it presents interesting and provocative features. The recording artists' complicated struggles to define themselves at different times as both employees and employers (depending on the stakes, law, and venue of a given issue) bring even more clearly to the foreground some of the problems associated with the politics of employment that arose in the previous chapter. In this section, to explain these problems, I discuss additional perspectives on employment and some of the basic distinctions between the employee and the independent contractor.

The democratic critique of employment as an institution of "civil mastery" and "civil subordination" (discussed in chapter 4) gives some very good reasons for recording artists (as employees) to fight for inalienable employee rights as limits on their subordination by employers.[84] In the struggle over the seven-year rule, an inalienable limit on the duration of recording contracts would have put a decisive limit on their subordination. It would have limited the amount of time for which they could alienate certain rights of self-government to a single employer. With that limit restored, the state would be prevented from enforcing the agreement by a recording artist to work for a record company for a period longer than seven years. But this effort also put recording artists in a paradoxical position: they were arguing for their recognition as employees in order to claim protections afforded employees by California labor law. However, as some democratic theorists argue, the employee's status is inherently subordinated, alienated, and politically derogated, and no amount of voluntarism or state protection can change this fundamental fact. In this view, to argue for recognition as employees, rather than to challenge the power of their employers to subordinate and alienate them, is to reify and reinforce the employment relation and its undemocratic principles. This kind of analysis suggests that the less people depend on subordinating employment for their livelihood, the less subordination there will be, and that society will be the more democratic on that account.

The logic of work for hire brings the subordinating power of employment into even sharper focus, with a further twist: it highlights the employer's superordinate position and associated power not only to control aspects of the employee's labor but also to appropriate the fruits of that labor. It highlights the relationship between domination and exploitation. The *Oxford English Dictionary* notes that one of the definitions of the verb "exploit" is to "make capital out of."[85] Thus, a company's ability to exploit an artist's work or persona, in Carole Pateman's analysis, "is a consequence of the fact that the sale of labour power entails the worker's subordination." You make capital out of the work or persona of another where you can make secure ownership claims; why make capital out of something if you are not sure of your rights to any associated profits? The contract is what puts one person in a position to make claims on the work or persona of another. The contract for employment enables the employer to engage in exploitation because it first creates the employer as "master," giving the employer "the political right to determine how the labour of the worker will be used."[86] Work for hire highlights this dynamic because the superordinate status of the employer allows the employer to claim ownership of the work or value created by the employee. Employment and work for hire allow the employer to alienate creative employees who might otherwise have some credible claim on authorial rights, under commonsense conceptions of authorship, creativity, and personality. Creative workers' feelings of ownership, rooted in Romantic discourses of creativity, charge work for hire with significance. The language of originary authorship that Crow used before arriving at her more structural arguments illustrates the discursive conflation of "creator" and "author." "The artist featured on a sound recording functions as the author of the work. Without the creative vision of that featured artist, there would be no sound recording," she argued.[87] And she added: "I am the author and creator of my work."[88] Work for hire splits author from creator: if an employee creates a work, then in the absence of a contract to the contrary, work for hire alienates the work from the employee-creator. The employee is the employer's instrument or medium of creation, the work is the employer's; the employer is the author and owner. The success of the recording artists in their bid to repeal the 1999 change to copyright law hinged not on arguments that creators should also be authors, but on their establishment of themselves as employers entitled to ownership based on their legal ability to alienate their employees.

Background to Employment

When Marx famously referred to the workplace as "the hidden abode of production, on whose threshold there stares us in the face [a sign reading] 'No admittance except on business,'"[89] he was highlighting the classic liberal conception of work and employment in capitalist society as essentially private affairs. Employment contracts, in this view, are understood to be enacted voluntarily, by free and juridically equal—that is, equal in the eyes of the law—private individuals. In the liberal common sense that Marx was confronting, and that is regaining its hegemonic status today under the banner of neoliberalism, no one but those directly involved in a given workplace or work relationship has any right to peer into it, let alone intervene in it.[90] Neoliberal thinkers, business people, and politicians continue to work to shield the social and political features of the private sector from public discussion and debate in the United States. The conception of the abstemious, industrious capitalist as beneficent altruist generously providing livelihoods to those sorry individuals who were insufficiently abstemious and industrious to become capitalists themselves seems as robust as ever.[91] That conception undergirds and justifies tax cuts for the very wealthiest and the derogation of everyone else.

The political dimensions of this arrangement between owners and non-owners, as well as misleading commonsense conceptions of it, remain largely unquestioned. Pateman explains that "the contradiction between lack of self-government in workplaces and its exercise in a democratic polity is not usually noticed because the question of democratization of the workplace is not on the political agenda."[92] The question "why, if the employment contract creates a free worker, [must he] 'abandon his liberty'?" does not get asked, because "for three centuries, contract doctrine has proclaimed that subjection to a master—a boss, a husband—is freedom."[93] For three centuries, relations of domination, hidden behind ideological conceptions of voluntarism, have nestled comfortably in our society's most liberal institution. There is a basic similarity between predemocratic monarchies, in which rulers governed in their own name and not in the name of their subjects, and contemporary workplaces, where essentially the same relations are the norm: "The employer governs in his own name, and is not selected by and does not represent the employees."[94] Political atavism is basic to employment. It is not just the relations of creative labor that appear as holdovers, not just the "craft"-style organization of creative workers that appears anachronistic.[95] The democratic analysis of employment discloses constitutional anachronisms and holdovers in the everyday relations of employment. The language of master and servant may have been largely replaced by that of employer and employee, and the feudal obligations of masters to servants may have been transmuted into reformist labor-protective legislation, but the undemocratic substance of the relationship remains essentially unchallenged: obey or suffer the consequences. In contrast to their appearances before California legislators where they sought protections against employer power, recording artists appearing before Congress invoked exactly employer power to secure control of the creative property they produce while under contract. The following sections explore themes of continuity and change in the employment relation in order to explain more fully the social dynamics encoded in work for hire.

The Common Law of Master, Servant, and "Free Labor"
The "free labor" at the heart of the conception of liberal society as systems of voluntary relationships is not only a relatively recent development, it also seems quite ambivalent.[96] The first century of American liberal legislation "demolished" many feudal structures with respect to politics and religion, spreading the franchise and freedom of conscience.[97] However, legislators were not as eager where labor relations were concerned. The law that covered the relations of employers and employees was imported almost entirely from

British common law, which derives mainly from judicial precedent and thus presents the deeply conservative orientation embodied in what was called the law of "master and servant" until the turn of the twentieth century. Master and servant law had developed over the course of many centuries of status-based labor traditions. Although the United States demonstrated a modern, liberal, and increasingly democratic legal system in many ways, the ancient provisions of master and servant law "were taken for granted and relied upon by the textile magnates and railroad barons in the nineteenth century, just as they had been relied upon by the landlords, master bricklayers, and wool merchants of the fifteenth century and by the ironmongers and cloth and tobacco and salt manufacturers of the seventeenth century."[98] These provisions, for example, conferred the status of criminal vagrant "upon those persons with the characteristics of being able-bodied and without other means of support." They protected the master's property interest in the labor of the servant over other claims, entitling the master to recover damages from a party responsible for any injury to the master's employee, "much as if the injury had been to his chattel or machines or buildings," and confirmed the principle that employment contracts were for labor "entire"—that is, "a worker hired for a stated job or period of time was not legally entitled to be paid for any labor performed until the job or term was completed."[99] In effect, the application of such provisions in the late nineteenth century radically constrained workers who were supposedly working in a regime of free contract and free labor.

Over the course of the nineteenth century, status distinctions that had previously accorded different rights to occupants of different social classes were replaced in American courts with "a uniform body of law that translated rights and obligations previously determined as a matter of status into implied contractual terms."[100] By the late nineteenth century, "contract became—at least in the language of the law—an organizing principle of as many social relationships as could be shoehorned into its framework of privately negotiated social relations."[101]

The ideology of contract holds that contracts are always voluntary and always take place between equals, and it thus imagines markets as power-neutral or nonpolitical (see chapter 4). But status appears to return through contract, which by assigning rights over employees to employers assigns each to distinct status groups. (This dynamic is particularly visible in the changing legal frameworks around intellectual property producing workers; "when it came to creative employees," writes Catherine Fisk, "the movement from status to contract was a movement from independence to dependence."[102]) The application of provisions of master and servant law to parties joined by modern, liberal contracts both confirms and extends employers' political power over employees, aggressively limiting the alternatives available to workers in the late nineteenth century. A provocative analysis of labor cases from the nineteenth and early twentieth centuries concludes that "the opinions in the labor decisions indicate that the judges believed that what was at stake [in labor disputes] was no less than the moral order of things, not merely the formal division of powers or the privileges of favorite social groups."[103] Because of the routine and unremarkable ascription to employees of subordinate status through a contract, liberal principles did not enter meaningfully into the workplace until the state's endorsement of collective bargaining and other labor legislation during the New Deal.[104]

Unfree Masters

However, the degree to which liberal principles entered in the employment relation even at this time is arguable. The Thirteenth Amendment to the Constitution may have eliminated involuntary servitude long before the arrival of the twentieth century, but it did not eliminate all forms of labor compulsion. The argument here is that old forms of compulsion have given way to new forms. English common law of the early modern era enabled the employer (as master) to engage in direct or personal legal compulsion of laborers through vagrancy laws (which virtually gave employers the power to conscript those without visible means of support), clauses mandating specific performance (the ability to compel fulfillment of the contract), and other forms of employee liability that have their roots in the earliest English labor legislation.[105] But an analysis of the changing terrains and conceptions of free labor shows how employers' legal power of compulsion—their power, for example, to beat or initiate criminal prosecution of workers who fail to perform—was gradually transformed and naturalized in the form of economic necessity. Employers' direct legal power to compel work "gave way to another form of legal regulation that offered workers greater formal autonomy but continued indirectly to place them at the disposal of those who owned productive assets"[106]—that is, it gave way to economic compulsion. In modern market society, in the words of James Brown, "if you don't work, you can't eat."[107] It seems to be internal need and not external force that compels people to work.

The transition from legal to economic compulsion was accompanied and assisted in cultural and conceptual registers by new, naturalistic metaphors that shifted the focus from the master's power to the servant's need. Voices from the intellectual movement driving this transformation of the concept of labor illuminate the discursive dimensions of this change. Direct coercion "is attended with too much trouble, violence, and noise," wrote a British thinker in 1786, "whereas hunger is not only a peaceable, silent, unremitted pressure, but as the most natural motive to industry, it calls forth the most powerful exertions. . . . Hunger will tame the fiercest animals, it will teach decency and civility, obedience and subjugation to the most brutish, the most obstinate, and the most perverse."[108] Another, more critically oriented German thinker of the nineteenth century pointed out that "the command of the slave owner has been replaced by the contract between worker and employer, a contract which is free only in form but not really in substance. Hunger makes almost a perfect substitute for the whip, and what was formerly called fodder is now called wages."[109] In the transition to a liberal free-market society, the traditional hierarchically ranked social system was to be transformed from a system of direct, personal, legal domination to one of indirect, impersonal, natural compulsion. In this brave new world, the subordination of people without means of their own to and by people with inherited or accumulated wealth was a voluntary arrangement, in which the choice not to starve was understood as entirely in the hands of the former.

A changing mix of freedom and unfreedom has characterized the employment relation in Anglo-American society for the last several centuries, with relations perceived as free at one time appearing unfree at another. Over the course of the last century, the formal autonomy of workers that is now the norm has been achieved through the gradual substitution of legal (or direct, nonpecuniary) compulsion by economic (or indirect, pecuniary) compulsion. Whereas legal compulsion is understood to have its source in man-made law "that authorizes or permits individuals and state officials to use physical violence or confinement to extract labor," it is "impersonal" market forces that are the source of economic compulsion. These market forces "are supposed to exert pressure in the way nature exerts pressure: If you do not work, you starve."[110] In this view, no individual whip-wielding person appears to compel others to do anything they would not otherwise do; people choose voluntarily to submit to the authority of employers on the basis of economic necessity. But the point is that both the indirectness of economic compulsion and its supposed comparative gentleness are questionable. Just like direct, personal, legal compulsion, indirect, abstract, economic compulsion has "its source in a set of legal rights, privileges and powers that place one person in a position to force another person to choose between labor and some more disagreeable alternative to the labor."[111] As I argued in chapter 3, the conditions in which such choices can be imposed are governed by law—that is, by people and institutions, not nature or the economy as some abstract, self-regulating entity. As with the line between creative and technical work in Hollywood's entertainment industries, the line between free and coerced labor is also a "matter of convention."[112] The degree of compulsion at work in different liberal regimes is greater or smaller, "but there are no logical grounds for saying that the performance of labor in one case is coerced and in the other it is voluntary."[113] The vaunted liberalism of the economic sector—in which there is no coercion and thus no politics; in which all action is undertaken consensually through the voluntary entry into contracts by juridical equals—can be understood, without posing any serious intellectual challenges, to be a matter of argument rather than fact.

Democracy and the Employment Relation

If the liberal nature of the employment relation is dubious, the reflection of democratic principles in the workplace is even more so. Pateman organizes her critique around the problem of the "political fiction" that people can somehow be separated from their labor without also separating them from their capacity of self-government.[114] David Ellerman proposes a related but differently inflected critique, sustaining a focus on problems of exploitation not directly addressed in Pateman's theorization. Ellerman puts forward a contrasting but complementary argument for workplace democracy based on a rehabilitated "labor theory of property."[115]

In standard accounts of authority in the workplace, imbalances of power in the employment relation often appear to derive from the unequal distribution of ownership of "the firm" or of "productive assets." In other words, bosses can tell workers what to do because, it seems, bosses own (or represent the owners of) the company. However, bosses' rights to govern are actually determined not by ownership of capital but by the "direction of the hiring contract."[116] This is a subtle but important distinction. "Capitalism is capitalist," Ellerman argues, "not because it is private enterprise or free enterprise, but because capital hires labor rather than vice-versa. Thus the quintessential aspect of our economy is neither private property nor free markets but is that legal relationship wherein capital hires labor, namely the employer-employee relationship."[117] Ellerman shares with Pateman a critique of the relationships of domination inherent in employment, but he explores that relationship from a different point of view. The focus on the "direction of the hiring contract" brings a different kind of lens to bear on the relationship, which helps explain the politics of work for hire.

The Rental of Persons

When the "hiring party" (usually capital) hires labor, the former is empowered by law—fraudulently, Ellerman argues—to deny employees the inalienable rights they enjoy as democratic citizens. It is widely understood that labor itself cannot be transferred—this is the basis of the Marxist concept of labor power, mirrored in Pateman's assertion that "a worker cannot send along capacities or services by themselves to an employer."[118] The employer buys not a worker's labor but a worker's capacity to labor and, with it, the control right to make sure that capacity is exercised to the employer's satisfaction. The right of a boss to fire you if you do not do the job well is one manifestation of the control right. Along with other, more mainstream economists, Ellerman understands the resolution of this quandary to be through the notion of rental: "When one rents a person for eight hours, one buys the labor services of eight man-hours (or person-hours), i.e., the right to employ or use the person within the limits of the contract for an eight-hour period." From this angle, "the labor market is the market for the renting of human beings."[119] The problem here, of course, is that "renting people treats them as if they were things."[120] Complementing Pateman's "political fiction" of property in the person, then, is what Ellerman calls the "fundamental myth" of capitalism.[121] This myth is that the employment relation creates the employee as the rented instrument of the employer. As an instrument, the employee surrenders responsibility for the positive and negative results of his or her intentional actions, including all claims on any thing or value produced while on the clock. However, this conversion takes place fictionally: "A person cannot in fact by consent transform himself or herself into a thing, so any contract to that effect is juridically invalid—even though it might be 'validated' by a system of positive law ([as was slavery in] the antebellum South)."[122]

The employment contract, in other words, is "invalid" because it attempts to do something—and is treated as if it does something—that it cannot do: transform a responsible person into a nonresponsible thing. A simple comparison that illuminates how the "fundamental myth" works demonstrates the invalidity of the employment, Ellerman suggests. Person A rents a van from Person B to commit a crime. Although A (if caught) can be found guilty,

B cannot: the rented van is a nonresponsible instrument, and B cannot be held responsible for what A did with it. However, consider the situation if A hires B to help commit a crime. In this case B cannot be excused from responsibility the way he could be when his van was used—even though, in every other way, the law considers the owner of the labor (that is, the owner and renter-out of "property in the person") to be identical with the owner of (property in) the van. In every situation in which A hires B to do something legal, the law treats B as a nonresponsible instrument. In the normal situation, A is the responsible person entitled to command and claim profits. If B (the employee) participates with A (the employer) in the commission of a crime, the former's de facto responsibility—which is fraudulently ignored during the normal course of work under the fundamental myth—cannot be avoided. At this point, as Supreme Court Justice Oliver Wendell Holmes put it, "the tortious servant emerges from the cocoon of non-responsibility metamorphosed into a responsible human agent."[123] Even though it is contrary to the basic theory of employment—to the fundamental myth—"to allow a servant to be sued for conduct in his capacity as such, he cannot rid himself of his responsibility as a freeman, and may be sued as a free wrong-doer."[124] This example shows that at bottom, our society, governors, and laws consider us responsible for our actions; the fundamental myth suspends and hides that responsibility in such a way that others may make use of us for their own ends without our noticing any mismatch between this situation and the liberal and democratic values correlated to public political rule.

The judicial principle of imputation is that people should be responsible for the positive and negative results of their intentional action. This judicial principle has an economic corollary: the labor theory of property. Of all the inputs that an enterprise purchases or rents, only labor is responsible. An enterprise can rent buildings, land, vans, equipment, and people to carry out its business, but it is a fundamental myth—a political fiction—that people can be divorced from their actions in the way that the owner of a van can be separated from responsibility for what the van does, along with the van itself, when he rents it out to someone else. "The notion of responsibility relevant to the structure of legal property rights" in the determination of who should own the products of labor, writes Ellerman, "is the normal nonmetaphorical juridical notion of responsibility that is used every day from 'the judicial point of view.'"[125] If the judicial view is carried over into economic life, especially into the private sphere of employment, then it becomes clear that "people should legally appropriate the positive and negative fruits of their labor." Regardless of the legal fictions that underlie the employment relation, people in liberal society remain, as demonstrated by the juridical consequences of their criminal acts, responsible for their actions: "The question of de facto responsibility, whether posed in a courtroom or outside, presupposes the understanding that persons act and things don't. Yet it is precisely the presupposition that is 'overlooked' in economic theory which treats both the services of human beings and the services of capital and land symmetrically as 'input services.'"[126] In law and social convention, the institution of employment not only puts some people in the position of commanding others, it also fraudulently distributes the products of labor and profits deriving from them by defining employed people as nonresponsible instruments. As the rental of human beings, it converts people into things without basic rights. The fraudulent nature of this legal myth is revealed when the employee commits a crime—his fictional nonresponsibility melts away and his actual, de facto responsibility becomes manifest.

Responsibility and the Conventions of Creative Labor

Authorship, like the commission and imputation of a crime, creates a powerful bond between the responsible person and the result of her act. The relation between the author and the product of her creative work is like that between a criminal and her crime: it has social, legal, cultural, and other forms of significance. De facto authorship coincides with legal authorship, as in the case of an artist who licenses his works to a publisher such as a record company. Authorship is opposed to alienation: by virtue of the 1976 Copyright Act's termination of transfers provision, his proprietary relationship to the works is inalienable.

Employment dissolves the worker's responsibility for virtually everything but his criminal acts. As work for hire makes clear, authorship is a claim that an employee may not make without a contract to the contrary—without, that is, his employer's approval. If criminal responsibility is a negative corollary to the inalienability of a person from the results of his actions, then authorship is a more positively-inflected one. Authorship and its definition and protection in copyright law guarantee the kind of responsibility that Ellerman asserts the employment system fraudulently denies employees. The author's right of termination of transfers at thirty-five years after the moment of licensing appears as inalienable as the murderer's obligation to bear responsibility for his criminal acts. The author's right could even be seen as more inalienable: an author's insanity or nonage would not throw responsibility into question.

By law, authors are owners; also by law, employers are authors, and employees are instruments. Struggles around work for hire and the allocation of authorship and ownership show that all creative work is not, or not simply, "ultimately irreducible to abstract value," as Bill Ryan argues.[127] Such struggles show that legal structures intervene in and condition the relations of creative work in ways that cut against simple conceptual linkages of creativity, autonomy, authorship, and proprietorship. Creative cultural-industry workers often see themselves as entitled to some rights to the fruit of their creative work. Work for hire is a way of making these workers submit to the kind of routine, dispossessive, political, and legal alienation to which most other working people have been long accustomed. It reduces transaction costs and increases efficiency, to be sure, but it requires that lines be drawn between authors and nonauthors; and between employers, independent contractors, and employees. The drawing of such lines has the effect of reifying and institutionalizing forms of dispossessive, political, and legal alienation. As the case of the "millennial flip flop" demonstrates, these lines are essentially political and historical.

The History of Work for Hire

The development of conventions and ideology of free labor did not automatically entail the alienation of employed creators of intellectual property from what they produce on the job. In fact, according to Catherine Fisk, "prior to the Civil War, no court recognized that an employer was entitled to copyright the works of its employees simply by virtue of the employment; indeed courts assumed just the opposite."[128] However, over the course of the six decades preceding the 1909 Copyright Act, courts managed a 180-degree shift in the default rule of authorship through an accumulation of incremental proemployer decisions that elaborated a new judicial notion of "implied contract."[129] No one of these cases was decisive, yet the development of contract law and contractarian thinking during this period "facilitated and legitimated a massive transfer of autonomy from creative workers to their employers."[130] This piecemeal development is significant because no one case during this period required a court or legislators to hear arguments over the allocation of ownership of intellectual property produced in the workplace and to choose, publicly and accountably, between a default position of employee or employer authorship.[131] Courts thus gradually "reallocated copyright ownership simply by rewriting the implied contract between employer and employee to include a principle of employer ownership as a matter of 'tacit assent'—rather than as a virtually inalienable right."[132] By the early twentieth century, the default rule of authorship had subtly but decisively shifted from employees to employers.

A variation of what Ellerman calls the "identity fiction"—whereby employer and employee are one person in law, and that person is the employer— "is given by the phrase: *Qui facit per alium facit per se* (that which is done through another is done oneself). This captures the instrumental role of the employee. The employer 'acts through' the employees."[133] Crow is "captain of the ship." "There is no confusion in the record industry," she testified, "as to who creates the sound recording. It is the featured artists. A sound recording is the final result of the creative vision, expression and execution of one person—the featured artist."[134] By placing the employee in "the legal role of a non-adult, indeed a non-person or thing,"[135] the employment relation not surprisingly dissolves the basis for employee claims of copyright for intellectual property created in the workplace.

For most workers in a liberal market society, even a partial claim on the product of their labor is so far removed from possibility that it never even presents itself as something to imagine, much less struggle for. What Robert Blauner called "ownership powerlessness"—the total disidentification of workers with owners and the rights that attach to ownership—"is a constant in modern industry, and employees, therefore, normally do not develop expectations for influence in this area."[136] For creative workers in the cultural industries, however, positioned at the point of the wedge of alienation, the viability of that kind of claim can mean the difference between the possibility of security and the promise of insecurity (which contributed to Mary Wells's destitution and early death), between the status of freeholder and that of precarious waged worker, between the status of *rentier* and proletarian.[137]

The Independent Contractor

An independent contractor "is somebody who works for herself instead of someone else." The US Fair Labor Standards Act excludes the independent contractor from the category of employee and thereby "deems her to be an employer"—an employer of herself, that is, as she contracts with those who desire her services or products. But in spite of its freedom from the kinds of alienation routinely associated with employment, the status of the independent contractor is uncertain and paradoxical: "Although the image of the independent contractor depicts a robust, risk-taking entrepreneur, a different picture may show a vulnerable worker with minimal bargaining power who has little choice but to accept that the risks of finding and keeping work have been shifted completely onto her shoulders."[138] Linder puts it more point-edly: "In light of the opportunities for self-exploitation available to the self-employed that are legally foreclosed to employees the independence of inde-pendent commodity producers can and does become so hollowed out as to render them de facto proletarians."[139] As close observers of independent con-tractors' economic lives point out, vulnerability, minimal bargaining power, and de facto proletarian status are indeed the lot of many if not most free-lance creative cultural-industry workers.[140]

Yet the obverse side of the coin is that they are not automatically subject to the alienated status of employment; under favorable conditions they may actually enjoy real proprietary rights over their work. And the conditions for successful recording artists are quite favorable, as their victory in 2000 sug-gests. Regardless of their classification at the level of state labor law, copy-right law does not consider them employees, and sound recordings are not on the list of commissioned works eligible for work-for-hire status. Except-ing the Copyright Act's nine categories of commissioned works, independent contracting is the political and economic foundation of, and corollary to, authorship.

Conclusion

In 1999, after ten years of trying, the RIAA succeeded in introducing a bit of legislation that redefined sound recordings as works made for hire when it was passed as part of a sprawling spending bill. This new law transformed the status of sound recordings by adding them to the list of types of com-missioned works eligible for work-for-hire status. Before this change, most observers understood copyrights of sound recordings to vest in their record-ing artist creators, by whom they were licensed to record companies. For decades, record companies had taken a "belt and suspenders" approach to securing control of sound recordings: contracts defined the sound record-ings around which the deal was orchestrated as works made for hire and also stipulated that, should they not turn out to be works for hire, the contract conveyed license to the sound recordings in perpetuity to the company. By changing copyright law as it did in 1999, Congress validated that standard contractual language, transforming thousands of recordings—many of them major hits—into works legally authored and controlled for the remainder of their copyright terms by major corporations. Most observers agree that this action was an attempt to stave off the impending reversion of those sound recordings to their natural authors, the recording artists, set to begin thirty-five years after the 1978 implementation of the 1976 Copyright Act. The 1976 act's provision for termination of transfers promises reversion, which was intended to give natural authors an opportunity to regain control of their work.

When their union lobbyist alerted recording artists and their allies to the 1999 change, they mobilized their celebrity and other forms of power and prevailed on Congress to hold a hearing on the substantiveness of the change and to consider reversing it. When the parties came together to hash it out, the record companies argued that their inability to concentrate corporate control of sound recordings under work for hire would cripple the industry. The companies argued that it would be impossible for them to sort out the heterogeneous worlds of artists, musicians, engineers, producers, and others and that the reconstruction and maintenance of clear title to profitable thirty-five-year-old sound recordings would be prohibitively expensive. Perhaps surprisingly, in response, the recording artists chose not to argue for authorship rights based on creativity, originality, or paternity. Rather, they chose to invoke their uncontested status as the employers of backup musicians, recording engineers, and producers, presenting themselves able, as employers, legally to dispossess their employees and concentrate authorship in themselves. They fought against their dispossession, through work for hire, by invoking their power, through work for hire, to dispossess others.

The apparent irreducibility of a given cultural practice—its resistance to capitalist rationalization and fragmentation—depends on historically, socially, and politically constructed structures of power. The lines between creative and technical labor, and between employee and author, are products of history. They may have much to do with our conceptions of what in culture is sacrosanct and what is not, but the relationship between each pole, in each binary, is one of mutual constitution. Rather than challenge the validity of work for hire as a general practice, which would have opened a Pandora's box, the recording artists whom Sheryl Crow represented in her testimony to the congressional subcommittee relied on the furniture of the employment relation to preserve themselves from dispossession. That is, they chose to take advantage of the historical power of the hiring party to consolidate their claims, harnessing employers' legally constituted power to certify their ownership of sound recordings by appropriating the products of their collaborators' labor.

I'm free!
To take lunch nearly whenever I want to
As long as I ask permission,
And don't take more than an hour.
—**Spot 1019,** "Wild Wild Workweek"

CONCLUSION

"I'm Free!"

This book proposes two answers to the question of why we should care about the status of the popular music performer. First, rather implicitly, the book shares with other scholarship on popular music some basic assumptions about the value of studying those who make music. For example, the status of popular music makers is worthy of study because the global popular music industry depends on their compositional and performance labor, and because they and their music are of great importance to people around the world. I offer the second, more explicit, answer in conjunction with critical conceptions of liberalism (the political-philosophical expression of capitalism) and liberal society (the corresponding form of society, in which individual freedom is proposed as the ultimate good). This answer considers the implications of this set of case studies for a critical political economy of employment in postindustrial capitalism. The answer holds that the constellation of characteristic forms taken by the narratives, social trajectories, and labor and property relations of popular music performers presents popular music as a field in which foundational liberal tensions are visibly and audibly performed by unfree masters. The capacity of popular music to function this way derives from the fact that it is a form of highly public expressive labor whose practitioners appear to enjoy rare degrees of pleasure, self-actualization, autonomy, and proprietorship, but who nevertheless appear to represent the ranks of everymen and everywomen to which most of us belong. Like the nineteenth-century husband analyzed by Carole Pateman, the recording artist is both master and servant; like the employee of the present, the recording artist simultaneously enjoys real freedoms and endures real subordination. Exploring the relationship between recording artists' freedom and subordination and those of other working people reveals analytically productive contrasts.

Jason Toynbee's observation that "people resolutely cleave to the promise of autonomy in popular music"[1] captures something quite freighted along these lines. Individual autonomy is liberalism's primary postulate and its fundamental promise, yet it is precisely individual autonomy that must be limited, alienable, and commodified in order for the institutions of a liberal market society to function. This book has presented detailed case studies that not only examine and explain the basis for and operation of popular music's promise of autonomy, but that also show how popular music brings a core liberal contradiction into high relief. In John Stuart Mill's words (cited in chapter 4), "[t]he principle of freedom cannot require that [one] should be free not to be free,"[2] but liberal freedom is the freedom to subject oneself to a master. Part I of this book focused on the ways in which aspiring and professionalizing popular music makers seek to establish and maintain a non-negligible baseline of autonomy (in line with popular music's promise), all the while negotiating with powerful individuals and institutions who are motivated by diverging and sometimes conflicting interests. Tellingly, media representations like *American Idol* and the rockumentary *Dig!* present themselves as practical guides for the successful navigation of liberal market society's signature condition: the getting of a living. Part II focused on the forms these negotiations take when successful artists become indispensable to the revenue flows of their companies, and when the laws that limit the alienability of the rights undergirding artists' autonomy come to be seen as susceptible to influence. In these interactions, the structures that underlie and set limits on popular music's promise of autonomy become starkly visible. In a way, then, *Unfree Masters* offers a theoretical analysis of two political economies of music: one in which qualified labor is plentiful and aspiring performers compete for employment (part I), and another in which the labor of stars is in high demand and employers are in competition (part II). The common dynamic is that in both situations, employers—often with the support of the state and popular discourse—pursue strategies for shifting burdens of cost and risk onto employees of all kinds: newcomers, established stars, and everyone in between.

The proposition that popular music makers "make their living by selling their services to record companies and promoters"[3] locates popular musicians in the same durable but changing political economy inhabited for centuries by working people in the English-speaking world, and in which workers around the world now find themselves. The professional or aspiring performer of popular music is a working person positioned in the same world of work, and subject to the same laws and logics, as most other working people. Like most other working people, she has value to companies only to the degree they can gain profits from her employment; she depends on some company or other to perceive her value or its promise in order to be hired and to earn. Like most other working people, she says to prospective employers, "exploit me please." Yet the position of the mass-mediated popular music performer in this ordinary, shared world of work is extraordinary. She is at once a public symbol of the outer limits of autonomy and proprietorship possible in work and an object of aggressive forms of contractual control and subordination.

A central argument of this book has been that, in this paradoxical extremity of heightened freedom and domination, the popular music performer, especially the successful one, presents a limit case of work in liberal market society. The situations of Courtney Love, Patti Austin, Don Henley, Sheryl Crow, and their cohort of stars; those of the subordinate ranks of middling acts like the Dandy Warhols and the Brian Jonestown Massacre; and baby acts such as those young *American Idol* wannabes bring to light primary themes in our society's dominant institutions and ideologies. The struggles and strivings of these music makers illuminate relations of authority and property that are rooted in the historical and political foundation and the philosophical heart of liberal society, relations that condition the lives of most individuals not born into wealth. They illustrate the idea that capital is not a thing—not an accumulation of goods or wealth—but a relation: the separation of people from the means of subsistence. Those of us without independent wealth depend on others—employers—to give us access to the means of making a living so that we can survive. The exertions of the music makers studied here show how paid work and upward social mobility require us to navigate complex power relations, to deal with employers' rights to make demands on us (and their efforts to relieve themselves of obligations to us). Studying their exertions reminds us that we give up basic political and authorial rights when we enter the workplace, becoming less than full legal persons. The accounts presented here have drawn on political-theoretical analyses that suggest that "liberal democracy," if not exactly an oxymoron, is a contradictory concept whose load of assumptions must be clarified if its use is not to further confuse the discussion or issues at hand. A society in which we are compelled to give up democratic rights and freedoms in order to gain access to the means of making a living may have some democratic aspects but it is far from fully democratized.

The relationship of work and freedom is now coming back into focus in the face of a worldwide economic crisis and rates of unemployment not seen since the 1930s, during the Great Depression. In this context, work and the capacity to earn a living, the power of employers to grant or withhold access to the means of making a living, and their power to set the terms on which access will be granted, have become matters of desperate concern for growing numbers of people. Rather than acting to provide employment and support for vulnerable individuals and social groups, however, "policy makers are catering almost exclusively to the interests of *rentiers*—those who derive lots of income from assets, who lent large sums of money in the past, often unwisely, but [who] are now being protected from loss at everyone else's expense."[4] *Rentiers*, to clarify the point, derive income not from work (or from producing and selling products or services) but from rent. This category includes, obviously, landlords who rent out property and investors who rent out capital, but also the conglomerates that hold composition and sound recording copyrights, as well as those songwriters and recording artists who hold copyright on their valuable compositions and sound recordings. "Everyone else" includes not only working people but also conventional capitalists who derive income not from rents but from systems that depend on the employment of others. (This tendency is perfectly illustrated in the contemporary transformation of the music industry: more and more resources and efforts are being expended on the capture and control of intellectual property rights and licensing opportunities, as music industry layoffs continue and talent rosters remain relatively thin.) Capitalism itself appears to be undergoing an epochal transformation as financial and industrial capital differentiate and diverge. Some observers see a burgeoning neofeudalism in this divergence and the gargantuan political and economic power of *rentiers*—not only over working people, but over employers and states.[5] The financialization of the economy, whereby an increasing percentage of the world's profits and economic growth come from rents and interest rather than investment in industries and sectors that require employees and hence produce opportunities to earn livings, indeed represents an epochal transformation in market society. With the exception of Iceland—whose citizens decided by referendum to default on the staggering debt accrued in the run-up to the 2008 economic crisis—few nations or regions have been willing to confront this change head on.

Despite the trend toward financialization, businesses around the world still have vast numbers of employees, and the high levels of unemployment associated with financialization have unsettling consequences for those employees. In this context, the existing trends of individualization and casualization of work have become exacerbated: increased competition for jobs enables employers to offer less and less in exchange for the time, effort, and subordination of working people. More and more people are in the position to understand intimately the implications of a quip made by George Frayne, a member of the band Commander Cody and the Lost Planet Airmen: "The only thing worse than selling out . . . is selling out and not getting bought."[6]

Frayne's observation provides a point of comparison to the situations of those artists who not only "get bought" but who are themselves able to achieve *rentier* status through the achievement and careful management of success on the order of Negus's "rock aristocracy."[7] The continuum between these poles is a terrain of struggle, and to travel from one end to the other is to exercise social mobility on a striking scale: the value of one's performance labor changes, and so does one's relationship to the compositions and recordings (and other forms of intellectual property) that, in circulation, generate rental income. Appearing as a social role or type that encompasses this range of statuses, the popular music performer thus poses a political and economic conundrum: he is neither fish nor fowl, neither wave nor particle. Marc Linder asks: "What . . . is the categorical difference between one who sells—and has nothing else to sell but—his labor power, and one who contracts to sell the product of his labor? . . . What distinguishes someone who appears, depends, and takes all his risk on the labor market from someone whose livelihood hinges on a nonlabor commodity market?"[8] What is the difference, in other words, between a working person and a capitalist, or between a proletarian and an entrepreneur? Recording artists pose a paradoxical answer to this question because they do and are both. When viewed from the perspective of state labor law and their record contracts, they are (however counterintuitively) sellers of labor power in the form of recording services, bound to companies through exclusive, long-term, assignable employment contracts. When viewed from the point of view of federal copyright legislation, they are independent, proprietary commodity producers. In this dual manifestation, they could be called, following Engels's typology, "small masters"—they are "neither real proletarians, since they partially live on the labor of the apprentices, and sell not labor but the finished product, nor real bourgeois, since it is still in the main their own labor that maintains them."[9] In other words, they require the labor of their employed (and therefore politically, legally alienated) backup musicians and others, yet their own labor is necessary to the finished product, which they appear to sell through their licensing of it to their record company paymasters.

Successful recording artists are not exactly employees, not exactly partners, not exactly independent contractors, not exactly suppliers of inputs. Yet one thing is clear: despite the impossibility of assigning them, finally, to any one category, they remain subject to the superior market power of the monopsonistic league of buyers of their services and products. Sheryl Crow, Don Henley, Courtney Love, and others have made their employers hundreds of millions of dollars, and they have done well for themselves, too. But even at the height of their power, they remain subject to the still more powerful multinational conglomerates who hold their contracts and whose influence on lawmakers is more formidable. The success of stars like these often has much to do with the ways companies market their artistic autonomy, as well as with consumers' awareness and valuation of it. Yet for all their real autonomy and social and psychological dealienation, they remain vulnerable to forms of contractual (and therefore legally consensual) alienation that make up the most durable elements of the ancient relationship between master and servant.

Scholars have been arguing over the specificity (or specificities) of creative cultural work for decades, seeking to articulate what exactly it is about this kind of work that sets it apart from other kinds. I discuss some of these arguments in the introduction, where I suggest that some of the characteristic themes that emerge in this scholarship indicate an essential Janus-facedness to cultural work. Scholars perceive in cultural labor both atavistic and prefigurative elements, drawing readers' attention to archaic holdovers and new models. Yet provocative homologies of the political and economic status of recording artists—such as Engels's description of "small masters"—frequently pop up in legal, historical, and economic literature, pushing us to reconsider the scholastic and political value of debate over creative cultural work's specificities.

In Max Weber's taxonomy of pre-twentieth-century nonemployee workers, featured artists such as those discussed in this book would rank near the peak of independence, plausibly finding their opposite numbers in a group of "artisans producing for the bespoke trade" who "have disposition over raw materials and tools," known as *verlegte Preisworker* (Artisan Outworkers)." These artisans "produce to order for an entrepreneur, who monopolizes their labor power."[10] The entrepreneur's ability to monopolize in this way "often resulted historically from artisans' being indebted to entrepreneurs for their lack of access to the export trade."[11] This is a striking parallel to the situation of early-career major-label recording artists under long-term contracts, who exchange exclusive rights to their labor and its products for corporate entrepreneurs' access to and influence in the mass market. New artists typically owe hundreds of thousands of dollars that they have received as advances (which bankruptcy law looks on as essentially the equivalent of debts). This kind of family resemblance, linking statuses across social, historical, and political gulfs, has provoked some of this book's investigations and arguments about the relationship of creative cultural work to other, more mundane forms of work. Homologies and comparisons such as this, in other words, support the conceptual reintegration of creative workers in the cultural industries into the social division of labor.

The developing interest in labor on the part of cultural-industries scholars is exciting. However, in the context of economic crisis and attacks on worker (and civil and human) rights in the name of austerity and economic recovery, we must consider an alternate center of gravity. Instead of concentrating solely on the contradictions of the art-capital relation, this book has proposed a focus on a critical conception of the contradictions of the democracy-liberalism relation—or, more precisely, the democracy-employment relation—of the kind developed by some of the theorists discussed herein. The rationale is quite simple: the project of democratization involves "reducing subordination and creating a more democratic society."[12] Democratization thus involves enhancing the ability of individuals to say no to relationships desired, and commands issued, by others. But, as I noted in chapter 5, in James Brown's words, "you got to have a job: if you don't work, you can't eat."[13] Without income-producing wealth of your own, there are few options other than to subject yourself to the commands of others in order to survive. Subordination is the lot not only of employees but also of independent contractors who lack the market power to make equitable deals with the buyers of their services or products, and thus the lot of most creative workers as well as most workers throughout society.

What sets creative cultural-industry workers apart from working people in other more mundane sectors are differences not of kind but of degree. On the political continuum, creative workers often find themselves much further from the pole of subordination and much closer to the pole of democratic participation than most other working people. This insight is a political refraction of more familiar social-scientific conceptions of creative workers' exceptional autonomy. It is offered as a general assessment, not a hard and fast rule. The insight reflects the conviction that many of the conditions of creative cultural work combine to democratize it in meaningful (if incremental) ways relative to other forms of work. However, the distinctions are quantitative rather than qualitative, in my view. The public visibility and audibility of creative workers' labor processes and authority relations (particularly those of stars), their reduced social-psychological alienation, and the potential for many of them to enjoy legal or collectively bargained rights regarding the disposition of their creative works and associated incomes translate into greater degrees of self-determination and participation in workplace governance, within rather than outside the structure of liberal employment.

Cultural-industries scholarship may be correct in attributing creative workers' unusual autonomy to cultural capitalists' need for an uninterrupted stream of new cultural texts, but this, to my mind, is an epiphenomenal point. To study how creative workers struggle for that autonomy is to learn about the ways in which employers seek—and often manage—to exercise and enhance their power to control and dispossess even the most autonomous and proprietary workers. To study the themes, features, and details of these struggles is to learn about the bases for more widespread claims against employer power. David Hesmondhalgh suggests that studies of cultural production ought to "assess the degree to which cultural production is organized in a socially just manner."[14] The study of work in the cultural industries undertaken with this priority as a lodestone "may encourage the formation of partnerships with organizations representing the interests of often exploited staff and build bridges between the goals of university researchers and nonuniversity activists."[15] By bringing the study of cultural work more in tune with critical perspectives on the structures and politics of employment in liberal society, *Unfree Masters* seeks to further these goals of assessment, dialogue, and progressive social change.

The employment contract is not the simple bargain imagined by most economists, politicians, and pundits (in which I give you my X in exchange for your Y). This is because, as Carole Pateman points out (as noted in chapter 5), no worker can "send along capacities or services by themselves to an employer," as if they were discrete, alienable items being exchanged. "A disembodied piece of property is not what is required," she writes; "the employer must also have access to the knowledge, skills, and experience of the worker if the capacities are to be used as the employer desires."[16] The fact that some sets of skills and attributes are simultaneously so valuable and so difficult to find substitutes for that their bearers enjoy considerable privileges should not obscure another fact: that the system of value that creates this ranking is itself a human, historical creation. It is a historical anomaly that the popular music performer can discover herself to be a valuable mechanism of entertainment industry accumulation on a global scale, and a target of corporate capture and control at the same time. Prior to the development of commercial mass media, the status of such performers' skills and abilities—as well as the widespread perception of them as members of servant classes—was not that different from those of other laboring people. In fact, in some European regions during the late medieval and early modern period, singers, musicians, and other performers were of very low social value and status.[17] But just as their historically marginal status has much to teach us about the contours and limits of economic and cultural systems in the past, the marginal status of present-day popular musicians enables them to serve as a lens through which we may perceive otherwise obscure truths about our own economic and cultural systems. Today, what recording artists (and other creative workers in the cultural industries) have to teach us about new models of work is not necessarily that we should behave more like artists, but that we should embrace flexibility and total self-responsibility and quit making demands on employers, the state, and each other. Rather, what I hope we take from their mass-mediated and state-archived social relations, experiences, and arguments are intellectual tools that can help us (citizens, scholars, working people, creative people—everyone) to learn more about how to perceive opportunities for and to argue for "reducing subordination and creating a more democratic society." What I hope we take from their stories and struggles are tools with which we can begin to pry open, enlarge, and enter the magic circles of autonomy and participation currently inhabited by successful recording artists and other creative workers in the cultural industries, and to reject the vulnerability that numerous state and corporate actors want to impose on us.

NOTES

Introduction: Popular Music and (Creative) Labor

1. Davidov, "The Three Axes of Employment Relationships," 380. As work fragments into a wide range of increasingly complicated relationships between suppliers and users of labor, "employment" as a clear-cut sociological and legal category describes a shrinking number of those relationships. And it is precisely that clear category that entitles its members—shrinking though their numbers may be—to benefits and protections like unemployment insurance and workers' compensation. Nevertheless, this book's political concern with work has mainly to do with introducing aspects of and perspectives on it that are rarely addressed outside of specialist literatures. For that reason, despite the rapid proliferation of new forms and institutions, the considerations here remain somewhat simplified.

2. Quoted in Macpherson, *The Life and Times of Liberal Democracy*, 48.

3. Under the heading of the "360 deal," new developments widen the scope of the contract beyond recording to include touring, public appearances, and other forms of performer labor and income. See Karubian, "360 Deals"; Stahl and Meier, "The Firm Foundation of Organizational Flexibility."

4. Pateman, *The Sexual Contract*, 142.

5. Harvey, *A Brief History of Neoliberalism*, 5.

6. See e.g., Ouellette and Hay, *Better Living through Reality TV*.

7. In the chapters to follow I refer frequently to the neoliberalizing society and economy as it forms a critical backdrop to the analyses offered herein. While I use varying terms to refer to this broad social transformation in order to inflect a given invocation with a particular thrust (e.g., postindustrial, postwelfare, deinstitutionalized, neoliberal), the principal themes are those illuminated by political economists and sociologists of culture: that transformations of markets and institutions are necessarily accompanied by and enabled through transformations in cultural conceptions and values having especially to do with work and the working self. These linked perspectives are exemplified in the work of David Harvey and Richard Sennett, respectively. See Harvey's *A Brief History of Neoliberalism* and Sennett's *The Culture of the New Capitalism*.

8. Blauner, *Alienation and Freedom*, 15.

9. Ibid., note 1.

10. Ibid., 52. See also Macpherson, *Democratic Theory*, 4–10, and *The Life and Times of Liberal Democracy*, chap. 3.

11. Hesmondhalgh, *The Cultural Industries*, 2nd ed., 199.

12. Miege, *The Capitalization of Cultural Production*, 78.

13. Ibid., 29. See also Ross, "The Mental Labor Problem," 6–7.

14. Hesmondhalgh, *The Cultural Industries*, 2nd ed., 199.

15. Ibid., 6.

16. Employment here is opposed to independent contracting. See the discussion of these forms and associated citations in chapter 5.

17. See also Negus's brief but illuminating discussion in *Producing Pop*, 149–50.

18. Toynbee, "Fingers to the Bone or Spaced Out on Creativity?," 39–40.

19. Toynbee, *Making Popular Music*, 6.

20. Toynbee, "Fingers to the Bone or Spaced Out on Creativity?," 44. In the early 21st century, musicians' economic independence is threatened by the terms of the emerging "360" or "multiple rights" deal. Under this new form of recording contract, a musician signs away percentages and sometimes control of all her incomes, recording as well as non-recording related. The contract thus becomes an encirclement that can constrict access to markets for skills and reputations, radically increasing performers' vulnerability and dependence. See Stahl, "Primitive Accumulation, the Social Common, and the Contractual Lockdown of Recording Artists at the Threshold of Digitalization"; Stahl and Meier, "The Firm Foundation of Organizational Flexibility: The 360 Contract in the Digitalizing Music Industry."

21. Toynbee, "Fingers to the Bone or Spaced Out on Creativity?," 44.

22. Keightley, "Reconsidering Rock," 134.

23. Ibid., 45. Employer subsidy through employees' external sources of income has a long history under the guise of "self-provisioning," whereby members of a nascent working class resisted full integration into wage labor through their production—

through gardening, for example — of much of what they needed to get by. As Michael Perelman explains, however, "many agents of capital soon recognized that household labor could serve a useful purpose once workers were engaged in wage labor. Capital could use the household economy to provide for some of the workers' needs. In this way, household production could allow money wages to fall below subsistence level, thus raising the rate of surplus value" (*The Invention of Capitalism*, 104).

24. Toynbee, "Fingers to the Bone or Spaced Out on Creativity?," 50.

25. Keightley, "Reconsidering Rock," 134.

26. Orren, *Belated Feudalism*.

27. Curtis, *Your Future in Music*, 9.

28. Miege, among others, makes similar points: insecurity is based on the industries' abilities "at any time to call upon the 'pool' of artistic talent" (*The Capitalization of Cultural Production*, 45), "the conditions of employment of artists are among the worst and their levels of remuneration are very low" (89), and "salaried work remains the exception in the cultural industries" (91). And Hesmondhalgh notes: "Creative workers . . . trade in financial reward and security for creative autonomy" (*The Cultural Industries*, 1st ed., 167).

29. M. Jones, "The Music Industry as Workplace," 148.

30. Stephanie Bunbury, "Rock Gone Wild." *The Age*, April 10, 2005. www.theage.com.

31. Attali, *Noise*, 31, 41.

32. Lash and Urry, *Economies of Signs and Space*, 123.

33. Sennett, 10.

34. Ibid., 10.

35. Ibid., 12.

36. Sennett, *The Culture of the New Capitalism*, 5.

37. Menger, *Portrait de l'Artiste en Travailleur*, 10 (translation by Jane Stahl).

38. This critical view is shared by Andrew Ross (see, for example, "The Mental Labor Problem") and Angela McRobbie (see, for example, "Clubs to Companies").

39. Deuze, *Media Work*, 10–11.

40. Ibid., 22–23.

41. Ibid., 7.

42. "We do not form or join unions anymore," according to Deuze. "We simply move to a different area, city, or country when we become dissatisfied with our working conditions" (ibid., 8). The "we" that Deuze constantly refers to in his book is not everybody, though he never makes clear exactly who he means.

43. Briefs, *The Proletariat*, 39.

44. Banks, *The Politics of Cultural Work*, 95.

45. Ibid., 99–100.

46. Ibid., 4, 167, 184–85.

47. Ryan, *Making Capital from Culture*; Hesmondhalgh, *The Cultural Industries*, 2nd ed., especially 12–15.

48. Miege, *The Capitalization of Cultural Production*, 33.

49. Writing about practices of subcontracting that are not widespread in the relations of commercial musical production under investigation here, Andrew Ross holds that "Labor history is full of vicious little time warps, where archaic or long foresworn practices and conceptions of work are reinvented in a fresh context to suit some new economic arrangement" ("The Mental Labor Problem," 12).

50. Faulkner, *Hollywood Studio Musicians*, 6.

51. Ryan, *Making Capital from Culture*, 40.

52. Hesmondhalgh, *The Cultural Industries*, 2nd ed., 67.

53. Banks, *The Politics of Cultural Work*, 31.

54. Quoted in Negus, *Producing Pop*, 140.

55. Miege, *The Capitalization of Cultural Production*, 67.

56. Ibid., 81.

57. Ibid., 40–41.

58. Jameson, "Marxism and Historicism," 68.

59. Ibid.

60. Ibid., 69.

61. Jameson, *Postmodernism*, 307.

62. Ibid.

63. The determination of who is and who is not an employee (and, complementarily, an employer) is not made by contract or defined by the persons or institutions involved in the contract. Rather, it is a matter of fact determined by a number of criteria (which differ in different national and sectoral arenas) as applied, for example, by judges in the form of judicial "tests." See Davidov, "The Three Axes of Employment Relationships."

64. Rubin, *Essays on Marx's Theory of Value*, x (emphasis in original).

65. Blauner, *Alienation and Freedom*, chapter 2.

66. Banks, *The Politics of Cultural Work*, chapter 3.

67. Ibid., chapter 5.

68. Pateman, *The Sexual Contract*, 7.

69. Perhaps this is what Banks means in his formulation of "the forces of art," which he sees as arrayed against those of "commerce" (*The Politics of Cultural Work*, 8). See also Stahl, "Cultural Labor's 'Democratic Deficits.'"

70. As Michael Burawoy puts it, "too little separation" of conception from execution "threatens to make surplus transparent" (*The Politics of Production*, 49).

71. Hesmondhalgh writes that the "combination of loose control of creative input, and tighter control of reproduction and circulation constitutes *the distinctive organizational form of cultural production during the complex professional era*. The form developed in the early twentieth century, persisted and became much more widespread" (*The Cultural Industries*, 1st ed., 56, italics added).

72. Huws, "The Spark in the Engine."

73. Weir, *Singlejack Solidarity*, 187.

74. Ellerman, *Property and Contract in Economics*, 106.

75. Taylor, *The Ethics of Authenticity*, 62.
76. Toynbee, *Making Popular Music*, x–xi.
77. Curtis, *Your Future in Music*, 10.

Part I: Representation

1. Meizel, *Idolized*.
2. Sennett, *The Culture of the New Capitalism*.
3. Rousseau, *The Social Contract and Discourses*, 90.

Chapter 1: American Idol and Narratives of Meritocracy

1. *American Idol*, September 4, 2002. For more on *Idol*'s reverential dimensions, see Katherine Meizel's "A Singing Citizenry." The first season had two hosts, Seacrest and Brian Dunkleman (a stand-up comic). Seacrest often toes the reverential line; Dunkleman, who was often given to cynical and sardonic reflections on the nature of the contest, judges, audience, and contestants, did not rejoin the show for the second or any subsequent seasons.
2. Ratings declined slightly in 2009 and 2010, but the program has remained in the top three since 2003.
3. Quoted in Bill Carter, "Fox Mulls How to Exploit the Mojo of 'American Idol,'" *New York Times*, May 23, 2003.
4. Meizel, *Idolized*, 28.
5. See Fairchild, *Pop Idols and Pirates*.
6. Dyer, "*A Star Is Born* and the Construction of Authenticity," 137.
7. This binary approach to *American Idol*'s modes of social sorting and rhetoric is related (though not entirely homologous) to Nick Couldry's perception in *Big Brother* of what he calls "rituals of incorporation" and "rituals of vilification" ("Teaching Us to Fake It," 96).
8. See Carla Hay, "'American Idol' Weds Reality TV and Music," *Billboard*, August 3, 2002.
9. Fred Bronson, "Chart Beat," *Billboard*, September 21, 2002.
10. Hay, "'American Idol' Weds Reality TV and Music."
11. For a helpfully thorough critical introduction to neoliberalism, see Harvey, *A Brief History of Neoliberalism*.
12. Hendershot, "Belabored Reality," 244.
13. Ouellette and Hay, *Better Living through Reality TV*, 31.
14. Hearn, "Reality Television, *The Hills*, and the Limits of the Immaterial Labour Thesis," 66. See also Raphael, "The Political Economic Origins of Reali-TV."
15. Hearn, "Reality Television," 71.
16. Couldry, "Teaching Us to Fake It," 86.
17. Ouellette and Hay, *Better Living through Reality TV*, 127.

18. It is, obviously, about producing new music audiences, too. See Lipsitz, *Footsteps in the Dark*, chapter 1; Fairchild, *Pop Idols and Pirates*, chapter 5.

19. Forman, *One Night on TV Is Worth Weeks at the Paramount*, 267, 261. Interestingly, relations between music and television industries were ambivalent from their earliest linkages. As Ted Mack, a talent show host, told a tap-dancing violinist contemplating her attachment to her day job, "I have to tell you the truth, it's a pretty precarious business" (quoted in ibid., 269).

20. See Meizel's illuminating discussion of amateurism and professionalism in *American Idol* in *Idolized*, 28–30.

21. Ibid., 2.

22. This is Ouellette and Hay's term (*Better Living through Reality TV*, 127).

23. See Fairchild's *Pop Idols and Pirates* for more on how the music industry is struggling to preserve the value of its familiar commodities while experimenting with new forms.

24. Jameson, *The Political Unconscious*, 85.

25. Jameson, "Reification and Utopia in Mass Culture," 130–48.

26. Sennett, *The Culture of the New Capitalism*, 46.

27. *American Idol*, September 3, 2002.

28. Caryn James, "On 'Idol,' the Only Losers Are the Audience's Ears," *New York Times*, September 1, 2002.

29. Regev, "Producing Artistic Value." See also Bourdieu, *The Field of Cultural Production*.

30. Regev, "Producing Artistic Value," 87.

31. Matthew Gilbert, "'Idol' Has the Crass to Make It Must See," *Boston Globe*, September 4, 2002.

32. My analysis here departs from Meizel's discussion of authenticity in *American Idol*, which considers more musicologically relevant themes such as song selection and performance style (*Idolized*, 51–80).

33. Andrejevic, "The Kinder, Gentler Gaze of Big Brother."

34. Ibid., 266.

35. See also Negus's useful discussion in *Producing Pop*, 69–79.

36. Zanes, "Too Much Mead?"

37. Bendix, *In Search of Authenticity*, 7.

38. Gamson, *Claims to Fame*, 15. See also Gamson, *Claims to Fame*, 28–39, and his later discussion of "production awareness" (142–71).

39. Forman, *One Night on TV Is Worth Weeks at the Paramount*, 261.

40. Meizel, "Making the Dream a Reality Show," 477.

41. *American Idol*, May 21, 2003.

42. Hendershot, "Belabored Reality," 246.

43. In later seasons, such home visits were restricted to the last few weeks of each season. However, other aspects of contestants' lives (such as their church and family) still appear throughout the season.

44. *American Idol*, July 23, 2002. In seasons 6, 7, and 9, in an event called "American Idol Gives Back," the Fox network and several of the program's advertisers donated funds to a number of relief organizations (Meizel, *Idolized*, 201–6). See also Ouellette and Hay, *Better Living through Reality TV*, 32–62.

45. In later seasons, these vignettes of contestants interacting with and in the real world were superseded by a weekly Ford video. These productions—which sometimes appear modeled on segments from *A Hard Day's Night* or *The Monkees*—often show contestants interacting in cute, friendly ways (riding in Ford cars together, running from crazy fans together, and so on).

46. *American Idol*, August 27, 2002.

47. Ibid., September 4, 2002.

48. A charge leveled by critics of television cartoons that featured and promoted children's toys. See Hendershot, *Saturday Morning Censors*, 96.

49. Lipsitz, *Time Passages*, chapter 5.

50. Simon Head's characterization of the economic structure of neoliberalism. Head, *The New Ruthless Economy*.

51. Dyer, "*A Star Is Born* and the Construction of Authenticity."

52. Leach, "Vicars of 'Wannabe.'"

53. Tregoning, "'Very Solo.'"

54. *American Idol*, June 11, 2002.

55. But see Meizel's *Idolized* for nuanced discussions of racialized, sexualized, and gendered dimensions of the program.

56. See Young, *The Rise of the Meritocracy*; Lemann, *The Big Test*.

57. Miller, *Humiliation*, 142.

58. Ibid., 144.

59. *American Idol: The Best and Worst of American Idol*.

60. Miller, *Humiliation*, 61.

61. Ibid., 50.

62. Ibid., 142–43.

63. Stahl, "Authentic Boy Bands on TV?"

64. *American Idol: The Search for a Superstar*.

65. Fine, Mortimer, and Roberts, "Leisure, Work and the Mass Media," 238.

66. Ibid.

67. Ellerman, "*Translatio* versus *Concessio*," 462.

68. Sennett, *The Corrosion of Character*. See also Barley and Kunda, *Gurus, Hired Guns, and Warm Bodies*.

69. Forman, *One Night on TV Is Worth Weeks at the Paramount*, 259–60.

70. Lusted, "The Glut of the Personality," 253 (emphasis in original).

71. Wallulis, *The New Insecurity*.

72. Dyer, "Entertainment and Utopia," 278 (emphasis in original).

73. Ibid., 273.

74. Sabo and Jansen, "Images of Men in Sport Media," 181.

75. Ibid., 183.

76. Herrnstein and Murray, *The Bell Curve*. See, for example, Fischer et al., *Inequality by Design*.

77. Macpherson, *The Political Theory of Possessive Individualism*.

78. Mascuch, *Origins of the Individualist Self*, 22–23.

79. Sennett, *The Corrosion of Character*, 84.

80. Côté and Allahar, *Generation on Hold*, 48. Isabel Sawhill puts it this way: two factors—"the increase in social mobility and the decline in economic mobility—have affected prospects for the youngest generation. The good news is that people are increasingly free to move beyond their origins. The bad news is that fewer destinations represent an improvement over where they began. For those concerned about the material well-being of the youngest generation, this is not a welcome message" ("Still the Land of Opportunity?," 11).

81. Côté and Allahar, *Generation on Hold*, 82, emphasis in original.

82. Fine, Mortimer, and Roberts, "Leisure, Work and the Mass Media"; Harter, "Self and Identity Development."

83. Mitroff et al., *Prime-Time Teens*, 7.

84. Ibid., 40.

85. Ibid., 222.

86. Ariès, *Centuries of Childhood*; Plumb, "The New World of Children"; Zelizer, *Pricing the Priceless Child*.

87. One could also argue that such deprivations are or will be intensified by new limitations on civil rights and privacy in the post-9/11 world.

88. "Adultolescent" appears to have been coined in the 25 March 2002 *Newsweek* article "Bringing Up Adultolescents" by Peg Tyre, Karen Springen, and Julie Scelfo.

89. Kamenetz, *Generation Debt*, 9.

90. Kamenetz, *Generation Debt*, 13. See also Draut, *Strapped*.

91. The "disheartening" Labor Department report of the small number of jobs added to the American economy in May 2011, was rendered even more disheartening by analysts' reports that "up to 30,000 of the 54,000 jobs created [that month] were the result of a hiring spree by the hamburger chain [McDonald's]" (Aliyah Shahid, "McDonald's April Hiring Spree Could Have Accounted for Half of May's Job Growth," *New York Daily News*, June 4, 2011).

92. *American Idol*, May 21, 2003.

Chapter 2: Rockumentary and the New Model Worker

1. Sawyer, "Battle of the Bands," 47.

2. The relationship between the categories of rock and pop music in the decades since the critical construction of rock as an esteemed art form (which took place around 1965) and the complementary critical disparagement of pop as an ephem-

eral commercial form have been the subjects of wide discussion. See, for example, Keightley, "Reconsidering Rock"; Regev, "Producing Artistic Value."

3. Melanie Clarin DeGiovanni, interview with author (1 July 1999), describing touring with a rock band.

4. This is the status enjoyed by the elite consultants studied by Barley and Kunda, *Gurus, Hired Guns, and Warm Bodies.*

5. Sennett, *The Culture of the New Capitalism*, 80.

6. Reich, *The Future of Success*, 69.

7. Richard Leacock, "A Search for the Feeling of Being There," 1997, http://www .afana.org/leacockessays.htm.

8. Quoted in Lawrence Van Gelder, "Maysles: Filming the Impossible," *New York Times*, October 18, 1987.

9. Allen and Gomery, *Film History*, 234.

10. Ibid., 233.

11. Quoted in ibid.

12. Honneth, "Organized Self-Realization," 468.

13. Frank, *The Conquest of Cool*, 10.

14. Ibid., 28.

15. Honneth, "Organized Self-Realization," 470.

16. Giddens, *Modernity and Self-Identity*. Eli Zaretsky sees this development of "personal life" as having been inaugurated somewhat earlier, through the process of "proletarianization" that he sees taking place in the early twentieth century: "By splitting society between work and life, proletarianization created the conditions under which men and women looked to themselves, outside of the division of labor, for meaning and purpose. Introspection intensified and deepened as people sought in themselves the only coherence, consistency, and unity capable of reconciling the fragmentation of social life" (*Capitalism, the Family, and Personal Life*, 49).

17. Frank, *The Conquest of Cool*, 11.

18. Ibid., 13.

19. Quoted in Levin, *Documentary Explorations*, 196.

20. Drew, *Primary*, DVD special features. In another interview included in the special features on this DVD, Robert Drew said of Leacock, Pennebaker, and the Maysles brothers that they "can sense an interesting situation, find characters within it, sense what is about to happen, be there when it happens, render it on film or tape, with art and craft and insight and intelligence as it happens, return with this material, and edit a film that will put across a feeling of what it was like to be there." See also Saunders, *Direct Cinema*.

21. Quoted in Levin, *Documentary Explorations*, 226.

22. Like many contemporary filmmakers, former employees of Drew Associates supported themselves between more glamorous projects with commissions from business and the state. They produced or worked on non-theatrical films for

AT&T; Western Electric; the Departments of State and of Health, Education, and Welfare; IBM; the National Institutes of Health and the National Institute of Mental Health; Standard Oil; and the New York Stock Exchange—as well as television commercials. Although these films represent a relatively large proportion of the filmmakers' bodies of work, very little is known about most of them. See Heide Solbrig, *Film and Function*.

23. See Heide Solbrig, *Film and Function* for more on this and other lesser-known Maysles industrial films.

24. Both the makers and reviewers of these films often use the term "verité" to describe them. See A. O. Scott, "Seeking Fame with Amps and Attitude" (*New York Times*, March 26, 2004); Chris Barry, "Battle of the Battling Bands"; C. Bottomley, "Dig!: Behind the Music" (VH1.com, October 7, 2004, http://www.vh1.com/news/articles/1492021/1 . . . 4/article.jhtml); Stephanie Bunbury, "Rock Gone Wild" (*Age*, April 10, 2005, http://www.theage.com.au/news/Film/Rock-gone-wild/2005/04/07/1112815672469.html). In a panel discussion on rockumentary at the London Film Festival, Timoner remarked: "We were around so much and there's nearly 2,000 hours of footage, so it's true verité, you know?" (London Film Festival, "Rockumentary Debate Live Online").

25. Barnouw, *Documentary*, 254–55.

26. London Film Festival, "Rockumentary Debate Live Online."

27. Wertsch, "Collective Memory," 228.

28. Nichols, *Representing Reality*, 33.

29. Hall, "Realism as Style."

30. Nichols, *Representing Reality*, 33.

31. McConvey, "*Dig!*" Timoner pitched her *Cut* project to the MTV network and was rebuffed, but before long MTV's VH1 channel was promoting its next hit, *Bands on the Run*—a reality/game show in which four local, unsigned bands, staked to a certain amount of money and other resources, had to tour and sell merchandise for the duration of a season. See Wurster, "See Band Run." Timoner discusses this series of events in a number of interviews, including London Film Festival, "Rockumentary Debate Live Online."

32. London Film Festival, "Rockumentary Debate Live Online."

33. Anton Newcombe, in Timoner, *Dig!*

34. London Film Festival, "Rockumentary Debate Live Online."

35. Newcombe, in Timoner, *Dig!*

36. Ondi Timoner interview "After the Release: Ondi at the L.A. Film Festival" in *Dig!* DVD special features, ibid.

37. Zia McCabe, in Timoner, *Dig!*

38. "Major indie" is a label that has major label distribution (and maybe even part ownership by a major) but signs and develops acts on its own. Many writers understand this relationship as a way for the major label to outsource risk. See, for example, Hesmondhalgh, "Indie."

39. The Who similarly became proprietors, "developing [a hall] and renting it out as specially-designed rock-tour rehearsal space, complete with stage, lighting banks, etc." (Frith, *Sound Effects*, 145). See also Negus's provocative discussion of the "rock aristocracy" in *Producing Pop* (138–41).

40. That is, all their advances have been paid off, and they're now collecting royalties.

41. Peter Holmstrom, in Timoner, *Dig!*

42. Adam Shore, in Timoner, *Dig!*

43. Quoted in Pizello, "Production Slate," 26.

44. London Film Festival, "Rockumentary Debate Live Online."

45. Mohr, "Docmaker Branches Out," 14.

46. Bunbury, "Rock Gone Wild."

47. Ondi Timoner interview "After the Release: Ondi at the L.A. Film Festival" in Timoner, *Dig!* DVD special features.

48. Timoner interview "After the Release: Ondi at the L.A. Film Festival."

49. Pizello, "Production Slate," 26.

50. Bourdieu, *Distinction.*

51. Timoner interview "After the Release: Ondi at the L.A. Film Festival."

52. London Film Festival, "Rockumentary Debate Live Online."

53. Geoffrey Macnab, "When Good Rockers Go Bad," *Independent*, October 27, 2004, http://global.factiva.com/redir/default.aspx?P=sa&an=IND0000020041026e0aro003i&cat=a&ep=ASE.

54. Timoner interview "After the Release: Ondi at the L.A. Film Festival."

55. Before I go any further, I have to point out that the vast weight of evidence in the film is that amateur diagnoses of Newcombe as suffering from various syndromes and disorders hold water. This makes it very difficult to argue for any agency at all on his part: in the face of this overwhelming argument, at what point can I or anyone else using this film as "evidence" be even partially certain that what he's doing or saying is not simply a product of his apparent pathologies?

56. Honneth, "Organized Self-Realization," 472.

57. Interestingly, viewed through the lens offered by David Riesman in his influential 1950 volume, the positions occupied by these two bandleaders may both be considered "well-adjusted"—Taylor to the dominant "other-directed" character structure of the late twentieth century and Newcombe to the now largely outmoded "inner-directed" character structure. See Riesman, *The Lonely Crowd*, 240–43.

58. Timoner in "The Reckoning," in Timoner, *Dig!* DVD special features. It is worth pointing out here that Maysles's first film was of patients in a psychiatric hospital in Russia, and that one of Pennebaker's first films after he left Drew Associates, *Elizabeth and Mary* (1965), was a medical film about twin girls, one of whom was only partially sighted and the other of whom was blind and severely brain damaged. As of 1970, this was one of Pennebaker's favorites of his films. See Levin, *Documentary Explorations*, 230.

59. For a fascinating discussion of how Robbie Robertson of The Band made use of his appearance in Martin Scorsese's rockumentary *The Last Waltz* (1978) for the enhancement of his career in the entertainment industry, see Severn, "Robbie Robertson's Big Break."

60. Laura Sinagra, "Almost Famous: Two Indie Bands Struggle to Survive the Industry and Each Other," *Village Voice*, October 5, 2004.

61. Nina Ritter, in Timoner, *Dig!*

62. Timoner interview "After the Release: Ondi at the L.A. Film Festival."

63. Commentary, in special features, ibid.

64. Honneth, "Organized Self-Realization," 472, 468.

65. The distinction between wanton and productive excess is, of course, a complicated one, and it may in fact only be justifiably applied in retrospect, when one is in a position to see how a given example of excess either hindered or facilitated progress according to the rules of the field.

66. Sennett, *The Culture of the New Capitalism*, 80; Reich, *The Future of Success*, 142.

67. Sinagra, "Almost Famous."

68. This kind of productivity is not to be identified with or reduced to material production, however: as Timoner points out, Newcombe's BJM finished twelve albums in the amount of time it took the Dandys to make four.

69. "Bonus Footage," in Timoner, *Dig!* DVD special features.

70. Courtney Taylor, in Timoner, *Dig!*

71. Evelyn McDonnell, "Filmmaker's S. Florida Family the Inspiration for her Success," *Miami Herald*, January 27, 2005.

72. Timoner, "The Diary of a Guerilla [*sic*] Filmmaker."

73. Zia McCabe, in Timoner, *Dig!*

74. Timoner, "The Diary of a Guerilla [*sic*] Filmmaker."

75. Ibid.

76. As well as later ones, as shown in Robert Drew's poignant *On the Road with Duke Ellington.*

77. Timoner interview "After the Release: Ondi at the L.A. Film Festival" in Timoner, *Dig!* DVD special features.

78. Posted to the Brian Jonestown Massacre's website in 2004; archived at: http://web .archive.org/web/20050214022514/http://www.brianjonestownmassacre.com/ bandinfo.html.

79. Posted to the Brian Jonestown Massacre's website in 2004; archived at: http://web .archive.org/web/20050301021629/http://www.brianjonestownmassacre.com/ dig_statement.html.

80. Nichols, *Representing Reality*, 44, 56.

81. Frank, *Conquest of Cool*, 123.

82. Honneth, "Organized Self-Realization," 467–68.

83. Keightley, "Reconsidering Rock" and "Manufacturing Authenticity."

84. Frank, *One Market under God.*

85. Menger, *Portrait de l'Artiste en Travailleur*, 35 (translation by Jane Stahl).

86. Ibid., 31 (translation by Jane Stahl).

87. See, for example, Klaprat, "The Star as Market Strategy," 353; Ryan, *Making Capital from Culture*, 65–69.

88. Menger, *Portrait de l'Artiste en Travailleur*, 31 (translation by Jane Stahl).

89. Ibid., 44 (translation by Jane Stahl).

90. See also Reich, *The Future of Success*; Sennett, *The Culture of the New Capitalism*.

91. Burger, *Les oubliés du XXIe siècle ou La fin du travail*.

92. Gorz, *Reclaiming Work*.

93. Nichols, *Representing Reality*, 140.

94. See, for example, Hochschild, *The Time Bind*.

95. Weber, *The Protestant Ethic and the Spirit of Capitalism*, 72.

96. Perelman, *The Invention of Capitalism*.

97. Barley and Kunda, "Design and Devotion"; Kraft, "To Control and Inspire"; Honneth, "Organized Self-Realization."

98. Beck, *The Brave New World of Work*.

99. In Grant Gee's *Meeting People Is Easy*, a rockumentary about Radiohead, a member of group talks about "bands now that own hotels, and you know . . . have investment companies and more businesses. There's this documentary done recently about Pink Floyd, and when it was shown to Pink Floyd they refused to have it released, because it basically showed them going in and out of business meetings and boardrooms and discussing moving money around."

Part II: Regulation

1. Recording artists Patti Austin and Courtney Love, *Personal Service Contracts: Seven-Year Rule; Exception for Recording Artists: Informational Hearing before the California State Senate Select Committee on the Entertainment Industry, September 5, 2001* (Sacramento: Senate Rules Committee, 2001), 54, 177.

2. "Handy" refers not to "useful" but to W. C. Handy. See the Blues Foundation's website at http://www.blues.org/#ref=hart_index.

Chapter 3: Carving Out Recording Artists from California's Seven-Year Rule

1. Given their importance to the music industry, it is surprising that contracts have been so little studied outside of legal scholarship. Exceptions include Cohen's ethnographic portrait of Liverpool-based indie bands' lives before and after signing a contract (*Rock Culture in Liverpool*, 102–34); Negus's brief discussion in *Producing Pop* (42–43); Webb's sociological analysis of royalty rates and accounting (*Exploring the Networked Worlds of Popular Music*, 206–12); and Fairchild's analysis of the contract's role in the assignment of intellectual property rights and in the various *Idol* franchises (*Pop Idols and Pirates*, 61–63, 96, 111, 114). Hull's analysis

detects some of the political problems associated with the recording contract but refrains from sustained analysis (*The Recording Industry*, 143–46).

2. Suchman, "The Contract as Social Artifact," 100.
3. Greenfield and Osborn, *Contract and Control in the Entertainment Industry*, 177.
4. Burston, "Synthespians among Us," 257.
5. Suchman, "The Contract as Social Artifact," 99.
6. Quoted in Perelman, *The Invention of Capitalism*, 21.
7. Quoted in Dannen, *Hit Men*, 142.
8. Ibid.
9. Motown Record Corporation v. Teena Marie Brockert, 160 Cal. App. 3d 123, 207 Cal. Rptr. 574 (1984).
10. Negus, *Producing Pop*, 55.
11. Denisoff, *Tarnished Gold*, 89. The legal terms for trying to woo an artist away from a company include "inducement to breach of contract" and "tortious interference with contractual relations."
12. Martin, *Sounds and Society*, 255. Martin cites Durkheim for this point.
13. Frith, *Sound Effects*, 106. Kemper (*Hidden Talent*) and Carman ("Independent Stardom") discuss some entertainers' power to drive favorable bargains.
14. Clark, "Medieval Labor Law and English Local Courts," 332.
15. Castel, "The Roads to Disaffiliation," 521.
16. Clark, "Medieval Labor Law and English Local Courts," 333.
17. It could be fairly pointed out that today's contracts are voluntary, while those of the fourteenth century were compulsory. The validity of this distinction is taken up in chapter 4.
18. Motown Record Corporation v. Teena Marie Brockert. See also Stahl, "Primitive Accumulation, the Social Common, and the Contractual Lockdown of Recording Artists at the Threshold of Digitalization."
19. Ellerman, *Property and Contract in Economics*, 22–30.
20. Blauner, *Alienation and Freedom*, 33. See also Seeman, "On The Meaning of Alienation."
21. Jones, "The Music Industry as Workplace." See also Faulkner, *Hollywood Studio Musicians*.
22. Jones, "The Music Industry as Workplace," 151.
23. Ibid., 153.
24. Blauner, *Alienation and Freedom*, 3.
25. Polanyi, *The Great Transformation*, 73.
26. Ellerman observes: "The system of renting people is our system, the employer-employee system. Of course, we do not *say* people are rented; we say people are 'hired.' Students would have had no difficulty thinking of an economic system where workers are hired. The difference a word makes! When applied to things rather than persons, the words 'rent' and 'hire' are synonyms. One could say either 'rent a car' or 'hire a car' with the only difference being that Americans favor 'rent

a car' while the British will tend to 'hire a car.' But American and British usage agrees that when people are rented, one says 'people are hired'" (*Property and Contract in Economics*, 61).

27. Banks, *The Politics of Cultural Work*, 7.

28. Quoted in Perelman, *The Invention of Capitalism*, 25.

29. Olivia de Haviland v. Warner Bros. Pictures, Inc., No. 487685, Los Angeles County Super. Ct. Mar. 14, 1944. The plaintiff's name is actually spelled de Havilland; the misspelling is the court's and it remains the spelling on the decision.

30. See Davidov, "The Three Axes of Employment Relationships."

31. Shemel and Krasilovsky, *This Business of Music*, 10. Whether person A is an employee of person B or the two are in an independent contracting relationship is sometimes unclear until certain judicial "tests"—such as that found in CCNV v. Reid (490 U.S. 730, 751 [1989])—have been applied; see Davidov, "The Three Axes of Employment Relationships," for a thorough discussion of such legal tests. Cutting against appearances is the fact that companies and artists often meet before legislators to fight over aspects of the California Labor Code that govern relationships between employers and employees. See chapters 3 and 4 and Stahl, "Primitive Accumulation, the Social Common, and the Contractual Lockdown of Recording Artists at the Threshold of Digitalization."

32. Orren, *Belated Feudalism*, 79, 71, 79.

33. Ryan, *Making Capital from Culture*, 134–41. Ryan's distinction between "contracted artists" and "professional creatives," however, doesn't quite capture the dynamic here.

34. Krasilovsky and Shemel, *This Business of Music*, 23.

35. In a fascinating example cited by Pateman (*The Sexual Contract*, 73), some colliers (employees in coal mines, not slaves) in eighteenth-century Scotland were bonded (employed) for life, and could be sold by employers along with the rest of the enterprise.

36. The "key man" clause can also work in favor of the "man." The "key man" clause that tied Whitney Houston's contract with RCA/Arista to Clive Davis made Davis indispensable to the company. See Dannen, *Hit Men*, 261.

37. Negus, *Producing Pop*, 150.

38. Krasilovsky and Shemel, *This Business of Music*, 12, 25. Option contracts remain the norm in the digitalized music industry.

39. Greenfield and Osborn, "Understanding Commercial Music Contracts," 17.

40. Quoted in Passman, *All You Need to Know about the Music Business*, 99. In the context of these critical views, Negus seems excessively optimistic. "In principle," he writes, the system of option periods "is to safeguard the artist against a company which might sign and retain them on an exclusive contract without investing in them" (*Producing Pop*, 43).

41. The survival of this rule into the early twenty-first century is probably almost entirely due to the importance of star labor to the state's entertainment industry.

Though numerous legal scholars (many of whom are cited below) have explored the scope and meaning of the rule, none has yet unearthed its history in detail.

42. California Labor Code, section 2855 (enacted 1937).

43. Olivia de Haviland v. Warner Bros. Pictures, Inc. 67 Cal. App. 2d 225; 153 P.2d 983 (1944).

44. Ibid., 237.

45. Ibid., 232.

46. Blaufarb, "The Seven Year Itch," 657.

47. Olivia de Haviland v. Warner Bros. Pictures, Inc. 67 Cal. App. 2d 225; 153 P.2d 983 (1944), 235.

48. Senator Kevin Murray argued in a "Committee Background Paper" prepared for a 2001 hearing on the seven-year rule that the 1872 version was originally intended to protect employers: "Ironically, it was first enacted in order to protect employers from being obligated to their employees who came west at their suggestion" (reprinted in California State Legislature. Senate. Select Committee on the Entertainment Industry. *Personal Service Contracts: Seven-year Rule; Exception for Recording Artists.* Senate Publication # 1121-S. Sacramento: Senate Rules Committee, 2001, n.p.n.) (hereinafter *Personal Service Contracts Hearing*). I have found no corroboration of this suggestion, but it is plausible. The fact is that both employers and employees had obligations and virtual property interests in the contracted benefits of the other under master and servant agreements. See Mooney, "The Search for a Legal Presumption of Employment Duration or Custom of Arbitrary Dismissal in California 1848–1872."

49. Hull, *The Recording Industry*, 123.

50. Organizational sociologists have taken an interest in this phenomenon from a different perspective. See Peterson and Berger, "Measuring Industry Concentration, Diversity, and Innovation in Popular Music"; Dowd, "Concentration and Diversity Revisited"; Lopes, "Innovation and Diversity in the Popular Music Industry."

51. Chapple and Garofalo, *Rock 'n' Roll Is Here to Pay*, 84.

52. Quoted in ibid.

53. Cornyn, *Exploding*, 79.

54. Frith, *Sound Effects*, 148.

55. Cornyn, *Exploding*, 199.

56. Eliot, *Rockonomics*, 177.

57. Tschmuck, *Creativity and Innovation in the Music Industry*, 135.

58. Denisoff, *Tarnished Gold*, 108.

59. Straw, "Popular Music as Cultural Commodity," 197.

60. Denisoff, *Tarnished Gold*, 150.

61. Straw, "Popular Music as Cultural Commodity," 210.

62. Denisoff, *Tarnished Gold*, 125.

63. Ibid., 146. See also Frith's discussion of the "platinum strategy" (*Sound Effects*, 147).

64. Straw, "Popular Music as Cultural Commodity," 213–14.

65. Eliot, *Rockonomics*, 198.

66. Quoted in Denisoff, *Tarnished Gold*, 146.

67. Quoted in ibid.

68. Eliot, *Rockonomics*, 198.

69. Garofalo, "From Music Publishing to MP3," 343.

70. Robert Christgau, "Rock 'n' Roller Coaster: The Music Biz on a Joyride," *Village Voice*, February 7, 1984.

71. Quoted in Eliot, *Rockonomics*, 197.

72. Tschmuck, *Creativity and Innovation in the Music Industry*, 160, 161.

73. Cooper, "Recording Contract Negotiation," 51.

74. Eliot, *Rockonomics*, 117–18.

75. Cooper, "Recording Contract Negotiation," 51.

76. Blaufarb, "The Seven Year Itch," 663.

77. Ibid., and note 56.

78. Quoted in Krasilovsky and Shemel, *This Business of Music*, 267.

79. Ibid. In contrast, the authors note, "the multiple for the acquisition of an existing master [recording] that has been released in the past may be quite low, even as little as 3 to 5 times average net earnings" (268).

80. Quoted in Eliot, *Rockonomics*, 191.

81. Although the "artist development" model of career cultivation was ascendant in the rock world, deals requiring two albums per year were not unusual at this time in the pop world, where cycles of release and promotion were more rapid; options were typically written so that the record company was empowered to demand as many as two records per year. Melissa Manchester's 1973 deal with Arista called for as many as two albums per year for seven years. See Light, "The California Injunction Statute and the Music Industry," 150. Today, under the "360 deal," by which companies secure rights in most or all of an artist's incomes (recording and non-recording alike), contracts increasingly specify numbers of tracks rather than albums.

82. Steinberg, "Injunctions," 92.

83. MCA Records v. Olivia Newton-John, 90 Cal. App. 3d 18; 153 Cal. Rptr. (1979), 155.

84. See Manchester v. Arista Records, Inc., No. CV 81–2134-RJK-Kx. (1981).

85. Steinberg, "Injunctions," 104.

86. The Newton-John case triggered a series of related cases as artists sought to replicate her back-door success in achieving free agency: Donna Summer (1980), Melissa Manchester (1981), Sammy Hagar (1981), and Tom Scholz of Boston (1984) all sought relief with varying degrees of success (see McLane and Wong, "Practice Tips: How Recording Artists Have Broken Their Contracts"). In the years following the 1987 carve out, another handful of artists attempted to exit their contracts through lawsuits. Of these, the George Michael case in 1992 (which took place in the United Kingdom) is the best known and most studied. In the United States, Luther Vandross (1992), Don Henley (1993), Glenn Frey (1994), Metallica (1994),

the Smashing Pumpkins (1997), and, most notoriously, Courtney Love (2000), as well as others, sought to challenge the carve out and achieve free agency (see Cappello and Thielemann, "Challenging the Practices of the Recording Industry"). At present, the carve out remains intact; chapter 4 deals in detail with a failed 2001–4 attempt by recording artists and sympathetic legislators to repeal the 1987 legislation.

87. Phillips and Graham, "New Developments in Recording Contract Negotiations," 16; see also Krasilovsky and Shemel, *This Business of Music*, 101; Webb, *Exploring the Networked Worlds of Popular Music*, 209. In his 1980 volume, *The Musician's Manual: A Practical Career Guide*, Mark Halloran perceptively wrote: "A recent case involving a dispute between Olivia Newton-John and her record company (MCA) suggests that California courts may no longer allow a record company to extend the term of a recording contract beyond its stated length on account of the Artist's failure to deliver product on time." He predicted that "if any California court clearly so decides, the record companies will surely change the standard term of their recording contracts to give them the maximum rights under the law" (148).

88. Webb, *Exploring the Networked Worlds of Popular Music*, 209; Ben McLane and Venice Wong, "'Gimme' a Break," 1998, http://www.benmclane.com/BreakCon.htm.

89. Knab and Day, *Music Is Your Business*, 111, emphasis in original. This trend is evident in a comparison of sample contracts and contract clauses reprinted in a number of reference guides. For example, compare those found in Derenberg, *Practical Legal Problems in Music & Recording Industry*, published in 1971, to the later examples reproduced in the 2008 edition of Halloran, *The Musician's Business & Legal Guide*.

90. Straw, "Popular Music as Cultural Commodity"; Keightley, "Long Play."

91. Passman, *All You Need to Know about the Music Business*, 101.

92. Blaufarb, "The Seven Year Itch," 659–60.

93. Van Beveren, "The Demise of the Long-Term Personal Service Contract in the Music Industry," 407. As noted above, the important George Michael case (Panayiotou v. Sony Music Entertainment [UK] Ltd., 13 Ch. 532 [Ch. 1994]) took place in the United Kingdom; therefore it does not set a precedent for US cases.

94. Frith and Marshall, "Making Sense of Copyright," 14.

95. California Labor Code, section 2855, subsection (b)(1).

96. Ibid., subsection (b)(3).

97. Ibid., subsection (b)(2).

98. *Personal Service Contracts Hearing*, 59–61.

99. Jay Cooper, statement at California State Senate Committee on the Judiciary, Hearing on California Labor Code Section 2855: "Informational Hearing SB 1246 (Murray): Legal Issues," March 19, 2002. Audio recording on file at the California State Archives.

100. The California State Archive contains a wealth of material pertaining to the two

bills' trajectory through committees, the two houses of the Legislature, and the governor's office. However, material on one point is strikingly absent. How was Dills persuaded to introduce this legislation and then to steer it through a two-and-a-half-year process? All contact between the RIAA and Dills prior to the bill's introduction is considered by the state to fall under the heading of "personal" and may be released only (if at all) by the senator or his family.

101. Chester Migden to Ralph C. Dills, February 20, 1985 (Industrial Relations Committee Bill File SB 469, California State Archive).

102. Neal Burraston, bill analysis of April 8, 1985 (Committee on Labor and Employment Bill File SB 469, California State Archive), 1, 3.

103. It is interesting to note that one of the original partners of the law firm, Martin Gang, who—representing Olivia de Havilland—provoked the strikingly pro-employee 1944 interpretation of the law. See Olivia de Haviland v. Warner Bros. Pictures, Inc., No. 487685, Los Angeles County Sup. Ct. Mar. 14, 1944 and Olivia de Haviland v. Warner Bros. Pictures, Inc. 67 Cal. App. 2d 225; 153 P.2d 983 (1944).

104. Gang, Tyre, and Brown and JLA Advocates, "Background Paper in Support of Senate Bill 469 (Dills)" (Industrial Relations Committee Bill File SB 469, California State Archive), 4.

105. Ibid., 21. This escalation continued apace throughout the early 1990s. Garofalo writes: "Ever since *Thriller*, the music industry has been stuck in a notion of artist development that demands superstardom. Consequently, record companies spent the early nineties ponying up millions for contracts that were as unprecedented as they were unrecoverable" ("From Music Publishing to MP3," 347).

106. Jay Cooper, "Background Paper in Opposition to Senate Bill 469" (Industrial Relations Committee Bill File SB 469, California State Archive), 2.

107. McLane and Wong, "Practice Tips"; Capitol Records, Inc. v. Hagar, Marin County Sup. Ct. No. 100486 (December 22, 1980); Cooper, "The Right of a Recording Company to Enjoin an Artist from Recording for Others"; Discreet Records, Inc. v. Dalton LA Sup. Ct. No. 122 536 (1976).

108. Cooper, "Background Paper in Opposition to Senate Bill 469," 4.

109. Ibid., 10-11.

110. Quoted in Cornyn, *Exploding*, 270-71.

111. Cooper, "Background Paper in Opposition to Senate Bill 469," 11.

112. Ibid., 8.

113. Ibid., 8-9. Foxx v. Williams, 244 Cal. App. 2d 223; 52 Cal. Rptr. (1966); Motown Record Corporation v. Teena Marie Brockert. See also Stahl, "Primitive Accumulation, the Social Common, and the Contractual Lockdown of Recording Artists at the Threshold of Digitalization," 344-46.

114. Cooper, "Background Paper in Opposition to Senate Bill 469," 14.

115. Quoted in Tusher, "Personal-Service Contracts Bill Not a Dead Matter Yet," 4. See also Tusher, "Amended Proposal Clears Senate Committee with a Major Compromise Added."

116. Quoted in Tusher, "Amended Proposal Clears Senate Committee with a Major Compromise Added," 15.

117. Oscar De La Hoya v. Top Rank, CV 00–9230-WMB, CV 00–10450-WMB (2001).

118. Quoted in Tusher, "Amended Proposal Clears Senate Committee with a Major Compromise Added," 15.

119. Hirsch, "Processing Fads and Fashions."

120. Keightley, "Long Play," 377.

121. Quoted in ibid., 381.

122. Dobb, *Studies in the Development of Capitalism*, 23–25.

123. Jeff Ayeroff, statement at "Informational Hearing SB 1246 (Murray): Legal Issues"; Cooper, statement at "Informational Hearing SB 1246 (Murray): Legal Issues."

124. Miege, *The Capitalization of Cultural Production*, 30, 83, 90–91; Hesmondhalgh, *The Cultural Industries*, 1st ed., 56.

125. Ryan notes: "The employment of artists in whatever technical form necessitates recognizing and preserving their named, concrete labor. They cannot be employed as labor-power, as anonymous production factors functioning under the sway of capital" (*Making Capital from Culture*, 44).

126. Clark, "Medieval Labor Law and English Local Courts," 333.

127. Carruthers and Stinchcombe, "The Social Structure of Liquidity," 355. The recession that began in 2007 is a convincing demonstration of the degree to which, for example, the value of a bundle of home mortgage debts is socially constructed.

128. Hesmondhalgh, "Indie."

129. Carruthers and Stinchcombe, "The Social Structure of Liquidity," 356.

130. Quoted in ibid., 355.

131. Ibid., 356.

132. Ibid., 356.

133. Gang, Tyre, and Brown and JLA Advocates, "Background Paper," 4.

134. Quoted in Perelman, *The Invention of Capitalism*, 31.

135. Suchman, "The Contract as Social Artifact."

Chapter 4: Freedom, Unfreedom, and the Rhetoric of the Recording Contract

1. Cappello and Thielemann, "Challenging the Practices of the Recording Industry."

2. *Personal Service Contracts: Seven-Year Rule; Exception for Recording Artists: Informational Hearing before the California State Senate Select Committee on the Entertainment Industry, September 5, 2001* (Sacramento: Senate Rules Committee, 2001), (hereinafter *Personal Service Contracts Hearing*), 54.

3. Ibid., 177.

4. Pateman, *The Sexual Contract*, 71.

5. *Personal Service Contracts Hearing*, 43.

6. Steinfeld, *Coercion, Contract, and Free Labor in the Nineteenth Century*, 14.

7. Ibid., 16.

8. Quoted in Pateman, *The Sexual Contract*, 74–75.

9. Steinfeld, *Coercion, Contract, and Free Labor in the Nineteenth Century*, 37.

10. In other words, if an artist has completed three albums and the contract provides for one album "firm" (that is, the album which begins the relationship, specified in the contract) plus six options, then the company can demand damages on the remaining four albums out of the total of seven, even if the company never picked up the options on those four records and never asked the artist to produce them.

11. Quoted in Brewer, "Bankruptcy & Entertainment Law," 600. See also Stahl, "Primitive Accumulation, the Social Common, and the Contractual Lockdown of Recording Artists at the Threshold of Digitalization," 346–48.

12. Other legal issues brought the situations of recording artists into public discourse, including two major class-action lawsuits. One, originating in 1993 against the American Federation of Television and Radio Artists (AFTRA) over underpayment of royalties and mismanagement of pension and healthcare funds, was finally making its way to trial around this time. Largely spearheaded by elderly and relatively impoverished African American recording artists—including Sam Moore of Sam & Dave, Curtis Mayfield, Jerry Butler of the Impressions, and Carl Gardner of the Coasters, as well as the estates of Jackie Wilson, Mary Wells, and Sam & Dave's David Prater—this lawsuit helped engender awareness of the highly racialized politics of the recording industry and sympathy toward recording artists (Bill Holland, "AFTRA Suit Heads toward Trial," *Billboard*, March 27, 1999). As Sam Moore told *Billboard*, "after decades of performances, I am hoping to see a day when my efforts can be rewarded by the security of a pension and health care benefits. I am sure many of my peers feel the same way" (quoted in Marilyn A. Gillen, "'60s Artists Sue Unions, Labels for Health Benefits," *Billboard*, November 13, 1993). A class-action suit brought against Decca Records for nonpayment of royalties by Peggy Lee in 1999 was also progressing at the time. Other members of the class included such popular and sympathetic figures as Louis Armstrong, Billie Holiday, Patsy Cline, Ella Fitzgerald, Bill Haley, Mary Martin, and Pearl Bailey (Ann O'Neill, "Judge Clears Music Royalties Settlement," *Los Angeles Times*, June 26, 2002; and Ann O'Neill, "Peggy Lee Class-Action Suit Settlement Stalled," *Los Angeles Times*, May 8, 2002). As this suit was nearing resolution, the *Los Angeles Times* reported that "the proposed settlement comes at a time when record company business practices are under heavy scrutiny. Such acts as Courtney Love and the Dixie Chicks have alleged similar questionable accounting practices and filed lawsuits that could turn a spotlight on industry tactics" (Ann O'Neill, Jeff Leeds, and *Times* staff writers, "Judge Clears Proposed Settlement in Royalty Suit against Universal," *Los Angeles Times*, January 16, 2002). The time must have seemed ripe indeed to revisit the 1987 amendment to the seven-year rule.

13. Courtney Love testified in 2001: "I signed . . . to the Geffen label, a little white cottage on Sunset Boulevard. . . . And then I was sold to liquor. And then I was sold to

sewage, all right? So that's my journey, all right. And maybe I'll be sold to grapes tomorrow" (*Personal Service Contracts Hearing*, 82).

14. Ibid., 28.
15. Ibid., 37.
16. Ibid., 55.
17. Ibid., 87.
18. Recording Artists' Coalition, "Position Statement on Senate Bill 1246" (Assembly Committee on the Judiciary Bill File SB 1246, California State Archive), 5.
19. *Personal Service Contracts Hearing*, 45.
20. Ibid., 60–61. Jay Cooper, another artists' attorney, asked: "How can you now sue for damages for albums in which you have not exercised an option? And that is my problem. They have not made a commitment themselves" (ibid., 176).
21. Ibid., 95–96.
22. Ibid., 59.
23. Ibid., 61.
24. Ibid., 93.
25. "There is a variety of artists," Mark Goldstein said, "that in the last 10 years, to give us a big enough time to look at, that have pretty consistently delivered a record a year, or, at least, six records within seven years. We have Neal Young [*sic*], who over the space of eight years, delivered eight records. Van Morrison, over the space of nine years, delivered nine records. Garth Brooks, delivered eleven records over eleven years, one of them was a greatest hits, but, that's still during the period there were eight records in eight years. Allen Jackson [*sic*] also nine records in nine years. REM, in their early career, delivered a record a year for eight years. Reba McIntyre [*sic*], for a couple of decades, has pretty much delivered a record a year. Blues Traveler, has delivered seven records in eight years. Master P, has delivered ten records in ten years. George Strait, has delivered pretty much a record a year for a couple of decades" (ibid., 137).
26. *Personal Service Contracts Hearing*, 116.
27. Ibid., 101. This language strikingly recalls language used to justify the draconian 1349 statute of laborers, promulgated after the Black Death had killed one-third of the English laboring population and the subsequent rise in power of the remaining laborers. The law was said to correct problems created by servants who "to their ease and singular covetise, do withdraw themselves to serve great men and other, unless they have . . . wages to the double or treble of that they were wont to take the said twentieth year . . . to the great damage of the great men, and impoverishing all the said commonalty" (quoted in Linder, *The Employment Relationship in Anglo-American Law*, 47).
28. *Personal Service Contracts Hearing*, 103.
29. Ibid., 165.
30. Dorothy Geller has drawn attention to the violence lurking within Copeland's industry-speak of "breaking" artists. "Talent," she writes, "is raw and wild in its

isolated form but must be 'broken' in order to reach a 'public.'" She continues: "It is the artist who is 'broken' in a manner that . . . clearly involves the person and body associated with the labor of music. Here 'breaking' signifies 'training,' as in the 'breaking in' of a colt or some other animal. Only after a process of the conversion of raw material, or 'raw' talent, to be more precise, 'can the manager cash in'" ("Antinomies of Globalization," 70–71).

31. *Personal Service Contracts Hearing*, 166.

32. "SENATOR MURRAY: What you were trying to do is enforce a contract for a number of albums to which you think you're entitled—MR. HARLESTON: Or to have the opportunity to seek damages" (ibid., 121).

33. Ultimately this included several bills: the initial repeal legislation (SB 2080) and SB 1246, a "spot bill" declaring the intention of the legislature to review the application of the 1987 law to recording artist contracts. A spot bill serves as a placeholder to allow debate on a bill to be introduced in the future. Despite being only a spot bill, SB 1246 occasioned the vigorous debate that I discuss below.

34. Chuck Philips and Dan Morain, "Measure on Music Contracts Planned," *Los Angeles Times*, October 19, 2001.

35. SB 1246, 2002 Leg., Reg. Sess. (Cal. 2002).

36. De Haviland v. Warner Bros. No. 487685, Los Angeles County Sup. Ct. Mar. 14, 1944. As noted in chapter 3, the court's spelling of the plaintiff's name as "De Haviland" is incorrect (it should be "de Havilland"). Nevertheless, this remains the name of the case.

37. SB 1246, 2002 Leg., Reg. Sess. (Cal. 2002).

38. Chuck Philips, "Bill on Free Agency for Artists Dies," *Los Angeles Times*, August 16, 2002.

39. For a thorough analysis of this bill and resulting law, see Sorenson, "California's Recording Industry Accounting Practices Act, SB 1034."

40. The bill was intended to secure artists' rights to audit their record labels and collect unpaid royalties. "'This is the first time artists have a statutory right to anything in their contracts,' Murray said. 'This is the artists' ability to verify their earnings. This gives them the realistic right to audit.' . . . Since Murray introduced the bill in February 2003, Warner Music Group, Universal Music Group and BMG Entertainment have outlined actions to reform and make their royalty and accounting systems more transparent to artists" (Tamara Conniff, "Artist Rights Bill Advances: Full Assembly Will Vote on Monday," *The Hollywood Reporter*, June 16, 2004). The bill passed July 1 and was signed by Governor Arnold Schwarzenegger on July 15, 2004.

41. Ray Haynes, statement at California State Senate Committee on the Judiciary, Hearing on California Labor Code Section 2855: "Informational Hearing SB 1246 (Murray): Legal Issues," March 19, 2002. Audio recording on file at the California State Archives.

42. Pateman, *The Sexual Contract*, 15.

43. Ibid., 39–40, emphasis in original.

44. Ellerman, "*Translatio* versus *Concessio*."

45. Pateman, *The Sexual Contract*, 15.

46. Friedman, *Capitalism and Freedom*, 5.

47. Pateman, *The Sexual Contract*, 33.

48. Byron Sher, statement at "Informational Hearing SB 1246 (Murray): Legal Issues."

49. Pateman, *The Sexual Contract*, 15.

50. Robert Nozick argues that "a free system will allow [one] to sell himself into slavery" (quoted in Ellerman, "*Translatio* versus *Concessio*," 453–54).

51. Kevin Murray, statement at "Informational Hearing SB 1246 (Murray): Legal Issues."

52. Ibid.

53. There are problems with Murray's blurring of the line between domination and exploitation that are too subtle to take up in this context. Pateman writes that domination precedes and grounds exploitation: "Wage slavery is not a consequence of exploitation—exploitation is a consequence of the fact that the sale of labour power entails the worker's subordination. The employment contract creates the capitalist as master; he has the political right to determine how the labour of the worker will be used, and—consequently—can engage in exploitation" (*The Sexual Contract*, 149).

54. *Personal Service Contracts Hearing*, 126–27.

55. Olivia de Haviland v. Warner Bros. Pictures, Inc. 67 Cal. App. 2d 225; 153 P.2d 983 (1944), 237.

56. Jeff Ayeroff, statement at "Informational Hearing SB 1246 (Murray): Legal Issues."

57. Ibid.

58. These ideas about "ownership" are controversial, and they are central to the account and analysis offered in chapter 5.

59. Jeff Ayeroff, statement at "Informational Hearing SB 1246 (Murray): Legal Issues."

60. Ibid.

61. Cooper, statement at "Informational Hearing SB 1246 (Murray): Legal Issues."

62. Karl Widerquist puts this in starkly different terms, presenting work not as an individual exchange by juridically equal property owners, but as a resource necessary to satisfy human needs that, in a capitalist society, is privately controlled. Widerquist writes: "Suppose B controls the only watering hole in the desert and refuses to let A drink unless A does X. A is effectively forced to do X, perhaps as certainly as if A were B's slave. All human beings have needs. If any person or group can put conditions on A's access to the resources that can secure her needs, they can effectively force A to do nearly anything" ("Effective Control Self-Ownership," 5). To this some people will object that there are many employers and many opportunities to work; people are free to choose in the real world. Widerquist responds by saying okay, then "suppose that 10 people control the only 10 watering holes in the desert, and each one refuses to let A drink unless A does X.

A is still forced to do X for somebody. Competition will probably be good for A, but it does not free A from the need to serve one of the owners. She enters trade with her more powerful neighbors not out of voluntary consent but out of socially created necessity" (ibid., 7–8).

63. Martha Escutia, statement at "Informational Hearing SB 1246 (Murray): Legal Issues."

64. Davidov, "The Three Axes of Employment Relationships," 393. This situation is intensified under the increasingly common "360 deal," which encircles a performer such that the contracting company may claim percentages in all the artist's revenue-generating activity, not just in recording-related incomes. See Stahl, "Primitive Accumulation, the Social Common, and the Contractual Lockdown of Recording Artists at the Threshold of Digitalization."

65. Quoted in Greenfield and Osborn, *Contract and Control in the Entertainment Industry*, 182.

66. Anorga, "Music Contracts Have Musicians Playing in the Key of Unconscionability," 745–47.

67. Greenfield and Osborn, "Understanding Commercial Music Contracts," 6.

68. Greenfield and Osborn, *Contract and Control in the Entertainment Industry*, 93.

69. Ray Haynes, statement at "Informational Hearing SB 1246 (Murray): Legal Issues."

70. Ibid.

71. Pateman, *The Sexual Contract*, 33.

72. Ray Haynes, statement at "Informational Hearing SB 1246 (Murray): Legal Issues."

73. Ibid.

74. Jay Cooper, statement at "Informational Hearing SB 1246 (Murray): Legal Issues."

75. Ibid.

76. Ray Haynes, statement at "Informational Hearing SB 1246 (Murray): Legal Issues."

77. Later in the hearing, Sher pressed Cooper on his rationale for legislative "interference" in the free contracting between artist and label, pinning Cooper to the ambiguity at the heart of the artists' argument. Sher asked if Cooper and the artists would like the Legislature "to interfere with your contractual negotiations as far as the compensation" goes. "No, not at all," Cooper replied. "But," said Sher, "the original statute *does* interfere with the ability of the parties to decide for how long a period it can be enforced, and you want us to interfere with that" (Byron Sher, statement at "Informational Hearing SB 1246 [Murray]: Legal Issues"). In other words, if you want the market to set the compensation, why should it not set the duration too?

78. Perhaps ironically, at the same time as Murray and the recording artists were failing to reclaim their formerly inalienable right under 2855, the seven-year rule was powerfully affirmed in the case of Oscar De La Hoya and the subsequent denial of Top Rank's appeal. Top Rank had tried to claim that renegotiations of the initial contract constituted "novation"—the creation of a new contract and the resetting, therefore, of the seven-year clock. The courts found, in close keeping with the de

Havilland decision, that "seven years" means "seven years," period, and that re-negotiations do not constitute the testing of one's value on an open market (Oscar De La Hoya v. Top Rank, CV 00–9230-WMB, CV 00–10450-WMB [2001]).

79. Pateman, *The Sexual Contract*, 7.

80. Olivia de Haviland v. Warner Bros. Pictures, Inc. 67 Cal. App. 2d 225; 153 P.2d 983 (1944), 237.

81. Simon Renshaw, statement at "Informational Hearing SB 1246 (Murray): Legal Issues."

82. Cooper, testimony.

83. *Personal Service Contracts Hearing*, 6–7. Cappello and Thielemann write: "Today, film actors enjoy the equitable compensation and creative freedom espoused by Section 2855(a) and De Haviland; contemporary music artists do not. Section 2855(b) has prevented one class of employees (recording artists) from enjoying the very freedoms for which Section 2855(a) was meant to provide. Every other employee in the state of California enjoys these freedoms and can seek other employment after seven years without exposure to liability" ("Challenging the Practices of the Recording Industry," 16).

84. For more on work as a mode of social and political inclusion, see Shklar, *American Citizenship*; Sayers, "The Need to Work."

85. Quoted in Chris Ayres, "Music Giants Face Shake-Up on Contracts," *The Times* (London), August 27, 2001.

86. *Personal Service Contracts Hearing*, 14–15.

87. Ibid., 40.

88. Ibid., 73–74. Perhaps the most far-reaching argument against the 1987 law was offered by Senator Richard Alarcon in the 2001 hearing: "I believe that if an average person lives to be 70 years old, [then] the seven year period represents basically 10 percent of their lives. I don't think the intent was for people to dedicate more than 10 percent of their life and be owing one particular relationship, one contract with one company. And I believe that's really the fundamental essence of the seven year period. So for me, if somebody is locked into something longer than seven years, it really flies in the face of the notion of them having freedom of will, and freedom of choice, with regard to their God-given talents, abilities and just their life, in general. And so, I am deeply concerned. In this hearing I have to say, that I am getting a strong sense that there is what is tantamount to 21st Century indentured servitude" (ibid., 129).

89. Olivia de Haviland v. Warner Bros. Pictures, Inc. 67 Cal. App. 2d 225; 153 P.2d 983 (1944), 235.

90. Pateman, "Self-Ownership and Property in the Person," 22.

91. Pateman, "Why Republicanism?," 6, and "The Equivalent of the Right to Land, Life, and Liberty?"

92. Pateman, *The Sexual Contract*, 147.

93. Ibid.

94. Quoted in ibid., 25.
95. In fact, Macpherson argues that the Lockean conception of property in the labor of the person is an essential component of the development of liberal market society (*Democratic Theory*, 129–30).
96. Ray Haynes, statement at "Informational Hearing sb 1246 (Murray): Legal Issues."
97. Pateman, "Self-Ownership and Property in the Person," 33.
98. Ibid.
99. Ibid., 49.
100. Ibid.
101. Or, as Ellerman puts it, "the employment relation legally alienates decision-making just as it legally alienates responsibility—even though both are factually inalienable"; moreover, "the actual inalienability of responsible human action and decision making is independent of the duration of the contract," whether for seven weeks, seven years, or seven decades (*Property and Contract in Economics*, 139). See also Ellerman, "*Translatio* versus *Concessio*," 463.
102. Pateman, *The Sexual Contract*, 150.
103. Ibid., 8.
104. Ibid., 12.
105. Ibid., 12–13.
106. Ibid., 13. In "Self-Ownership and Property in the Person," Pateman argues that the critical concept of "self-ownership" actually depoliticizes late-twentieth-century political theory because in discussions of self-ownership, "little attention is given to ownership and what follows from owning"—for example, "alienability, inalienability, and contract" (21). In contrast, "property in the person" foregrounds the central liberal postulate that individuals encounter each other in the market as "owner occupied" (26) bearers of alienable property that they sell or rent to employers. "Property in the person" succeeds as a critical concept because it more clearly represents how liberal principles and institutions (for example, employment) entail not only exploitation but domination through the requirement of individuals' alienation of their democratic rights to self-govern.

Chapter 5: Recording Artists, Work for Hire, Employment, and Appropriation

1. See Davidov, "The Three Axes of Employment Relationships," for elaborations on each category. It is important to note here that under the auspices of a union contract (either with the American Federation of Musicians or the American Federation of Radio and Television Artists) and based on particular formulas, performers are entitled to employer contributions to—and expect future payments from—union-administered health and retirement funds. See the home pages of the American Federation of Musicians and Employers' Pension Fund (http://afm-epf.org) and the American Federation of Radio and Television Artists' Health and Retirement Funds (http://aftrahr.com).

2. Linder, *The Employment Relationship in Anglo-American Law*, xiv, note 6.

3. Ibid.

4. Ibid.

5. David Harvey coins this phrase in *The New Imperialism*, 137.

6. Any music, in the form of "composition" or "sound recording," can be considered a work for hire when carried out by an employee. Without a contract expressly granting the employee some rights, the employer is the owner, just as if the employee were writing advertising copy. The recording artist's double status—employee under state law, independent contractor for the purposes of copyright—is a convenience more than a paradox, if only for the reason that in all the decades of argument in the two venues, no consequential argument has ever succeeded in tipping the balance one way or the other.

7. See Marshall, "Metallica and Morality."

8. Field, "Their Master's Voice?," 146.

9. Quoted in Eric Boehlert, "Four Little Words," *Salon.com*, August 28, 2000, http://www.salon.com/2000/08/28/work_for_hire.

10. US copyright's focus on words and melody privileges certain forms and makers of music and disadvantages others along racialized lines. See, for example, Gitelman, "Reading Music, Reading Records, Reading Race"; Greene, "Copyright, Culture & Black Music."

11. The establishment of this right detached the property from the physical object of the tape and simultaneously extended the property to all physical instances of the sound recording. For a more detailed discussion, see Drahos, *A Philosophy of Intellectual Property*.

12. Halpern, "The Sound Recording Act of 1971," 971.

13. See Sanjek and Sanjek, *American Popular Music Business in the 20th Century*, 12.

14. Halpern, "The Sound Recording Act of 1971," 968.

15. Quoted in ibid., 964.

16. CCNV v. Reid 490 U.S. 730, 751 (1989).

17. Hamilton, "Commissioned Works as Works Made for Hire under the 1976 Copyright Act," 1291.

18. Stewart, "The Freelancer's Trap."

19. United States Congress. House. Committee on the Judiciary. Subcommittee on Courts and Intellectual Property. *United States Copyright Office and Sound Recordings as Work Made for Hire: Hearing before the Subcommittee on Courts and Intellectual Property of the Committee on the Judiciary, House of Representatives*, 106th Cong., 2nd sess., May 25, 2000 (Washington: Government Printing Office, 2000) (hereinafter *Work Made for Hire Hearing*), 112.

20. Hull, "Termination Rights and the Real Songwriters," 309.

21. A. Jones, "Get Ready Cause Here They Come," 128.

22. Stewart, "The Freelancer's Trap."

23. Bill Holland, "Acts' Reps Decry C'right Clause," *Billboard*, January 15, 2000.

24. A "greatest hits" compilation—even of pre-1972 recordings—is eligible for copyright as a compilation; the act of compilation does not create a copyright in the underlying (individual song) sound recordings. As of this writing, it appears unclear whether remastering or digitizing pre- or post-1972 sound recordings creates a new copyright (as a "derivative work") and hence a "restarting" of a copyright term. One point of contention is whether the remastered work meets the criteria of originality. See Comis, "Copyright Killed the Internet Star."

25. Ripley, "Moving to the Beat"; Ed Christman, "A&M Octone CEO Diener: 360 Deal Needs to be Industry Standard," *Billboard.biz*, May 16, 2010, http://www.billboard .biz/bbbiz/content_display/industry/news/e3i417b9e1bf4bfc8ecbda5e23a8b6a0799.

26. Strohm, "Writings in the Margin (of Error)," 131.

27. See Mentzer, "Sound Recordings and Unintended Consequences of the Anti-cybersquatting Consumer Protection Act," 20, and the cases cited in that article.

28. Bill Holland, "Work-For-Hire Law Merits Debated," *Billboard*, June 3, 2000.

29. *Work Made for Hire Hearing*, 78.

30. Bill Holland, "Artists Claim Progress with Hearing," *Billboard*, June 10, 2000.

31. "Cybersquatting" describes the practice of registering someone else's name as an Internet domain name in order to extort from that person an exorbitant payment to obtain the domain name.

32. *Work Made for Hire Hearing*, 185.

33. Ibid., 140.

34. Ibid., 129.

35. Ibid.

36. Backup musicians hired as members of the American Federation of Musicians are entitled to a range of benefits, including (through residuals) forms of partial, quasi-ownership claims. See Stahl, "Privilege and Distinction in Production Worlds."

37. Typically, where producers, engineers, managers, or others have worked in exchange for "points," their cut is subtracted from the recording's royalties from the moment those royalties begin to accumulate. This means these participants begin earning income from the recording before the artist has "recouped," before the artist's royalty share has paid back the record company's recording advance and thus before the artist sees a penny.

38. See e.g., D. Nimmer and Menell, "Sound Recordings, Works for Hire, and the Termination-of-Transfers Time Bomb" and Randy S. Frisch and Matthew J. Fortnow, "The Time Bomb in the Record Company Vaults."

39. Quoted in Hunter, "Culture War."

40. Bernard Weinraub, "For the Industry, Less to Celebrate at the Grammys," *New York Times*, February 25, 2002.

41. *Work Made for Hire Hearing*, 129.

42. Ibid., 130.

43. Kretschmer and Kawohl, "The History and Philosophy of Copyright."

44. *Work Made for Hire Hearing*, 131.

45. Ibid., 214–17.

46. Bill Holland, "Seagram Contributes Big to Candidates," *Billboard*, July 29, 2000; and "Work-For-Hire Repeal Near?," *Billboard*, July 29, 2000.

47. Michael Greene, *Work Made for Hire Hearing*, 181.

48. *Work Made for Hire Hearing*, 137.

49. However, through collectively bargained arrangements for residuals, some employee collaborators dispossessed by copyright become entitled to "residual" or "reuse" payments—which are distinct from wages—whose amounts are dictated by the market performance of the given recording, television program, or other intellectual property at issue. See Stahl, "Privilege and Distinction in Production Worlds."

50. Moreover, there is no disincentive for record companies to withhold royalties against the terms of contracts. When recording artists who can afford the tens of thousands of dollars it costs to pursue an audit of their contracting label find that the label has shorted them on royalties (as they almost invariably do, according to one accountant who has conducted dozens of such audits), the most they can claim is what they are owed. They are entitled to no penalties, and they can't even demand to be reimbursed for the costs of the audit (see California State Legislature. Senate. Committee on the Judiciary and Select Committee on the Entertainment Industry. *Record Label Accounting Practices, July 23, 2002.* Senate Publication #1187-S. Sacramento: Senate Rules Committee, 2002 [hereinafter *Record Label Accounting Practices,* first hearing]; Clover, "Accounting Accountability").

51. Melville Nimmer, however, points out that case law with respect to motion pictures suggests that "if [minor contributors] never contributed copyrightable expression, then they failed to qualify as 'authors' later entitled to terminate" (*Nimmer on Copyright,* § 5.03[B][2][a], note 121.85).

52. U.S. Const., art. 1, § 8.

53. *Work Made for Hire Hearing*, 149.

54. Contributing to a sense of recording artists' political awakening perceptible in the context of the work for hire contest, the terms "artist community" and "artist manager community" appear first to be applied to recording artists and their managers by Bill Holland, "Acts' Reps Decry C'right Clause," *Billboard*, January 15, 2000.

55. Ibid., 194. Artists, their representatives, and accountants who work for firms that audit record labels on behalf of artists have described at length the multifarious, Byzantine means by which record labels withhold royalties and other payments to artists. For example, see the testimony of Linda Becker and Charles Sussman, both certified public accountants, in California State Legislature. Senate. Committee on the Judiciary and Select Committee on the Entertainment Industry. *Record Label Accounting Practices, September 24, 2002.* Senate Publication # 1210-S. Sacramento: Senate Rules Committee, 2002 (second hearing). According to the

litigator Don Engel's testimony before California State Senators, "the intentional underpayment of royalties to all recording artists is a pervasive, consistent policy and practice of each of the five record conglomerates that, together, control the worldwide record industry. These are not accounting errors. They are systematic, outright thievery" (*Record Label Accounting Practices*, first hearing, 91).

56. See, for example, Dave Hoekstra, "The Last, Lonely Years: Misfortune Took Its Toll on Mary Wells," *Chicago Sun-Times*, August 2, 1992; Sam Moore (of Sam and Dave), *Record Label Accounting Practices*, July 23, 2002, written testimony, 1–12.

57. These arguments took place in what Anne Chaitovitz of the American Federation of Television and Radio Artists called the "CARP [copyright arbitration and royalty panel] from hell" (telephone interview with author, April 24, 2004). See Delibero, "Copyright Arbitration Royalty Panels."

58. Quoted in Holland, "Artists Claim Progress with Hearing."

59. *Work Made for Hire Hearing*, 160.

60. Ibid.

61. Ibid., 161.

62. Ibid., 164.

63. Ibid.

64. Ibid.

65. See Rose, *Authors and Owners*, particularly chapter 7; Woodmansee, "The Genius and the Copyright."

66. *Work Made for Hire Hearing*, 165.

67. Ellerman, *Property and Contract in Economics*, 93–94. Major label recording artists do not hire capital in exactly the same way that other entrepreneurs do; what the artists return to lenders is not interest. Nevertheless, Crow was arguing that the relationship between entrepreneur and investor is the appropriate analogy for that between recording artist and record company.

68. *Work Made for Hire Hearing*, 166. The recording process has been described and narrated in numerous different ways. For another perspective and a detailed account, see Stokes, *Starmaking Machinery*.

69. *Work Made for Hire Hearing*, 166, emphasis added.

70. Toynbee, *Making Popular Music*.

71. Locke, "Second Treatise of Government," section 27. See also Macpherson, *The Political Theory of Possessive Individualism*, 214.

72. Locke suggests that the property one has in one's labor is sufficiently like what one could have claimed through mixing one's labor with external stuff—that the fact that all the stuff is used up does not weaken the justification for its original appropriation (Macpherson, *The Political Theory of Possessive Individualism*, 200–201).

73. Macpherson, *The Political Theory of Possessive Individualism*, 214. The historical basis of copyright in "literary property" was the need by booksellers in the seventeenth and eighteenth centuries of an originary source of manuscript that could decisively and exclusively be alienated (see Rose, *Authors and Owners*).

74. Macpherson, *The Political Theory of Possessive Individualism*, 221. Absolute conceptions of intellectual property exist in tension with the Constitutional logic of copyright, which prioritizes the benefit to society of—and therefore the rights of persons to—cultural material. The short initial copyright terms underscore the importance of the social to the Constitution's framers. See Kretschmer and Kawohl, "The History and Philosophy of Copyright."

75. Locke, "Second Treatise of Government," section 28.

76. Zaretsky, *Capitalism, the Family, and Personal Life*, 57.

77. Without direct evidence to support it, my belief is that representatives of the record companies and the RIAA did not push this argument because it would have contradicted too radically the commonsense understanding of recording artists as entrepreneurs to be accepted, regardless of the status and conditions set out in California labor law.

78. *Work Made for Hire Hearing*, 181.

79. Ibid., 173.

80. Ibid., 190–91. Castel writes of the period of the transition to capitalism: "In the country at least, the recourse to wage labor always indicates a grave precariousness of conditions, and the more one is a wage laborer, the more one is impoverished" (*From Manual Workers to Wage Laborers*, 117). There is evidence from the early industrial era that weavers, potters, and other artisans defended their threatened status as independent artisans rather than employees on the basis of their control over assistants (sometimes their own children), whom they classified as employees (Rick Biernacki, interview with author, La Jolla, CA, May 5, 2005; see also Biernacki, *The Fabrication of Labor*, 82–83).

81. *Work Made for Hire Hearing*, 222–24.

82. Writers Guild of America, "Residuals Survival Guide."

83. Quoted in Stahl, "Non-Proprietary Authorship," 98.

84. Pateman, *The Sexual Contract*, 7.

85. Definition 4b, *Oxford English Dictionary*, online edition.

86. Pateman, *The Sexual Contract*, 149.

87. *Work Made for Hire Hearing*, 161.

88. Ibid., 164.

89. Marx, *Capital: Volume 1*, 176. See also Marx, "On the Jewish Question."

90. Antisweatshop activism brings this principle into focus. See, for example, Bender, *Sweated Work, Weak Bodies*.

91. Head, *The New Ruthless Economy*; Henwood, *After the New Economy*.

92. Pateman, "Self-Ownership and Property in the Person," 46.

93. Pateman, *The Sexual Contract*, 146.

94. Ellerman, *Property and Contract in Economics*, 107.

95. See Banks, *The Politics of Cultural Work*, 31; Miege, *The Capitalization of Cultural Production*, 67, 81.

96. Orren, *Belated Feudalism*; Steinfeld, *The Invention of Free Labor* and *Coercion, Contract, and Free Labor in the Nineteenth Century*.

97. Orren, *Belated Feudalism*, 41.

98. Ibid., 70.

99. Ibid., 74, 81, 84.

100. Fisk, "Authors at Work," 21.

101. Fisk, *Working Knowledge*, 78.

102. Ibid., 9.

103. Orren, *Belated Feudalism*, 114.

104. Orren, *Belated Feudalism*.

105. For more on this fascinating legislation, its subsequent amendments and intensifications, and its ultimate transformation into quasi-liberal terms, see Robertson, *The Laborer's Two Bodies*; Castel, *From Manual Workers to Wage Laborers*; Orren, *Belated Feudalism*; and Linder, *The Employment Relationship in Anglo-American Law*.

106. Steinfeld, *The Invention of Free Labor*, 9.

107. Brown, "You Got To Have A Job."

108. Quoted in Perelman, *The Invention of Capitalism*, 102.

109. Quoted in ibid., 103.

110. Steinfeld, *Coercion, Contract, and Free Labor in the Nineteenth Century*, 19.

111. Ibid.

112. Ibid., 26.

113. Ibid.

114. Pateman, *The Sexual Contract*, 147.

115. Ellerman, *Property and Contract in Economics*, 20.

116. Ibid., 32. See also Dahl, *A Preface to Economic Democracy*.

117. Ellerman, *Property and Contract in Economics*, 93–94.

118. Pateman, "Self-Ownership and Property in the Person," 33.

119. Ellerman, *Property and Contract in Economics*, 94–95.

120. Ibid., 137.

121. Ibid., 21.

122. Ibid., 127.

123. Quoted in ibid., 128.

124. Ibid.

125. Ellerman, "Myth and Metaphor in Orthodox Economics," 63.

126. Ellerman, *Property and Contract in Economics*, 41.

127. Ryan, *Making Capital from Culture*, 44.

128. Fisk, "Authors at Work," 32.

129. Fisk, *Working Knowledge*, 81–82.

130. Ibid., 79.

131. Fisk, "Authors at Work," 44.

132. Ibid., 45.

133. Ellerman, *Property and Contract in Economics*, 131.

134. *Work Made for Hire Hearing*, 165.

135. Ellerman, "*Translatio* versus *Concessio*," 462.

136. Blauner, *Alienation and Freedom*, 17.

137. Stewart, "The Freelancer's Trap."

138. Dau-Schmidt et al., *Labor Law in the Contemporary Workplace*, 115.

139. Linder, *The Employment Relationship in Anglo-American Law*, 7.

140. Menger, "Artistic Labor Markets and Careers"; Banks, *The Politics of Cultural Work*, 57.

Conclusion: "I'm Free!"

1. Toynbee, *Making Popular Music*, 6.

2. Quoted in Pateman, *The Sexual Contract*, 75.

3. Frith, *Sound Effects*, 66.

4. Paul Krugman, "Rule by Rentiers," *New York Times*, June 6, 2011.

5. See, for example, Hudson, "The Counter-Enlightenment."

6. Quoted in Stokes, *Starmaking Machinery*, 219.

7. Negus, *Producing Pop*, 140.

8. Linder, *The Employment Relationship in Anglo-American Law*, 5–6.

9. Quoted in ibid., 7.

10. Quoted in ibid., 9.

11. Ibid., 29, note 45.

12. Pateman, "Self-Ownership and Property in the Person," 22.

13. Brown, "You Got To Have A Job."

14. Hesmondhalgh, *The Cultural Industries*, 1st ed., 34.

15. Ibid., 2nd ed., 308.

16. Pateman, "Self-Ownership and Property in the Person," 33.

17. Salmen, "The Social Status of the Musician in the Middle Ages." See also the discussions of minstrels and vagrancy in Baldwin, *Paying the Piper*, especially 79–87.

BIBLIOGRAPHY

Allen, Robert C., and Douglas Gomery. *Film History: Theory and Practice.* New York: Knopf, 1985.

American Idol: The Best and Worst of American Idol, Seasons 1–4. DVD. Burbank, CA: Capital Entertainment Enterprises, 2005.

American Idol: The Search for a Superstar. DVD. Portland, OR: Respond2 Entertainment, 2002.

Andrejevic, Mark. "The Kinder, Gentler Gaze of Big Brother: Reality TV in the Era of Digital Capitalism." *New Media and Society* 4, no. 2 (2002): 251–70.

Anorga, Omar. "Music Contracts Have Musicians Playing in the Key of Unconscionability." *Whittier Law Review* 24 (Spring 2003): 739–73.

Ariès, Philippe. *Centuries of Childhood: A Social History of Family Life.* Translated by Robert Baldick. New York: Knopf, 1962.

Attali, Jacques. *Noise: The Political Economy of Music.* Translated by Brian Massumi. Minneapolis: University of Minnesota Press, 1985.

Baldwin, Elizabeth. *Paying the Piper: Music in Pre-1642 Cheshire.* Kalamazoo, MI: Medieval Institute Publications, Western Michigan University, 2002.

Banks, Mark. *The Politics of Cultural Work,* New York: Palgrave Macmillan, 2007.

Barley, Steven R., and Gideon Kunda. "Design and Devotion: Surges of Rational and

Normative Ideologies of Control in Managerial Discourse." *Administrative Science Quarterly* 37 (September, 1992): 363–99.

———. *Gurus, Hired Guns, and Warm Bodies: Itinerant Experts in a Knowledge Economy*. Princeton: Princeton University Press, 2004.

Barnouw, Erik. *Documentary: A History of the Non-fiction Film*. New York: Oxford University Press, 1993.

Barry, Chris. "Battle of the Battling Bands." *Montreal Mirror*, December 23, 2004–January 5, 2005. http://www.montrealmirror.com/2004/122304/film2.html.

Beck, Ulrich. *The Brave New World of Work*. Translated by Patrick Camiller. Malden, MA: Polity, 2000.

Bender, Daniel E. *Sweated Work, Weak Bodies: Anti-Sweatshop Campaigns and Languages of Labor*. New Brunswick, NJ: Rutgers University Press, 2004.

Bendix, Regina. *In Search of Authenticity: The Formation of Folklore Studies*. Madison: University of Wisconsin Press, 1997.

Biernacki, Richard. *The Fabrication of Labor: Germany and Britain, 1640–1914*. Berkeley: University of California Press, 1995.

Blaufarb, Jonathan. "The Seven Year Itch: California Labor Code Section 2855." *Communication/Entertainment Law Journal* 6, no. 3 (1983–84): 653–93.

Blauner, Robert. *Alienation and Freedom: The Factory Worker and His Industry*. Chicago: University of Chicago Press, 1964.

Bourdieu, Pierre. *Distinction: A Social Critique of the Judgment of Taste*, translated by Richard Nice. Cambridge: Harvard University Press, 1984.

———. *The Field of Cultural Production: Essays on Art and Literature*. Edited and introduced by Randal Johnson. New York: Columbia University Press, 1993.

Brewer, Theresa. "Bankruptcy & Entertainment Law: The Controversial Rejection of Recording Contracts." *American Bankruptcy Institute Law Review* 11 (Winter 2003): 581–606.

Briefs, Goetz. *The Proletariat: A Challenge to Western Civilization*. New York: McGraw-Hill, 1937.

Brown, James. "You Got To Have A Job." *The Singles. Volume* 5: 1967–1969 (CD). Santa Monica, CA: Universal Music and Video Distribution, 2008.

Burawoy, Michael. *The Politics of Production: Factory Regimes under Capitalism and Socialism*. London: Verso, 1985.

Burger, Jean-Claude. *Les oubliés du XXIe siècle ou La fin du travail* [For man must work or The end of work]. Brooklyn, NY: First Run/Icarus Films, 2000.

Burston, Jonathan. "Synthespians among Us: Re-thinking the Actor in Media Work and Media Theory." In *Media and Cultural Theory*, edited by James Curran and David Morley, 250–62. London: Routledge, 2006.

California State Legislature. Senate. Committee on the Judiciary and Select Committee on the Entertainment Industry. *Record Label Accounting Practices, July 23, 2002*. Senate Publication # 1187-S. Sacramento: Senate Rules Committee, 2002.

California State Legislature. Senate. Committee on the Judiciary and Select Committee on the Entertainment Industry. *Record Label Accounting Practices, September 24, 2002.* Senate Publication # 1210-S. Sacramento: Senate Rules Committee, 2002.

California State Legislature. Senate. Select Committee on the Entertainment Industry. *Personal Service Contracts: Seven-year Rule; Exception for Recording Artists.* Senate Publication # 1121-S. Sacramento: Senate Rules Committee, 2001.

Cappello, A. Barry, and Troy A. Thielemann. "Challenging the Practices of the Recording Industry: Recent Lawsuits by Recording Artists Question the Legality of Their Contracts." *Los Angeles Lawyer* 25 (May 2002): 14–19.

Carman, Emily. "Independent Stardom: Female Film Stars and the Studio System in the 1930s." *Women's Studies* 37, no. 6 (2008): 583–615.

Carruthers, Bruce, and Arthur Stinchcombe. "The Social Structure of Liquidity: Flexibility, Markets, and States." *Theory and Society* 28, no. 3 (1999): 353–82.

Castel, Robert. *From Manual Workers to Wage Laborers: Transformation of the Social Question.* Translated and edited by Richard Boyd. New Brunswick, NJ: Transaction, 2003.

———. "The Roads to Disaffiliation: Insecure Work and Vulnerable Relationships." *International Journal of Urban and Regional Research* 24, no. 3 (2000): 519–35.

Chapple, Steve, and Reebee Garofalo. *Rock 'n' Roll Is Here to Pay.* Chicago: Nelson-Hall, 1977.

Clark, Elaine. "Medieval Labor Law and English Local Courts." *American Journal of Legal History* 27, no. 4 (1983): 330–53.

Clover, Corrina C. "Accounting Accountability: Should Record Labels Have a Fiduciary Duty to Report Accurate Royalties to Recording Artists?" *Loyola of Los Angeles Entertainment Law Review* 23, no. 2 (2003): 395–442.

Coates, Norma. "Teenyboppers, Groupies, and Other Grotesques: Girls and Women and Rock Culture in the 1960s and 1970s." *Journal of Popular Music Studies* 15, no. 1 (2003): 65–94.

Cohen, Sara. *Rock Culture in Liverpool: Popular Music in the Making.* Bloomington: Indiana University Press, 1991.

Comis, Alexander G. "Copyright Killed the Internet Star: The Record Industry's Battle to Stop Copyright Infringement Online; A Case Note on UMG Recordings, Inc. v. MP3.com, Inc. and the Creation of a Derivative Work by the Digitization of Pre-1972 Sound Recordings." *Southwestern University Law Review* 31 (2001–2): 754–80.

Cooper, Jay. "Recording Contract Negotiation: A Perspective." *Loyola Entertainment Law Journal* 1, no. 1 (1981): 43–78.

———. "The Right of a Recording Company to Enjoin an Artist from Recording for Others." *Loyola Entertainment Law Journal* 3 (1983): 79–86.

Cornyn, Stan. *Exploding: The Highs, Hits, Hype, Heroes, and Hustlers of the Warner Music Group.* New York: Harper Entertainment, 2002.

Côté, James E., and Anton Allahar. *Generation on Hold: Coming of Age in the Late Twentieth Century.* New York: New York University Press, 1996.

Couldry, Nick. "Teaching Us to Fake It: The Ritualized Norms of Television's 'Reality'

Games." In *Reality TV: Remaking Television Culture*, edited by Susan Murray and Laurie Ouellette. 2nd ed. New York: New York University Press, 2009, 82–99.

Curtis, Robert E. *Your Future in Music*. New York: Richards Rosen, 1962.

Dahl, Robert A. *A Preface to Economic Democracy*. Berkeley: University of California Press, 1985.

Dannen, Fredric. *Hit Men: Power Brokers and Fast Money inside the Music Business*. New York: Vintage, 1991.

Dau-Schmidt, Kenneth C., et al. *Labor Law in the Contemporary Workplace*. St. Paul, MN: Labor Law Group, 2009.

Davidov, Guy. "The Three Axes of Employment Relationships: A Characterization of Workers in Need of Protection." *University of Toronto Law Journal* 52, no. 4 (2002): 357–418.

Delibero, Jeremy. "Copyright Arbitration Royalty Panels and the Webcasting Controversy: The Antithesis of Good Alternative Dispute Resolution." *Pepperdine Dispute Resolution Law Journal* 5, no. 1 (2005): 83–113.

Denisoff, R. Serge. *Tarnished Gold: The Record Industry Revisited*. New Brunswick, NJ: Transaction, 1986.

Derenberg, Walter. *Practical Legal Problems in Music & Recording Industry*. New York: Practising Law Institute, 1971.

Deuze, Mark. *Media Work*. Cambridge: Polity, 2007.

Dobb, Maurice. *Studies in the Development of Capitalism*. London: Routledge and K. Paul, 1963.

Dowd, Timothy J. "Concentration and Diversity Revisited: Production Logics and the U.S. Mainstream Recording Market, 1940–1990." *Social Forces* 82, no. 4 (2004): 1411–55.

Drahos, Peter. *A Philosophy of Intellectual Property*. Brookfield, VT: Dartmouth, 1996.

Draut, Tamara. *Strapped: Why America's 20- and 30-Somethings Can't Get Ahead*. New York: Doubleday, 2006.

Drew, Robert. *On the Road with Duke Ellington*. DVD. 1974. New York: Docurama, 2002.

———. *Primary*. DVD. 1960. New York: Docurama, 2003.

Dyer, Richard. "Entertainment and Utopia." In *The Cultural Studies Reader*, edited by Simon During. London: Routledge, 1993, 271–83.

———. "*A Star Is Born* and the Construction of Authenticity." In *Stardom: Industry of Desire*, edited by Christine Gledhill. London: Routledge, 1991, 132–40.

Eliot, Marc. *Rockonomics: The Money behind the Music*. Rev. and updated ed. New York: Carol, 1993.

Ellerman, David P. "Myth and Metaphor in Orthodox Economics." In David P. Ellerman, *Intellectual Trespassing as a Way of Life: Essays in Philosophy, Economics, and Mathematics*, 49–68. Lanham, MD: Rowman and Littlefield, 1995.

———. *Property and Contract in Economics: The Case for Economic Democracy*. Cambridge, MA: Blackwell, 1992.

———. "*Translatio* versus *Concessio*: Retrieving the Debate about Contracts of Alienation with an Application to Today's Employment Contract." *Politics and Society* 33, no. 3 (2005): 449–80.

Fairchild, Charles. *Pop Idols and Pirates: Mechanisms of Consumption and the Global Circulation of Popular Music.* Aldershot, Hampshire, England: Ashgate, 2008.

Faulkner, Robert. *Hollywood Studio Musicians: Their Work and Careers in the Recording Industry.* Chicago: Aldine-Atherton, 1971.

Field, Corey. "Their Master's Voice? Recording Artists, Bright Lines, and Bowie Bonds: The Debate over Sound Recordings as Works Made for Hire." *Journal of the Copyright Society of the U.S.A.* 48 (1–2) (2000): 145–89.

Fine, Gary, Jeylan Mortimer, and Donald F. Roberts. "Leisure, Work and the Mass Media." In *At the Threshold: The Developing Adolescent,* edited by S. Shirley Feldman and Glen R. Elliott. Cambridge: Harvard University Press, 1990, 225–52.

Fischer, Claude S., et al. *Inequality by Design: Cracking the Bell Curve Myth.* Princeton: Princeton University Press, 1996.

Fisk, Catherine. "Authors at Work: The Origins of the Work-For-Hire Doctrine." *Yale Journal of Law and the Humanities* 15, no. 1 (2003): 1–70.

———. *Working Knowledge: Employee Innovation and the Rise of Corporate Intellectual Property, 1800–1930.* Chapel Hill, NC: University of North Carolina Press, 2009.

Forman, Murray. "'One Night on TV Is Worth Weeks at the Paramount': Musicians and Opportunity in Early Television, 1948–1955." *Popular Music* 21, no. 3 (2002): 249–76.

Frank, Thomas. *The Conquest of Cool: Business Culture, Counterculture, and the Rise of Hip Consumerism.* Chicago: University of Chicago Press, 1997.

———. *One Market under God: Extreme Capitalism, Market Populism, and the End of Economic Democracy.* New York: Doubleday, 2000.

Friedman, Milton. *Capitalism and Freedom.* 1962. Chicago: University of Chicago Press, 2002.

Frisch, Randy S., and Matthew J. Fortnow. "The Time Bomb in the Record Company Vaults," in *Entertainment, Publishing and the Arts Handbook* 111 (1993–94), 115–16.

Frith, Simon. *Sound Effects: Youth, Leisure and the Politics of Rock'n'Roll.* New York: Pantheon, 1981.

Frith, Simon, and Lee Marshall. "Making Sense of Copyright." In *Music and Copyright,* edited by Simon Frith and Lee Marshall, 1–18. 2nd ed. New York: Routledge, 2004.

Gamson, Joshua. *Claims to Fame: Celebrity in Contemporary America.* Berkeley: University of California Press, 1994.

Garofalo, Reebee. "From Music Publishing to MP3: Music and Industry in the Twentieth Century." *American Music* 17, no. 3 (1999): 318–54.

Gee, Grant. *Meeting People Is Easy.* DVD. Hollywood, CA: EMI, 1998.

Geller, Dorothy. "Antinomies of Globalization: Possible Fictions, Ideological Placements, Musical Labor." PhD diss., George Washington University, 2007.

Giddens, Anthony. *Modernity and Self-Identity: Self and Society in the Late Modern Age.* Cambridge: Polity, 1991.

Gitelman, Lisa. "Reading Music, Reading Records, Reading Race: Musical Copyright and the U.S. Copyright Act of 1909." *Musical Quarterly* 81, no. 2 (1997), 265–90.

Gorz, Andre. *Reclaiming Work: Beyond the Wage-Based Society*. Malden, MA: Blackwell, 1999.

Greene, K. J. "Copyright, Culture & Black Music: A Legacy of Unequal Protection." *Hastings Communications and Entertainment Law Journal* 21, no. 2 (1998–99): 339–92.

Greenfield, Steve, and Guy Osborn. *Contract and Control in the Entertainment Industry: Dancing on the Edge of Heaven*. Brookfield, VT: Ashgate, 1998.

———. "Understanding Commercial Music Contracts: The Place of Contractual Theory." *Journal of Contract Law* 23, no. 3 (2007): 248–68.

Hall, Jeanne. "Realism as Style in Cinema Verite: A Critical Analysis of 'Primary.'" *Cinema Journal* 30, no. 4 (1991): 24–50.

Halloran, Mark. *The Musician's Business and Legal Guide*. 4th ed. Upper Saddle River, NJ: Prentice-Hall, 2008

———. *The Musician's Manual: A Practical Career Guide*. New York: Hawthorn Dutton, 1980.

Halpern, Melvin L. "The Sound Recording Act of 1971: An End to Copyright on the High C's?" *George Washington Law Review* 40, no. 5 (1972): 964–94.

Hamilton, Marci. "Commissioned Works as Works Made for Hire under the 1976 Copyright Act: Misinterpretation and Injustice." *University of Pennsylvania Law Review* 135, no. 5 (1987): 1281–329.

Harter, Susan. "Self and Identity Development." In *At the Threshold: The Developing Adolescent*, edited by S. Shirley Feldman and Glen R. Elliott. Cambridge: Harvard University Press, 1990, 352–87.

Harvey, David. *A Brief History of Neoliberalism*. Oxford: Oxford University Press, 2005.

———. *The New Imperialism*. Oxford: Oxford University Press, 2003.

Head, Simon. *The New Ruthless Economy: Work & Power in the Digital Age*. Oxford: Oxford University Press, 2003.

Hearn, Alison. "Reality Television, *The Hills*, and the Limits of the Immaterial Labour Thesis." *Cognition, Communication, Co-operation* 8, no. 1 (2010): 60–76.

Hendershot, Heather. "Belabored Reality: Making It Work on *The Simple Life* and *Project Runway*." In *Reality TV: Remaking Television Culture*, edited by Susan Murray and Laurie Ouellette. 2nd ed. New York: New York University Press, 2009, 243–59.

———. *Saturday Morning Censors: Television Regulation Before the V-Chip*. Durham, NC: Duke University Press, 1998.

Henwood, Doug. *After the New Economy*. New York: New Press, 2003.

Herrnstein, Richard, and Charles Murray. *The Bell Curve: Intelligence and Class Structure in American Life*. New York: Free Press Paperbacks, 1996.

Hesmondhalgh, David. *The Cultural Industries*. 1st ed. London: Sage, 2002.

———. *The Cultural Industries*. 2nd ed. London: Sage, 2007.

———. "Indie: The Institutional Politics and Aesthetics of a Popular Music Genre." *Cultural Studies* 13, no. 1 (1999): 34–61.

Hirsch, Paul. "Processing Fads and Fashions: An Organization-Set Analysis of Cultural Industry Systems." *American Journal of Sociology* 77, no. 4 (1972): 639–59.

Hochschild, Arlie Russell. *The Time Bind: When Work Becomes Home and Home Becomes Work.* New York: Holt, 2001.

Honneth, Axel. "Organized Self-Realization: Some Paradoxes of Individualization." *European Journal of Social Theory* 7, no. 4 (2004): 463–78.

Hudson, Michael. "The Counter-Enlightenment: Its Economic Program—and the Classical Alternative." *Progress*, April 2010, 4–25.

Hull, Geoffrey. *The Recording Industry.* 2nd ed. New York: Routledge, 2004.

———. "Termination Rights and the Real Songwriters." *Vanderbilt Journal of Entertainment and Technology Law* 7, no. 2 (2005): 301–322.

Hunter, Dan. "Culture War." *Law, Social Justice, and Global Development* 2 (2004), http://www2.warwick.ac.uk/fac/soc/law/elj/lgd/2004_2/hunter.

Huws, Ursula. "The Spark in the Engine: Creative Workers in the Global Economy." Keynote address at the Digital Labour: Workers, Authors, Citizens conference, University of Western Ontario, October 17, 2009, London, ON.

Jameson, Fredric. "Marxism and Historicism." *New Literary History* 2, no. 1 (1979): 41–73.

———. *The Political Unconscious: Narrative as a Socially Symbolic Act.* Ithaca: Cornell University Press, 1994.

———. *Postmodernism, or, The Cultural Logic of Late Capitalism.* Durham: Duke University Press, 1991.

———. "Reification and Utopia in Mass Culture." *Social Text* 1, no. 1 (1979): 130–48.

Jones, Abbot Marie. "Get Ready Cause Here They Come: A Look at Problems on the Horizon for Authorship and Termination Rights in Sound Recordings." *Hastings Communication and Entertainment Law Journal* 31, no. 1 (2008): 127–52.

Jones, Mike. "The Music Industry as Workplace: An Approach to Analysis." In *Cultural Work: Understanding the Cultural Industries*, edited by Andrew Beck, 147–56. New York: Routledge, 2003.

Kamenetz, Anya. *Generation Debt: Why Now Is a Terrible Time to Be Young.* New York: Riverhead, 2006.

Karubian, Sara. "360 Deals: An Industry Reaction to the Devaluation of Recorded Music." *Southern California Interdisciplinary Law Journal* 18, no. 2 (2009): 395–462.

Keightley, Keir. "Long Play: Adult-Oriented Popular Music and the Temporal Logics of the Post-War Sound Recording Industry in the USA." *Media, Culture & Society* 26, no. 3 (2004): 375–91.

———. "Manufacturing Authenticity: Imagining the Music Industry in Anglo-American Cinema, 1956–62." In *Movie Music, The Film Reader*, edited by Kay Dickinson. New York: Routledge, 2003, 165–80.

———. "Reconsidering Rock." In *The Cambridge Companion to Pop and Rock*, edited by Simon Frith, Will Straw, and John Street, 109–42. New York: Cambridge University Press, 2001.

Kemper, Tom. *Hidden Talent: The Emergence of Hollywood Agents.* Berkeley: University of California Press, 2010.

Klaprat, Cathy. "The Star as Market Strategy: Bette Davis in Another Light." In *The American Film Industry*, edited by Tino Balio, 351–76. Rev. ed. Madison: University of Wisconsin Press, 1985.

Knab, Christopher, and Bartley F. Day. *Music Is Your Business: The Musician's FourFront Strategy for Success.* 3rd ed. Seattle: FourFront Media and Music, 2007.

Kraft, Philip. "To Control and Inspire: U.S. Management in the Age of Computer Information Systems and Global Production." In *Rethinking the Labor Process*, edited by Mark Wardell, Thomas L. Steiger, and Peter Meiksins. Albany: State University of New York Press, 1999, 17–36.

Krasilovsky, M. William, and Sidney Shemel. *This Business of Music.* 10th ed. New York: Billboard, 2003.

Kretschmer, Martin, and Friedermann Kawohl. "The History and Philosophy of Copyright." In *Music and Copyright*, edited by Simon Frith and Lee Marshall. 2nd ed. New York: Routledge, 2004, 21–53.

Lash, Scott, and John Urry. *Economies of Signs and Space.* London: Sage, 1994.

Leach, Elizabeth. "Vicars of 'Wannabe': Authenticity and the Spice Girls." *Popular Music* 20, no. 2 (2001): 143–67.

Lemann, Nicholas. *The Big Test: The Secret History of the American Meritocracy.* New York: Farrar, Straus and Giroux, 1999.

Levin, G. Roy. *Documentary Explorations: 15 Interviews with Film-Makers.* Garden City, NY: Doubleday, 1971.

Light, Jeffrey B. "The California Injunction Statute and the Music Industry: What Price Relief?" *Columbia Journal of Art and the Law* 7, no. 2 (1982): 141–78.

Linder, Marc. *The Employment Relationship in Anglo-American Law: A Historical Perspective.* New York: Greenwood: 1989.

Lipsitz, George. *Footsteps in the Dark: The Hidden Histories of Popular Music.* Minneapolis: University of Minnesota Press, 2007.

———. *Time Passages: Collective Memory and American Popular Culture.* Minneapolis: University of Minnesota Press, 1990.

Locke, John. "Second Treatise of Government." 1689. In John Locke, *Two Treatises of Government*, edited by Mark Goldie, 115–240. Everyman ed. London: J. M. Dent, 1993.

London Film Festival. "Rockumentary Debate Live Online." 2004. http://www.lff .org.uk/news_details.php?NewsID=39. Archived at: http://web.archive.org/web/ 20050205001711/http://www.lff.org.uk/news_details.php?NewsID=39.

Lopes, Paul D. "Innovation and Diversity in the Popular Music Industry, 1969 to 1990." *American Sociological Review* 57, no. 1 (1992): 56–71.

Lusted, David. "The Glut of the Personality." In *Stardom: Industry of Desire*, edited by Christine Gledhill. London: Routledge, 1991, 251–58.

Macpherson, C. B. *Democratic Theory: Essays in Retrieval*. Oxford: Clarendon Press of Oxford University Press, 1973.

———. *The Life and Times of Liberal Democracy*. Oxford: Oxford University Press, 1977.

———. *The Political Theory of Possessive Individualism: Hobbes to Locke*. Oxford: Clarendon Press of Oxford University Press, 1962.

Marshall, Lee. "Metallica and Morality: The Rhetorical Battleground of the Napster Wars." *Entertainment Law* 1, no. 1 (2002): 1–19.

Martin, Peter. *Sounds and Society: Themes in the Sociology of Music*. New York: Manchester University Press, 1996.

Marx, Karl. *Capital: Volume 1*, Introduced and edited by Ernest Mandel and translated by Ben Fowkes. New York: Vintage Books, 1977.

———. *The Economic and Philosophical Manuscripts of 1944*, edited by Dirk J. Struik and translated by Martin Milligan. New York: International Publishers, 1964.

———. "On the Jewish Question." In *The Marx-Engels Reader*, edited by Robert C. Tucker, 26–52. 2nd ed. New York: Norton, 1978.

Mascuch, Michael. *Origins of the Individualist Self: Autobiography and Self-Identity in England, 1591–1791*. Stanford: Stanford University Press, 1996.

McConvey, Joel. "*Dig!*" *Eye Weekly*, October 7, 2004. http://archives.eyeweekly.com/archived/article/26880.

McLane, Ben, and Venice Wong. "Practice Tips: How Recording Artists Have Broken Their Contracts." *Los Angeles Lawyer* 22 (April 1999): 27–55.

McRobbie, Angela. "Clubs to Companies: Notes on the Decline of Political Culture in Speeded Up Creative Worlds." *Cultural Studies* 16, no. 4 (2002): 516–31.

Meizel, Katherine. *Idolized: Music Media and Identity in "American Idol."* Bloomington: Indiana University Press, 2011.

———. "Making the Dream a Reality Show: The Celebration of Failure in *American Idol*." *Popular Music and Society* 32, no. 4 (2009), 475–88.

———. "A Singing Citizenry: Popular Music and Civil Religion in America." *Journal for the Scientific Study of Religion* 45, no. 4 (2006): 497–503.

Menger, Pierre-Michel. "Artistic Labor Markets and Careers." *Annual Review of Sociology* 25 (1999): 541–74.

———. *Portrait de l'Artiste en Travailleur: Métamorphoses du Capitalisme*. Paris: Seuil, 2002.

Mentzer, Stefan M. "Sound Recordings and Unintended Consequences of the Anti-cybersquatting Consumer Protection Act." *Computer & Internet Lawyer* 18, no. 7 (2001): 14–43.

Miege, Bernard. *The Capitalization of Cultural Production*. New York: International General, 1989.

Miller, William Ian. *Humiliation: And Other Essays on Honor, Social Discomfort, and Violence*. Ithaca: Cornell University Press, 1993.

Mitroff, Donna, et al. *Prime-Time Teens: Perspectives on the New Youth-Media Environment*. New York: William T. Grant Foundation, 2004.

Mohr, Ian. "Docmaker Branches Out." *Variety*, January 3–9, 2005, 14.

Mooney, Donna R. "The Search for a Legal Presumption of Employment Duration or Custom of Arbitrary Dismissal in California 1848–1872." *Berkeley Journal of Employment and Labor Law* 21, no. 2 (2000): 633–76.

Negus, Keith. *Producing Pop: Culture and Conflict in the Popular Music Industry*. London: Arnold, 1992.

Nichols, Bill. *Representing Reality: Issues and Concepts in Documentary*. Bloomington: Indiana University Press, 1991.

Nimmer, David, and Peter S. Menell. "Sound Recordings, Works for Hire, and the Termination-of-Transfers Time Bomb." *Journal of the Copyright Society of the USA* 49, no. 2 (2001): 387–416.

Nimmer, Melville B. *Nimmer on Copyright: A Treatise on the Law of Literary, Musical and Artistic Property, and the Protection of Ideas*. 2 vols.; loose-leaf (consulted on March 4, 2005). Albany, NY: M. Bender, 1978/2005.

Orren, Karen. *Belated Feudalism: Labor, the Law, and Liberal Development in the United States*. New York: Cambridge University Press, 1991.

Ouellette, Laurie, and James Hay. *Better Living through Reality TV: Television and Post-Welfare Citizenship*. Malden, MA: Blackwell, 2008.

Passman, Donald. *All You Need to Know about the Music Business*. 6th ed. New York: Free Press, 2006.

Pateman, Carole. "The Equivalent of the Right to Land, Life, and Liberty? Democracy and the Idea of a Basic Income." 90th UCLA Faculty Research Lecture, April 18, 2001, Los Angeles, CA.

———. "Self-Ownership and Property in the Person: Democratization and a Tale of Two Concepts." *Journal of Political Philosophy* 10, no. 1 (2002): 20–53.

———. *The Sexual Contract*. Stanford: Stanford University Press, 1988.

———. "Why Republicanism?" *Basic Income Studies* 2, no. 2 (2007): 1–6.

Perelman, Michael. *The Invention of Capitalism: Classical Political Economy and the Secret History of Primitive Accumulation*. Durham: Duke University Press, 2000.

Peterson, Richard A., and David G. Berger. "Measuring Industry Concentration, Diversity, and Innovation in Popular Music." *American Sociological Review* 61, no. 1 (1996): 175–78.

Phillips, L. Lee, and Jody E. Graham. "New Developments in Recording Contract Negotiations: Reflections of a Changing Economic Profile." *Entertainment and Sports Lawyer* 2, no. 3 (1984) 1, 5–17.

Pizello, Chris. "Production Slate: Sex Fiends and Rock 'n' Roll Rivals: Battle of the Bands." *American Cinematographer* 85, no. 10 (2004): 26–30.

Plumb, J. H. "The New World of Children." In *The Birth of a Consumer Society: The*

Commercialization of Eighteenth-Century England, edited by Neil McKendrick, John Brewer, and J. H. Plumb, 286–315. Bloomington: Indiana University Press, 1982.

Polanyi, Karl. *The Great Transformation*. 1944. Boston: Beacon, 1965.

Raphael, Chad. "The Political Economic Origins of Reali-TV." In *Reality TV: Remaking Television Culture*. 2nd ed., edited by Susan Murray and Laurie Ouellette, 123–140. New York: New York University Press, 2009.

Regev, Motti. "Producing Artistic Value: The Case of Rock Music." *Sociological Quarterly* 35, no. 1 (1994): 85–102.

Reich, Robert B. *The Future of Success*. New York: Knopf, 2000.

Riesman, David. *The Lonely Crowd: A Study of the Changing American Character*. Rev. ed. New Haven: Yale University Press, 1961 [1950].

Ripley, Kathleen. "Moving to the Beat: Digital Media and Changing Tastes Force Publishers to Fine-Tune Strategies." *IBISWorld Industry Report 51223: Music Publishing in the US*, October 2010. http://clients.ibisworld.com/industryUS/default.aspx?indid=1253.

Robertson, Kellie. *The Laborer's Two Bodies: Labor and the "Work" of the Text in Medieval Britain, 1350–1500*. London: Palgrave Macmillan, 2006.

Rose, Mark. *Authors and Owners: The Invention of Copyright*. Cambridge: Harvard University Press, 1993.

Ross, Andrew. "The Mental Labor Problem." *Social Text* 18, no. 2 (2000): 1–31.

Rousseau, Jean-Jacques. *Discourse on the Sciences and Arts (First Discourse) and Polemics*. Edited by Roger D. Masters and Christopher Kelly. Translated by Judith R. Bush, Roger D. Masters, and Christopher Kelly. Hanover, NH: University Press of New England, 1992.

———. *The Social Contract and Discourses*. 1755. Translated by G. D. H. Cole. London: Dent, 1973.

Rubin, Isaac. *Essays on Marx's Theory of Value*. 1928. Translated by Miloš Samardźija and Fredy Perlman. Montreal: Black Rose, 1973.

Ryan, Bill. *Making Capital from Culture: The Corporate Form of Capitalist Cultural Production*. New York: de Gruyter, 1992.

Sabo, Donald, and Sue Curry Jansen. "Images of Men in Sport Media: The Social Reproduction of Gender Order." In *Men, Masculinity, and the Media*, edited by Steve Craig, 169–84. Newbury Park, CA: Sage, 1992.

Salmen, Walter. "The Social Status of the Musician in the Middle Ages." In *The Social Status of the Professional Musician from the Middle Ages to the 19th Century*, edited by Walter Salmen, 3–29. New York: Pendragon, 1983.

Sanjek, Russell, and David Sanjek. *American Popular Music Business in the 20th Century*. New York: Oxford University Press, 1991.

Saunders, Dave. *Direct Cinema: Observational Documentary and the Politics of the Sixties*. London: Wallflower, 2007.

Sawhill, Isabel. "Still the Land of Opportunity?" *Public Interest*, Spring 1999, no. 135, 3–17.

Sawyer, Miranda. "Battle of the Bands: On the Road to Hell with the Monsters of Rock." *New Statesman*, July 4, 2005, 47.

Sayers, Sean. "The Need to Work: A Perspective from Philosophy." In *On Work: Historical, Comparative, and Theoretical Approaches*, edited by R. E. Pahl, 722–41. New York: Blackwell, 1988.

Seeman, Melvin. "On the Meaning of Alienation." *American Sociological Review* 24, no. 6 (1959): 783–91.

Sennett, Richard. *The Corrosion of Character: The Personal Consequences of Work in the New Capitalism*. New York: Norton, 1998.

———. *The Culture of the New Capitalism*. New Haven: Yale University Press, 2006.

Severn, Stephen E. "Robbie Robertson's Big Break: A Reevaluation of Martin Scorsese's *The Last Waltz*." *Film Quarterly* 56, no. 2 (2003): 25–31.

Shemel, Sidney, and M. William Krasilovsky. *This Business of Music*. New York: Billboard, 1971.

Shklar, Judith. *American Citizenship: The Quest for Inclusion*. Cambridge: Harvard University Press, 1991.

Solbrig, Heide. *Film and Function: A History of Industrial Motivation Film*. PhD dissertation. San Diego, CA: University of California, San Diego, 2004.

Sorenson, Lon. "California's Recording Industry Accounting Practices Act, SB 1034: New Auditing Rights for Artists." *Berkeley Technology Law Journal* 20, no. 1 (2005): 933–52.

Stahl, Matt. "Authentic Boy Bands on TV? Performers and Impresarios in *The Monkees* and *Making the Band*." *Popular Music* 21, no. 3 (2002): 307–29.

———. "Cultural Labor's 'Democratic Deficits': Employment, Autonomy, and Alienation in U.S. Film Animation." *Journal for Cultural Research* 14, no. 3 (2010): 271–293.

———. "Non-Proprietary Authorship and the Uses of Autonomy: Artistic Labor in American Film Animation, 1900–2004." *LABOR* 2, no. 4 (2005): 87–105.

———. "Primitive Accumulation, the Social Common, and the Contractual Lockdown of Recording Artists at the Threshold of Digitalization." *Ephemera* 10, nos. 3–4 (2010): 337–55.

———. "Privilege and Distinction in Production Worlds: Copyright, Collective Bargaining, and Working Conditions in Media Making." In *Production Studies: Cultural Studies of Media Industries*, edited by Vicki Mayer, Miranda J. Banks, and John T. Caldwell, 54–67. New York: Routledge, 2008.

Stahl, Matt, and Leslie M. Meier. "The Firm Foundation of Organizational Flexibility: The 360 Contract in the Digitalizing Music Industry." *Canadian Journal of Communication*, forthcoming.

Steinberg, Robert. "Injunctions—Unjust Restraints on Entertainers in California." *Loyola Entertainment Law Journal* 1, no. 1 (1981): 91–111.

Steinfeld, Robert J. *Coercion, Contract, and Free Labor in the Nineteenth Century*. New York: Cambridge University Press, 2001.

———. *The Invention of Free Labor: The Employment Relation in English and American Law and Culture, 1350–1870*. Chapel Hill: University of North Carolina Press, 1991.

Stewart, Johanna Fisher. "The Freelancer's Trap: Work for Hire under the Copyright Act of 1976." *West Virginia Law Review* 86, no. 3 (1984): 1305–16.

Stokes, Geoffrey. *Starmaking Machinery: Inside the Business of Rock and Roll*. New York: Vintage, 1976.

Straw, Will. "Popular Music as Cultural Commodity: The American Recorded Music Industries 1976–1985." PhD diss., McGill University, 1990.

Strohm, John P. "Writings in the Margin (of Error): The Authorship Status of Sound Recordings under United States Copyright Law." *Cumberland Law Review* 34 (2003–4): 127–56.

Suchman, Mark C. "The Contract as Social Artifact." *Law and Society Review* 37, no. 1 (2003): 91–142.

Taylor, Charles. *The Ethics of Authenticity*. Cambridge MA: Harvard University Press, 1992.

Timoner, Ondi. "The Diary of a Guerilla [*sic*] Filmmaker." Movienet, 2004. http://web .archive.org/web/20040917035803/http://www.movienet.com/dig.html. Accessed April 16, 2012.

———. *Dig!* DVD. Los Angeles: Interloper Films, 2004.

Toynbee, Jason. "Fingers to the Bone or Spaced out on Creativity? Labor Process and Ideology in the Production of Pop." In *Cultural Work: Understanding the Cultural Industries*, edited by Andrew Beck. New York: Routledge, 2003, 39–55.

———. *Making Popular Music: Musicians, Creativity and Institutions*. London: Arnold, 2000.

Tregoning, William. "'Very Solo': Anecdotes of Authentic Identity." *M/C Journal* 7, no. 5 (2004). http://journal.media-culture.org.au/0411/04-tregoning.php. Accessed May 6, 2006.

Tschmuck, Peter. *Creativity and Innovation in the Music Industry*. Dordrecht, the Netherlands: Springer, 2006.

Tusher, Will. "Amended Proposal Clears Senate Committee with a Major Compromise Added." *Variety*, June 13, 1985, 1, 15.

———. "Personal-Service Contracts Bill Not a Dead Matter Yet." *Variety*, June 12, 1985, 4.

United States Congress. House. Committee on the Judiciary. Subcommittee on Courts and Intellectual Property. *United States Copyright Office and sound recordings as work made for hire: hearing before the Subcommittee on Courts and Intellectual Property of the Committee on the Judiciary, House of Representatives, 106ᵗʰ Congress, 2nd session, May 25, 2000*. Washington: U.S. G.P.O., 2000. http://commdocs.house.gov/ committees/judiciary/hju65223.000/hju65223_0.HTM. Accessed April 19, 2012.

Van Beveren, Theresa. "The Demise of the Long-Term Personal Service Contract in the Music Industry: Artistic Freedom against Company Profit." UCLA *Entertainment Law Review* 3, no. 2 (1996): 377–425.

Wallulis, Jerald. *The New Insecurity: The End of the Standard Job and Family*. Albany: State University of New York Press, 1998.

Webb, Peter. *Exploring the Networked Worlds of Popular Music: Milieu Cultures*. New York: Routledge, 2007.

Weber, Max. *The Protestant Ethic and the Spirit of Capitalism*. Translated by Talcott Parsons. New York: Scribner, 1958.

Weir, Stan. *Singlejack Solidarity*. Edited and with an afterword by George Lipsitz. Minneapolis: University of Minnesota Press, 2004.

Wertsch, James. "Collective Memory: Issues from a Sociohistorical Perspective." In *Mind, Culture, and Activity: Seminal Papers from the Laboratory of Comparative Human Cognition*, edited by Michael Cole, Yrjo Engestrom, and Olga Vasquez. New York: Cambridge University Press, 1997, 226–32.

Widerquist, Karl. "Effective Control Self-Ownership: Freedom as the Power to Say No." Unpublished manuscript, 2008.

Woodmansee, Martha. "The Genius and the Copyright: Economic and Legal Conditions of the Emergence of the 'Author.'" *Eighteenth-Century Studies* 17, no. 4 (1984): 425–48.

Writers Guild of America. *Residuals Survival Guide*. Los Angeles: Writers Guild of America, West, 2005. http://www.wga.org/uploadedFiles/writers_resources/residuals/residualssurvival05.pdf.

Wurster, Jon. "See Band Run: 'Bands on the Run.'" *Independent Weekly*, June 27, 2001. http://web.archive.org/web/20080726200425/http://www.indyweek.com/durham/2001-06-27/music2.html. Accessed 4/16/2012.

Young, Michael D. *The Rise of the Meritocracy*. New Brunswick, NJ: Transaction, 1994.

Zanes, R. J. Warren. "Too Much Mead? Under the Influence (of Participant Observation)." In *Reading Rock and Roll: Authenticity, Appropriation, Aesthetics*, edited by Kevin J. H. Dettmar and William Richey, 37–71. New York: Columbia University Press, 1999.

Zaretsky, Eli. *Capitalism, the Family, and Personal Life*. New York: Perennial Library, 1986.

Zelizer, Viviana A. R. *Pricing the Priceless Child: The Changing Social Value of Children*. New York: Basic, 1985.

INDEX

Beatles, the, 40, 68, 77, 80, 189, 192
Bendix, Regina, 47–48
Bentham, Jeremy, 106
Berle, Adolph, 138–39
Berman, Howard, 191
Berman, Steve, 157
Bertelsmann Music Group (BMG), 121, 257n40
Billboard pop chart, 40
"bird-freedom," 11
Black Death (1348), 108, 256n27
Blauner, Robert, 6, 22–23, 110–11, 223
blockbuster model of entertainment marketing, 27, 109, 120–22, 124–25, 130, 135–37, 139, 140, 153, 253n105. *See also* recording industry
Blues Foundation, 104
Blur (band), 77
boilerplate, 130–31, 135, 186, 197. *See also* standard contract
Bomp Records, 76, 88
Born in the USA (album), 120
Boston Globe, 46
Bourdieu, Pierre, 16, 46
Branca, John, 157
Brian Jonestown Massacre (BJM) (band), 26, 34, 64, 75–81, 83–84, 87–92, 94–95, 102, 105, 228, 246n68
Briefs, Goetz, 14
Brown, James, 216, 232
Browne, Jackson, 118
Burston, Jonathan, 106

California Federation of Labor, 128
California Labor Code, section 2855. *See* seven-year rule
California Labor Code, section 2855(b) ("carve out"), 126–27, 135, 143–44, 149, 151, 155, 164, 170
Candid Camera (TV program), 43
capital: 228; contractarian view of, 168, 178; cultural, 34, 88, 93, 103; in cultural industries, 15–16, 102, 110, 112; in democratic theory, 181, 212, 218–19, 265n67;

in economic theory, 221; "featured artist" identification with, 204, 207; indie cultural producers and, 81–82, 84–85; labor shortage and, 136; neoliberalizing, 96, 98, 102; reality TV and, 41–42; record industry, 107, 117–18; *rentiers* and, 229; self-actualization and, 92–93; self-provisioning and, 236n23; social, 93, 103; social authorship and, 9; in television production, 44–45. *See also* "art-capital relation," contradictions in; capitalism
capitalism: creative work and, 10, 12; development of, 266n80; direction of hiring bargain in, 218–19; freedom in, 97–98, 136, 181; liberalism and, 226; Marx on, 181; neoliberal transformation of, 41, 229, 236n7; "new" capitalism, 12, 33, 45, 67; nonsynchronicity and, 17–18; reality TV and, 41; welfare, 62, 64
Capitol Records, 76, 84, 131, 135, 253n107
career and professional guides, music, 11, 122–24, 125, 132, 249n40, 252n87, 252n89
Carey, Mariah, 39
Carruthers, Bruce, 138–39
catalog. *See* sound recordings
CBGB (nightclub), 77
CBS Records, 121
Chaitovitz, Ann, 152, 265n57
Chapple, Steve, 117
Christgau, Robert, 121
cinema verité, 73, 244n24
cinema verité, American. *See* direct cinema
civil mastery, 23, 173, 211. *See also* civil subordination
civil society, 159–60, 206
civil subordination, 23, 159, 173, 179, 211. *See also* indentured servitude
Civil War, U.S., 144, 222
Clark, Elaine, 137
Clarkson, Kelly, 36–38, 40, 45, 50, 53
Clash, the (band), 65
class: in *American Idol*, 53, 58; copyright and, 187; democratic theory and, 180; in

de Haviland v. Warner Bros. Pictures, 116–17, 133, 136, 161–62, 169, 173, 176

deinstitutionalization, 5, 70, 82, 89, 93–94, 96–97, 236n7. *See also* individualization; neoliberalism

De La Hoya, Oscar, 133, 259n78

democracy: democratic discourse, 43; democratic social relations, 45; employment and, 4, 103, 211–12, 214, 218–20, 232–33; lawmakers in, 21; liberalism and, 14–15, 27–28, 38, 53, 141, 174, 215, 229; political processes in, 69; promises of, 2, 5, 38, 47, 53; responsibility and, 219–20; theory and theorists of, 2, 6–7, 23, 35, 148, 172, 177, 212, 214, 218–20

democratization, 174, 177, 182, 214, 232–34; of modernist impulse, 70–71

Denisoff, Serge, 119

Deuze, Mark, 13, 15, 237n42

Dig! (film), 26, 33–35, 64–67, 69, 72–77, 79, 81–83, 85–87, 89, 91–96, 98–99, 105, 227

Dills, Ralph (California state senator), 127–29, 134, 252n100

direct cinema, 67–69, 72–74, 80, 91, 96; conventions of, 71; reformism of, 89; as technique of *Dig!*, 85; as "text genre," 73, 97. *See also* documentary (film genre)

Directors Guild of America, 128

disco, 118–19

Discreet Records, 131

Disney, 189

dispossession, 6, 103; as element of work for hire, 185–87, 225. *See also* accumulation by dispossession

division of labor, 7, 15–17, 95, 187, 211, 232, 243n16

Dixie Chicks, 202, 255n12

Dobb, Maurice, 136

documentary (film genre), 34, 64, 67–68, 71–74, 89, 91, 93, 95; rhetoric of, 97. *See also* direct cinema

domination, 109, 154; in contract, 105, 160, 162–63, 180–81; as controversial in creative work, 19, 23; as feature of employ-

ment, 112; obscuring by market forces, 217–19; paradoxical endurance of by recording artists, 228, 258n53, 261n106; as precursor to exploitation, 212, 214; re-naturalization of, 28. *See also* appropriation; exploitation

Dont Look Back (film), 68

Drew, Robert, 68, 243n20

Drew Associates, 68–69, 71, 74, 243n22

drug use: as "productive excess," 86, 91, 246n65; as "wanton excess," 86–87, 246n65

Dunkleman, Brian, 53, 239n1

Dyer, Richard, 38, 52, 58, 241n51, 241n72

Dylan, Bob, 1, 68, 121

Eagles, the (band), 118

economic crisis, 229–30

economic security, 96

Elektra Records, 118, 132

Ellerman, David, 159, 182, 218–21, 223, 248n26, 261n101

employee: legal status of, 185, 212; as protected status, 185; social status of, 230

Employee Barriers to Good Service (film), 72

employment: atavism of, 214; boundary between servitude/slavery and, 173, 177, 218; as central liberal institution, 24; command and obedience in, 175; democratic critique of, 211, 214, 218, 229; deregulation of, 174; domination and, 112, 217–18; as exchange of properties, 178; as impediment to democratization, 177; as object of public policy, 114–17; political liberalization and, 174–75; regulation of, 185; relation to democratic principles, 4, 229; as rental of persons, 219–21, 248n26; social benefits attached to, 174; subordination and, 232–33; as system of private rule, 112, 212–14, 219, 234; work for hire and, 190, 262n6

End of the Century (film), 73

Guarini, Justin, 40, 45, 50
Guirenot, Jim, 174

Habitat for Humanity, 50
Hagar, Sammy, 131, 251n86
Hamilton, Marci, 193, 200
handicraft. *See* artisanal "craft" production
Handy Artists Relief Trust, 104
Harleston, Jeff, 150, 154, 157
Harvey, David, 5
Hay, James, 41–42
Haynes, Ray (California state senator), 146, 157–61, 163, 165–66, 168–72, 176, 178–79
Hearn, Alison, 41–42
Hendershot, Heather, 49
Henley, Don, 104, 150–52, 157, 194, 200–202, 228, 231, 251n86
Herrnstein, Richard, 59
Hesmondhalgh, David, 7, 16, 31, 233, 237n28, 238n71
Hirsch, Paul, 135
Holmes, Oliver Wendell (Supreme Court Justice), 220
Holzman, Jac, 132
Honneth, Axel, 69–70, 72, 82, 86, 92, 97
house arrest, 161
Houston, Whitney, 46, 249n36
Hull, Geoffrey, 191, 247n1
humiliation: definition of, 54; in *American Idol*, 26, 38–39, 45, 48–49, 51–52, 54–55
Hung, William, 48
husband, socio-legal status of, 3–4, 180, 214, 227

I Am Trying to Break Your Heart (film), 73
"identity fiction," 223
imputation, judicial principle of, 220
indentured servitude: contrasted with employment, 128, 260n88; contrasted with voluntarism, 164; as function of recording contract, 151; as legitimate under contractarianism, 182; as object of labor law, 158, 161, 174; as rhetorical critique of employment, 148, 153; rhetorical invo-

cation by recording artists of, 27, 103, 144–46, 160, 173, 179–80
independent contracting: contrasted with employment, 57, 122, 184, 194–95; distinction between employment and, 129; as preference of neoliberal employers, 185
independent contractor: bargaining power of, 223–24; social status of, 230; subordination and, 232–33
individualism, 43, 58–60, 69–72
individualization: democratic-theoretical critique of, 180; "mass," 70–72; in neoliberalism, 5, 99; in popular musical narrative, 82, 97; the production of celebrity and, 50; of work, 12–15, 19, 94, 240
institutional autonomy, 8–9. *See also* autonomy
Intel Corporation, 87
intellectual property, 3, 230, 266n74; in *American Idol* contracts, 247n1; appropriation by record companies, 150, 195–96; as basis of rents, 99; market performance of as basis for residual payments, 274n49; as object of work for hire, 10, 23, 28, 186–91, 215–16; possessive individualism and, 206; as product of creative labor, 25; in recording industry, 229–30; retention of rights to by recording artists, 57; as right of natural authors, 211; rights in contrast with worker rights, 184; as social institution, 4, 9; sound recordings protected as, 192; as workplace product, 222–23
Interscope Records, 157, 165
Irell and Manella (law firm), 157

Jackson, Michael, 120, 122, 189
Jackson, Randy, 39
James, Caryn, 46
Jameson, Fredric, 17–18, 44
Jansen, Sue Curry, 59
Janus (deity), 10, 17, 19, 231

Marenberg, Steve, 157
Marshall, Lee, 126
Martin, Ricky, 48
Marx, Karl, 22, 97–98, 110, 112, 140, 181, 213
Mascuch, Michael, 59–60
mass society critique, 69–72, 82; commercial career of, 93; in direct cinema, 69
master: employer as, 212–16; husband as, 3, 213; recording artist as, 3, 227, 231. *See also* master and servant, law of
master and servant, law of, 10, 113, 139, 214–16, 250n48, 267n105. *See also* labor law; master
master recording, 188–89
Matsushita, 121
Maysles, Albert, 68–69, 71–72, 245n58
Maysles, David, 68, 72, 245n58
MCA Records, 109, 117, 120–23, 140, 150, 154, 157, 252n87
McCabe, Zia, 76, 86–88
"McJobs," 56–57
McKibbin, Nikki, 56
Means, Gardiner, 138–39
medieval Europe, 256n27; patterns of labor in, 136–37; status of musicians in, 234
Meeting People Is Easy (film), 73, 247n99
Meizel, Katherine, 33, 43–44
Menger, Pierre-Michel, 12–13, 15, 93–96
meritocracy, 52–53, 54, 58–59
Metallica (band), 65, 73, 98, 251–52n86
Metallica: Some Kind of Monster (film), 73, 98
Michael, George, 125, 251n86, 252n93
Miege, Bernard, 7, 15–17, 237n28
Mill, John Stuart, 2, 6–7, 148, 171, 227
"millennial flip flop" in copyright law, 187, 192, 222
Miller, William Ian, 54–55
Minutemen, the (band), 65
Mitchell, Joni, 118, 194
mobility, of labor: 13, 15; in conditions of labor shortage, 136–37; recording artists and, 8, 139, 151–52
mobility, social: 35; in medieval England,

103; meritocracy and, 59; in neoliberalism, 4, 57, 242n80; in popular music narrative, 26, 33, 37–38, 47, 54, 60, 65–66, 96, 103; of popular music performers, 230; postwar, 70, 94; power relations and, 174, 228; rules of, 55, 87. *See also* class
Monkees, The (TV program), 56, 241n45
Monterey Pop (film), 65, 68
Motown Records, 107–9, 201
MTV, 121, 165, 244n31
Murray, Charles, 59
Murray, Kevin, 143–45, 149–50, 155–57, 160–63, 169, 172–73, 176

National Academy of Recording Arts and Sciences (NARAS), 176
Nature of the Beast (film), 78
Negus, Keith, 16, 114, 230, 249n40
"neofeudalism," 229
neoliberalism, 4–6, 236n7; *American Idol* and, 38, 49, 59, 63; creative workers and, 12–13, 28–29, 33; "deinstitutionalization" in, 82; as dominant discourse, 160, 172–73, 185, 213; economic supernumeraries in, 96; erosion of social entitlements in, 41; image of working person in, 5; individualist subjectivity and, 82–83, 89; individualization in, 70; precarious conditions of workers under, 174; "push" and "pull" of, 5; reality TV as expression of, 40–42; segmentation and ranking of work force in, 94; self-actualization in, 70
Newcombe, Anton, 75–81, 83–87, 90–91, 94–96, 245n55, 245n57, 246n68
New Deal, 216
Newton-John, Olivia, 27, 109, 117, 122; contract with MCA, 123; lawsuit against MCA, 123–25, 132, 137, 140–41, 252n87
New York Times, 46
Nichols, Bill, 73–74, 97
nonalienation. *See* de-alienation
nostalgia, for 1960s, 80, 84

Oasis (band), 77
opportunity, in popular music narrative, 42
Ordinance of Labourers (1349), 10
"ordinariness" of stars, 48, 52
Orren, Karen, 113
Osborn, Guy, 167–68
Ouellette, Laurie, 41–42

participation: democratic, 3, 47, 59, 69, 157, 163, 187, 201, 233; in recording industry income flows, 195, 263n37. See also royalties
Pateman, Carole, 3–4, 23, 101, 105, 143, 158–59, 169, 173, 177–81, 212, 214, 218–19, 227, 234, 249n35, 258n53, 261n106
paternalism, 169–70
Peace, Steve (California state senator), 157
pedagogy, in mass media, 38, 82
Pennebaker, D. A., 68, 71–72, 245n58
personal service, 115–16, 126, 128, 134, 162, 166. See also contract, employment; contract, recording
Peters, Marybeth, 193
piano roll, as mechanical reproduction, 189
Polanyi, Karl, 111
Police, the (band), 121
political economy, 3, 6, 20–22, 27, 95, 135, 226–28; definition of, 21
Pop Idol (TV program), 39–40
popular culture: reification in, 44; utopia in, 44, 58
popular music culture: democratic promise in, 47, 53; utopian values of, 18
possessive individualism, 60
postindustrial capitalism, 6, 60, 226, 236n7
precariousness, 266n80; of musical work, 11, 340n19. See also employment; neoliberalism
prefiguration, perception of in creative labor. See creative labor
privatization, 182
"privileged poor," 85

professionalism, 102
professionalization: of music makers, 21, 26, 28, 32–34, 47, 49, 56, 65, 102, 106, 227, 240n20; of Ondi Timoner, 34, 95. See also career and professional guides, music
professional sports, 59
proletarianization, 243n16
proletarians, 66, 136, 207, 223, 224, 230–31
property, labor theory of, 218, 220
property in the person, 178–79, 220; contrasted with self-ownership, 261n106; political fiction of, 180
Pyromania (album), 121

Radiohead (band), 65, 73, 247n99
RCA Records, 121, 249n36
reality TV: ideology and, 41–42; neoliberalism and, 41–42. See also American Idol
record companies: as creators of markets, 165; as investors in artist careers, 163–64; as owners of sound recordings, 164; purchase and sale of, 122. See also recording industry
recording artists: advocacy groups, 187; as "artisan outworkers," 232; as "artist community," 200, 264n54; "breaking" of, 155, 256n30; as commodity, 111; contract lawsuits of, 251n86; contradictory employment status, 57, 230–32; as double figure, 2–3, 4; as employees, 57, 112–13, 129, 184–85, 211–12; as employees in need of protection, 162; as employers, 187, 202, 204, 207–11; as entrepreneurs, 202, 265n67; as "exemplary agents," 25; as "featured artist," 195, 202–5, 208, 213, 223; as independent commodity producer, 231; as independent contractors, 25, 57, 112–13, 129, 184–85, 211–12; narrative of professionalization, 33; as political interest group, 201; as rentiers, 25, 247n99; as responsible agent, 204; as rock aristocracy, 16, 230, 245n39; and "selling out," 103; in social division of

Scruggs, Earl, 193

Seacrest, Ryan, 36, 53, 239n1

self-actualization vs. alienation, 6–7; in Millian democracy, 2, 38, 65, 227; in narratives of music-making, 25, 32–33; in the new individualism, 69–70, 72, 74, 82, 96–97, 99; rhetoric of in rocku-mentary, 89–94

self as symbolic project, 97

self-exploitation, 224

self-expression, 3, 6–7, 24, 99, 106. *See also* autonomy

self-governance/government, 5, 23, 25, 63, 179, 214, 218, 261n106. *See also* self-responsibility

self-identity, 60

"self-ownership," 181, 205–6, 261n106. *See also* property in the person

self-responsibility, 5, 93–94, 97, 234. *See also* self-governance/government

"selling out," 230

Sennett, Richard, 12, 33, 45, 60, 67, 236n7

servant, 108, 144, 161, 214–16, 220, 256n27; recording artist as, 3, 227, 231, 234. *See also* master and servant, law of

Seven Arts, 116

seven-year rule, 27, 109, 143–44, 155, 212; "absolute" interpretation (de Haviland v. Warner Bros, 1944), 115–16; hearings on, 149–54; history of, 116; legislative history of, 129, "naturalness" of duration limit, 176, 260n88; as protection from coer-cion, 161–63, 170, 173. *See also* Califor-nia Labor Code, section 2855(b) ("carve out"); labor law, California

Sex Pistols, the, 65

Shemel, Sidney, 112–14, 122

Sher, Byron (California state senator), 157, 159, 169–70, 172

Simon, Carly, 132, 154–55

slavery: "civil,"145–48, 151, 159–60, 173, 177, 179–80; commodification of labor and, 249; in contractarian view, 258n50; contrasted with waged labor, 144, 151,

173, 176–77, 180; objectification and, 219; rhetorical invocation by recording art-ists of, 27, 103, 144–46, 160, 179; "tack-ing" of successive contracts and, 133; "wage," 181, 258n53

Smith, Joe, 132

social authorship, 205. *See also* authorship

social capital, 87, 93, 103. *See also* cultural capital

Sony, 121, 125, 252n93

sound recordings: as "catalog," 119–20, 138, 164, 192, 199; collaborative author-ship of, 203; as commissioned works, 184, 192; copyright status of, 186; counterfeiters of, 188; legal status of, 188–89, 192–93, 197, 224. *See also* social authorship

Spears, Britney, 53

"specialness" of stars, 48, 107, 116

Spector, Ronnie, 193

Spice Girls, 40, 52–53

Spice World (film), 40

Springsteen, Bruce, 120, 202, 204, 209–10

standard contract, 167–68, 199. *See also* boilerplate; contract, recording

state of nature, 159

Statute of Labourers (1351), 10, 108

Steinfeld, Robert, 147–48

Stinchcombe, Arthur, 138–39

stock options, 87

stratification, systems of, 45

Straw, Will, 119–20

Sundance Film Festival, 83

Synchronicity (album), 121

"tacking," of successive contracts, 133–35, 141, 149, 259n78. *See also* contract, recording

Taylor, Charles, 25

Taylor, Courtney, 76–78, 80–81, 83, 87–88, 90–91, 245n57

Teena Marie (Brockert), 107–8, 132–33

termination of transfer (in copyright), 191, 194, 221. *See also* Copyright Act of 1976

MATT STAHL is assistant professor of Information and Media
Studies at the University of Western Ontario.

Library of Congress Cataloging-in-Publication Data
Stahl, Matt.
Unfree masters : recording artists and the politics of work / Matt Stahl.
p. cm. — (Refiguring American music)
Includes bibliographical references and index.
ISBN 978-0-8223-5328-7 (cloth : alk. paper)
ISBN 978-0-8223-5343-0 (pbk. : alk. paper)
1. Popular music — Writing and publishing — United States. 2. Popular
music — Economic aspects — United States. 3. Intellectual property —
United States. 4. Sound recording industry — United States. I. Title.
II. Series: Refiguring American music.
ML3477.S725 2012
338.47'780973 — dc23   2012011603